After the Fact

After the Fact

The Holocaust in Twenty-First Century Documentary Film

Brad Prager

Bloomsbury Academic
An imprint of Bloomsbury Publishing Inc

BLOOMSBURY
NEW YORK · LONDON · NEW DELHI · SYDNEY

Bloomsbury Academic

An imprint of Bloomsbury Publishing Inc

1385 Broadway	50 Bedford Square
New York	London
NY 10018	WC1B 3DP
USA	UK

www.bloomsbury.com

BLOOMSBURY and the Diana logo are trademarks of Bloomsbury Publishing Plc

First published 2015

© Brad Prager, 2015

All rights reserved. No part of this publication may be reproduced or transmitted in any form or by any means, electronic or mechanical, including photocopying, recording, or any information storage or retrieval system, without prior permission in writing from the publishers.

No responsibility for loss caused to any individual or organization acting on or refraining from action as a result of the material in this publication can be accepted by Bloomsbury or the author.

Library of Congress Cataloging-in-Publication Data
Prager, Brad, 1971–
After the fact: the Holocaust in twenty-first century documentary film/Brad Prager.
pages cm
Includes bibliographical references and index.
ISBN 978-1-62356-932-7 (hardback: alk. paper) – ISBN 978-1-62356-444-5 (pbk.: alk. paper)
1. Holocaust, Jewish (1939–1945). 2. Documentary films–History and criticism. I. Title.
D804.3.P69 2015
070.4'499405318–dc23
2014031365

ISBN: HB: 978-1-6235-6932-7
PB: 978-1-6235-6444-5
ePUB: 978-1-6235-6925-9
ePDF: 978-1-6235-6833-7

Typeset by Deanta Global Publishing Services, Chennai, India

The views and opinions expressed in this book and the context in which the images are used do not necessarily reflect the views or policy of, nor imply approval or endorsement by, the United States Holocaust Memorial Museum

Contents

Acknowledgments	vi
Introduction: The Holocaust Documentary: In Stages	1
1 Touring Sites: Revisiting the Concentration Camps in *KZ* and *Martin*	27
2 Mediated Memories: The Influence of Spielberg's Hollywood Hit on *Inheritance* and *Spielberg's List*	69
3 Forgiveness on Film: Resentment and Reconciliation in *Forgiving Dr. Mengele* and *Landscapes of Memory: The Life of Ruth Klüger*	111
4 Family Issues: Oedipal Confrontations in *2 or 3 Things I Know about Him* and *The Flat*	149
5 Rescreening Perpetrator Images: Witnessing the Past in *A Film Unfinished* and *Photographer*	187
Conclusion	225
Notes	231
Selected Filmography	267
Works Cited	271
Index	285

Acknowledgments

I wish to thank Katie Gallof, the Commissioning Editor for Film and Media Studies at Bloomsbury, for supporting this project from the start and for keeping me on track. I am very grateful to her.

The work in these pages benefited from colleagues' insights and feedback. For insights they offered at conferences, colloquia, and on other occasions, I am indebted to Maya Barzilai, Stephanie Craft, Jaimey Fisher, Margit Grieb, Sara Hall, Amanda Hinnant, Jennie Hirsh, Andreas Huyssen, Irene Kacandes, Brett Kaplan, Lutz Koepnick, Manuel Köppen, Sven Kramer, Lisa Nicoletti, Anson Rabinbach, Eric Rentschler, Christoph Ribbat, Michael Rothberg, Stephan Schindler, Christiane Schönfeld, Vincent Slatt, Yasemin Yildiz, and Markus Zisselsberger. I am particularly appreciative of Jennifer Kapczynski, Erin McGlothlin, and Susanne Vees-Gulani for regularly exchanging ideas with me, electronically and in person. For guidance on this project in particular, I was fortunate to be able to turn to David Bathrick, Dagmar Herzog, and Michael D. Richardson.

At the University of Missouri, I appreciate, as always, my colleagues in the Department of German & Russian Studies and the Dean of the College of Arts and Science. They continually provide me with the time and resources I need. I am especially grateful to Lauren Bartshe, for having been an outstanding and able research assistant, and to Kristin Bowen for her editorial work. Above all, I owe thanks to Andrew Hoberek and Anne Myers for their kindness and support.

Part of Chapter 4 appeared in *Colloquia Germanica* (vol. 43, no. 3 [2010]: 215-234), and part of Chapter 5 appeared in *New German Critique* (no. 123 [2014]: 135-157). Those sections appear here with the permission of those journals.

Introduction

The Holocaust Documentary: In Stages

On November 29, 1945 the prosecution at the Nuremberg Trials introduced a documentary film into evidence and played it for the court. The documentary, *Nazi Concentration Camps*, begins with a static shot of a typewritten affidavit, which states that the images in the film have not been tampered with. George Stevens, a Hollywood director, compiled the film from footage taken by members of the United States Army Signal Corps, and his signed statement asserts that the images "have not been altered in any respect since the exposures were made." We are then shown a second affidavit, signed by Navy Lieutenant Edgar Ray Kellogg, who was also employed by 20th Century Fox. He states that he has carefully examined the motion picture, and that its images "have not been retouched, distorted or otherwise altered."[1] The film presented to the court required attestation because it was being entered into evidence, yet as the filmed images of these documents are presented on screen, we simultaneously hear their contents read into the soundtrack. The actual documents were turned over to the court at trial, but they are also reproduced, visually and aurally, in the film. Lawrence Douglas argues that the prosecution was attempting to turn the documentary into a "privileged witness," one that would be "competent to swear to the truth of its own images."[2] The film they were screening was intended to serve as an eyewitness, and its pictures were meant to "speak for themselves."[3]

That documentary's images, of course, could not speak for themselves. Like all films or photographs, their reception was determined by how they were framed and in what context they appeared. Prior to the film's screening, the prosecutor, Thomas J. Dodd, explained to the court that the "fear and terror and nameless horror of the concentration camps were instruments by which the defendants retained power and suppressed the opposition to any of their policies."[4] Dodd's observations are right, yet the film shows little of German civil society under the Third Reich; it contains mostly scenes from the camps. He may have chosen his words with the idea that the court would respond to

Nazi Concentration Camps with a mixture of fear, terror, and horror. Moreover, the film's narration goes a long way toward determining its images' reception. However stark and clinical the narrator's intonation may be, the documentary's script hardly hesitates to speculate into the perpetrators' states of mind.

The prosecution surely had many reasons for screening such a vivid and grim film. They might have wanted to "reinfuse drama into the proceeding," as has been asserted, or it might have been intended to publically shame the perpetrators, who were seated in the dock.[5] Most of the reporters in the court that day were persuaded of the film's impact. The *New York Times* summarized that the audience in the courtroom gasped as they concluded what was "probably the most horrible hour that they had ever spent." It had been "too appalling even for tears." The *Times*'s article ends with a particularly harsh observation: "Most of the audience remained silent for a few minutes, too stunned to express emotion. But one soldier remarked: 'God, this makes me feel like killing the first German I meet.'"[6] The soldier's sentiment is regrettable, but it might not have been the images alone that provoked his reaction. The manner of their presentation was intended to awaken ire, whether it was toward the defendants, the German populace, or both.

Today we are far removed from that courtroom. If *Nazi Concentration Camps* outrages or wounds contemporary viewers, then it does so differently. It is hard to put ourselves in that place. Although some of the courtroom's spectators had been exposed to shocking material before, and some had even been at the camps at the time of their liberation, few would have seen a compilation film like this one, and filmmakers had not been confronted with this type of material. The Nuremberg Trial also took place long before the extensive public reception of survivor testimonies, as at the Eichmann Trial, and long before the widespread publication of memoirs.[7] Filmmakers and their audiences thus had little understanding of what went on behind the barbed wire, let alone the ability to distinguish between concentration and extermination camps, which are among the most significant issues where the production and reception of the earliest Holocaust films are concerned. It took a number of years until historians began to understand what had happened.

The other significant problem that dogged the form at its inception was that the images filmed by the Allied photographic teams in Western Europe and by Soviet film crews at Auschwitz and Majdanek were not images of the crime, but rather of the aftermath. Cameras arrived on the scene after the gates had been opened, so the images were already belated. Furthermore, although there are many photographic records of German concentration camps such as Buchenwald and Neuengamme while they were functioning, what went on in the extermination camps went unfilmed, and most of those sites were dismantled before the war's end. The location of the killing machinery at Bełżec, for example, had been planted over with trees by the summer of 1943. Viewers thus had to adduce the truth from its traces. The chief questions with which documentarians were forced to contend had to do, on the one hand, with establishing the facts of the matter, which remains an ongoing challenge, and, on the other hand, with answering questions as to how one could envision so much that had been concealed.

The legacy of these questions endures. Although the present study is concerned with contemporary Holocaust documentaries, one has to look at newer works in light of past ones. Since the time of the camps' liberations, the first films and photographs have been integrated into other films, appearing in new contexts and subject to reinterpretation based on the various standpoints and nationalities of a broad array of directors who are concerned with a wide body of themes. Holocaust documentaries have a specific history that includes the earliest postwar films, and they continue to draw on a distinct but expanding archive. Each filmmaker stages their presentation of the past in his or her own way, responding, whether implicitly or explicitly, to those who came before, and the works of major figures such as Alain Resnais, who directed the watershed film *Night and Fog* (1955), and Claude Lanzmann, who made the epic nine-and-one-half hour work *Shoah* (1985), continue to impact today's documentaries. Understanding why *Night and Fog* was a turning point, why Lanzmann subsequently took the position he did, and how these types of discussions have developed over time are essential for studying the Holocaust documentary today.

Witnessing witnesses

The earliest films of the liberations, which have been called "newsreel form" films or "compilation films," were the Western world's introduction to the concentration camps.[8] Because much of that footage has been included in other films over the years, many viewers immediately associate the Holocaust with those stark images. There were several of these films, among them *Nazi Concentration Camps* and *Death Mills* (1946).[9] The latter film, the German version of which was entitled *Die Todesmühlen*, has a distinctive tone that, more than most, aims to reproach the perpetrators.[10] The images in these films were meant as windows onto a horrific reality that one might see but not believe. Starving, emaciated survivors appear alongside piles of corpses. The films' narrators report on the startling numbers of fatalities, about which they, at that time, could only speculate. The camera encounters massive stacks of bodies laid atop one another, ones that had not been treated respectfully, but as waste. Much of the footage showed people, including former perpetrators, engaged in the ghastly task of relocating and interring the cadavers.

Another similar film was housed in the archives of the British Imperial War Museum and it drew renewed public attention when it screened in 1984 and was given the title *Memory of the Camps*.[11] Alfred Hitchcock's name had been attached to that film, although his role was limited.[12] He acted as a consultant and proposed that the filmmakers avoid complex editing, because some viewers might already be disinclined to believe what they were seeing.[13] That film also depicts Germans being forced to clean up corpses after the liberation. Its narration, based on a text written contemporaneously with the film's production but voiced later by Trevor Howard, explains that the Germans we see in the film remained mostly silent during the war, not speaking up against the violence when it took place. Germans, including perpetrators, city administrators, and civilians view piles of bodies, gazing at the consequences of their respective action or inaction. Many of its images overlap with *Death Mills*, which was initially part of an interconnected project, and in the English language version of that film the narrator informs us: "Nazi party leaders and office holders were commanded by Allied military authorities to visit concentration camps in their own cities. They were forced to see with their own eyes crimes whose existence they had indignantly denied."[14] In one now famous sequence, the narrator explains that the residents of Weimar near Buchenwald were told that they were going on a picnic, but that they soon learned the truth. We watch them view the aftermath of the murders, to which they react by covering their noses and mouths. The script for *Die Todesmühlen* was written with the German public in mind, and near the end of that film, the narrator reproaches his audience forcefully, speaking in the first person: "I marched with them. . . . I watched as they took away my neighbor." He concludes with a rhetorical question meant to accuse his German viewers: "what did I do against it?"[15]

Most of this footage obliged audiences to gaze in a certain way at violence and its consequences. To their intended spectators, whether they were German or Allied, these films said: "look at this," or "believe the unbelievable." The mission of *Die Todesmühlen* was to compel Germans to confront the brutal truth, but it might not have been all that effective. Ulrike Weckel argues that some of these films had a shaming effect, which led more to concealment and avoidance than it did to any real discussion of guilt and responsibility.[16] Moreover, they may have only struck a chord with certain parts of the population. Citing a report by the US Information Control Division, Kay Gladstone observes that with respect to *Die Todesmühlen*, "workers, intellectuals and soldiers who had witnessed horrors on the Eastern Front" composed the majority of those who found the film "credible and necessary."[17] Members of the lower-middle classes, who had been early supporters of Nazism, responded less well. Gladstone writes, "The final ICD report concluded that although few doubted the authenticity of the atrocities in the film, hardly anyone accepted responsibility for them. Even though the film had apparently succeeded better than any other attempt to make the Germans aware of the guilty nature of the Hitler regime, it had failed in its aim to awaken in Germans a consciousness of their own individual and collective guilt for the atrocities."[18] Filmmakers approached the problem with different audiences in mind, yet they all had to confront the same question: how could one frame these apparently incomprehensible images so they would awaken some form of comprehension; how could one encourage viewers to *look* at the images so that they might also be *seen*?

These first documentaries, filmed at the camps' liberations, were governed by the principle that it was essential to depict someone in the process of observing what had happened. The presence of witnesses was an inbuilt, even vital part of these films' approaches. Just as few filmmakers would make a film about a natural wonder without including a human figure for scale, no one at that time made a film about Nazi atrocities without including witnesses, ones touring the scene, whether they were ordinary Germans or Allied soldiers, culpable parties or simply living beings wandering among the dead. *Memory of the Camps* and *Death Mills*, which include many overlapping shots, each adhered to a similar model, calling on numerous witnesses. Proxies for the viewers were ever-present, mediating the audience's response to horror.

The groundbreaking film *Night and Fog*, which was directed by Resnais with a screenplay by Jean Cayrol, took a different approach. Their film might be mistaken for a compilation film, because it draws on so many archival sources, yet they had studied several earlier compilation films, and they were thus attempting to do something distinctive.[19] In *Night and Fog*, the viewer is expected to take on the role of the witness. Resnais and Cayrol's documentary about deportations and concentration camps demonstrates an acute awareness of the earlier filmmakers' dilemma. One could not simply look at horrific footage and comprehend the crime that had taken place. If filmed images and photographs of Holocaust victims are meant to speak for themselves, then it is by no means clear what they say. The one who is being made to look, to make sense of the atrocities, is no longer the perpetrator, soldier, or bystander who appears in the film, but is rather those audience members to whom the film is addressed; the burden falls back on them. The film viewer's position as witness becomes central. Some of *Night and Fog's* most famous images are haunting because they appear to have no point of view, and Libby Saxton describes a tendency toward "complicit onlooking" in the film, whereby the many partially excluded bodies, the persons who half-appear in the frame, are meant to provoke the viewer by calling into question the very possibility of a neutral bystander.[20] *Night and Fog* not only challenges its audiences in these ways, but it also seeks a point at which the viewer's gaze can come into contact with that of the victim, particularly that of the deportee arriving at the camps. One now famous image, a detail from an identity photograph at the Auschwitz museum, depicts a close up of a deportee's eyes, and the film's narrator, Michel Bouquet, exclaims: "First sight of the camp. It is another planet."[21] Here, the challenge of empathizing and thinking ourselves into the position of the deportee is made explicit. Resnais and Cayrol thus give themselves two tasks, which may even contradict one another: they position viewers such that they are forced to imagine how it must have felt to see all of this for the first time as a prisoner and, simultaneously, they challenge their audience members to think of themselves as implicated witnesses, who potentially might have been drawn into the crime.

The film's use of music, its poetic narration, and its alternation between color and black and white are all designed to unsettle, but viewers are also meant to pay close attention to the images. Audiences are supposed to study what they see on the screen and ask, along with the narration written by Cayrol, whether the Nazis' surgical barracks could be mistaken for an actual clinic, whether the crematorium today looks like a picture postcard around which tourists have themselves photographed, and what might it mean to look upon these ruins, "as though there were a cure for the plague of these camps." The contention that the camps represent a plague with no cure is meant to be disquieting. It suggests either that what caused Auschwitz has not yet disappeared, that the victims' suffering is not yet at an end, or perhaps both. Debarati Sanyal argues that there are parallels between Resnais and Cayrol's intentions and those expressed in the French survivor Charlotte Delbo's poetry about Auschwitz, where we are enjoined, "Try to look. Just try and see, but also try to look so that you may see."[22] The narrator not only wants us to look, he wants us to look longer and more intensely. If Resnais and Cayrol's constellations of texts and images, their poetry and montage, calls for decoding, then the shocking footage surely cannot be expected to speak for itself. Whether viewers had ever before seen any of the film's archival material—and when the film premiered in 1956 the vast majority had not—they were encouraged to look again.

Holocaust aniconism

The montages and compositions in *Night and Fog* are surely provocative, but viewers may, as a consequence of watching Resnais's work, imagine that they have seen or understood the worst of the violence. The film's images of deportations and gas chambers awaken strong reactions, yet they are only photographs and film stills, and on their own they cannot convey the truth. Moreover, *Night and Fog*, although it was extremely well informed for the time, did not address itself to a substantial part of the Nazis' concentrationary project, specifically to a number of killing centers in the East such as Bełżec and Treblinka. In response to these issues, Lanzmann sought a different position, one that circumvents the problem of photomediation.[23] Released three decades later, *Shoah* attempted to sidestep the limitation that photographs impose on the imagination; he wanted to force his audiences to listen to testimony, particularly about the extermination camps, and in so doing he aimed to challenge conventional approaches and supersede all prior Holocaust film.[24] In the early compilation films, audiences were expected to watch perpetrators, soldiers, and bystanders react at the sight of victims and survivors. *Night and Fog*, in turn, challenged that model, asking the audience not to witness witnesses, but rather to become a witness. In *Shoah*, this process of observation takes yet another turn: viewers are asked to *not* bear witness to the filmed and photographic record of violence. They are encouraged instead to look at what seem to be empty spaces—overgrown train stations, or fields where killing machines once stood—and to watch subjects conjuring up with their words and gestures crimes that happened decades earlier. As Henry Pickford notes, *Shoah* is a process of observing witnesses "imagining themselves seeing, experiencing what they saw during the Holocaust."[25]

Lanzmann's model still determines much of the language with which we discuss Holocaust documentaries today. He has reedited and added supplementary footage to unseen outtakes from *Shoah* for release as new films, including *A Visitor from the Living* (1997), *Sobibor* (2001), *The Karski Report* (2010), and *The Last of the Unjust* (2013). There are hundreds of hours of outtakes from *Shoah* in the collection of the US Holocaust Memorial Museum, and in this way the film has itself become an archive. As the art historian Georges Didi-Huberman points out, future historians will benefit from the information in the film, not least from those many hours of unreleased footage.[26] Lanzmann's major legacy, however, has stemmed from his attempt to legislate others' filmmaking practices. His belief, which has come to seem like a commandment, is by now well known: filmmakers ought not reproduce filmed and photographed images of Jewish wartime suffering. He asserts that if he were to come into possession of footage of Jews dying in gas chambers, he would destroy it.[27] Reproducing images of that sort, he asserts, risks distancing us even further from the crimes, and thereby erasing the past.[28] Lanzmann's position shares similarities with that of the cultural anthropologist Cornelia Brink, who argues that many of these older, black and white images have by now been sacralized as though they were religious icons, and that they have, "pushed themselves between ourselves and reality" as would a protective layer; we are, by now, blind to them.[29] Filmmakers should, according to Lanzmann, refrain from using archival material.

The German word *Bilderverbot*, or the "ban against images," has been applied to Lanzmann's aniconic position, and it relates to two issues fundamental for the present study. One motivation behind Lanzmann's thinking concerns the question of who took the photographs and footage we commonly see. Where one sees images of the camps or ghettos, perpetrators were typically the ones behind the cameras, and they enframed their prisoners in genocidal narratives. These images, despite the fact that they depict victims and survivors, can be described as "perpetrator photographs."[30] And although there are instances of Jews photodocumenting their own experience, including pictures of ghettos and deportations taken by prisoners such as Arie ben-Menachem or Mordechaj Mendel Grossman, such documents are comparatively uncommon.[31] Perpetrators are responsible for the overwhelming percentage of surviving images of German and Eastern European Jews taken from 1939 until the liberation of the camps, whether they were photographing for purposes of propaganda, out of historical interest, or as soldiers' keepsakes. Following this argument's logic, one might say that there are few if any true photos and films of the Holocaust: the images are missing, because those we encounter are essentially part of a larger lie.[32] The other major motivation behind the ban concerns the notion that the crime itself was unimaginable: no one who did not live through the experience can picture what it was like, and it is thus beyond representation, or, after a manner of speaking, sublime.[33] Picturing the Holocaust's horrors diminishes them, turns them to kitsch, and prolongs the treacherous illusion that it is possible, from our standpoint, to comprehend what took place.

But Lanzmann has recently changed his course. The centerpiece of *The Last of the Unjust*, which is partly composed of outtakes from *Shoah*, is Lanzmann's 1975 interview with Benjamin Murmelstein, the only surviving elder of the Jewish Council in the Theresienstadt ghetto.[34] During the Holocaust, Murmelstein was in a difficult spot: he had to make life and death decisions about the ghetto's prisoners, ostensibly ensuring the survival of the community while keeping the Nazis satisfied. As with many prisoners in similarly privileged positions, he was pilloried after the war for having collaborated. At the film's beginning, Lanzmann explains that these long hours of conversations have continued to linger in his mind and haunt him. Early in the film, which includes much of that interview material, Lanzmann edits in some scenes from *Theresienstadt: A Documentary Film from the Jewish Settlement Area*, a propaganda film about the lives of Jewish prisoners produced in Theresienstadt in 1944 under Nazi oversight. Although that newsreel style propaganda film nominally had a Jewish director, Kurt Gerron, the Nazis had ordered him to make the film and deported large numbers of Jews to the camps so that Theresienstadt would appear to be sufficiently livable.[35] Lanzmann includes several minutes of this deceitful propaganda film in *The Last of the Unjust*, and the words "Mise en scene Nazi" ("Staged by Nazis") appear in the corner of the frame the whole time.

In earlier films, Lanzmann had avoided incorporating this kind of footage. He could have included it in *A Visitor from the Living*, a film he released 16 years earlier in which he interviewed a Red Cross inspector who wrongly gave his seal of approval to conditions in Theresienstadt; yet Lanzmann chose not to. Lanzmann now includes the propaganda film in his more recent film, having apparently decided that it has something to say, and that rescreening it for us tells us more than excluding it would. It is a valuable document owing to the insight it offers into life in Theresienstadt, and perhaps even more so for its gaps and ambiguities. One can reasonably ask whether there were moments in these victims' daily lives when they did not feel the impact of their persecution, and whether it is possible that they were trying to communicate wordlessly with the film's present or future viewers.[36]

The idea that one must choose between, on the one hand, showing images of the Nazis' victims that were filmed and photographed during the war or, on the other hand, refusing to show those same images has by now lost much of its sway. Libby Saxton observes that the aniconic position is "rapidly losing critical currency."[37] She writes that appealing to those boundaries, "perpetuates a reductive moral framework which promotes the application of interdictions and taboos, while shielding us from more difficult questions about complicity and responsibility."[38] Didi-Huberman argues against the image ban, asserting that we should try to comprehend images such as these, ones that do exist, and read them against their grain, thereby defying the intentions of Nazis, who concentrated on "obliterating every remnant."[39] The formal choices of Lanzmann's *Shoah*, he writes, have by now "served as alibis for a whole discourse," but the existing images should be examined. Like the survivors themselves, they are *"surviving images."*[40] He argues that it is more constructive to look at these images, to talk about the context in which they were produced and how they have been continuously reproduced, than it is to turn away from them. The images of life in Theresienstadt, for example, are hardly *true* insofar as the Nazis staged everything we see for propaganda purposes; yet the film contains some of the only surviving images of these victims, many of whom were immediately thereafter deported. The very context of its production sheds light on what happened there. On this basis, Lanzmann seems to have cast aside his own directive, and now, in the twenty-first century, he too can be described as being in a "post-Lanzmann" phase.

Lanzmann worked on *Shoah* for close to 12 years, starting in 1973, when Alouph Hareven, the director-general of Israel's Ministry of Foreign Affairs, approached him with the idea for the project.[41] Elements of Lanzmann's style were firmly in place even before he set out to make a Holocaust documentary. His first major film *Pourquoi Israël* (1973) is 185 minutes long and makes extensive use of interviews. His approach to documentary was already different from that of the German-born director Erwin Leiser, who made *Mein Kampf* (1960), an assemblage of archival footage depicting the Nazis rise to power and the persecution of the Jews, or Frédéric Rossif, the French filmmaker who made *The Time of the Ghetto* (1961), which extensively used perpetrator images that had been assembled for propaganda purposes. Rossif's film is powerful, yet it egregiously fails to explain the provenance of the propagandistic source on which it relies. As Lanzmann embarked on *Shoah*, he had a number of other approaches to consider, including Marcel Ophüls's *The Sorrow and the Pity* (1969), which makes use of both lengthy interviews and archival footage.[42] Between

Night and Fog and *Shoah* a number of high-profile documentaries were released, including the Russian documentary *Ordinary Fascism* (1965), which played in western Europe in the late 1960s and early 1970s; the Israeli film *The Eighty-First Blow* (1975), which supplements testimony from survivors at the Eichmann trial with striking images of pogroms and persecution that were mostly taken by perpetrators; and the Academy Award nominated US film *The Yellow Star: The Persecution of the Jews in Europe, 1933-1945*, which opened widely in 1981. All of those films, with varying degrees of self-consciousness, use archival footage to recount atrocities and cast them in historical terms. Some of them pay heed to the origins of their filmed material, and some of them obliquely refer to the limitations on any contemporary viewer's capacity to comprehend the horrors depicted in photographs and footage of camps and ghettos, but all of them rely on substantial amounts of archival images, including them in their attempts to depict wartime events.

The taboo associated with using archival images has by now become historical. Filmmakers today have been finding new contexts for old images, in part because documents are continually being unearthed, and in part because those documentarians are of a younger generation, one that connects different experiences and ideas to wartime and immediate postwar images. Even if some filmmakers agree with Lanzmann's overall sentiment that introducing such materials also introduces a host of vexing problems, many have returned to the image archive with the goal of reexamining films and photographs from the past and analyzing the "the gaps and ambiguities that reside in those images."[43] The films studied in these pages offer new contexts and new interpretations. Rather than redeploying images seen many times over and having us gaze upon them in mute astonishment, recent Holocaust documentaries have tended toward interpreting archival images, either challenging or complementing the work of historians. Several films examined here, especially Dariusz Jablonski's *Photographer* (1998) and Yael Hersonski's *A Film Unfinished* (2010), incorporate archival material in their films precisely in order to bring about a reconsideration of how historians have interpreted films and footage from the past. Twenty-first century documentarians have been reluctant to treat the distinction between Lanzmann's and Resnais's approaches as an either/or and have returned to the archives, offering new and inventive ways of exploring their contents.

Owing to the tremendous breadth of approaches, I prefer to think of the interrelation of Holocaust documentaries as something akin to a system, rather than a genre. The films and their filmmakers respond to one another's propositions, particularly concerning how atrocities can be observed and made legible. They view one another's perspectives with the act of observation in mind, as had both *Night and Fog* and *Shoah*. Each film responds to how the last one surveys its object, and as each emerges, it takes a new approach to observation.[44] In new films, a shot of a tranquil landscape, a monument, or even a view through the window of a moving car carries with it a history. Most documentaries thus speak to prior films' observational practices. As in a drawing by M. C. Escher, the observation of others' observations is a potentially interminable process, and the progression of practices is particularly distinctive where Holocaust representation is concerned, because Holocaust representation begins with a void at its center. As is the case with many films discussed in the present study, Holocaust documentaries are in the position of reconstructing atrocities, exploring sites of unrecovered memories, and depicting observers, those who come along after the fact, in the process of doing the same. These contemporary documentaries are, of course, influenced by other factors as well. They can be affected by changing cultures of victimhood, by transformations in film style, or by historically varied perspectives on survivor testimony.[45] It is thus important to remain open-minded when one studies these films and how they came to be. But each of the documentaries chosen for examination in the following chapters is shadowed by an interconnected set of historical questions as to whether and how the Holocaust can be observed, and, as each one takes up that question, it interacts and communicates with the films that preceded it.

Defining Holocaust documentary

What do I mean by "documentary," and how do documentaries differ from "documents"? One answer can be drawn from an example: a short film of an Einsatzgruppe action from 1941 connected with the German invasion of the Soviet Union directly depicts Holocaust atrocities.[46] The footage was filmed in Libau, Latvia, when Nazis and Latvian collaborators were in the process of exterminating the local Jewish population. There is only 1 minute and 39 seconds of this footage, which shows Jews shot to death by a firing squad. We see prisoners dismounting a truck, descending into a ditch and being fired upon, while soldiers and policemen watch from the pit's edge. The victims' bodies are then partially covered over with sand. A German naval officer, a *Kriegsmariner*, named Reinhard Wiener happened to take the footage while on a walk in the park, between the town and the beach.⁴⁷ There are few, if any, other filmed documents of this type of murder, largely because Heinrich Himmler banned the filming of executions at the end of 1941. Although the Nazis believed that posterity would prove them right, they recognized the criminal character of what they were doing. Joshua Hirsch, in his study of Holocaust films and trauma, discusses the "vicarious trauma" Wiener's comrades experienced when they saw the footage and were upset by it.⁴⁸ If for no other reason than because the filmmaker rewatched it, reacted to it, and later attempted to explain it, studying the footage affords us insight into the Germans' mindset.

Yet the Wiener fragment, also referred to as "Execution of Jews in Liepaja," as a product of amateur filmmaking, contains neither narration, nor a commentary track for context. Because it is unframed, I would not describe it as a documentary. In an abstract sense, all films are framed insofar as when we view them, we do so from particular standpoints, and our horizon of understanding enframes our reception. For practical purposes, however, this film has no frame. All the elements necessary for incorporating it into a context, historical or otherwise, are missing: there is no narration, exposition, or intertitles. It should not be treated as a documentary, but rather as a document.

Bill Nichols proposes a definition of documentary film that deals with both the subjects involved and the filmmaker. He writes that documentary, "speaks about situations and events involving real people (social actors) who present themselves to us as themselves in stories that convey a plausible proposal about, or perspective on, the lives, situations, and events portrayed. The distinct point of view of the filmmaker shapes this story into a way of seeing the historical world directly rather than into a fictional allegory."⁴⁹ Nichols's definition is comprehensive, and to some extent it describes *Shoah*, in which people surely present themselves to us as themselves.⁵⁰ The case of the Holocaust, however, is somewhat atypical, because many of the people involved, the social actors, are dead and cannot speak for themselves. These subjects are gone, and, more and more, those who can speak on their behalf, those who witnessed the killings, are gone as well. This absence is already at issue in *Night and Fog*: even though Cayrol, the author of the spoken text of the film, was a survivor of Mauthausen and he allowed his experience to shape the narration, the true subjects of the film are the dead. Traces of their faces appear, as do the impressions left by the scratching of their nails on the walls of the execution chambers, but they are not called upon to testify, nor are they able to "present themselves to us as themselves."

One can, on the other hand, always speak about a filmmaker's point of view, even in the case of "Execution of Jews in Liepaja." In spite of the document's silence we can draw some conclusions. The man holding the camera does nothing, for example, to intervene in the horrific crime. Given the circumstance, we would not have expected him to, but the simple facts that he stood by and filmed, and that the camera does not definitively avert its gaze when the killings take place, illuminate the filmmaker's state of mind. Although we cannot describe Wiener's perspective with certainty, these elements provide us with a basis for conjecture. What is missing, however, and what makes this a document rather than a documentary, is that the footage is not placed in a context. It is not employed as part of a line of argumentation, or, as the documentary theorist Michael Renov would assert, the material is not reorganized in conformity with a particular interest or desire.[51] Had the footage been taken up by a filmmaker like Resnais, or the Israeli documentarian Yael Hersonski, or the experimental German filmmaker Harun Farocki, who reedited and reframed footage from Westerbork concentration camp in the film *Respite* (2007), or even if it had been retitled and screened as part of an installation, one could begin to describe the work in terms of documentary film. As it is, "Execution of Jews in Liepaja" is a document. The earliest films of the liberations such as *Nazi Concentration Camps*, *Death Mills*, and *Memory of the Camps*, order and present their nonfictional material, and, for this reason, I would call them documentaries. Although a number of the social actors involved could not speak for themselves, these films articulate their producers' perspectives on the real world, and they selectively compile historical footage in the interest of conveying that standpoint.

Although documentaries can be diverting, they tend to present themselves as contributions to our historical understanding of events. In that sense they are more likely than feature films to incorporate archival materials and to concern themselves with accuracy. *Night and Fog* used some archival images in a way that has been contested. There has been discussion, for example, about whether the film makes it clear that a British soldier rather than a German is driving a bulldozer that was on one occasion used to move corpses at Bergen-Belsen. Because the bulldozer is the closing image of *Nazi Concentration Camps*, discussions of its various employments can be found throughout the scholarship; the bulldozer discussion is now enshrined in the critical literature. Writing about *Night and Fog*, Sylvie Lindeperg correctly remarks that, when one pays attention to the narration, Resnais's depiction is as it should be: the scene appears immediately following the narrator's statement that the Allies have opened the camp's gates.⁵² Still more discussion, however, surrounds an image that appears when the narrator is describing the selection process and says: "These pictures were taken a few moments before extermination." One of the photographs we are shown at that point was taken in October 1942 and is from a ravine south of Rivne, now in Western Ukraine, where Jews from the Mizocz ghetto were executed. It is by now a well-known photograph, and its title in the USHMM's photo archive reads: "Naked Jewish women, some of whom are holding infants, wait in a line before their execution by Ukrainian auxiliary police." It is not, in other words, a photo of persons on their way to the gas chamber, and it seems chronologically out of place. Griselda Pollock points out that the photo today has an iconic function, in part owing to this use in *Night and Fog*, and that our continued fascination with it calls for deeper explanation.⁵³ Didi-Huberman sees in its potentially misleading placement an opening for a photographic archaeology, or a chance to restore the image's original context.⁵⁴

I draw attention to this moment because it is an example of how later documentaries can insert themselves into an ongoing discussion. In Romain Icard's *Shoah by Bullets* (2008), a team of researchers goes to the Ukraine, and the film's central figure, Father Patrick Desbois, speaks to elderly Holocaust bystanders with the help of an interpreter. The film is concerned with assembling testimony about mass executions in the East, and in its project of historical recovery it resembles *Shoah*. At points in the film Desbois asks the local witnesses specific questions, such as whether prisoners were kneeling or standing when they were shot, and how precisely the victims fell into the death pits. As in *Shoah*, witnesses perform their memories for the camera. When the camera crew reaches the area near Mizocz, the now familiar photos are incorporated into the film, including the image of exposed women prior to their execution. After one resident directs the film crew to what he believes to be the ravine where the shootings took place, the image dissolves, very convincingly, from a black and white photograph of corpses—a photo from that same set of photos—to an image of the landscape as it appears today. Desbois, it would seem, has succeeded in locating the hitherto unknown site of the murders amid the woodsy, rural terrain, and the archival photo acts as his witness. On the heels of the very real acts of archaeology depicted in the film, Icard's *Shoah by Bullets* conducts a cinematic archaeology, and in doing so it communicates with several films that preceded it.

Archival documents are one major form of documentary currency; testimony is the other. Thomas Trezise describes a contemporary "anxiety of historical transmission," which owes itself to the fact that living memory, the witnesses and survivors, may soon be extinguished. "This anxiety," according to Trezise, "accounts in large part for the accelerated production of testimony in the past two or three decades, most notably through the establishment of extensive video archives but also through the publication of written memoirs."[55] Testimony, preferably the account of a witness or survivor, is still a hallmark of authenticity, and it remains one of the ways documentaries meet the demands of what Aaron Kerner calls "the realistic imperative" that drives many Holocaust films.[56] Because of the seriousness of the subject matter, audiences assume that Holocaust documentaries are not playing games with the truth: if there is a witness, we expect that they are who they say they are, and that their story corresponds to reality, even if it is highly subjective. But audiovisual testimony takes on a dual role in documentary films, one that perhaps distinguishes it from audiovisual testimony viewed in an archive or at a museum: on the one hand, it is constative insofar as it is part of establishing the truth about what happened, yet it is, on the other hand, an audiovisual representation integrated into a narrative, and it thus makes impressions that leave room for and even inspire speculative interpretation.[57] Testimonies in documentaries play both roles, especially as they are incorporated into documentaries and become part of a narrative construction.[58] They inform us, yet they are subject to the filmmakers enframing and the various spectators' acts of reading.

If talking heads are less frequently found in contemporary Holocaust documentaries, this may have to do with the expansion of testimonial archives, including the Fortunoff Video Archive for Holocaust Testimonies and the USC Shoah Foundation. Filmmakers tend to distance themselves from the hallmarks of that form.[59] One should, under no circumstances, diminish the importance of the talking head, which, as the key mode of audiovisual testimony, remains one of the most "geopolitically significant ... venues for the attestation, reception, and mitigation of social suffering."[60] But if the image of the witness seated on the couch, telling his or her story is diminishing in prominence as a documentary technique, the "return documentary" is not. Hearkening back to *Shoah* or to Peter Morley's groundbreaking documentary *Kitty: Return to Auschwitz* (1979), recent documentaries continue to bring survivors back to sites of traumatic incidents, usually concentration or death camps.[61] Directors generally do this in the hope that something cinematic will happen. As Janet Walker points out, "the project of a return documentary is to occasion testimony, be it spoken, gestural, or silent."[62] As is common on "reality television," a filmmaker sets the stage, creating the preconditions for drama. In James Moll's *Inheritance* (2006), for example, a survivor and a perpetrator's daughter are taken back to the site of the concentration camp at Płaszów in the hopes of capturing a unique encounter on camera. Ruth Klüger, in *Landscapes of Memory* (2011), is made to go to Bergen-Belsen, where she was never actually imprisoned, in the hopes of motivating a more authentic interview. Finally, and perhaps most startlingly, the film *No Place on Earth* (2012), in its finale, submerges a number of its survivor-witnesses, all of whom are well over 80 years old, into the Ukrainian caves in which they once hid from Nazis, in order to stumble upon what all of these films' filmmakers are looking for: a personal disclosure, a swell of memory, or a revelation about the past that would have otherwise remained buried.

Insofar as audiovisual testimonies admit the broad array of interpretive responses, studying documentaries is distinct from studying fictional features. Documentaries often put viewers in the peculiar situation of making judgments about real people, whose real lives are depicted on film. One has to approach the matter with care: we have available to us only two-dimensional representations of persons as they appear in the moving frames of a film, which is a limited source of information. No matter how much the subjects tell us, no matter how openly they speak about their lives on screen, the picture will never be full. We only know what people say, not who they are. We can evaluate their statements and their gestures, but we can only speculate about their motivations, and about the depths of their wounds. Some responses are well founded, and others are projections. One cannot know whether Martin Zaidenstadt, the late survivor who roams the grounds of Dachau's memorial museum in *Martin* (1999), had dubious motives, or whether Monika Hertwig, the daughter of Amon Göth, who appears in both *Inheritance* and *Hitler's Children* (2011), is truly tormented by guilt. Zaidenstadt, it seems, may have been a difficult personality, and Hertwig comes off as very troubled, but these are only impressions. About the facts of matters, such as whether someone is a survivor, or about how many actually died in a camp, everyone should agree, but apparently telltale signs about the characters of persons involved, or about the states of mind of those interviewed, are little more than red herrings. If personal histories are, as Siegfried Kracauer once wrote about the subjects of photographs, buried beneath a blanket of snow, then documentary subjects' psyches are likewise hidden, perhaps beneath sheets of ice as well.[63] The screen offers us only its two dimensions: it provides no access to the depths.

To analyze the documentaries referred to in this study, I am relying on some particularly helpful terms developed by Bill Nichols.[64] Nichols's language offers convenient reference points for describing the position of the filmmaker vis-à-vis his or her subject, as well as the extent to which the organization of a filmmaker's material is openly colored by his or her subjective experience. Nichols identifies several modes, and the ones that are central here include: the *observational* mode, in which the director shows events as they ideally would have transpired irrespective of the presence of the filmmaker and his or her crew (as in films by the documentarian Frederick Wiseman); the *expository* mode, which aims to clarify, as objectively as it can, the matter at hand, often relying on a "voice-of-god" commentary (as in most newsreels or scientific documentaries); the *participatory* mode, which is marked by the active input and involvement of a film's subjects, specifically where those subjects speak directly to the camera, travel with the filmmaker, or act as performers (as in Joshua Oppenheimer's *The Act of Killing* [2012]); the *performative* mode, in which the filmmaker places him or herself right into the world of the film, allowing events to be shaped by his or her actions (as in Morgan Spurlock's *Super Size Me* [2004]); and the *poetic* mode, which focuses on the subjective and sensory impressions the real world makes on the filmmaker, who constructs his or her documentary in accord with impressionistic or esthetic attitudes (as in Godfrey Reggio's *Koyaanisqatsi* [1982]). Nichols, in identifying the different modes of documentary film follows Kracauer, who observed that there were different types of "films of fact," some of which were objective and conducive to reporting, and others that shaped material in accord with the filmmakers' "inner images," and were marked by more personal views.[65] Documentaries can seldom be confined to any one of these categories. Nichols observes that they are not mutually exclusive, but rather complementary.[66] Filmmakers usually employ many modes in the same film, shifting between, for example, the rational argumentation of a case and allowing themselves the latitude to awaken an audience's esthetic response.

Holocaust documentaries tend to shift between modes when they draw on the images and language of the first Holocaust films, on the wide landscapes and intrusive interview style that characterize Lanzmann's work, and on an iconography inherited from a range of Holocaust feature films. The early compilation films, however, were primarily expository. The commentary in *Nazi Concentration Camps*, for example, was intended to serve as evidence, and it soberly explains its images, one after the next, doing its best to avoid digressions or personal asides. *Night and Fog*, on the other hand, puts viewers into the position of the deportee; we are meant to think of the term "night and fog" less as it applies to the eponymous historical Nazi decree that called for deportations of the Reich's opponents, but more in terms of how the victims perceived their largely incomprehensible and overwhelming persecution. The poetic arrangement of image, text, and music is employed to awaken our sympathy and to communicate the prisoners' experience. Nichols writes that one might think of *Night and Fog* as expository, but that "the haunting, personal quality of the commentary moves it toward the performative." He adds, "It calls for an emotional responsiveness from us that acknowledges how understanding this event within any preestablished frame of reference is an utter impossibility."[67] The knowledge that Cayrol authored the narration, and that Resnais had made a prior film about Van Gogh, might also incline a viewer to categorize *Night and Fog* as poetic.[68] If its opening image, which shows us how "even a tranquil landscape ... with crows flying" can lead to a concentration camp intentionally calls to mind Van Gogh's painting *Cornfield with Crows* (1890), then Resnais is relying on cinematic poetry to hit deeply discordant notes.[69]

After the fact

The editors of a recent collection of essays entitled *After Testimony* point out that the word "after" in their title refers to the idea that we are, "nearing an age 'after testimony,' an age where first-person accounts by Holocaust survivors will no longer be forthcoming." They add, however, that the word "after" has yet another meaning, "referring not to chronology but to artistic creation: a painting 'after' Michelangelo is one that situates itself self-consciously in a position of imitation or homage." In this way, they conclude, "all works dealing with the Holocaust must in some way come to terms with the historical reality that the accounts of survivors have tried to communicate."[70] For them the word evokes the problems associated with mimesis. It refers to an attempt to approximate something that inhibits its re-creation. Film cannot mimetically reproduce or re-create the events in question, and in a very real, historical sense, nearly all of our images of the Holocaust originate "afterwards," because most come from the period following the liberation. Documentaries about the Holocaust thus approach their obscure historical object without being able to capture it. Although film is never equivalent to life itself, the problems of achieving presence and verisimilitude are particularly profound when it comes to atrocities because the gaps between history and its representation seem that much greater. Holocaust documentarians chase after something elusive, attempting to produce its aura through testimony or re-creation, but they always remain removed from it.

A fact is something that is not in dispute. The word *factus* means having been done or made, and it gives the word "manufacture" its root. Historians construct and agree on the facts of the matter, determining what is and is not uncertain. They are, to the best of our abilities, manufactured through a process of dialogue, debate, and reconstruction. Berel Lang observes that ascertaining the facts is the most pressing obligation for those who write about the Holocaust, and that establishing "a bare chronicle of the event—what *happened*," remains "the single most important task of all writing about that event."[71] To think from the standpoint of Lang's imperative, the chief importance of *Shoah* is not its esthetic contribution, but rather how it adds to our knowledge of the facts. Yet Berel Lang also cites a remark by Jean-Paul Sartre that, "the fact of genocide is as old as humanity."[72] Why was Sartre motivated to include the words "the fact of" in this oft quoted phrase? He could surely have simply referred to "genocide itself." "Fact," in this circumstance, is an intensifier. When we refer to genocide as a fact, we are meant to think of its irreversibility. It denotes something that cannot be changed, and something as final as death, particularly mass death, has a fact's immutable finality.

Facts must thus be agreed upon, but they are also absolute. Didi-Huberman cautions against being absorbed by the idea of their finality insofar as we should not over-focus on the machinery of killing as the sole "fact" of the Holocaust. Mass murder by gas was not the only event that took place in those years, and in speaking of it this way, one loses sight of larger contexts. In Didi-Huberman's view there was more to the Holocaust than that notorious act. It was "an infinitely large, complex, multiform phenomenon, ranging from radical evil to banality."[73] In this sense, the fact of the attempted extermination of the Jews is immense and undeniable, because it includes the hateful policies of the Nazis from the 1930s, the deportations to the ghettos and camps, as well as the event's long aftermath. The fact's boundaries are broad, and we can think of the event as extending into the lifetime of its survivors. We are perhaps only now truly arriving, for the first time, at a moment truly after the fact, after most of the survivors have passed. Many documentarians who are now making films have no personal memory of the event, and many were born 20 and 30 years later, such as Arnon Goldfinger, who made *The Flat* (2011) and Omer Fast, who made *Spielberg's List* (2003). Their films are informed by an acute awareness of their historical distance from the Holocaust, as well as the consciousness that their responses are highly mediated, not only by others' films, but also by the specific cultures in which they now live.

The coinage "postmemory" is frequently associated with Holocaust representations that come after the fact and after the first generation of witnesses. Marianne Hirsch was among the earliest to use the term, and when she writes about visual representations of the Holocaust that initially made a strong impression on her, she writes about having been fascinated by *Shoah* while *Night and Fog* was still "burned into [her] eyelids."[74] In her writing, postmemorial connections with the past are often rooted in contact with family members who were survivors. Relationships of "filiation" are central to her work, although her writings also leave room for those who have come into contact with the past through relationships of attachment and affiliation.[75] It is thus not only second-generation witnesses like Art Spiegelman who might stand in postmemorial relation to historical events, but "secondary" ones as well. Anyone who comes into contact with personal memories of the past can be wounded by it, even if they are not traumatized by it. And one surely need not be a traumatized subject to have a connection to the past that is "mediated not by recall but by imaginative investment, projection, and creation."[76] The term also appears in Andrea Liss's study of post-Holocaust photographic art, *Trespassing through Shadows,* and for Liss it refers specifically to artists who return to images from the past, reusing them in their work. Postmemories, according to Liss, "constitute the imprints that photographic imagery of the Shoah have created within the post-Auschwitz generation."[77] I use the term adjectivally in this study, because postmillennial filmmaking belongs to a postmemorial era: the films discussed here belong to an age wherein most of those who depict or enframe narratives about the Holocaust did not themselves live through it. It is a neutral term insofar as it is assigned to mediated Holocaust memories in general, and mediated memories, regardless of how affecting and emotionally involving they may be, can either be approached with a critical eye or uncritically appropriated. Documentarians surely do both.

As the generation of firsthand witnesses vanishes, it leaves the present, younger generation with the question of whether one can adopt someone else's trauma as one's own. Trauma cannot be transferred. Someone's painful story can surely trigger painful memories in someone else, for example, the memory of child abuse, and disparate stories touch one another in this way, but trauma, of course, cannot be given away. In order to transfer trauma, one would have to start from the beginning with the creation of trauma. Holocaust survivor

Jean Améry puts it best when he points out that torture is impossible to convey, and that it "mark[s] the limit of the capacity of language to communicate."[78] The only way for him to explain to you the torture he endured would be to make you endure it. In these discussions, terms that recall the act of mediation are helpful, including Gary Weissman's "fantasies of witnessing," and Alison Landsberg's "prosthetic memory."[79] Concepts such as these underscore the extent to which the reproduction of wounds is artificial, or even an illusion. Much of our contemporary museum culture, not to mention our fascination with talk shows, operates from the expectation that viewers will partake in a traumatic affect. However, mediated experience is not experience, and hearing about torture is not the same as having been tortured. The proliferation of theories about these issues are symptoms of a culture looking for an appropriate language with which to describe and preserve a relation to the past, a relation that has long been predicated on elusive ideals of authentic witnessing. It is not unexpected that one would fall into a faint on a tour of a concentration camp memorial. When confronted by these sites and their histories, we feel inclined to act as though we are taking traumas upon ourselves. We should, in those moments, feel an equal or greater obligation to bear in mind the significant historical distinctions between our positions and those of the victims.

The following five chapters closely examine films that are constructed around a set of themes particular to newer Holocaust documentaries. The films analyzed here also tend to reflect on how Holocaust film has dealt with these same themes in the past. The first chapter examines documentaries that depict concentration camp tourism, and the two films under discussion highlight the peculiar side-effects of the Holocaust's ongoing musealization. In *Shoah* and *Night and Fog*, the sites of former camps were presented as overgrown and untended. In recent films, filmmakers have been less concerned with neglect, and more with the sites' integration in the cultures that surround them. Many former camps in Germany and Austria have been preserved as memorial sites and they are popular destinations, but the majority of visitors are disconnected from the Holocaust, and they are usually little acquainted with its history. They go there hoping to come in contact with others' trauma. *KZ* (2005) depicts this tourist culture at the Mauthausen Memorial and Museum in Austria, which, in the film, appears to receive visitors as though it were on autopilot. The film specifically looks at the Memorial's impact on the lives of the guides who work there. *Martin* deals with the Dachau Concentration Camp Memorial Site in Germany, and it pays particular attention to a curious man, Martin Zaidenstadt, whose bids for attention seem to trade on tourists' fascination with authenticity. Both documentaries ask how film itself can convey the problems and contradictions associated with tourist culture, especially in light of the fact that cinema, like tourism, is also a mode of mediation.

Chapter 2 analyzes documentaries that are closely related to the feature film *Schindler's List* (1993). Both of the films explored in that chapter address the medial aftereffects of Steven Spielberg's highly mediated, Hollywood Holocaust melodrama. *Schindler's List* was a high-priced re-creation, and Lanzmann openly criticized him for his approach, opening the door to other filmmakers' critical engagements. Documentarians in the twenty-first century are continuing to deal with that film's legacy, and this chapter explores whether documentaries that pick up this theme have a responsibility to correct Spielberg's errant representations. *Inheritance*, which tells the story of an encounter between two people impacted by the story of Oskar Schindler and Amon Göth, sees itself as a project interconnected with Spielberg's film. However, the documentary and the story surrounding it reveal a much more complicated picture than Spielberg's streamlined version was capable of conveying. Omer Fast's *Spielberg's List*, which is not a documentary but rather a work of video art, is a direct engagement with Spielberg's adaptation of history for the screen, one that uses the trope of translation and mistranslation as a means of articulating its objections. Using two-channel video, Fast immanently critiques Spielberg's Hollywood practices.

This study's third chapter analyzes documentaries centered on forgiveness and resentment. The documentaries discussed in that chapter each feature an older survivor who contemplates the extent to which they are still driven to reflect on or engage with the long shadow of the perpetrators. Both films discussed in that chapter are documentary depictions of how survivors negotiate their resentments, and how memory and loss still haunt them. The chapter looks specifically at the issues raised by the participatory documentaries *Forgiving Dr. Mengele* (2005) and *Landscapes of Memory: The Life of Ruth Klüger*. The former film is about a woman who imagines letting go of her antipathy, and the latter one focuses on a woman who is willing to acknowledge its persistence. In each case the film's subject, its protagonist, plays a role in determining the shape and tenor of the film. This is true of the films discussed in Chapter 4 as well. The states of affairs in the documentaries *2 or 3 Things I Know about Him* (2004), a German film about the family of a perpetrator, and *The Flat* (2011), an Israeli film about the legacy of one family's flight from Germany, are remarkably parallel, despite the lines that typically divide perpetrators from victims. In both of these cases, a family member playing the role of the provocateur sullies the family nest. These documentaries show how the silences that followed from difficult Holocaust legacies continue to divide mothers from sons, and siblings from one another. They are largely performative films in which the filmmaker creates a confrontation, stepping right into the most difficult familial situations.

The fifth and final chapter explores two films that revisit archives, thereby returning us to and rebuffing the key element of Lanzmann's famous injunction. In these films, *A Film Unfinished* and *Photographer*, the viewer does not watch witnesses gaze at the aftermath of atrocities, but is rather placed in the position of watching survivors in the present look at images of victims in the ghettos, images filmed and photographed during the war, in times and places when those survivors were present. Both of these films stage scenes of metaspectatorship, and they are remarkable reflections on the processes associated with photomediation, insofar as they place particular emphasis on how both the survivors and the documentary's spectators become invested in what they see. These films intercut color with black and white, as had Resnais in *Night and Fog*, yet in these cases the survivors are prompted to testify about the extent to which they can comprehend or come to terms with the now alien worlds they see portrayed.

I have chosen to analyze a very specific group of recent films that exemplify key tendencies in postmillennial Holocaust documentary filmmaking. These represent only a small subgroup of the films that have been produced. Philippe Mesnard asserts that from 1985–95, the decade following Lanzmann's *Shoah*, no less than 1,194 films were made that dealt in one way or another with the Holocaust.[80] I sought out, first of all, films that illuminate where Holocaust documentaries are today, 70 years after the liberations, but also films that acknowledge that the form has a past. The traces of those earlier films can be seen and heard in newer ones; it would be impossible to approach them without some knowledge of what came before. Secondly, these films represent several different national approaches to the question, including Anglophone, Israeli, Germanic, Polish, and French ones. As Lanzmann acknowledged by traveling to America, Israel, Germany, Poland, and France when conducting his interviews for *Shoah*, the aftermath of the Holocaust is distinctively transnational. It resulted in a diaspora of the survivors, the majority of whom landed far away from places they once called home. The films chosen here reflect the event's transnationality. Every cinematic response to the Holocaust is filtered through a particular cultural lens, and they are each inflected in unique ways depending on the origins of the filmmakers: Arnon Goldfinger, an Israeli filmmaker, has to contend with his feelings about historical Zionism and with the displacement of his grandparents; Malte Ludin, a German filmmaker addresses his family's legacy of perpetration and their unwillingness to accept the truth; and, the children of the American survivors in these films find themselves alienated from their parents' experience, because they were raised thousands of miles from Auschwitz.

In the most thorough study to date of the impact that historical Holocaust imagery has had on melodramatic feature films, Tobias Ebbrecht argues that our mediated memories behave like a self-referential system akin to a hall of mirrors. Cinema, in his view, repeats and distorts historical images, rescreening them again and again until we take them to be more real than the real thing.[81] Despite their various ideological limitations, I argue that documentaries are less a hall of mirrors than they are works in dialogue, and the documentarians aspire to avoid falsifying history or pretending to produce archival footage on a studio set. Rather than dressing up in period-appropriate uniforms, most of the filmmakers studied here are seeking new, alternate approaches to reconciling history and memory. My contention is not that documentarians should be understood as historians, even though many viewers have learned their history lessons from Resnais and Lanzmann. The specifically cinematic quality of these films is what makes them fascinating. Documentaries are exceptionally open to dynamics of cinematic contingency. Scenes and sequences interact with one another in unexpected and evocative ways, and they call to mind an archive of images; today's landscapes and testimonial performances awaken memories of other, older landscapes and testimonial performances. In these ways, although they are concerned with getting at the truth, they challenge, destabilize, and often exceed the constative work of empirical research. I have aspired to attend to the merits as well as the pleasures associated with those contingencies in each of the following readings.

1

Touring Sites: Revisiting the Concentration Camps in *KZ* and *Martin*

In *Shoah* (1985) Claude Lanzmann's camera surveys, among other locations, the sites of former death camps. At times, the director lingers silently on apparently empty spaces, now and again nearing well-known locations, including the ruins of crematoria or the black wall at Auschwitz, where many were murdered. He relies on handheld cinematography to destabilize the viewer, and the camerawork may be meant to mirror, even if only obliquely, the disorientation of prisoners who would have been forced to walk the footpaths approaching the gas chambers. Seen from another perspective, that same destabilization can be interpreted as an attempt to draw attention to the disjunctions imposed by a gap of many decades. Where should we, today's intruders in space and time, Lanzmann asks, position ourselves relative to the victims? At yet other points in his nine-and-a-half-hour documentary, Lanzmann's perspective seems more detached. His extreme long shots of wide-open landscapes suggest that the violence has been almost completely effaced. Rabbits forage contentedly among the blades of grass, and if one did not know what had happened, one might not, years later, be prompted to ask. In their silence, these images of fields lend support to the idea that we need films such as Lanzmann's to tell us precisely what happened. The overwhelming calm and quiet are readable as replies to the director's own most pressing questions. It is because of this effacement that he needed to make this film; it is because of the silence that *Shoah* was necessary.

The idea that concentration and death camp tourism would later become an industry hardly seems to have been on Lanzmann's mind. He focused his attention on exposing the vile behavior of perpetrators and bystanders, and on the still unheard stories of the victims. Not too long into the new millennium, however, other questions have also become central for filmmakers, including the concern as to whether the ruins of camps and the museums around them are appropriate tourist attractions. In recent years, diverse documentary filmmakers from multiple nations including Rex Bloomstein, Ra'anan Alexandrowicz, Romuald Karmakar, and Jes Benstock have taken up this question.[1] Auschwitz, the former Nazi concentration and extermination camp, was opened as a museum in 1947, not long after the war. The number of visitors today reaches record highs, and that number has tripled what it was in 2001. Unsurprisingly, large numbers of Internet users are also visiting the Auschwitz Memorial page on Facebook. Although Lanzmann's film unearthed questions and answers about what precisely had happened and who should be held responsible, the question of how cultural memory is formed in the digital age has since surfaced as an issue. More and more, consumer culture transforms our mode of interacting with the past: Justin Bieber visited the Anne Frank House in 2013, writing in the guest book that he hoped Anne would have been a "belieber," the term for his impassioned fans, and the *New Yorker*'s Ruth Margalit reported on a satirical Facebook page devoted to poking fun at tourists who take "selfies" at Auschwitz.[2]

Holocaust tourism has its critics: a 1998 artwork by the British artist Alan Schechner entitled *Souvenirs from Poland (Lousy T-Shirts)* consists of white t-shirts displayed on rods each with the name of a famous location of a concentration or death camp on it and featuring a familiar slogan, for example, "My daughter went to Treblinka and" (Figure 1.1). The souvenir's sentence is unfinished; it trails off into the white space of the shirt. The meaning of the work is initially obvious: almost any family member who went to these death camps died there; they brought back nothing. But by breaking off in the middle of the sentence, the artwork indicates the complications connected with concentration camp tourism. By choosing the most frivolous souvenir, the shirts draw attention to the trivialization that goes hand in hand with any act of Holocaust merchandising. Tim Cole's book *Selling the Holocaust: From Auschwitz to Schindler. How History is Bought, Packaged and Sold*, published in 1999—on the cusp of the new millennium—was a comment on the status of the Holocaust in the postmemorial era. Cole subjected the commercial aspects of Yad Vashem, Auschwitz, and the United States Holocaust Memorial Museum (USHMM) to critical assessments. Even Henryk Broder, a German Jew who is particularly concerned by left wing anti-Semitism and whose parents were Holocaust survivors, provocatively compares tourism at Auschwitz to Disneyland, noting that the camps are a distraction from contemporary Judaism's real concerns, particularly the swell in worldwide anti-Semitism. Satirically comparing the idea that Auschwitz should never happen again with the resolution that the *Titanic* should never sink again, he describes

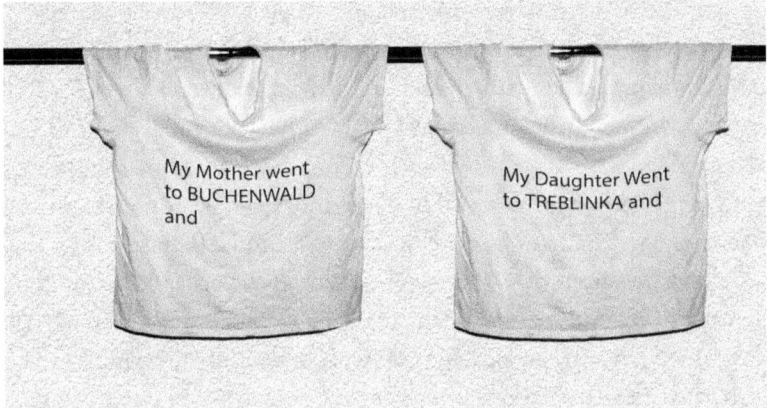

Figure 1.1 Artwork by Alan Schechner, *Souvenirs from Poland (Lousy T-Shirts)* (1998) © Alan Schechner. Image courtesy the artist. www.dottycommies.com

today's Auschwitz as "a Disneyland of death, where visitors can shudder without danger."[3] Broder's invective is obviously geared toward getting attention, but his taboo-breaking position is a symptom: tourists regularly parade past these sites, visiting Dachau, Auschwitz, and other locations every day. To judge from the changing subject of Holocaust documentaries, the question of whether the commodification of Holocaust cultural memory is problematic, repugnant, or simply inevitable has become an important one for contemporary filmmakers.

I do not mean to suggest that questions concerning Holocaust memory, site preservation, and tourism were not discussed prior to the end of the Cold War. They certainly were. As early as *Night and Fog* (1955), for which Auschwitz is central, the film's narrator enjoins the viewer to reflect on the fact that tourists are having their photographs taken in front of crematoria. Tim Cole observes that Auschwitz became a major pilgrimage site, especially in the 1970s, because it was "*the* symbol of the Holocaust" in Western consciousness, citing famous uses of the name by Theodor Adorno in 1955 as well as by Sylvia Plath in 1965.[4] In her 1977 book *On Photography,* Susan Sontag includes an excerpt of a 1974 article from the *New York Times* with the dateline: Oswiecim, Poland. The author of that article notes that now nearly 30 years have passed since the Auschwitz camp was closed down, and that "the underlying horror of the place seems diminished by the souvenir stands, Pepsi-Cola signs and the tourist-attraction atmosphere." The crowds, the author adds indignantly, "troop through the former prison barracks, gas chambers and crematoria, looking with interest at such gruesome displays as an enormous showcase filled with some of the human hair the SS used to make into cloth.... At the souvenir stands, visitors can buy a selection of Auschwitz lapel pins in Polish and German, or picture postcards showing gas chambers and crematoria, or even souvenir Auschwitz ballpoint pens which, when held up to the light, reveal similar pictures."[5] Sontag includes this *Times* excerpt among an array of other quotations, but perhaps she means to comment on it by way of its proximity to a 1973 quote from Marshall McLuhan, who writes that, "The media have substituted themselves for the older world. Even if we should wish to recover that older world we can do it only by an intensive study of the ways in which the media have swallowed it."[6] The two quotations, as they appear, side-by-side with one another, highlight the extent to which tourism is mediation, as well as how Sontag seemed to be sympathetic to McLuhan's assertion that analyzing the medium itself—exploring tourism as one among the many beasts that swallows experience—has to take priority over engaging in any act of "recovery."

One can, of course, reach even further back: the various camp memorial sites and museums each have their own storied history. The Dachau memorial, for example, was first established in 1965 and the Mauthausen Museum in Austria was opened a decade later. In no case has the establishment of a museum been a simple matter; people, particularly the Germans and Poles who have to maintain these sites, do not always wish to be reminded of painful parts of the past. The German author Peter Weiss, as early as 1965, had attempted to depict the vexations associated with visiting the Auschwitz camp memorial. Weiss, who is perhaps most famous for his 1965 play *The Investigation*, which depicts the Frankfurt Auschwitz Trials that were concluded in that year, was of Jewish heritage and spent most of the war in exile in Sweden. His short prose piece about Auschwitz entitled "My Place" ("Meine Ortschaft") was a contribution to a literary collection entitled *Atlas*, which was published that year and also featured contributions by Heinrich Böll, Anna Seghers, and Nelly Sachs.[7] Weiss's reflections are shaped by the knowledge that he too would have been deported to Auschwitz had he stayed in Germany.[8] His essay is permeated with the sense that his fate was only narrowly avoided. Now, he writes, he arrives at the camp of his own free will, 20 years too late. He attempts to perceive Auschwitz with what the narrative theorist F. K. Stanzel would have called a "camera-eye" technique in which the author-narrator attempts to bracket out his own feelings.[9] Weiss writes, for example, "Without thoughts. Without any impressions beyond the fact that I am standing here alone, it is cold, the ovens are cold, the wagons are stiff and rusted."[10] His sentences are short, and he occasionally omits verbs, emphasizing austere descriptions over actions. Weiss seems to fear that allowing too much space for subjective impressions opens the door to clichés in place of the truth. Trying to make his standpoint palpable to the reader, Weiss reiterates the word "here": "*Here* the washroom, *here* the stone aisle. . . . *Here* the steps leading down to the bunkers."[11] In studying this style of narration, Stanzel observes that one can only *aspire* to depict a complete lack of reflection and emotion. Where writing is concerned, imagery cannot be unencumbered by a subject, and the technique, he asserts, "can never be carried as far in literature as in film."[12] Weiss, however, attempts it, and he writes as though his visit were being taken in through the lens of a documentarian's camera.

At times Weiss's "camera-eye text" evokes the bluntness of Alain Resnais's *Night and Fog*, had that film been stripped of its music.[13] Weiss seeks to communicate only what *is*. He tries to approximate the position of the living person who approaches this site as an intruder. Auschwitz is a terrain that belongs to the dead. He concludes, "The living person who comes here, from another world, possesses nothing but his knowledge of figures, of written reports, of testimonies, they are a part of his life, he grapples with them, but can only comprehend what happens to himself."[14] The unbridgeable distance from the dead is, of course, the tourist's central problem: what can the subject, who visits these places so many years afterward, make of it? Even those who, like Weiss, were destined for the camps and escaped them, cannot comprehend what happened there. If, however, that is the case—if, as we learn from Weiss, the living cannot truly comprehend these sites of annihilation—then what is the purpose of camp memorials? Where are we, the members of later generations, to stand in order to view them, and, given such constraints, what can documentary films about the sites ever hope to communicate?

The themes of camp tourism and memorial preservation have only recently been taken up by film, and one could well imagine that a film that called the Holocaust tourist industry to account would have, at an earlier point in time, met with a fair amount of resistance or skepticism. The demand made by the narrator of *Night and Fog*, that we must look upon the ruins of the camps and remain vigilant so that the nightmare not recur, was, for many years, the only mindful way of perceiving those camps. It was not until long after Resnais's film, after *Shoah*, after *Kitty: Return to Auschwitz* (1979), and after the end of the Cold War (a relevant historical detail insofar as many of these camps were east of the Iron Curtain) that filmmakers began to engage explicitly in a second order of reflection on the marketing and merchandizing of those spaces depicted in *Night and Fog*. Rex Bloomstein's *KZ* (2005) is one example of this type of postmillennial meta-analysis. For what purpose do European governments maintain these sites, and is there any way for the visitors to position themselves so that they learn from them?

Both Bloomstein's *KZ* and Ra'anan Alexandrowicz's *Martin* (1999) are about such sites. They deal with the locations of the former concentration camps—*Konzentrationslager*, hence the abbreviation "KZ"—at Mauthausen in Austria and at Dachau in Germany, respectively. Because our knowledge of those sites is linked to our exposure to them as filmed images and photographs, Bloomstein's and Alexandrowicz's documentaries are also about how those visits are mediated by film. Visiting the sites is, of course, a mediated experience, and watching films about them can be described as a remediation insofar as our knowledge of the camps is, for the most part, determined or predetermined by the long history of these images' receptions, which are, in turn, framed by the films' directors. Few visitors come to such sites without foreknowledge of what they are about to see and, in general, they have a sense of the affect with which they are meant to respond to them. Tourists hope to come into contact with the past and feel something authentic. Gary Weissman refers to this desire as a "fantasy of witnessing," and he describes, as one example, the experience of a son who expected that he might share with his father, a survivor, a sense of the horrors that were endured at Mauthausen. He discovers instead that "the camp appeared neither as his father remembered it nor as he had fantasized it would." The "tidy camp," he observes, had "the cold soul of a museum."[15] What strikes Weissman, and what motivates him to write his book, is the widespread interest in mimicking victims' experiences, whether in person or through film. When Weissman, at a later point in his book, discusses the fantasies associated with films, he notes that they too can make you feel as though you had witnessed something, and that Holocaust films, particularly Steven Spielberg's *Schindler's List*, but to some extent even Lanzmann's *Shoah*, willfully conflate cinematic spectatorship with historical experience.[16]

The documentaries *KZ* and *Martin* take divergent approaches to a similar problem: *KZ* is about trying to re-represent the experience of the contemporary tourist in all of its strangeness. Consistent with Weissman's perspective concerning fantasies of witnessing, *KZ* draws attention to the curious character of our attempts to reproduce sensations from the past. *Martin*, on the other hand, deals with the filmmaker's encounter with a survivor he meets at the Dachau memorial, and that film, at nearly every turn, thematizes the director's investment in the degree to which a survivor can or cannot provide visitors with privileged or authentic access to history. The two films each engage with a specific kind of postmillennial problem: what good are concentration camp memorial sites today and whom precisely do they serve? In the case of *KZ*, Bloomstein tries to maintain a distance, to reproduce the eerie automation and self-perpetuating tourist mechanisms that are involved in marketing this illusory experience, while in *Martin*, the filmmaker is more concerned with highlighting his own complicated desires and subjecting his own affective investments to scrutiny.

"You feel it?": Touring Mauthausen in Rex Bloomstein's *KZ*

KZ is *not* a film about the Holocaust. Bloomstein's documentary centers on the tour guides and tourists affected by the atmosphere at the memorial to the camp at Mauthausen, which is in the area known since 1940 as Mauthausen-Gusen in Upper Austria, not far from the more populous city of Linz. Austria has its own troubled and complex relationship to Holocaust atrocities. In Austria's cultural memory, it seems—in relation, for example, to the election of President Kurt Waldheim, a former Wehrmacht intelligence officer—that much of that nation's population has difficulty accepting obvious evidence about their massive collaboration with the Nazis and still today view Austria as foremost among National Socialism's victims.[17] Concerns about the legacy of Austrian perpetration arise not only in connection with debates around Waldheim or the late xenophobic politician Jörg Haider, but also in connection with discussions surrounding the site of the former concentration camp Mauthausen. Although this stone quarry near Linz in which hundreds of thousands of prisoners were worked to death was not one of the horrific industrial killing centers in the East, conditions there were overcrowded and catastrophic. Bloomstein's film deals with the Mauthausen Memorial and Museum, the way tours are conducted there, and even with the daily life of the ordinary Austrians who live in the long shadow cast by the camp. It is geared toward compelling its viewers to look anew at the memorial site itself. The film represents the encounter with the museum and its surroundings, and it does not concern itself, as had *Shoah*, with the more abstract philosophical issue of whether film could ever truly be capable of representing the Holocaust.

The film is not concerned with unearthing the facts of the matter; it does not establish a chronicle of what *happened*. Nor does it mean to serve as the documentation of a tour; it is not a virtual sightseeing expedition.[18] It objectifies the activity of visiting Mauthausen, turning the museum's status as a tourist destination into an object of scrutiny. Bloomstein's film attempts to account for the expectations involved when the tour guides attempt to transfer trauma, and it also means to account for the impact this attempted transference has on the guides themselves. In this way, the film is both something *more* and *less* than the tour. It gives its viewers less access to the location—as a conventionally expository documentary about a tour might—yet it succeeds in capturing unacknowledged truths about the museum and its environs, inquiring into what a visit there accomplishes. Its subject, in this way, could not be farther from the events of the Judeocide. It is not concerned with the idea that the atrocities should never be repeated, but it is instead engaged with the implicit and explicit rationales that justify these perpetually repeated expeditions back in time. What, it asks, is the goal of reproducing aspects of the original trauma as it affected the camp's prisoners? Do visitors approach Mauthausen, those who come to the town or to the site of the former camp, in order to learn to feel and enact trauma? Are visitors learning, at that site, to perform traumatization?

The film's subject is a tourist destination that appears to function on autopilot, and, as such, Bloomstein stages a critical encounter with contemporary trauma culture.[19] Viewers of the film are likely aware that its topic is the Holocaust, and yet the Holocaust is not even obliquely referenced in the film's initial images, apart from the viewers' knowledge that we are most likely looking at footage filmed in or near the Austrian market town of Mauthausen. *KZ* begins idyllically with a shot of a roller skater as seen from a boat cruising along a placid river. Not a single on-screen intertitle announces the location, and few if any steps are taken to orient viewers temporally. The portrait is simply that of an idyllic park, sometime around the "now" of the film; this is a time and a place that is unlikely to open onto the space of a concentration camp memorial. It turns out, however, that these initial scenes allude to an absence, or a past that has been effaced. The residents appear to think of other things besides the mass murder that took place on their doorstep, and the filmmaker offers no heavy-handed reproach of them, as Lanzmann might have. This is, after all, a portrait of another generation, one removed by many decades from the original event.

Watching Bloomstein's film one becomes acutely aware that the camera's gaze is often attached to no single subject's perspective. Early on, the film's lack of focalization seems acute. In these first riverfront images, we are aligned with neither a face nor a narrative voice, and in the shot that immediately follows, the third image in the film, we are shown a ship's automatic door opening and closing. Someone has activated it, yet it seems to be moving on its own. The automatic door is not the only thing we see operating mechanistically in the film. *KZ* seems to bear witness to a compulsive repetition. One can interpret Bloomstein's style—these images that are seemingly shot from the perspective of no one in particular—as studies of automata. These are ghostly, thanatographic portraits and, given the context, they may be seen to convey the impression that spirits of the past haunt these spaces. Still more important, however, is that the director uses this type of imagery to foreshadow the chief characteristics of the world he is about to depict: everything we see seems to behave mechanistically. Like other tourist cultures, this one rehearses the past over and over again. It is a culture driven by its tourist industry, and the motivation for preserving the past is presumed but unspoken. The memorial culture that everywhere surrounds this camp museum simply lurches forward, and its existential rationale, that one learns from the past so that one does not repeat it, is unceremoniously coupled with commercial interests. The vacant gaze of Bloomstein's camera suggests the film's inability to get near its historical object. The residents of Mauthausen are, for the most part, indifferent to the history that surrounds them, and the Holocaust's survivors are not to be found here—at least not in this film.

Bloomstein begins by painting a larger picture, and by drawing our attention to the appeal of old-fashioned tourism in Austria. We see a traditional historical tour, and the film at this point seems to be poking fun at its quaint charm. As it does this, it is also contextualizing the tour of the concentration camp as simply one museum tour alongside others. Among the film's very first shots is a tracking shot of a corridor on a cruise ship, a hallway that opens up onto a dining room in which passengers luxuriate, and in which everyone has enough to eat. We then see sightseers, perhaps the same ones who approached the town along its river, being led around a well-preserved historic town center—an *Altstadt*—by a guide. Bloomstein is steering us along a course: into what sort of day, and along with what other attractions, would a tourist's trip to a concentration camp be integrated? Visitors to the town learn about the lives of Hapsburg monarchs and they then get on buses and proceed to the camps. While it at first seems as though Bloomstein means to draw our attention to the difference between the one sort of tour, one that takes general historical interest as its object, and the one the travelers are going to receive at Mauthausen, in which they will expose themselves to narratives of murder and trauma, Bloomstein's point has more to do with the overall similarity between the two. Both of these activities combine didacticism and diversion, education and entertainment.

Although most Holocaust documentaries emphasize the difference between perpetrators and victims, the two major groups represented in *KZ* are the tourists and the locals. The local residents seem to partake of a disproportionate enchantment with Austria's long premodern history, insofar as they evince far less interest in its recent past. Before the film even sets foot in the camp memorial, Bloomstein edits in an interview with a woman who appears to be one of Mauthausen's less than 5,000 inhabitants. She wears her traditional Austrian garb (her *Tracht*), speaks with a characteristic vernacular, and proudly proclaims that Mauthausen's history goes back a thousand years, adding that with all its ups and downs, Mauthausen has always muddled through ("Mauthausen is' no' net untaganga"). Images and interviews of this sort run counter to the stereotypes about Holocaust memorial culture, which notoriously lingers on the deepest wounds of the twentieth century. Bloomstein follows this first interview with others: residents are asked whether they feel they live in a normal place, and they explain that they find it exceptionally nice. The consensus depicted here is that Mauthausen is a scenic town, and the film hardly aims to level judgments against those who live today in its modest homes. It would be unfair to condemn them on that basis, yet something more is at work here: Bloomstein's film makes the tacit assumption that these residents should be the caretakers of memory. It is difficult to watch these scenes and not bring to bear the presumption that living so close to the former camp comes with a responsibility that one should be attuned to the local history of violence. Here *KZ* already plays with our expectations. We expect to find in the film a tone of reproach and are likely to project it onto these interviews. Bloomstein does not have to rebuke these residents; most of his viewers will do that reflexively.

The film then conveys us to the camp, and in doing so it highlights the extent to which tourism is, *pace* McLuhan and Sontag, an extraordinarily mediated practice. Tourism is mediation by definition; subject to translation, facilitation, and other interference, the tourist never truly makes contact with his or her object. Bloomfield's perspective is made abundantly clear when he loads us, via his camera, onto a bus headed for the Mauthausen Memorial less than 2 miles from the town's center (Figure 1.2). The guide explains that when the tour of the camp begins, his voice will be heard on Channel 1 of their headsets. Highlighting the technological aspects of the tour emphasizes the numerous strata of mediation; this tour cannot truly be an encounter with the past, and the guides

Figure 1.2 Arriving at the Mauthausen memorial by bus in *KZ* (2005).

are technologically abetted *remediators*, simultaneously aiding and inhibiting the tourists' experience.[20] Visitors' connections to history and to the site of the camp itself are mitigated by the infinite gap that separates the lives and deaths of the prisoners from the dispassionate gazes of these half-bored tourists.

With this in mind *KZ*'s camera scrutinizes visitors to the memorial in 2004, asking how they expect to meet two contradictory aims at once: to understand what it was like to have been in the camps, while at the same time standing, of necessity, at a marked distance from it. The documentary is concerned with tourists' interest in nearing the edge, stepping closer to the atrocities. Because it is trying to create a feeling or mood, rather than make an argument, the documentary is, at least in part, in what Bill Nichols would describe as the poetic mode: its interest lies in establishing a tone, one that communicates the addled disposition of the tourist.[21] Yet the film, in doing so, also criticizes and objectifies, taking its own distance from those who believe that they can or will fall into the space of trauma. In this regard, the film's opening credits sequence is noteworthy: subsequent to observing the advance of the tour bus, we hear a peculiar mechanized voice, one that, it turns out, is associated with the museum's own tour.[22] We first hear a hiss—a background noise associated with analog recording—and a voice declares: "You have come here, and that is good. . . . There is no need to grasp the full extent of the tragedy, which took place here; there is a safety device inside you, which will protect you, and that is a good thing. Otherwise there would be the danger that one might lose one's mind. But we want you to return home safely with a sound mind, and to use it later on for the cause of freedom, justice and truth." As this recorded voice speaks, the two letters "KZ" appear on the screen and spin clockwise, eventually landing in their final, readable position. The film's viewer is drawn into the void between the K and the Z, into the geometric space between the letters. They zoom toward us, and engulf the theater in a darkness, which then dissolves into an image of a fog-covered landscape. The notably automated voice's effect is hypnotic, vertigo inducing, and it is meant to throw us off balance. Its discourse is one-way, a monologue; the machine addresses the visitor, appearing to self-consciously stand in for the entirety of the tourist experience as depicted in the film. The process turns the tourist into a mechanism, and it is no coincidence that the voice refers to a "safety device," one that shields visitors from understanding the true nature of the drama that unfolded there. But it remains unclear precisely what this device is meant to protect against: is it historical truth, or the perils of one's own imagination?

The film's cinematography accentuates the mechanization that attends these ritualized practices. The machine-like character of Bloomstein's images—the world that is depicted here—recalls cinematography associated with filmmakers such as Harun Farocki, who emphasizes surveillance in his films, and Nikolaus Geyrhalter, whose documentaries about hospital practices and factory food production are almost entirely free of commentary and narration. Many of those two documentarians' films aim to depict their worlds as self-perpetuating mechanisms.[23] Bloomstein's camera is at its most automatous at this point in the film, as he approaches the camp through the fog. It is a gray day, and the doors to the bus open, as if on their own, similar to the cryogenic sleep pods in the movie *Alien* (1979). They then empty the tourists onto the parking lot, and the visitors proceed as though they were acting in accord with subconscious directives. As the film presents it, they are subordinated to a process. They are turning themselves over to a trauma culture that cycles and recycles on its own, akin to a watch that is wound by an unseen hand.

Bloomstein's sound editing plays a part in his cinematic expression of alienation. The transitions throughout *KZ* generally take place without music, and they thrust the viewer forward, from image to image, often connecting sequences via loosely linked ambient noise. It seems that we are moving through the space of the museum from one empty, reverberating chamber to the next. At no point is the tour naturalized or normalized, as a non-diegetic musical score would typically do. Bloomstein cuts from the parking lot to a group of Anglophone students, arrayed in front of the camera, as though they were the audience for a performance. They appear to have been sent there from central casting: they wear T-shirts with brand names, some have bared midriffs, and others chew gum. For viewers who carry an archive of Holocaust images in their heads, whether from documentary photography or from Hollywood films such as *Schindler's List*, this group's movement into formation is a postmodern parody of a roll call on the *Appelplatz*. It is parodic insofar as these tourists do not seem to have stepped out of the past; they are deeply in the thrall of the present. They are artifacts of 2004, and any tour's ability to transport them to another time and place—if that is indeed the *desideratum*—is doubtful. Any circumvention of this group's wholesale presentness seems unlikely. As they are depicted in the film, these travelers do not look as though they are prepared to recognize much beyond their own here and now.

By some standards the measure of the tour's success is its ability to approximate traumatization. Those affiliated with the Mauthausen memorial site are duty-bound to offer a simulacrum of the former prisoners' distress. Florian Panhölzl, the tour guide, is only slightly older than this group of students. An employee of the camp museum—a young man doing his state-sponsored civil service—Panhölzl leads tours with a grave and sober affect (Figure 1.3). We later find out that his grandfather had served in the Waffen-SS.[24] He speaks, and Bloomstein's camera lingers on the students. His shaved head and his accent appear less as part of his personality than as part of an adopted persona: from the students' perspective he likely makes for a more than appropriate tour guide, somehow authentically connected to this place. His tone is grim, as is commensurate with his charge, and he explains to the tourists how members of the camp population were defined as "asocial." As he speaks, the visiting students begin to look unwell. He tells them that the camp was constructed with stone from the quarry, adding that every stone they see before them is historically connected with death. However accurate his interpretation may be, his rhetoric intersects with that of a ghost story; wherever they look, they are now meant to see murder.

As Panhölzl speaks of the famous "stairs of death" in the quarry, he says that this is the symbol of Mauthausen, this "stair," but insofar as he is trying to convince them to see differently—or as Charlotte Delbo would say, to try to look so that they may see—we might hear him saying the word's homophone, *stare*. The ghostly stairs stare back at the visitors, and the guide's intention, here even more than elsewhere, seems to be to produce the sensation of trauma. He then waves the teenage sightseers onward, to the next station. The group assembles, and he speaks to them in graphic terms about the prisoners' treatment and about their complete degradation at the hands of the SS, explaining that people were

Figure 1.3 Florian Panhölzl leads a tour of the Mauthausen memorial in *KZ*.

starved, frozen, left naked, and forced to learn the international camp language: beating. As the camera surveys the visiting students' faces, one has to wonder what it is that he means for these students to be doing with themselves. Some look around, others look down. They hear about the various torments and the attack dogs, and Panhölzl makes reference to Georg Bachmayer, the sadistic SS captain, who was notorious for unleashing bloodhounds on inmates. At this point, one of the young students falls into a faint. This induced trauma manifests itself like an illness. She loses her footing and has to be supported by the other students. As she collapses, the camera lingers on her, but only momentarily before it starts panning left, forging forward steadily and indifferently with the group. The tour moves on and so, deliberately, does the filmmaker's gaze. Bloomstein, in a deftly handled attempt to display a deficit of empathy—to highlight his documentary's camera-eye narration—simply leaves her behind, pressing on without her.

This visitor's response can hardly be called inapt. For what reason does one come to the KZ memorial museum apart from learning to perform responses to trauma? Film is, of course, a poor diagnostic tool, and one cannot know for sure, but we might argue that the young woman here makes a decision—that her response is not entirely involuntary. Visitors to the museum may not be traumatized, but they may instead be learning to behave in a way that mimics reactions to trauma. Perhaps for this reason, owing to the gaps between the violent scenes from the past and contemporary sightseeing tours, *KZ* is hardly concerned with reproducing the viewpoint of its prisoners and deportees. At its onset, as the camera approaches the former camp, first seen through the front window of a bus, and a diegetic voice, that of the driver or a guide, explains that such buses today approach the site differently from the path by which the prisoners arrived. We are not traveling in their footsteps. The film thus makes clear that it does not aim to be *Night and Fog*, with its depictions of the entry gate at Auschwitz, nor is it *Shoah*, with its nearly obsessive focus on the arrivals of trains. The subjective mindset of the deportee is of little interest here. This is a postmillennial and postmemorial film, and as such it is only concerned with distant aftereffects and with belated rehearsals of Holocaust trauma. Although *KZ* inherits a long history of past films' sign systems and image archives, its chief interests lie in the present.

One of the museum's more seasoned tour guides, Harald Brachner, is symptomatically depressed. If there is subject through whom *KZ* is focalized, he is it. Bloomstein's camera accompanies Brachner on a drive in which he describes the large numbers of videos and books he has about the Third Reich, and how his interests have now reached the level of an addiction. He concludes that he has given more than 100 percent to his job for the last 8 years, but that things have recently started to go downhill. Unlike the town of Mauthausen itself, Brachner is in decline. He has been taking antidepressants and has become an alcoholic. Following this revelation, there is a long pause. Bloomstein shows us the road ahead seen through the windshield of a moving car. The redoubling of the screen via the windshield recalls the mediated nature of the act of tourism. We are being pushed forward and the motion underscores the feeling of helplessness.[25] This shot is then followed by a cut: two tourists pose for a photo, setting the programmed timer of their camera in proximity to one of the camp's stone walls (Figure 1.4). The shutter of the tourists' automated camera takes the picture, and Bloomstein's decision to cut from the car to the timed portrait suggests that the memorial site is one among several self-perpetuating systems. When it comes to this institution, no one can clearly articulate the purpose of this perpetually moving mechanism.

Inasmuch as we can know the subject of a documentary—that is, if any part of Brachner's inner life can be understood via the narrow window of time over which we come to know him—this tour guide is presented to us as vulnerable and abandoned; he can neither fight his depression nor can he properly edify the community of Austrians who live around the memorial. One of the film's most poignant moments comes when Brachner stands in the open field that Franz Ziereis, Mauthausen's notorious commandant, once ordered encircled with wire to keep Hungarian Jews and Russian soldiers sleeping in the open, killing them through exposure to the cold (Figure 1.5). Brachner laments that hardly anyone

Figure 1.4 A timed portrait, taken by tourists in *KZ*.

Figure 1.5 Harald Brachner in front of an empty field in *KZ*.

visits this site anymore, but that, on the other hand, there is really nothing to see "in this abominable place" (*in diesem extrem scheusslichen Bereich*). The camera then pans across the terrain and, as is one of Bloomstein's hallmarks, it lingers. There is nothing, the director is showing us, that is by nature "abominable" about this place—it is a field, it may even be a pretty one. Its inclusion recalls how *Shoah* also trafficked in absences. There are no evident wounds there; we see little more than a bright green plain beneath a steel gray sky. The field's emptiness is a figure for the fact that the camp is, for visitors today and for the residents of Mauthausen, a projection surface. The landscape itself just lies there. On its own, it will create no new wounds, and it is likely to be ignored. Brachner's poignant speech is followed by a cut to a billboard featuring McDonald's golden arches.

On the sign is written "McDrive Mauthausen." It is a pointed cut; Bloomstein is indicating that the passage of time and the expansion of commerce have blunted the past's capacity to wound.

Although the film is critical of Mauthausen and its culture, it neither condemns nor censures the tourists who come through. What precisely is to be feared from those who do not behave "appropriately," or from those who take photographs at crematoria and adjust their clothing so that they look their best when in the process of posing next to an oven? The film provides no clear answers to this question. In surveying visitors to Mauthausen Bloomstein is hardly cruel. He interviews, for example, a group of South African tourists who make sensible comments about how small acts of discrimination lead to worse atrocities. What they say is thoughtful and true. A benevolent but self-involved tourist from Los Angeles earnestly explains his rationale for visiting the camp on Yom Kippur. He is a quintessential Californian tourist whose remarks are meant to be reverent, even though they are uttered with the affect of a caricatured Hollywood executive.

Bloomstein's camera, however, seems to take a dimmer view of a number of other residents, and he returns us to Mauthausen's inhabitants later in the film. Decades have come and gone since 1945, and some of this town's residents seem impervious to the lingering traces of trauma. The ones we see are hardly conscious of their affiliation with the perpetrators. They can be read as somewhat milder, updated versions of the duplicitous bystanders in *Shoah*. In some cases they are simply naïve, although other responses are more troubling. Some of Bloomstein's interviewees are people who happen to own homes that were once inhabited by the SS. The questions raised by these interviews presuppose certain ethical conundrums: what responsibility, if any, does this group of persons have for the crimes committed at that place and for the memory of the dead? Bloomstein shows us an interview with a couple that resides in a cozy cottage. They explain that some of their friends made jokes about the history of the house when they first moved in, and the interviewer wryly, and in a style that vaguely recalls Lanzmann's, asks for specifics, at which point they good-naturedly reproduce dark attempts at humor—jokes they attribute to friends—concerning what they might have inadvertently dug up or about their home's system of gas heating. Asked whether the past is a burden to them, they promptly reply that it is not; one partner refers to "all of what happened here" (*was alles hier passiert*) and the second then offers a correction: "could have happened" (*. . . sein könnte*), a phrase that leaves things safely in the realm of the unknown. The two simply state their hope that no cruelties took place in the home in which they now live. A long pause then follows. Bloomstein's lingering is a form of reframing, one that denaturalizes in that it resists the urge to cut away. It objectifies the subjects, drawing our gaze toward them, and it also underscores the silence with which such apparently normal remarks are met. We can imagine that these interviewees were supposed to fill the empty space with their contrition, but the film never makes that explicit. It is a presupposition that viewers are likely to bring to the film.

In yet another interview, a woman speaks about having toured Israel, and she relates how she was asked by the tour guide not to tell anyone that she was a visitor from Mauthausen. She describes visiting a place that, from her description, sounds like Yad Vashem and that she remembers seeing the name Mauthausen writ large on the floor. She had, of course, a "wrong" or inappropriate reaction: she was "full of happiness" (*voller Freude*) as a resident of the town. But, she then recounts, the tour guide looked at her as if to say, "please, don't say anything." In this narrative, she is victimized: shame has been thrust upon her. As the interviewee explains her negative response to the tour guide's censorship, it is clear that the writing at the memorial at Yad Vashem apparently had exactly the opposite effect it was meant to; it made her prouder. One can look at the story from multiple perspectives and it is hardly clear which position Bloomstein's film means to adopt: is this woman a victim, or does she suffer from a shortfall of historical consciousness and shame? It is certainly not easy for her to tell this story. Both the information she provides and her "performance"—of pride, of victimization—make it difficult for the viewer to find footing, either to identify with or to condemn her.

Perhaps the least flattering interview is with a woman who had been married to a member of the SS. A dark-haired woman, likely in her late seventies, sits with two friends of the same generation, all of them witnesses who were there at the time, or ones to whom the German term *Zeitzeugen* ("contemporary witnesses") would apply. These testimonies are not of value because they offer facts about the past. Such information would be, in any case, unreliable. As J. Hillis Miller points out, testimony is performative, not constative: we can only assume that the subject believes what he or she is saying is true.[26] The question here is *how* the information is presented. The affect of the interview subjects says as much or more than the interview's content. These women speak proudly and comfortably where certain aspects of the past are concerned. It turns out that one of them met her husband, who was an SS man, at the camp. She describes the beautiful wedding with its soft music, adding that an SS guard accompanied her on either side during the ceremony. She recalls the occasion and how handsome her betrothed was, elaborating that there were, after all, 700 men working at the camp, so she had her pick. The women go on to explain what a boon it was to the community to have the camp there. They had been poor and now their fathers had jobs, all of which helped bring about a warm reception for Hitler's policies. One of the three women, however, seems to have a lot of knowledge about the machinery of destruction, explaining that when the bodies were being burned at the camp, the whole town stank. The ovens were going all day, she says, and here she makes a gesture with her hand, sweeping it across the table, which indicates that she knows how the bodies were fed into the crematoria. As she goes into detail, the other two marvel at how much she seems to know about it. The one who was married to the SS man acts as though she's hearing for the first time about murder at Mauthausen. The real issue, as is made apparent by the contradictory tendencies in this interview, is these subjects' conflicted attitudes of nostalgia and embarrassment. The witnesses go back and forth between the two, privileged to choose whether or not their memories are marred by this history of violence.

Among the scenes of residential life, however, the sorriest portrait, and perhaps the centerpiece of the film, is the depiction of the Frellerhof, an inn where hard cider is served, not far from the memorial and museum. Before we enter, we hear the whooping and screeching of celebration, which, given the context, strangely echo sounds of pain. The concept depicted here is tradition, particularly in the form of a dancing ritual that involves participants slapping one another. Bloomstein captures on film a folk music production number that shares similarities with the traditional Watschentanz, complete with Lederhosen, accordion, loud shoe-stomping, and pantomimed slapping. A trio sings: "The tavern up here by the camp/ is really quite splendid and fine/ everyone happily drops by/. . . ./ A tasty wurst from the spit/ drink a dreamy cider with it" [*Die Moststub'n heroben beim KZ / Die ist wirklich herrlich und nett / Da kehr'n heut' die Leut' gern ein (. . .) / A knackig Würschtel vom Rost / Und dazu ein' traumhaften Most . . .*].[27] Brachner stands apart from all this, framed as an outsider to the fun that's being had inside. The farm, the Frellerhof, once produced food for the camp, and it was also a place where the SS would eat and drink. Brachner points out that today is not all that different from 60 years earlier, and, he adds, he can't help but laugh. The residents' praise for "the cider house (the *Moststub'n*) by the KZ" is remarkable. It is hard to begrudge these residents their traditions, and Bloomstein never comments explicitly, yet the film depicts them as being entirely unselfconscious about their proximity to the site. The atmosphere of commerce and community, the air of sociability or *Gemütlichkeit*, stands in sharp contrast with Brachner's own isolation. Not at home at the inn, the film finds him alone in a wide field keeping company with ghosts. For these Mauthauseners, the alternatives seem to be complete denial, as goes on at the cider house, or deep depression.

In reviewing the film, the critic Thomas Blum writes that this inn is where the people of Mauthausen conduct their "folksy nonsense" (*Volkstumsquatsch*). It may be only accidental that Bloomstein captures this pantomimed face slapping on camera, but the traditional dance can also be seen as one of the film's central metaphors. Leading tours at Mauthausen, even visiting Mauthausen, is akin to slapping one's own face. Most of the visitors, especially upon exposure to Florian Panhölzl's guided tour, or upon looking at the photos in the museum's exhibit, look as though they have come a long way for self-punishment, and the self-flagellation—the images of Austrians striking one another's faces—comes across as though it were a calculated mise-en-scène. It recalls a position taken by Martin Walser, the famous German author who courted controversy in 1998 when he wrote that the chief purpose of mentioning National Socialist crimes in Germany was the exploitation of German shame in the service of fashionable ends. Commemoration of the past had become, as far as he was concerned, a uniformly applicable basis for intimidation or a moral cudgel.[28] Exposure to the crimes connected with Auschwitz had become an obligation. The German idiom about drawing a *Schlussstrich*, or a "final line," beneath it was often introduced into the debates on Holocaust commemoration, especially by those who wanted to cease examining their culpability. Walser's opinion can be read as symptomatic of a trans-generational confusion, one that is highlighted by the multiple older and younger subjects in Bloomstein's film: at the end of the twentieth century, to look at such things becomes less a matter of debt and duty than it is a matter of choice. For his part, Walser does not feel obligated to remember, and he certainly does not like being pushed around. He was, however, in the Wehrmacht, and one could certainly argue that he is obliged to remember insofar as he played a part, even if only a small one, on the side of the perpetrators. The choice to remember is a matter of privilege, and in his aversion, he seems to have confused himself with someone much younger. Members of his generation often look preposterous when asserting their right to remain ignorant or indifferent—when asserting that they have no interest in punishing themselves for the past.

The one person who is punishing himself more than any other, the person who takes up the cudgel, is Brachner. His choices seem to be part of a constant project of self-flagellation. He lives and works in proximity to the site, and he feels that he has been driven to alcoholism. When Brachner describes what goes on at the Frellerhof, he says, "I don't really like it," but as he speaks this mild condemnation an engine guns in the background, subduing his voice and drowning him out. It is difficult not to sympathize with this man. He becomes, after a point, *KZ*'s central character, and the extent to which he keeps company with ghosts can be seen as a part of a search for companionship. We find ourselves with him again at the film's conclusion. The camera follows him through one room of the museum after the next, informing anyone who remains that the museum is about to close. He then explains to the filmmaker, "Sometimes I think I'm living in this time. Really. . . . Voices. Footsteps." Then, in the silence, he tries to present to the camera the ghostly presence of the past: "That's what I mean," he says, "You feel it?" But *KZ* is neither *Paranormal Activity* (2007) nor is it *The Blair Witch Project* (1999). No one haunts these empty spaces, and it is, in the end, about deliberately attempting to see specters, or about the extent to which one might or might not choose to punish one's self with the past.

KZ shifts back and forth between the poetic mode, showing us a mood, approximating the feelings of disorientation and vertigo connected with the attempt to induce Holocaust trauma in twenty-first century tourists, and, on the other hand, a participatory approach, whereby its documentary subjects become our sympathetic guides. In this way, in shifting back and forth between atmospheric imagery and testimony, it reproduces the contradictory impulses of the tour itself, simultaneously occupying a number of positions: it wants to force us to stare, to unflinchingly observe the mechanisms that perpetuate this culture, the ones that alternately allow for or necessitate the locals' indifference, while also sympathizing with these guides who have elected to act as ambassadors to the past and, as a consequence, suffer beneath its weight. Its subjects' testimonials work against the grain of the film's ostensibly automated point of view and against its "camera eye" style of narration. Despite the film's unusually impersonal and perhaps even cynical take on its milieu, the words and attitudes of those who spend day in and day out at the site of the camp may convince the film's viewer that he or she should aspire, in Brachner's words, to "feel" it.

The man from Dachau: Ra'anan Alexandrowicz's *Martin*

Writing in 2002 Volkhard Knigge, the German historian, points out that the experience we expect to have when we visit memorial museums at concentration camps is something denoted by the German word *Betroffenheit*, which is often translated as "shock" or "sadness." Knigge adds, however, that the term has two not completely coincident meanings in German: on the one hand it signifies something that unleashes a compassionate wave of feeling, but, on the other hand, it is connected with something that has concrete consequences, as when one is "impacted" by something, such as a financial or other, similar event.[29] These two definitions can be applied to our conception of how a museum or camp memorial site is meant to confront us: the experience is supposed to be mainly emotional, but we also hope that such sites will have a concrete effect, perhaps on public policy, and for this reason Germany, Poland, and other nations continue to invest in preserving them.

In the present situation, expectations are determined by that fact that we stand in a postmemorial relation to the Holocaust. Visitors are typically not survivors, whose numbers are diminishing, and this has a transformative role where museums as transmitters of the past are concerned. Can such sites counter the effect whereby the distant past grows ever more distant? Can a museum fight the apparently inescapable temporal erosion whereby history rapidly, through lack of real contact with witnesses, becomes ancient? Knigge notes that there is presently a drive to meet the need for more "reality" at such institutions, by including piles of shoes, glasses, and suitcases, all of which feed visitors' "hunger for reality" (*Realienhunger*), and which makes itself felt in the deliberate fabrication of objects from the past. Museums, in other words, may be willing to install replicas of period-appropriate railcars. This drive finds its parallel in those melodramatic feature films that strive to make the past more and more realistic the farther it recedes.

Museums cropped up at camps throughout the 1950s and 1960s. Although numerous memorial sites were dedicated immediately after the war, their establishment as state-funded museums—whether in Germany, Poland, or elsewhere—was often a long road, one that was generally marked by fights and contestations with local communities, communities that, in general, would have preferred not to think about recent history and their role in it. A separate question, perhaps, from that developmental history is the history of meta-reflection on the function that such museums and memorial sites serve. While the question is often raised as to whether institutions of this nature should be established and funded, there is a different question as to what they are supposed to *mean*. What does one take away from visits to these places? Adorno's 1966 essay "Education after Auschwitz" is one attempt to contend with the question of what is to be gained by interacting with the past, especially for Germans. Adorno appeals for a form of enlightenment that would be defined by "an intellectual, cultural, and social climate in which a recurrence would no longer be possible, a climate, therefore, in which the motives that led to the horror would become relatively conscious."[30] Conscious comprehension of the mechanisms that made Auschwitz possible is thus necessary, "as is knowledge of the stereotypical defense mechanisms that block such a consciousness."[31]

The goal of education after Auschwitz is to bring the hidden preconditions of fascism into the light. It is unclear, however, that museums help accomplish this goal. The conceptual artist Jochen Gerz, who was born in 1940 in Berlin, mounted in 1972 an exhibition with the title *Exit/Dachau* at an art museum in Bochum. According to the art historian James Young, the exhibition consisted of "a long hall with twenty tables in two rows of ten, each with a chair underneath and a dimly lit light bulb dangling overhead." On each table there was a photo album, handcrafted by Gerz, featuring images he had taken at the Dachau concentration camp memorial's museum earlier that year. Young continues, "Without explicit directions, visitors to the installation would seat themselves at the tables and begin to leaf through the photographs in the albums. Because the albums were bound in freshly cut wooden covers and the chairs themselves were newly fashioned of unsanded wood, splinters were rife in both hands and seat."[32] At first glance, Gerz appears to be reflecting on the relative similarity between the concept of the museum, with its orderly presentation and its rules, and that of the concentration camp. The mere constellation is provocative, even bordering on offensive, insofar as everyone would agree that the rules of museum attendance are hardly as violent and oppressive as the regulatory regime that dictated concentration camp behavior. The suggestion is, on its face, tasteless, so one would have to assume that the stakes lie elsewhere. The exhibit might much more be about the concept of camp museums and memorials, specifically how they dictate viewers' responses. As Young observes, it is not the artist's own past that he was subjecting to scrutiny, but rather "the experience of the present moment as explicitly controlled and shaped by the museum."[33]

This argument, one that is probably applicable to most museums—that is, that they dictate the terms of their reception—is of particular interest where Holocaust memorials are concerned. We tend to hold out high and perhaps unrealistic hopes for such places: they should make visitors reflect on causes, and prompt a reconsideration of what it is in culture that leads to atrocity.

A museum that dictates its responses potentially reproduces the authoritarianism it means to criticize. Young surmises that Gerz's assertion is that these memorials are really "less about history than how to comport ourselves in its vicinity."[34] But the provocation can be taken farther: museums do not simply impose an interpretation upon visitors without assistance from those visitors. Whether one learns anything at all from a visit to a memorial site is a process of dialogue between the visitor and the site. The more visitors and spectators look for moments of impact, for instances of authenticity and transformation, the more they shape and even delimit what can be learned at those places. The narrowness of our expectations constricts our gaze; the expectations one brings simultaneously form and deform the encounter.

Documentary film has been a major part of the dialogue about what one is supposed to learn from the camps. Bloomstein's *KZ* looks at tourist culture at the site of the Mauthausen memorial, and in 1999 the Israeli director Ra'anan Alexandrowicz released *Martin*, which documented part of his excursion to Dachau, the small city of 45,000 residents just 16 miles north of Munich, which was once home to a concentration camp. Alexandrowicz is particularly interested in recording his feelings about the memorial site, as well as his interactions with the townspeople who live near it, and with a man, Martin Zaidenstadt, who was present at that site nearly every day, talking to visitors. The film is a reflection on the question of what expectations we bring to the memorials and museums, and how those expectations shape the information we receive.

Alexandrowicz was attending a short film festival in Germany in 1996 when he went to the Dachau concentration camp memorial and encountered Zaidenstadt, a man who was then in his mid-eighties. Zaidenstadt gave unauthorized tours of the site from his perspective as a Polish-Jewish camp survivor. The director was so intrigued by his first encounter that he went back with his camera and shot a documentary about this provocative tour guide as a means of exposing both the camp's own aggressively imposed narrative of the past and the surrounding community's aversion to addressing the toughest questions.[35] Owing to the distinctions between the official narrative of what the camp is supposed to mean and Zaidenstadt's decidedly more difficult memories, Alexandrowicz himself describes the film as "a journey into the void between the terms 'memory' and 'commemoration.'"[36] He adds that in Israeli culture memory and commemoration are "not differentiated and are mixed up," noting, "you have these national memories of various kinds; the way that they're passed to you makes them somehow seem to you to be your own memories."[37] For

Alexandrowicz, the adoption of others' memories is rooted in the desire for an ever-closer encounter with authentic voices from the past, and the second-hand witness also bears responsibility for the problematic or even false memories he or she adopts. In the search for impact, for authenticity, and simply for those same experiences that might preoccupy any tourist of history, people are open to accepting truths they might not otherwise accept.

When dealing with this sort of encounter with the past, in the person, for example, of an apparently authentic witness at a camp museum, one typically engages less with history than with empathy. Visitors to Dachau are rarely informed enough to ask detailed questions. They prefer to console Zaidenstadt and to take a souvenir photograph with him. Although one can argue, as does the historian Dominick LaCapra, that the truth of an account provided by a witness can be less important than the "empathic unsettlement" the listener experiences, one should not confuse accounts provided by witnesses, however moving they might be, with the historical truth.[38] Both the witness and their empathic listener bring expectations to the encounter, and because Alexandrowicz is intensely aware of what expectations he brought with him to Dachau and of the type of encounter he was hoping to have there, *Martin* becomes a performative documentary.

With respect to Zaidenstadt, who has by now passed away, the issue was not so much that his tours were unauthorized, but rather that this lack of authority was directly connected to the possibility that he was not a legitimate witness. Timothy W. Ryback's book *The Last Survivor: Legacies of Dachau* (2000) is nearly entirely focused on Zaidenstadt, and it appeared at approximately the same time that Alexandrowicz released his film. At some point Ryback, an expert on European history and culture who provides a long and sometimes personal account of his interactions with Zaidenstadt, begins to wonder about whether the information he is getting, however moving and even unsettling it may be, is trustworthy. An acquaintance reminds him: "There are some people who have read and seen so much about the Holocaust that they begin to confuse themselves with the victims.... It wouldn't surprise me if your friend Martin were one of those people."[39] This revelation is presented as a surprise to readers of the book, but at this point Zaidenstadt, as he appears in Ryback's study, begins to seem a little like Bruno Dössekker, also known as Binjamin Wilkomirski, the author of *Fragments* (1995), a fabricated memoir for which he invented a Holocaust past either because he believed it to be true—that is, because he so desperately wanted the recognition and empathy that comes to survivors that he talked himself into believing he was one—or for more cynical, mercenary reasons. In either case, Dössekker's claims were being refuted at the end of the 1990s, around the same time at which Ryback was writing about Zaidenstadt, and, insofar as both cases correspond to a phenomenon whereby people had been reluctant to question information coming from an ostensibly authentic source, these two stories shared similarities.

Zaidenstadt, as he appears in the film and the book, was a somewhat cantankerous man who insisted that the horror of the camps, as it had been generally made known to tourists, was hardly as horrific as his very real experience. Ryback investigates, as a journalist pursuing the truth. He tries to gather evidence about Zaidenstadt's past from the memorial museum's director, Barbara Distel, and he reports: "Distel apologizes that her colleagues couldn't help me, and she is sorry that she cannot help me either, but the fact is that they have never been able to find Martin Zaidenstadt in [Dachau's] registry of names compiled from the Nazi registration cards after the war, and they are not about to begin looking now."[40] Distel eventually tells him: "Martin says he is a survivor. . . . If he thinks he is, and I don't have the records to prove that he is not, I must accept that he is. . . . And anyway, at his age does it really matter?"[41] This skepticism, and the treatment Zaidenstadt received, is the starting point for Alexandrowicz's film. On the one hand, the director is forced to reflect on his mixed feelings and growing skepticism about Zaidenstadt, and, on the other hand, he has to consider whether Zaidenstadt has been treated with skepticism by others because he has been long telling a story that the institution and the residents of Dachau did not want to hear. His tour, Zaidenstadt argued, was of the "real" camp at Dachau, unadorned and with descriptions of screaming victims. Alexandrowicz found it was important simply to film, "this person who remembers," because, "the environment has a reason not to be happy with these memories and try to paint it in some different way."[42] Taking Zaidenstadt's claims at face value, regardless of whether they were true or false, opened the door for Alexandrowicz to investigate matters differently.

Martin resembles Bloomstein's *KZ* in that it looks both at the camp memorial and museum and at the local residents, many of whom are neither particularly enthusiastic nor knowledgeable about the past. At one point in the film, Alexandrowicz includes an image of himself positioned beneath a street sign that reads "Avenue of the Concentration Camp Victims" (*Straße der KZ-Opfer*) on the east side of town, close to the camp, and he remarks that it must be strange to live in a town that bears this name. In order to find out more, he and his traveling companions, a woman named Artemis and a cinematographer, go to the central square where the locals are friendly and welcoming. A Christmas market is in full swing, and, precisely as Bloomstein had discovered in *KZ* when he visited the beer garden adjacent to Mauthausen, these locals have no problem enjoying themselves in proximity to the site where atrocities took place. Alexandrowicz summarizes that, "Tourists come to the south of Germany to do various things, not only look at Holocaust commemoration museums. And so they hang out in Munich and they have whatever fun they have and they know that they have to devote certain time to having certain sentiments about the Holocaust. And they go and do it in Dachau, of course, and the people living in Dachau feel that they sort of carry the blame for the people of Munich. So they are pushed into this situation." He adds, "if they would wake up one morning and the memorial site, the remains of the camp, would just have disappeared in the night, I don't think they would complain."[43]

Neither Bloomstein nor Alexandrowicz has unearthed a "new" resistance. In the case of Dachau, this friction has a past. The historian Harold Marcuse has researched the long record of antipathy between the town and its memorial site, noting, for example, a piece written in January 1952 by Joachim Steinmayr, then an editor of the *Süddeutsche Zeitung*. Steinmayr had collected a number of quotations critical of the extent to which the memorial, which was not yet officially a museum, had become a tourist attraction of horrors. A representative of the State Restitution Office expressed some resentment when he told Steinmayr that, "he personally was dissatisfied with the exhibition, but ... that the German authorities were at the mercy of the Dachau survivors," adding, "If we change any part, foreigners would storm the barricades. They will say: the Germans want to cover up their guilt." Marcuse notes that the piece strongly implied that only foreign interests supported the exhibition. According to Marcuse, Steinmayr concludes his article with the demand that "something must be done," and, "an accompanying article made it quite clear that the 'horrors' drew the tourists, and it would be best if both disappeared."[44] This sentiment echoes Alexandrowicz's general impression that no one would complain if the camp were to simply go away. And although many have criticized the culture of Holocaust tourism, as Alan Schechner did with his "Souvenirs from Poland" t-shirts, the criticisms take on a different valence when they come from Germans themselves. They appear as intolerance, particularly coming from those who live, and those whose families lived in the vicinity of the camps and who may bear, if for no other reason than the hazard of geography, some responsibility to the absent and murdered victims.

One example of this tension surrounds a sculpture featured in Alexandrowicz's film, one that has by now become metonymically associated with the camp: a Fritz Koelle work, generally known by the name *Concentration Camp Inmate* (*KZ-Häftling*), but also sometimes called "The Unknown Prisoner." For reasons of ostensibly Bolshevist leanings in his art, the artist Koelle had been interned at Dachau, and his sculpture now stands in front of the crematorium. Harold Marcuse notes that this was not the first sculpture Koelle proposed as a memorial, and that he had initially offered a statue depicting "a clothed concentration camp inmate supporting a naked, emaciated comrade with his left arm." Marcuse writes that the composition recalled a pietà, but one transformed so as to be appropriate to its subject: the icon was altered such that it included symbols of camp suffering—the victim was emaciated, with "a shorn head, pajama-like uniform, and a sallow face with sunken eyes." Marcuse concludes that the statue "is not inwardly directed and meditative, but outward and aggressive."[45] Possibly because of the confrontational character, another one of Koelle's sculptures was selected, "a solitary inmate in a long, drooping coat. This 'unknown concentration camp inmate,' as the sculpture has come to be known, is fully clothed so that only his gaunt face betrays emaciation. The accusatory right hand of the earlier statue is now buried in the coat pocket; the knit brows and focused gaze of the earlier work have been raised in a dreamy, undirected look. . . . The accusatory presentation of the inhumanity that reigned in the Nazi camps and the solidarity among the prisoners have been replaced by a vague and palatable representation of a victim of a relatively 'clean' camp."[46] Marcuse's observations about this work's differences from the earlier, more confrontational work makes the later one seem like a toned down and neutered version, the kind of sculpture that does not aggressively challenge the visitors. *Martin* often lingers on Koelle's sculpture; it is the spot where most people like to take Zaidenstadt's photograph (Figure 1.6). With his overcoat on and his hand in his pocket, Zaidenstadt resembles the "unknown inmate." Alexandrowicz at one point dissolves from a close-up shot of the head of the sculpture to its representation on the cover of an informational brochure, on sale for three Deutsch Marks. For the tourists, Zaidenstadt is part of this scenery and he gives the visitors what they want, yet he also pushes too far; most do not want to see this sculpture brought to life, and they would rather leave the past in the past.

The residents of Dachau are, of course, entitled to enjoy their lives, and when approached by Alexandrowicz in *Martin*, they are, similar to the residents of Mauthausen, glad to discuss the very long history of their hometown. Getting

Figure 1.6 Martin Zaidenstadt being photographed in the company of a visitor to the Dachau Concentration Camp Memorial Site in *Martin* (1999).

them to discuss the history of the camp is, however, trickier. The scenes resemble similar scenes in *KZ*: older women, some of whom were there during the war, claim that they knew nothing of the camp, having only been told of its existence at the end of the war, and still others have their own narrative of victimization, explaining that they object to people picking on Dachau all the time, pointing out emphatically that nobody was even gassed there. Zaidenstadt presents himself as a contrast to the area's own will to disown the past, to forget about it, and to deny knowledge of it. In this way he offers something that the travelers to Dachau come there to hear: a hidden, authentic truth. Alexandrowicz is implicated in this as well. He acknowledges that his interest in Zaidenstadt came from this curiosity. Zaidenstadt is unauthorized, unofficial, and marginal. As Alexandrowicz tells the story, he went back with his camera to investigate. He sought out Zaidenstadt and most people assumed that he was doing so because he was irate that Zaidenstadt had taken money from him in exchange for the unauthorized tour. Alexandrowicz observed that most of the employees talked about him in this suspicious way, and even a stranger they met on the bus warned them away from Zaidenstadt with the words, "don't believe everything he says." Alexandrowicz says that the contrast between Zaidenstadt's will and the residents' opinions was clear. He recalled, "by the time I was on [Zaidenstadt's] doorstep, I felt that I understood the story: here was memory trying to survive in an environment of forgetting."[47]

Central to any discussion of the film is how both Dachau and Zaidenstadt address the debate about Dachau's gas chamber. Zaidenstadt maintains that the gas chamber was used, and that he heard the screams, even though the official position taken by the Dachau concentration camp memorial museum was that the chamber was not used. In the film, Barbara Distel explains that there is a controversy about the precise history of the chambers, and that they were perhaps only used once or twice by the SS doctor Sigmund Rascher, whose experiments on humans at Dachau were judged inhumane and criminal during the Nuremberg Trials.[48] As she appears in Alexandrowicz's documentary, Distel remains open to the possibility that people were gassed, but it seems to be important to the people of Dachau to assert that they were not. In the book *The Last Survivor*, Ryback writes that nearly everyone else with whom he spoke informed him that the chamber was not used, adding that a former Dachau mayor, "once argued that since the damn thing had never been used it should have been torn down, because it gave visitors the wrong impression."[49] The historian Falk Pingel has located the source of the claim that it was used by Rascher, which was the testimony of a doctor provided to the US Military court after the war.[50] There is no doubt about the huge numbers of dead at Dachau, that over 40,000 died there, and that the crematoria were certainly used to dispose of the dead even though it was not, by the standard definition, a death camp (a designation reserved for institutions devoted almost entirely to mass killing, such as Auschwitz and Treblinka). The status of the gas chamber enters into *Martin* because the discussion about it resonates with Zaidenstadt's status as provocateur. That Dachau was the site of a functioning gas chamber is something the Dachauers prefer not to hear. It is not Alexandrowicz's point that a gas chamber was used, but rather that the community wanted to see Zaidenstadt silenced for saying otherwise. For this reason, it was important to the filmmaker to take Zaidenstadt's claims at face value: the subject of the film is not the history of the Dachau camp, it is the present—the desire to avoid certain questions, to let matters lie.

When Alexandrowicz, in *Martin*, recounts his impressions of the museum at the camp, he narrates, "we entered the gas chamber," and the statement is self-conscious about mediated witnessing that goes hand-in-hand with museum visits. What he enters, of course, is not the gas chamber, but rather a museum exhibition featuring a gas chamber. Those who entered Dachau's gas chamber, whether it was only a few or many more, never came out. The director-narrator's curt statement gives one pause to reflect on the meaning of this type of re-creation and identification—the pathos of trying to re-experience the camps prosthetically. Of his museum visit, Alexandrowicz explains: "I was disappointed with the whole thing. Artemis said that what I am looking for cannot be found here. You can't understand hunger in a museum." He and Artemis are looking for something more, and they take responsibility for the fact that they were drawn in by Zaidenstadt's story.

At this point in the film, Artemis is depicted standing alone, staring out a window, and Alexandrowicz presents a still image transitioning to a moving one. As the film goes into motion a woman passes behind Artemis in the background, and the figure seems ghostly, partly because of the speed at which she moves, but partly because she goes entirely unnoticed. Zaidenstadt's appearance speaks to the need in Artemis's claim: you cannot understand hunger in a museum, so their encounter with a survivor represents the authenticity for which the director and his companions were looking. The transition from still images to moving images is part of thinking through this transformation: the museum, with its photographic exhibitions, its sculpture, and its essentially inert relationship to the past also cannot compare with the presence of the living witness. Zaidenstadt embodies suffering, and if a visitor to the museum is seeking to empathize there is no more convincing way to do that than through contact with this marginalized survivor. Photographs are taken to be true and evidentiary value is attributed to them, yet they pale in comparison with live witnesses from the living past. In comparison with embodied memory, images are deficient. For this reason, Alexandrowicz's film starts and ends with still images, some of which are video stills, others are photographs. In the film's opening moments, for example, we first see a bag, which appears to contain photographs. Hands then reach into the bag and pull out pictures (Figure 1.7), but this is all a conceit: these images are less photographs than they are stills culled from the moving images Alexandrowicz and his cameraman took on their visit; the story is initially narrated via a series of still frames from the moving video. Where one expects motion, there is stasis. On the one hand, this suggests that memory is fleeting and fragmentary—that we perhaps remember more in discrete instants than we do in long sequences—but it also reflects the fact that the day had not come alive for them prior to their meeting with Zaidenstadt.

All of the exchanges between still and moving images—that is, the fact that Alexandrowicz takes moving images, makes still images from them, and then films them or edits them in as part of another set of moving images—are enabled

Figure 1.7 A photographic still in *Martin*.

by the curious relationship he establishes between photography and memory. His choices recall the conceit of Andrzej Munk's Polish film *Passenger* (1963), which was completed not by Munk but by another director because Munk died before he could finish it. As part of assembling that film, that film's second director, Witold Lesiewicz, relied on still frames. He was indicating that he had difficulty reconstructing the late director's intentions, and something similar is at work in *Martin*, where the still images stand for a type of narrative openness: each image is, by itself, nothing more than a point on a line, and those lines—the narratives we attach to the photographs—can radiate in any direction. Stories can be constructed around photographs in a number of ways, and to make sense of them, they have to be assembled.

As Alexandrowicz's party arrives at the camp, we see, in a still frame and through the window of the S-Bahn (and thus doubly mediated), the train station's sign: Dachau. The image of the station sign is over-determined in this context. This type of arrival has an iconic history; we have seen this so many times in feature films, and the arrival is a self-conscious gesture. The director cannot reproduce the trauma of deportation. It is at this point that *Martin* transitions, bringing us up to date, by taking the still images out of the narrator's hands. We move from the paper package of stills with which the film had been introduced, to a series of unframed still frames, and eventually to still images of the exhibit at the memorial museum. As the framing layers fall away, we see Alexandrowicz standing in front of museum displays; he is in color, while the images are in black and white. One image depicts him as being quite small in front of a large portrait of barracks. He is looking up at it, but the shot is taken from the air, and the prisoners look tiny. It seems to emphasize the scale of things; everything is out of proportion. The prisoners in the panoramic image of the camps are small and inaccessible, and, at the same time, the picture is wall sized, and it makes the viewer feel small when standing next to it. The director looks despondent. What was Alexandrowicz supposed to do with such an image? From the tone of his laconic commentary—"Dachau was not exactly what I expected"—the disproportion vexes him. This type of interaction seems to strike the narrator as somehow false.

Why is this film so fascinated with still images? Alexandrowicz's documentary is bookended by photographs. It starts and ends with this same curious relationship to the image. Throughout their encounter Zaidenstadt alludes to photographs he has, ones that would verify that he was present at the camp at its liberation. Zaidenstadt is, however, reluctant to share them, possibly because he is made uncomfortable when he is forced to prove the veracity of his claims. The film suspends this problem until near its end, when Alexandrowicz finesses an invitation to join Zaidenstadt in his home. There, Zaidenstadt takes Alexandrowicz back to his study, reaches into a box, and pulls out photos taken in 1945. These photographs hardly have the evidentiary value Zaidenstadt believes they do. They are the same photos that are part of many archival collections including that of the USHMM. In one of them, for example, survivors explain the operation of the crematorium ovens (Figure 1.8). That photograph, a posed reenactment, was, according to the USHMM, taken by a committee of former Yugoslav prisoners for their records and then widely distributed to American soldiers.

The fact that Martin owns these is hardly evidence; many people have these photographs. They are fully reproducible and tell us nothing except that they exist. But this problem, it seems, was among the impetuses for the film. Alexandrowicz's aim is not to prove whether or not Zaidenstadt was in the place he says he was, but rather to ask what his presence reveals. The director says that when he explained about the photographs to the archivists at Yad Vashem, they said, "everyone has these pictures." Alexandrowicz says this was a turning point: "that's when I decided I was going to edit the film without any further research about Dachau; just use the material that I have and look for a perspective through that."[51] The photographs mean something to Zaidenstadt, and perhaps for this reason the compositions at this point, near the film's end, are similar to the

Figure 1.8 Survivors of the Dachau concentration camp demonstrate the operation of the crematorium by pushing a corpse into one of the ovens. Courtesy the USHMM, Photo Archive. Photograph no. 15026.

opening shots in which Alexandrowicz narrates his own memories while holding still images. Here too, Zaidenstadt holds the photos in his hands, narrating a series of still images, just as Alexandrowicz had. Zaidenstadt lingers on these same photographs, displaying them over and over again, as if the repetition served to further validate his claims. In the film, Alexandrowicz explains: "he showed us every copy he had, as if it were a new image to be looked at." Each repeated photo affirms his story owing to its evidentiary nature as a photograph. The contents of the photographs are less significant.

One image in the film is particularly emblematic when it comes to addressing the evidentiary character of photographs in *Martin*. Early on, while touring the museum, Alexandrowicz says, "I read in the guide that more than 32,000 people died here," and as he says this, the camera nears an image of the infamous tree-hanging punishment, a photo that was supposedly taken at another camp, at Buchenwald (Figure 1.9). This photo was not only *not* a photo from Dachau, but it may in fact be inauthentic; according to the historian Herbert Obenaus, the photo, of which there is more than one version, was staged after the war by the East German film production company known as the DEFA in conjunction with the production of a film. For Obenaus this was retrospectively obvious. A "critical and skeptical observer" of the tree-hanging photo, "would notice the bent legs of both of the prisoners. If the persons producing the photo of the tree hanging even once looked more closely at the drawings that were made by

Figure 1.9 The hanging torture photograph, as depicted in *Martin*.

the prisoners, it would have been clear to them that the bodies of the hanged men hang slack and that they don't bend their legs. The bent legs are probably to be chalked up to the techniques that were used to affix the men to the tree." Obenaus concluded that they were likely attached to the tree with a kind of belt, one that allowed them to bend their legs.[52] The photograph appears in literature about Buchenwald, Dachau, and elsewhere, and Obenaus uses the photograph's reception as an opportunity to discuss the circulation of such images, or their migration away from the source.[53] He writes of his concerns about the "marked tendency to rely less on the contemporaneous illustrations by prisoners, or ones completed from memory, than on a photo, the origins of and knowledge about which were always less than certain." Obenaus adds, "the great rarity of photographs showing abuse of detainees taken by the SS would have made one suspicious. . . . In this respect, the history of the photo of the tree hanging has a symptomatic meaning that should give cause for consideration and skepticism."[54]

One might perhaps be less concerned about whether this photograph misleads people into believing that tree-hanging or pole-hanging—a torture otherwise known as "strappado"—was a common form of punishment at Dachau. There is no question that it was, and this type of torture, for example, has been discussed in the accounts of Paul Martin Neurath, Josef Seuß, and others.[55] Of greater interest is the issue of what the reception of the photograph helps us understand. The image was taken to have been accurate, and its installation as part of the exhibition had an added force of authenticity, because, as Obenaus points out, images of SS men brutalizing people are more rarely seen than others; they are rarer than the photographs that were taken following the liberation and thus after the torturous fact. The more and the more closely *Martin* dwells on the evidence as supported by the museum (the idea that the gas chambers were rarely if ever used) and then on the evidence provided by Zaidenstadt himself (the curious and sketchy details of his own biography), truths begin to fragment and separate like the pixels that compose a digital photograph. Alexandrowicz, in including the image in his film, and in enacting, as his camera zooms in on the photo of the hanging tree, its dissolution, was likely not thinking about its possible falsity. He may, however, have been thinking about other types of gaps in our knowledge, especially about what it means to near a survivor's experience and to approximate any understanding of torture. It is easy to claim to "understand" how the tortured subject feels, and how awful torture must have been. But as Jean Améry, who was tortured by the Gestapo and who survived Auschwitz, points out, torture, particularly this kind of hanging torture (which he himself endured), is impossible to communicate. Writing that it would be senseless to describe the pain that was inflicted upon him, Améry concludes, "The pain was what it was. Beyond that there is nothing to say. Qualities of feeling are as incomparable as they are indescribable. They mark the limit of the capacity of language to communicate."[56] Something like this might have been occurring to Alexandrowicz as he looked at the image of the tree-hanging and wondered whether he could understand the experience of the victim, or, in the words of his companion Artemis, whether one can "understand hunger in a museum." Even with what can be described as his "extra-museal" experience of encountering Zaidenstadt, the truth—the understanding or coming to terms with experiences like hunger, degradation, and torture—remains at a distant remove. And the more closely Alexandrowicz's camera-eye investigates his own desire for proximity, the more rapidly everything falls apart.

    Alexandrowicz is aware that he has come to Dachau with preconceptions, and he describes earlier, informational documentaries, ones taken right after the war with the intention of convincing people—both those people watching the images, and the Germans seen in the images—that horrific events had actually happened. For these audiences the films were meant to be evidence, yet they, in their ever-changing contexts, take on a variety of changing meanings. A scene from an expository documentary that Alexandrowicz examines contains a shot of people viewing corpses piled high at Dachau, one that is nearly identical to shots that appear in *Death Mills* and in *Nazi Concentration Camps*. In the context of his own film, Alexandrowicz replays the sequence, which purports to show persons who have died in the gas chamber, this time slowing it down.[57] He reflects on the mise-en-scène and remarks, "I noticed the spotlight at the top of the frame. I could imagine the American director instructing the residents of Dachau to pass from left to right in front of the bodies.... Did he also tell them to shake their heads?" He reproaches himself that he had come to accept as truth whatever is said in the booming voice of the narrator, but it is hard not to see it—to see this scene with its enframed spotlight, which he includes twice in *Martin* so that we, along with him, can re-read it—as a reflection on the kind of documentary that Alexandrowicz himself has made; a self-reflective one that questions his need to see a certain way. The film questions his own investments, and we might ask whether his documentary is not still, even at this late date, decades after, a reaction to the earliest postwar documentaries, ones that linger in the mind's eye and still today shape our cultural memory.

Despite taking its title from the name of a survivor, *Martin* is not really Zaidenstadt's story. Looking at received images of Dachau's liberation, both filmed and photographed, it is more about that which stands in the way of gaining access to the past and to the kind of authentic truth that would make its director, a Jewish filmmaker from Israel, feel distinct from other visitors to Dachau, from those who "know that they have to devote certain time to having certain sentiments about the Holocaust," and who thus make their dutiful pilgrimages. The photographs in the film, whether they are at the museum or in Zaidenstadt's own collection, prove little. They are of value to Zaidenstadt, but they do not substantiate his claims. Such photographs are reproducible and subject to interpretation, and Zaidenstadt's own insistence on their significance only serves to make his claims less credible. He relies on them; he protests too much.

This overall impression about Zaidenstadt—that something in his story is not quite right—is also the impression one has while reading Ryback's *The Last Survivor*. Ryback leaves readers feeling that there are many gaps in Zaidenstadt's assertions about his past. The museum at Dachau has no way to help Ryback with his research. Regardless of what Zaidenstadt feels—that he was telling the truth, and that to him, as was the case with Bruno Dösseker, his truth was true to him—questions linger. Ryback looks into this matter, spending a fair bit of time on it and ultimately recounting Zaidenstadt's version: he grew up as Mordechai Zaidenstadt; he was from the small Polish town of Jedwabne, the site of an infamous 1941 pogrom; he was registered as the Polish soldier Mjetek Zaideta; and he arrived in Dachau sometime in the autumn of 1943.[58] His registration as a Polish soldier is significant because many prisoners identified as Jews were deported away from Dachau, to death camps in the East. One might speculate that he carries with him a degree of guilt for having avoided the fate of other Jews. Ryback can find little that confirms these details, however, and he simply "abandon[s] himself" to Distel's instinct that Zaidenstadt is probably a survivor.

Ryback uses Zaidenstadt's assertions as starting points to talk about anti-Semitism in Poland, up to and including the Jedwabne massacre. He goes so far as to travel to Jedwabne looking for traces, but he leaves much to speculation, and cannot quite assemble all the pieces of Zaidenstadt's past. Writing about Ryback's book, Jenny Edkins surmises that if Zaidenstadt's wife and child died at Jedwabne, then the fact that he repeatedly "tells the tale of how he heard the screams of those gassed in Dachau to anyone and everyone who will listen," is really a way of speaking about "what is absent: the silence, the void." She concludes: "The story he does tell functions perhaps in some way to conceal the tale he cannot tell. The screams he maybe didn't hear at Dachau stand for the screams he didn't hear at Jedwabne: the screams of his wife and child."[59] Ryback summarizes his findings this way: "In Dachau, Martin has seen and heard the worst of horrors that man ever committed against man, but they are nothing compared to his inner vision of the flaming barn that lit Jedwabne's night-time sky and cast its dancing flames against the rising twin-spired church. . . . Martin comes to the gas chamber, to this place of palpable horror, to escape the horrors he never knew, the screams he never heard but that have called to him every silent day, every silent hour of his long life, the cries of a wife he once loved, and possibly still does, the screams of a daughter whose age he cannot speak, whose name he cannot utter."[60]

The writing in Ryback's book is poetic, but on this point it is intensely speculative. There is much more information to be had, and documents from the International Tracing Service (ITS), which was not opened to the public until 2007, tell a more detailed story. Distel's instincts were right: Zaidenstadt is a survivor. The documents follow the course of his imprisonment and his various plans for emigration. One document shows Zaidenstadt as having spent the postwar period in Allach concentration camp, and being among the

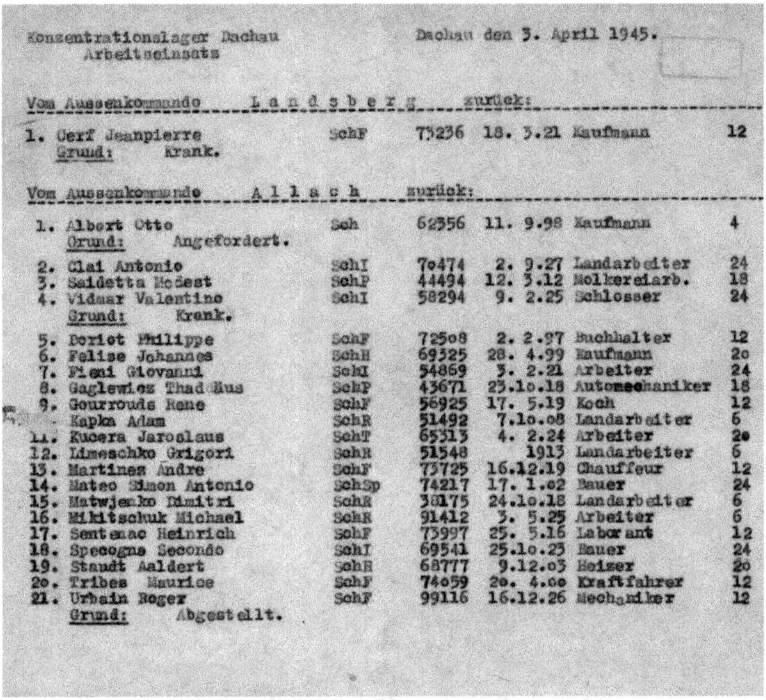

Konzentrationslager Dachau
Arbeitseinsatz

Dachau den 3. April 1945.

Vom Aussenkommando L a n d s b e r g zurück:

1.	Cerf Jeanpierre	SchF	73236	18. 3.21	Kaufmann	12
	Grund: Krank.					

Vom Aussenkommando A l l a c h zurück:

1.	Albert Otto	Sch	62356	11. 9.98	Kaufmann	4
	Grund: Angefordert.					
2.	Clai Antonio	SchI	70474	2. 9.27	Landarbeiter	24
3.	Saidetta Modest	SchP	44494	12. 3.12	Molkereiarb.	18
4.	Vidmar Valentino	SchI	58294	9. 2.25	Schlosser	24
	Grund: Krank.					
5.	Doriot Philippe	SchF	72508	2. 2.97	Buchhalter	12
6.	Felise Johannes	SchH	69325	28. 4.99	Kaufmann	20
7.	Pieni Giovanni	SchI	54869	3. 2.21	Arbeiter	24
8.	Gaglewicz Thaddäus	SchP	43671	23.10.18	Automechaniker	18
9.	Gourrouds Rene	SchF	56925	17. 5.19	Koch	12
[illegible]	Kapka Adam	SchR	51492	7.10.08	Landarbeiter	6
11.	Kucera Jaroslaus	SchT	65313	4. 2.24	Arbeiter	20
12.	Limeschko Grigori	SchR	51548	1913	Landarbeiter	6
13.	Martinez Andre	SchF	73725	16.12.19	Chauffeur	12
14.	Mateo Simon Antonio	SchSp	74217	17. 1.02	Bauer	24
15.	Matwjenko Dimitri	SchR	38175	24.10.18	Landarbeiter	6
16.	Mikitschuk Michael	SchR	91412	3. 5.25	Arbeiter	6
17.	Sentenac Heinrich	SchF	73997	25. 5.16	Laborant	12
18.	Specogna Secondo	SchI	69541	25.10.23	Bauer	24
19.	Staudt Aaldert	SchH	68777	9.12.03	Heizer	20
20.	Tribes Maurice	SchF	74059	20. 4.00	Kraftfahrer	12
21.	Urbain Roger	SchF	99116	16.12.26	Mechaniker	12
	Grund: Abgestellt.					

Figure 1.10 Work deployment of prisoners of KL Dachau in various detachments outside the camp, April 3, 1945, International Tracing Service Digital Collection, List Material Dachau 1.1.6.1, 9918881, Courtesy USHMM.

Polish nationals who were liberated.[61] There, he is listed as Modest Zaidetta from Jedwabno, born March 12, 1912. Other documents list him by the name Saidetta, indicating that he was a *Molkereiarbeiter*, or someone who is trained to work at a creamery or a dairy (Figure 1.10), and still others show the first name Modest or Mordechai. Another document, from May 1947 or 1948 shows him as a member of the Jewish community of Dachau.[62] Most important, however, is the "CM1," the "Care and Maintenance" form, dated November 9, 1949 in which he goes by Zaidenstadt, and which shows that he was interned in Dachau in 1943 (Figure 1.11). That form, which includes Zaidenstadt's photograph, indicates that he has no relatives left in Poland, and that he does not intend to go back.

In spite of websites that have denounced Zaidenstadt as a fake, viewing him as symptomatic of a commemorative culture too quick to accept anything as the truth, these ITS documents provide important evidence. The picture appears to be a certain match: the man in the photo *is* the man who introduced himself to

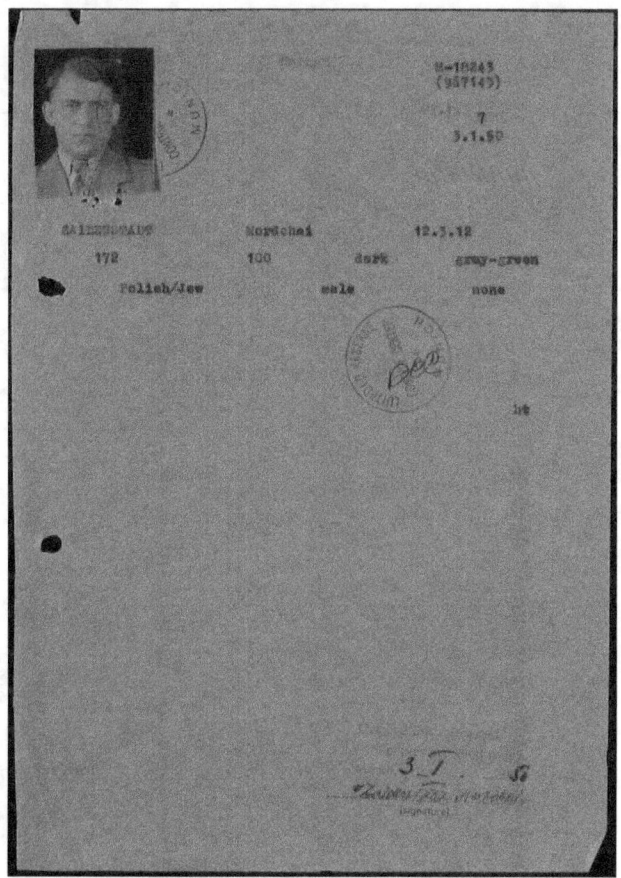

Figure 1.11 CM/1 Form Mordchai Zaidenstadt, September 10, 1951, International Tracing Service Digital Collection, CM/1 Files originating in Germany 3.2.1.1, 79942717, Courtesy USHMM.

Alexandrowicz as Zaidenstadt, the Jewish survivor. But Alexandrowicz's *Martin* is not interested in foregrounding that kind of evidence. It could have been devoted to proving the skeptics wrong, but the film instead focused on the effect Zaidenstadt's presence had on the community. According to Alexandrowicz, his conviction was, "there was something here that had to be made available, but it's not necessarily the testimony and the details." The photograph on the Care and Maintenance form seems dispositive (Figure 1.12), but what, in the end, does a photo tell us?

What is true about all concentration camp museums in the twenty-first century, but in particular about visits to the Mauthausen Memorial and the

Figure 1.12 Detail of ITS Document 79942717 alongside an image of Zaidenstadt as he appears in *Martin*. ITS Document courtesy ITS Digital Collection, USHMM.

Dachau Concentration Camp Memorial Site as they are captured on film is that one cannot walk in the victims' shoes; one cannot travel in time. The problems associated with confronting the past are here depicted as a kind of bad habit: museum consumption can become ritualized, or even mechanized, as it appears to have become in Mauthausen. Alternately, one develops the unenviable habit of hearing simply what one wants to hear, as seems to be the case in Alexandrowicz's depiction of Dachau. If the museums depicted in both of these films, in *KZ* and *Martin,* are going to challenge the defense mechanisms that stand in the way of coming to consciousness about the past, or if they are going to subvert the mechanisms that prevent us from understanding the causes of what happened, they might have to worry less about establishing facts than they do about confronting resistance, on the part of visitors and locals, to hearing anything more than the most convenient and conventional narratives.

2

Mediated Memories: The Influence of Spielberg's Hollywood Hit on *Inheritance* and *Spielberg's List*

If only as a noteworthy work of cinema, *Schindler's List* (1993) is a milestone. According to the American Film Institute, the Oscar-winning production is one of the ten best American films of all time, and it earned over 300 million dollars, which is exceptional revenue for a historical film. The project spawned the Survivors of the Shoah Visual History Foundation, which in 2006 partnered with USC and became the USC Shoah Foundation Institute for Visual History and Education. That vast archive of Holocaust testimony is a major resource for scholars and the public. Moreover, its commercial success had an impact on the economy of Kraków, where some of it was filmed, and the advertisement for that city's *Schindler's List* tour explains that the expedition involves a visit to Oskar Schindler's world, which, we are told, has "survived intact." That world includes Schindler's wartime apartment as well as "the eerie house that was the residence of Camp Kommandant Amon Göth."[1] As both a celebrated pedagogical tool and as a commercial product, the film continues to have an effect.[2]

If only because it is a noteworthy work of cinema, *Schindler's List* merits viewing. The film is regularly taught in cinema history courses, and film scholar Miriam Hansen, among others, has noted its stylistic and thematic debts to Orson Welles's *Citizen Kane* (1941).[3] In making the film, Spielberg brought to bear an arsenal of techniques, and the work's formal complexities frustrate those who would dismiss it as a pop cultural simplification of an enormously complex event. There has been a somewhat predictable tendency to compare it unfavorably to Lanzmann's *Shoah* because those two are without a doubt the most highly profiled benchmarks in the late twentieth-century story of cinematic Holocaust representation. Janet Walker summarizes that the two films are dually celebrated on the basis of their "modal difference," concluding that *Schindler's List* is seen as "the greatest historical *fiction film* on the Holocaust," while *Shoah* is perceived as the greatest documentary.[4] For her part, Hansen published a widely read essay with the title "*Schindler's List* Is Not *Shoah*: Second Commandment, Popular Modernism, and Public Memory." In that essay she anticipates and lays the groundwork for twenty-first century discussions insofar as she rejects the binary disagreement as to whether one may depict or is forbidden from depicting photographs of Holocaust atrocities. Those terms had been generated by Lanzmann's own longstanding anxiety about Holocaust representation, and they are part of *Schindler's List*'s reception because of Lanzmann's response to the film. He declared: "I sincerely thought that there was a time before *Shoah*, and a time after *Shoah*, and that after *Shoah* certain things could no longer be done. Spielberg did them anyway."[5] Hansen prefers to set aside Lanzmann's ban on images, drawing the conclusion that *Schindler's List* uses Hollywood representational techniques "in a relatively more intelligent, responsible, and interesting manner than one might have expected" (at least, "on the basis of Spielberg's earlier work").[6] For this and other reasons, she argues, it should not be viewed unfavorably in light of *Shoah*, nor should Lanzmann be permitted to have the final word.

While there are obvious grounds for comparison between the two films in that they are twin cinematic monuments, the discussion's terms tell us something about how the discourse of Holocaust feature filmmaking overlaps with that of Holocaust documentaries. Those who have seen atrocious images of the camps generally encountered them for the first time in compilation films like *Nazi Concentration Camps* or in *Night and Fog*. Viewers have been confronted by similar arrays of black-and-white archival footage and by similar sets of still photographs. They make up the public's archive and they form the basis of its collective memory. Additionally, feature filmmakers are often in need of instruction as to the extent to which these events are even representable. If *Night and Fog* declared itself capable of depicting atrocity on celluloid, then why would Spielberg not feel authorized to do this as well? Piles of eyeglasses are Resnais's synecdoche for piles of bodies; if they can be shown in one film, then why not in another? The fact that Spielberg may have derived some of his images from *Night and Fog* only serves to lend an air of documentary authenticity to his Hollywood production. While the "piles of glasses, shirts, shoes, gold teeth and other objects" seen in Spielberg's film might only be an indirect or even an unconscious reference to Resnais's work (as asserted by Sara Horowitz), the Polish onlooker who "draws his finger along his throat in a gesture representing death" stands in an even clearer relation to a similarly iconic and memorable moment in *Shoah*.[7] Whether or not we can call these moments in Spielberg's film "citations" of prior films, the archive of familiar Holocaust imagery, which seems at times to be composed of a finite array of signs and symbols, enables us to identify key points of intersection between the works.

More than most filmmakers, Spielberg drew on archival history, integrating material from a range of sources. For example, the legendary girl in the red coat, who is so memorable in *Schindler's List*, was based on a description provided as part of testimony at Adolf Eichmann's trial.[8] The incorporation and appropriation of images in *Schindler's List* is the primary reason the film has been described as authentic. It legitimates itself by way of its re-representation of the archive, and it seems to be the truest reconstruction of an era that viewers know via photographic and cinematic representations. Few can say with any authority whether Spielberg has captured the "truth" about events such as the liquidation of the Ghetto, the construction of the concentration camp at Płaszów, or the liberation by the Soviets, but most viewers would say that it looks like the past with which they believe themselves familiar, only sharper and more seamlessly depicted. The film's account of Oskar Schindler's activities, which constitutes the bulk of the film, seems true-to-life because it exhibits an appearance of authenticity, and because it is all rendered in black and white (or, rather, in shades of gray), which, many have asserted, seems to connect it closely to newsreel footage from the era it depicts.[9] The use of black and white recalls film noir and expressionism, yet World War II newsreels were indisputably among Spielberg's key reference points. Joshua Hirsch asserts that the film's pastiche, by which he means the artful integration of various familiar cinematic styles, "functions both to reinforce the authenticity of the film (on the postmodern assumption that the past is more real if it looks like past films) and to set the film up as the ultimate and authoritative Holocaust film that absorbs and replaces all previous Holocaust films."[10]

Schindler's List is deeply entangled with nonfiction film. Not only does it borrow from documents and documentaries, but at a certain point it even *becomes* documentary: at the narrative's end, once the war has come to a close and Schindler's prisoner-workers have been released, a passing Soviet soldier, in response to being asked what they should now do, tells the former prisoners to go neither east nor west, because they are wanted in neither direction. He then points off-screen and proposes: "Isn't there a town over there?" Spielberg then cuts to a wide-angle shot of the survivors crossing a field, and, as an indication of the location toward which they are now meant to be walking, we hear the folk song "Jerusalem of Gold."[11] Following a brief cutaway to a staging of Amon Göth's hanging and then some words about Schindler's eventual fate, the film returns to the Jews and dissolves to color, moving its narrative out of the past and into the present. The actors are suddenly replaced by their older counterparts, and at the bottom of the screen the title appears: "The Schindler Jews today." Spielberg thus concludes his feature film with documentary footage, cutting away to Schindler's real-life grave marker, as the still living Holocaust survivors, one by one and in many cases accompanied by the actors and actresses who played them, reverently lay small stones on the protagonist's grave. If the film's status as having been based on a true story were not enough to impress viewers as authentic, real, and close to its sources, its ending is intended to seal the deal.[12] Although it in some respects destabilizes the past-ness of the narrative, it also is an assertion that the film is reality-based, and it projects, in that moment, all the earnestness of documentary realism. The sequence even looks different, relying on natural lighting and on an image resolution associated with nonfiction film.

The ending is an allegorical return to origins: Spielberg's film, which traded on documentary film's legitimacy, now inserts itself into documentary history. It wants to be something larger, forgetting its own status as a feature, and in this respect the film's overall project can be seen as a double of Lanzmann's film.[13] Lanzmann does not like referring to his film *Shoah* as a documentary because one can hardly make a documentary about a horror of which there is little footage and about an event where the majority of witnesses were murdered. Owing to the lack of material and the elusiveness of the subject, he feels that he cannot represent such a thing. Making a similarly boundary-breaking gesture, Spielberg aimed to produce something *more* than a feature film. And if Spielberg indeed wants audiences to receive his historically based fiction as something more, then Lanzmann is right to claim that the project runs the risk of "fabricating" an archive.[14] *Schindler's List* replaces historical images with synthetic and palatable Hollywood ones. One should, of course, not be unfair: Spielberg is not trying to replace archives, and the most tangible effect of Spielberg's film was the subsequent establishment of a massive testimonial archive. However, the documentary moment at the end of the Hollywood film suggests that this feature film is meant to take up a place in the body of archival footage. It sheds light on Lanzmann's irritation with Spielberg for trying to create an archive. We may wish to separate the film's positive impact—that it spawned a new wave of documentation—from the question of whether and how it may have negatively impacted the twenty-first century's encounter with the trove of existing images.

If *Schindler's List* inscribes itself into a lineage of documentary films, then it is not surprising that that same body of work reciprocates and draws from it. Documentary film has, of course, responded to its imposing guest. As one example, Janet Tobias's film *No Place on Earth* (2012), which documents the travails of the Sterner family who spent the war years hiding in caves in Eastern Ukraine, ends with a visual quotation of *Schindler's List*: the actors playing the family in the dramatization that takes up much of the film, after having been liberated, cross an empty field in a single line, headed for freedom. The influence and resonance of Spielberg's film's final moments are unmistakable, and equally unmistakable is the similarity between the two films' formulations of their redemptive end titles, which explain how many children are today the descendants of the film's courageous survivors. *No Place on Earth* pays homage to *Schindler's List*, and the citation is a sign of deference and respect. The present chapter, however, looks at two films that have more complicated affiliations with Spielberg's film. The first of the two, James Moll's *Inheritance* (2006), is a contrivance—it is a document of a meeting between two people who would not likely have met if not for the international notoriety and acclaim of Spielberg's film. Moll's documentary gives viewers pause to reflect on the information provided by *Schindler's List*. It stands in a critical relationship to the appearance of authenticity and truth connected with the women's stories depicted in that film. The other work, *Spielberg's List* (2002), was not a documentary in the proper sense, but was rather a work of installation art that explicitly critiques Spielberg's approach to the past. It is a calculated confrontation with Spielberg's version of events and with the space his film assumes in our collective memory.

Meet me in Płaszów: James Moll's *Inheritance*

Inheritance begins with an open door: it is the door to Amon Göth's villa, where the Austrian-born SS officer lived when he was the commandant of the Płaszów concentration camp near Kraków. Viewers might recognize this architecture, more or less, from *Schindler's List*, for which it was meticulously copied and reconstructed. Spielberg changed some details for his film, placing, for example, the balcony from which Göth is depicted shooting his victims inside rather than outside the camp's limits. Watching Moll's documentary, the first thing that would occur to most viewers is its connection with Spielberg's film: it is a documentary that generated its storyline based on characters and locations viewers have come to know by way of a phenomenally successful Hollywood feature. The widespread acquaintanceship with *Schindler's List* mediates nearly every viewer's experience of *Inheritance*, and most people, when they think of Amon Göth, imagine the actor Ralph Fiennes. Given the extent to which *Schindler's List* informs our understanding of the Holocaust, how can our encounter with the people and the places depicted in *Inheritance* be anything but over-determined by Hollywood? Moll's work inherits its subject matter from Spielberg. Can the viewer learn anything about these events that is not already defined by its prior, big-budgeted depiction, and how does the documentary work with or against that knowledge?

Inheritance is nearly entirely responsible for its own storyline: the encounter depicted in the film would not have taken place were it not for the filmmaker's intervention. The film neither observes the daily lives of its subjects nor does it provide a detailed account of historical events—it is neither an observational nor an expository documentary—but is rather a film that invited and facilitated the participation of its subjects. It documents a prearranged encounter between Amon Göth's biological daughter, Monika Hertwig, and Helen Jonas-Rosenzweig, a survivor of the Płaszów camp who was a maid in Göth's villa, and whose experiences were similar to those of Helen Hirsch, the character of Göth's forced-labor housekeeper in the film, whose story was based on a real-life account.[15] Moll, a director and producer, apparently first got in touch with Hertwig in 2003 to ask her permission to use photographs of her father for a separate project, one that had to do with the preparation of *Schindler's List*'s video release. At around the same time, Moll was also introduced to Jonas-Rosenzweig through the Shoah Foundation, an organization he helped to create.[16]

In Moll's film, Hertwig reveals that her own knowledge about her father is highly mediated; she did not know her father and was raised by her mother. She only learned about Göth's atrocious and violent behavior second hand, and, as she tells it in *Inheritance*, her viewing of *Schindler's List* was the first time she was told the truth.[17] Prior to that film's release she seems to have been unaware of what a monster he was, and traces of her obliviousness can be found in the German public record. In a German magazine article about *Schindler's List*, one that is mentioned in Moll's film, one paragraph stands out. The article's author interviews Mietek Pemper, a survivor of the Płaszów camp who helped assemble

Oskar Schindler's real-life list. *Der Spiegel* quotes Pemper speaking somewhat derisively about Hertwig, recalling a letter she had written to that same magazine in 1983 declaring that her father and Schindler had been "best friends," and that the rescue of the Schindler Jews was really more to Göth's credit. Pemper contradicts her, explaining that he knew better, and that he was the one who informed Spielberg how it really felt when Göth "interrupted his dictation and reached for his hunting rifle."[18]

Hertwig had indeed written that letter to *Der Spiegel* in 1983, the year her mother committed suicide, partly as a response to the publicity around Thomas Keneally's 1982 book about Oskar Schindler, which later served as the basis for Spielberg's film. In the letter, Hertwig tries to correct the record. She asserts, "without my father ... the action taken to save the Jews at Płaszów would not have been possible. His silence also saved Mr. Schindler's life."[19] She subsequently learned much more about her father, and Hollywood history here converges with personal memory in the form of an unusual cinematic mise-en-abyme: Hertwig saw Ralph Fiennes play Amon Göth in *Schindler's List*, and she explains her reaction in Moll's *Inheritance*: "I knew from the first moment, this is my father. I had the photo of my father. It was the same profile, just the same." Spielberg, in making a Hollywood film, depicts the truth about Göth's victimization of the Jews, a truth about which Hertwig's mother never spoke to her. This screen image then replaced the image of her own father, just as it became the historical image in the minds of most viewers, especially in the minds of those who had never before heard of Göth. Hertwig's inner conflict became a crisis. She recounts: "I started to hate Spielberg. . . . Spielberg told me the truth. For telling me the truth, I attacked him. Because I didn't want to know."[20]

Göth's daughter thus underwent a very public Oedipal crisis, one that involved a Hollywood film and a popular German magazine. Her crisis also led to a published book-length interview conducted in German and given the title "But I Must Love My Father, Right?"[21] The story is personal to Hertwig, yet the turmoil she felt since 1993 came as the result of an effort to assemble an array of received images and truths. Her crisis was real, yet her oddly mediated position also echoes that of the viewer of *Inheritance*, who has, like Hertwig, come to know this part of the past primarily through Spielberg's depiction of it. *Schindler's List*, however much it alters the facts to fit its melodramatic narrative, becomes a central part of collective memory's fabric. It aimed to be as authentic as possible, and part of that authenticity was its unselfconsciousness about being history's intermediary. It encourages the viewer to forget that it is a representation—that it is not the past itself—and, as with most historical melodramas, it hopes to lead us to believe that we are looking through a window into history.

Schindler's List strives to set an authentic stage onto which we can enter, as if transported, down a hole through to the past. In that 1993 *Spiegel* article— the one that grabbed Hertwig's attention and which was part of the process of introducing *Schindler's List* to the German public—the Swiss journalist Urs Jenny describes, with reference to the US-produced television miniseries *Holocaust* (which aired in Germany in 1979 under the title *Holocaust—Die Geschichte der Familie Weiss*), the mediated memory-hole into which most German knowledge of the event has fallen. Writing about the enormous number of German camps in Poland, he remarks: "Germans, it would seem, had nothing to do with it—in their language there was for a long time not even a term for it. Decades later they agreed on the term 'Holocaust': it calls less to mind the reality than it does the television series, and the advantage of that word is that no one really knows what it means."[22] Akin to many Germans, Hertwig only learned about the past via melodrama. In her case, however, the difference was that this new knowledge had to compete with contradictory personal and familial memories: she had Spielberg and Fiennes to thank for rewriting her difficult relationship with her father and for compelling her to confront the past anew.

Seen from the viewer's perspective, rather than Hertwig's, the uncanniest part about watching *Inheritance* is the recognition of the film's "characters" from the roles they played in *Schindler's List*. When we see Jonas-Rosenzweig it is as though we are seeing, for the first time, the person on whom the role was based. This is, however, not quite the truth: Spielberg changed many of the details. The film's screenplay was based on Keneally's semi-fictionalized book, which, as an exemplar of a hybrid genre can be termed a historical novel. We are thus in the position of comparing the documentary with knowledge that was already once removed from historical fact, and which was then farther removed when it was adapted for the Hollywood screen. The book as well as the screenplay for *Schindler's List* provided Göth's character with a mistress named Majola who stays with him in his villa. The small role was based on Hertwig's mother, Ruth Irene Kalder, whom Göth called Majola, and many of the details were altered to fit the narrative.[23] The stories of the two Jewish maids who, in actuality, shared a room in the house, were condensed into one: that of Helen Hirsch, played by Embeth Davidtz.[24] Spielberg's film depicts Göth having been attracted to Hirsch. Hirsch, the real-life woman, did describe a sexual assault, but by most accounts her tormentor's desire for her, as depicted in the film, was exaggerated as a plot device.[25] In reality there were two prisoner-servants, both named Helen: Helen Hirsch Horowitz and Helen (Helena) Sternlicht Jonas-Rosenzweig.[26] The story of their victimization was simplified and eroticized for the sake of the narrative. In this case, Moll's documentary, when seen in connection with Spielberg's film, serves the laudable purpose of unpacking or even undoing the streamlining undertaken by Keneally, Spielberg, and the screenwriter Steven Zaillian. Whether or not the documentary consciously emends the historical record, it at least gives some of the actual persons room to speak without having to compete with the generic expectations of Spielberg's melodrama. In that respect, the film can be seen as a corrective.

Moll's *Inheritance* is thus an opportunity for the women involved in the story to represent themselves. This goes both for Hertwig, the daughter of a perpetrator, and for Jonas-Rosenzweig, a survivor. From another perspective, however, the entire premise of the film, the encounter between Göth's biological daughter and his prisoner, is predicated on a doubling effect that relies on Spielberg's fictionalization. The character of Amon Göth, that is, the fictionalized version of the real man, had an attractive live-in lover, yet he also had unfulfilled desires for his beautiful Jewish servant. His character thus pivots between the two women, both of whom live under the same roof, one as a hostage and the other by choice. In Moll's film, we are witnessing the upshot of this fictionalized libidinal entanglement. Although the standpoint is reductive, Spielberg depicts Ruth Kalder's affair as the flipside of Helen Rosenzweig's victimization. The scenario offers dramatic traction, but not historical truth.

Trading on our interest in this situation, Moll's film now stages a real-life encounter. Similar strategies are at work in films such as Beate Thalberg's *The Joel Files* (2000), which explores the case of the Jewish businessman Karl Joel, whose holdings had been legally but unethically appropriated or "Arianized" before the war by Josef Neckermann, a Nazi party member. In Thalberg's film, descendants of both families—including the world-famous pop star Billy Joel— meet in Vienna, nearly 70 years later, to discuss their Jewish and German pasts. Sequences in *The Joel Files* as well as in *Inheritance* center on the encounters between the films' central figures. Moll seems to support not only the idea that such people should be encouraged to be in dialogue with one another, but also the position that there are certain categories of persons, specifically victims, bystanders, and perpetrators, and that, on that basis, their stories can be seen as complementary; these films' moral judgments are made on the basis of categorizations. Lanzmann had preferred not to place victims, perpetrators, and bystanders in one place, because he did not want to provide the impression that he was leveling differences. Such interactions, in general, culminate in a particular type of scene: we witness either displays of continued resentment or cathartic forgiveness, and in presenting the confrontation everyone involved has to make a choice. Akin to reality television, such as confessional or confrontational talk shows, a documentary that brings together a child of a perpetrator and a victim does so in the hope that something will happen, regardless of whether its explicitly stated intention is to promote healing. Moll's film depicts the meeting between its two subjects as a summit: we watch Hertwig preparing to depart for Poland from the Munich airport, and we see Jonas-Rosenzweig along with her daughter simultaneously leaving from JFK in New York. The two sequences, the departures and arrivals, are edited in parallel with one another. The film thus dramatizes the meeting between them as a sort of climax, even though we are at this point only 20 minutes into the film.

Central to the film's story are two mother-and-daughter narratives, presented in tandem. On the one hand, the story in *Inheritance* concerns the influence that the absent Ruth Kalder had and still has over her daughter. Kalder is silent in Moll's film because she committed suicide immediately after her final interview, which was provided to Jon Blair for his documentary *Schindler* (1983). In Blair's film, made 10 years prior to *Schindler's List*, Kalder sits, poised before the camera (Figure 2.1). She seems to have seen herself as a film star, and in photos she often appears stylized after Elizabeth Taylor and others. Here, speaking with Blair, she offers what seems to be a candid interview. According to her daughter, she had been expecting questions about Schindler, but was surprised when Blair inquired deeply into Göth.[27] She struggles visibly with the truth about her former lover, with whom she shared romantic wartime memories and who posthumously became her husband.[28] Of course, she concedes, Göth disdained the Jews, conceiving of them as all SS men did: they were simply an expendable labor force. Given that she spent so much time there, the idea that Płaszów was a work camp, rather than an extermination camp was meaningful to her, and she appears to have relied on this in the decades after the war as an important moral distinction, as though it meant that the workers were not prisoners and were not executed in large numbers. Göth was not, she maintains, a brutal killer, and as to the question of where all the bodies at Płaszów came from, her answer is simply: "I don't know." Watching this soft form of Holocaust denial, which seems to come from a position of feigned or willful naiveté, it is easy to see how Hertwig grew

Figure 2.1 Ruth Irene Kalder being interviewed in Jon Blair's *Schindler* (1983).

up without any acquaintanceship with history. Kalder had been deeply attached to Göth, who was hanged for his crimes, and she even named her daughter after him (in familial circles "Amon" went by the affectionate diminutive "Mony").[29] In *Inheritance* Hertwig relates how her mother concealed the facts about her father from her, explaining that she eventually was forced to turn to her grandmother, Agnes Kalder, who enlightened her about the past.

Hertwig also appears in Chanoch Ze'evi's Israeli film *Hitler's Children* (2011). That documentary explores how difficult it must be to be a direct descendent of Nazis such as Goering, Himmler, or Höss, and Ze'evi's interview with Hertwig is revealing. In speaking about her fraught relationship with her mother, Hertwig lapses into an imaginary dialogue, practically embodying Kalder. She subtly begins to reenact how the two would argue, adopting two tones of voice to go with the two positions, one agitated, the other calm. They debate, with Kalder reminding her that Płaszów was only a work camp. Hertwig says that she was able to drive her mother crazy by asking exactly how many Jews Göth killed, and she explains that the very question would prompt Kalder to take out a cable of some sort and beat her with it. In her published interviews with Matthias Kessler, Hertwig speaks about provoking her mother when she was 20 years old by refusing to be bossed around, and answering Kalder's demands with "Hey, I'm not one of your servant girls from Płaszów."[30]

In Moll's *Inheritance*, Hertwig gazes directly into the camera and recalls one dispute in which Kalder declared that her daughter was temperamental like her father and that she would surely die like him. The insult is an odd one: it was unlikely that Hertwig would end up hanged by a Polish court, but the severity of the insult indicates the extent to which Kalder was willing to burden Hertwig with her own unhappiness. Looking at all the various interviews—in Blair's, Moll's, and Ze'evi's films—it is plain that the two women carry their life experiences quite differently: to judge from what we see, Kalder imitates film stars of an earlier era, while Hertwig comes across as a bundle of nerves. Kalder felt that her past life had been glamorous. She led her daughter to believe that Płaszów was akin to the plantation featured in *Gone with the Wind*, and she had compared Clark Gable's Rhett Butler with Amon Göth.[31] In Kalder's self-aggrandizing imagination, and in a vision adopted by her daughter, the life of the slaves on the plantation (in this case, the Jewish forced laborers) was good; they liked it there, and they needed the help of the plantation-owning family. Płaszów was, in her mind, a safe haven, because it was, after all, a work camp and not a death camp. Hertwig believed her mother's version of events until she secretly read *The Diary of Anne Frank*, and began to openly carry the burden of the prior generation's misdeeds.[32]

As though its two protagonists' stories could be better understood in parallel, Moll's film also tells the story of Jonas-Rosenzweig, who here appears with her daughter, Vivian Delman. Delman is a grown woman and a professional. The mother and daughter are comfortable traveling together, and Delman seems protective of her mother.[33] Jonas-Rosenzweig's personal history, specifically how she ended up at the Płaszów concentration camp, involves her own mother and sister: in late 1942, her mother and one of her older sisters were sent to work on the construction of the camp. She decided to try to sneak into Płaszów because she did not have the appropriate blue work ID card (*Kennkarte*). As she tells it, she had already "learned about the death trains to Bełżec, and was desperate to join her sister and mother. . . . She hid in a milk wagon going to the new camp but was discovered by the driver just before he got there. She managed to escape his grasp and made it into the camp, where she was given a job cleaning barracks."[34] Her mother and sister did not survive, but now, approximately six decades later and prompted by Moll's production, she is traveling back to Płaszów with her daughter. Delman seems to care for and support her mother without having adopted the affect of the traumatized subject. Based on what we see in the film, she does not over-identify with her mother to the point of mistaking a survivor's trauma for her own. The story of Delman's knowledge about her mother's past is also oriented toward the appearance of *Schindler's*

List. She explains, "I remember hearing things about the experiences my mother went through starting around 10 years old; she told me more after my dad's death in 1980, when I was 24 years old. . . . [T]he extent of the story was told in 1993, after the release of *Schindler's List*."³⁵

Unlike Delman, the daughter of the survivor, Hertwig's wounds are all very much on display. She is presented to us as leading a modest, respectable life in Weißenburg, Germany, close to where her husband works as an administrator in the forest service; yet it also seems that the past has been tough on her. Not only do we know about her mother's suicide, which might contribute to viewers' perceptions of her as a victim, but we are also informed that her own daughter has struggled with drug addiction, leaving Hertwig to care for her grandson.³⁶ The filmmakers also at that point probably did not know about the Afro-German daughter whom Hertwig had turned over to a Catholic orphanage in 1970. Now named Jennifer Teege, the child was the product of Hertwig's romance with a Nigerian man who was living in Germany. Teege later reconnected with Hertwig and wrote a memoir entitled *Amon: My Grandfather Would Have Shot Me* (2013).³⁷

Viewers of Moll's and Ze'evi's documentaries know only what they hear and see, but much of Hertwig's comportment is readable as an extension of a troubled legacy.³⁸ At the Sheraton Hotel in Kraków, before her meeting with Jonas-Rosenzweig, Hertwig lights a cigarette that dangles from her mouth in a way that bespeaks utter fatigue (Figure 2.2). She calls to make an appointment to meet Jonas-Rosenzweig at the monument at Płaszów camp, and already over the phone she begins to cry. Jonas-Rosenzweig is polite to her, perhaps even kind, and the traumatized victim, who is returning for the first time to the site of the trauma, thus finds herself in the curious position of comforting her tormentor's daughter.

For her part, Jonas-Rosenzweig does not adopt a posture of forgiveness akin to that of Eva Kor, the survivor of medical experiments whose personal journey is documented in *Forgiving Dr. Mengele* (2006). It is plain that Jonas-Rosenzweig is not coming to Poland to ease Hertwig's burdens, and that she does not want, like Kor, to share with the world a message of forgiveness. Jonas-Rosenzweig, years later, still spoke of suffering from bad dreams about Göth, which may have mitigated any desire she might otherwise have to comfort Hertwig.³⁹ She is prepared to offer Hertwig the harsh truth about her father, a truth that Hertwig, even after having seen *Schindler's List*, is not keen to accept. The former prisoner's standpoint is emphatic and unforgiving. She says, "He was a monster; he was a

Figure 2.2 Monika Hertwig in James Moll's *Inheritance* (2006).

living monster. He enjoyed what he was doing, but he did it out of pleasure.... I saw his face." Jonas-Rosenzweig does not want to understand, and she is not coming to Płaszów to absolve Hertwig. Hertwig, it should be pointed out, is no perpetrator, yet for a documentary such as this to accomplish its goals—for it to depict an encounter, a summit, and the possibility of a reconciliation—one has to understand that Hertwig feels culpability for the past. She is, of course, not guilty of any crime, yet she is the daughter of a woman who lived on the grounds of the camp, who benefited from Jonas-Rosenzweig's labor, and who never atoned for it. For these reasons, Hertwig is inclined to assume her mother's burden, and her acceptance of that burden makes the film's encounter possible.

Jonas-Rosenzweig has a good basis for her resentments. In her background is not only the loss of two of the most important women in her life, her mother and sister, but she has lost two important men as well. She speaks in the film about Adam Sztab, whom she describes as having been her boyfriend in Płaszów, and she describes his role in an underground group. The story about that loss is devastating in that Göth implicated her in the crime. One day he approached her on his famous white horse, asked where Sztab was. He then proceeded down the road, killed him, and displayed his body for others to see.[40] The story is grim, but it is made grimmer by the additional detail that Sztab knew the location of Jonas-Rosenzweig's mother's body, and that the knowledge of that location died with him. In Moll's film, Jonas-Rosenzweig explains: "Adam had been by my mother's side all the time when she was ill. And Adam was by her side when she died. And he told me that he buried her. But you see, because Amon Göth killed Adam, I can never find my mom's body." Sztab is one of two ghosts in her personal story. The other is her husband Joseph Jonas, who committed suicide in 1980. Moll's film includes a number of photographs of him, and Jonas-Rosenzweig tells that story tearfully, speaking directly into the camera: "Joseph tried hard to live a normal life, but he was troubled." She pauses to collect herself, describing his posttraumatic stress, though she does not refer to it in those terms. He was in the habit of writing his deceased father's name compulsively. She concludes, "That's what the Germans did to us." *Inheritance* thus has two comparable suicides in its background: Joseph Jonas in 1980 and Ruth Kalder in 1983. Although Jonas-Rosenzweig and Hertwig, the film's two central figures, do not map neatly onto one another as victim and perpetrator, they are here inscribed as two parallel cases; each of them a mother and a daughter, contending with the legacy of violence that Göth imposed on their families.

In therapeutic terms, it thus makes a certain amount of sense to return to the scene of the crime. And when the film brings all of its protagonists to Göth's villa, the location now made famous by Spielberg's film, it is Jonas-Rosenzweig's first return since the time she was a prisoner there. For the sake of the film, she is participating, to some extent, in a traumatic reenactment. She performs parts of her past, explaining how she would shiver when she heard Göth's footsteps, how she used to look out the window watching the forced laborers go to work, envying them because they had at least one another's company. She recalls how she was forced to hurry up the stairs, saying that she would take two at a time, to do it as quickly as she could. She does not elaborate here, but has elsewhere explained that this was a sadistic game Göth inflicted on his maids.[41] Here, although Moll is not visible in the frame, telling her to go up the stairs again, we know that he is standing behind the camera, and that he has conceptualized this encounter: in front of the daughter of her German tormentor, Jonas-Rosenzweig again ascends the very same stairs. She struggles to contain her distress, choking back tears, and in these moments it feels as though there may be something exploitative in Moll's project.

Where could such an encounter, between a victim and the child of her tormentor, lead? Hertwig, perhaps as a direct result of the contrived scenario, becomes her mother's deputy or spokeswoman, and, as she and Jonas-Rosenzweig discuss the past, Hertwig engages in some startling rationalizations. She carries with her a remarkable level of ambivalence about her mother. After the war, and after Göth was hanged for his crimes, Kalder took pains to have her name legally changed to his. Rather than run from or atone for his deeds, Kalder likely felt there was no reason to be ashamed of them. At the same time, there are also stories about her that lead one to believe that she did not want to see the two prisoner-maids abused, and that she may indeed have made some small attempts to mitigate their suffering.[42] As Hertwig looks around the villa's living room, she comments that Kalder most likely did not witness the murders. At that point, Jonas-Rosenzweig becomes exercised, explaining to her that of course Kalder would have heard the shots, that one couldn't have missed them. Her voice rises as she insists, "You know how many thousands of people died?" Hertwig only digs in further, reflexively parroting what her mother, and perhaps others, used to say, which was that it was only smaller numbers of Jews who were killed, and that it was chiefly owing to unsanitary conditions in the camp. Jonas-Rosenzweig then lays it out for her: "we were tortured and killed because we were Jews.... Stop thinking that way!" Delman finally chimes in with the word, "denial," implying, of course, that Kalder was in denial, and that she didn't want to see what was taking place, but the word, in this context, also resonates as Holocaust denial, which Hertwig is here perpetuating. In this moment, to judge from Jonas-Rosenzweig's strong reaction, it is as though Hertwig is the embodiment of Kalder, and she is now taking the opportunity to dispute with or speak back to Kalder via Hertwig, who acts—as she ventriloquizes her mother's rationalizations—as a surrogate. The film has thus managed to stage a confrontation, not only between Jonas-Rosenzweig and Hertwig, but also between Jonas-Rosenzweig and Kalder. As in *The Joel Files*, the victim gets to confront and correct the perpetrator in the form of her deputy. The more that Hertwig takes on the role of her mother, speaking her mother's part for purposes of the film, the more that scenario is enabled.

And this may not be entirely for the purposes of the film; it may serve a therapeutic goal as well. In order to better understand her dead mother two decades after her suicide, Hertwig has to wonder what she was thinking. The visit to the villa is similar to the scene in *Hitler's Children* in which Rainer Höss, the grandson of Rudolf Höss, returns to the family villa at Auschwitz to see what his father, as a child, would have seen. In order to understand, he, like Hertwig, has to stand where his parent once stood. It is also in the spirit of *Blind Spot: Hitler's Secretary*, the 2002 Austrian documentary which consists of an 87-minute interview with Hitler's partly apologetic secretary Traudl Junge. Inspired by the rebelliousness of Sophie Scholl, who was Junge's age, but stood up to the Nazis and was executed, Junge realizes that she could, at the time, have tried to learn more about what was happening. Hertwig's words, spoken directly into the camera, echo Junge's, and she says these very same words about her mother: "she could have known more." This sentence, which is spoken in English—the language of the interview and the film—cuts two ways: Kalder could possibly have known more than she let on, but she could have made an effort to find out more. More than likely, Hertwig means the latter, that her mother, like Junge, had a blind spot, and that she could have made a greater effort to know more, yet she took no steps in this direction. Hertwig then adds a statement that echoes the sentiment expressed by Oskar Schindler at the end of Spielberg's film: "before my mother died, she said she didn't do enough for the Jews." Hertwig surely does not mean to aggrandize her mother, or to praise her moral character, but here she articulates feelings of guilt on her mother's behalf.

By virtue of the form, Hertwig is forced to play a role. Although it is strange to speak of roles and characters where documentary films are concerned, it surely makes sense in this context. Given that the film is not observational, that is, that the filmmaker does not simply record unobtrusively what his subjects would happen to be doing in the absence of the camera, the scenario is a contrivance: nearly everything that happens owes itself to the film. The film's events can thus be described as staged. For that reason, one of the film's most interesting moments comes when a bee appears uninvited during the first encounter between Jonas-Rosenzweig and Hertwig, when the two meet at the site of the camp (Figure 2.3). Jonas-Rosenzweig is in the middle of explaining how, because of her position, she was attuned to Göth's habits, and that she knew precisely what hat he was going to wear when he was preparing to kill people. The story's rhythm suggests that she has told it before. She continues her exposition, "we lived with this man day and night," but at this point the bee's presence is simply too intrusive to be ignored. The two women, who had been cautious about maintaining a respectful distance from one another, are forced into an uncontrolled display of ordinary rather than performative empathy. Hertwig spontaneously assists Jonas-Rosenzweig, as would perhaps anyone, including even the daughter of

Figure 2.3 Monika Hertwig and Helen Jonas-Rosenzweig deal with a bee in *Inheritance*.

one's German torturer whom one is meeting for the first time. For a moment the two have to be themselves, and although it is unusual to speak of going "off script" in a documentary, that is precisely what happens. Jonas-Rosenzwieg, pausing from her story, says, "It will go away."

The many characters from *Schindler's List* to whom Moll's film indirectly exposes us—the real-life analogues of Göth's lover, Majola (who is almost, but not quite meant to be Ruth Kalder), and the real-life maid (who is almost, but not quite the Helen Hirsch we come to know in Spielberg's film)—perform their roles on two levels: they perform their emotional responses insofar as they, on the one hand, re-perform trauma (in the case of Jonas-Rosenzweig, who once again treads the villa's stairs), or, on the other hand, they perform the appropriate amount of concerned empathy (in the case of Hertwig, who displays her concern for Jonas-Rosenzweig). Yet their performances must also be understood relative to the images we have of the persons whose lives are depicted in the film, the Hollywood images of Kalder and Hirsch. The film introduces us to the real-life analogues of the characters we already know, and it also gives us more insight into Schindler and Göth, who are hardly in a position to speak for themselves: Schindler died in 1974, and Göth was hanged in 1946. All these documentary figures stand in a paratextual relationship to the characters in the Hollywood film. The women with whom we are familiar seem to acquire a voice, and the men acquire dimension through the inclusion of archival footage and photographs.

These photographic depictions, the images from the archive, lend Moll's documentary an air of historical authenticity. Black and white photographs of Göth appear throughout the film: he can be seen sunning himself, occasionally shirtless, and sometimes he poses with his high-powered rifle in a display of unassailable authority that is so familiar from Fiennes's memorable performance. The image that may linger longest in memory among these archival images, however, is the footage of Göth being hanged. He was tried in Poland in 1946, having been charged with, among other crimes, responsibility for the deaths of 8,000 persons in Płaszów many of whom died by his own hand, and for his liability for the liquidation of the Kraków Ghetto. Göth was found guilty, sentenced to death, and he was hanged on September 13 of that year. Moll includes footage of the execution in his film, which is difficult to watch because the rope was too long, and it required three attempts. The footage plays in near total silence and is quite impactful. Moll's film does not allow Hertwig to speak over the images. She is, after all, more her mother's deputy than she is her father's. After we see the last, successful attempt to hang him, Hertwig adds laconically, "now he's dead."

After Moll released his film, however, debate arose about whether the footage had been accurately identified. One can discern the smirk on the face of the man being led to the gallows, and it is hard not to think of Fiennes's performance, yet many now believe that Polish archivists mislabeled it. Indeed, upon closer inspection, the man being hanged closely resembles Ludwig Fischer, the Nazi governor of the Warsaw district in the occupied part of Poland, who was tried in Warsaw and hanged in March 1947 (Figure 2.4).[43] The condemned man looks thinner than Fischer does in some early photographs, but he had likely lost weight in the period following the war. There is a close resemblance to Fischer, as he is identified in 1946 trial footage, and the face of the hanged man certainly looks more like Fischer's than Göth's, but images are imperfect witnesses.

Spielberg, it should be recalled, stages Göth's execution in *Schindler's List*. In the Hollywood version, Göth says, "Heil Hitler," and then a Polish officer kicks

Figure 2.4 The man identified as Ludwig Fischer at his trial, from *Warszawa oskarża* [Warsaw Accuses (1946)] alongside an image from the contested footage of Göth's execution. Source: YouTube.

a chair out from under him. Although the story that "Heil Hitler" was Göth's last utterance is widely circulated, Spielberg and Zaillian obviously chose not to base their version on the Polish video. In their version, the hanging need only be attempted once, and it is successful. The video's existence makes it even more difficult to separate fact and fantasy. Because the footage is possibly mislabeled and thus entirely misleading, Spielberg's feature film might be a more faithful representation of the truth of the execution than the documentary, with its archival footage. The combination of archival confusion and embellished history draws attention to the extent to which these images are ciphers. We look at the blurry footage and see only the man who we, at this point, think we know, the one who had been in control for so long, and who is predictably indignant or impatient with the Poles as they botch his execution.

As it appears in the film, ostensibly as footage of Göth's execution, it stands in sharp contrast with the other images we have seen, such as the image of Göth on his white horse, as he appeared more than once in Moll's film (Figure 2.5). He was a king with a kingdom—a terrain that Kalder mistook for Margaret Mitchell's Tara—and he believed himself above all laws. When Jonas-Rosenzweig describes Göth's first arrest, when the Germans took him away in the fall of 1944 for black market activities stemming from activities in his own camps, she talks about the amazement with which she viewed his sudden helplessness. The war ended before the Germans could try him, but he then fell into the hands of the Poles.

Figure 2.5 Commandant Amon Göth rides his horse in the Płaszów concentration camp: Courtesy the United States Holocaust Memorial Museum, Photo Archive. Photograph no. 03373.

At his trial it became known that Göth was taking the food from prisoners to sell on the black market, and one witness testified that, "money coming from these exchanges [black marketeering] of sugar and other products like fat, was used for maintaining a beautiful horse and cattle breeding, and generally for the accused [Göth's] private use."[44] That very horse, in other words, was paid for with food taken from the prisoners, knowledge that makes those glamorous photos much less glamorous.

Both films are highly mediated: Spielberg fits his story into the narrative constraints of Hollywood melodrama, turning Oskar Schindler into Charles Foster Kane; James Moll tells a story that most viewers feel they already know based on their acquaintanceship with Spielberg's melodrama. Life similarly re-performs film in *Branko: Return to Auschwitz* (2013), a short film by Topaz Adizes, in which Branko Lustig, the producer of *Schindler's List,* travels back to the site of Auschwitz to celebrate the Bar Mitzvah that he was unable to have while he was imprisoned there as a youth. Lustig, an extremely successful producer who was also behind *Sophie's Choice* (1982), makes clear that he is not a particularly religious man. It is the symbolic character—the desire not be denied the right to have a ritual—that concerns him. The film is nine-and-a-half minutes long, and it is related to *Inheritance* insofar as it too is highly mediated through Spielberg. Adizes's film has an odd structure: it begins with *Schindler's List* receiving the Academy Award for best picture, and thus a journey for a survivor back to a camp begins after the release and success of *Schindler's List*. This is also, more or less, where the story of *Inheritance* begins. Hertwig hadn't known the extent of her father's crimes until she saw *Schindler's List*. We hear Harrison Ford's voice announcing the Academy Award, and we see Lustig accepting the prize on behalf of the people who "died in front of [him] at the camps." The film then transitions from color footage to the type of greyscale depiction similar to that seen in *Schindler's List*. The color palate is similar, as an homage. Is he here inserting himself into history—that the black and white (or, in this case, the variation on black and white) is our way of conceiving of the past, and thus appropriate to his journey back in time—or, is he inserting himself into a history that starts and ends with Spielberg's film? Like Kitty Hart Moxon in Peter Morley's film, Lustig needed to return to the site of the atrocity in order to properly come to terms with his experience. That it is a ritual resonates specifically with *Schindler's List*, insofar as there is, in that film, a wedding in the Płaszów camp; life goes on despite the atrocities. Is Lustig, by having his Bar Mitzvah at that place, imitating Spielberg's feature film? Are we subordinating truth to quasi-fictional narratives, or should documentaries such as Moll's and Adizes's be seen as correctives?

One thing is certainly corrected in Moll's film: even Kalder's once devoted daughter deems her mother's version of events utterly unreliable. Her memories, including her references to *Gone with the Wind*, are instructive only in that they reveal the extent of perpetrators' abilities to rationalize their actions. Hertwig had initially ventriloquized her mother's position, restating lies and excuses about the past, even putting them into print, but the film has succeeded in putting a wedge between a daughter and her mother. In *Inheritance*'s last moments, Hertwig speaks of her deep distrust. Following her return to Weißenburg, she talks about being optimistic that she will be able to tell her grandson, David Amon, the truth about his great-grandfather, and that it—whether she means having knowledge of his father's crimes, or his life in general—will be for the best. Her final thought, however, concerns a cigarette case with an etching of a street in Grinzing in Austria on it, a case that once belonged to her mother. Hertwig says that she once asked Kalder: "is this from the Jews?" Her mother said, "No, Monika, it's from your grandfather." Hertwig then adds, "But now I know. I wouldn't believe anything anymore."

Lost in translation: Omer Fast's *Spielberg's List*

Omer Fast's *Spielberg's List* (2003) is not a documentary but is rather a 65-minute work of two-channel video art, one that has been displayed in museums and elsewhere as an installation. Its two-channel structure, unlike most works of cinema, deliberately bifurcates the viewer's attention. Because of its self-conscious manipulation of time, containing interviews that unfold discordantly such that similar images of the same interview subject appear adjacent to one another yet occasionally staggered by mere moments, Fast's work should certainly be understood within the longer history of video art. However, it overlaps thematically with Holocaust documentaries such as *KZ* and *The Holocaust Tourist*, and it shares commonalities with Moll's *Inheritance*. Fast's artwork, akin to Moll's film, raises the issue of how viewers can engage with Holocaust images in the wake of *Schindler's List*. Filmmakers such as Lanzmann and Jean-Luc Godard have criticized Spielberg for his Hollywoodization of atrocity, specifically for the act of translating the Holocaust into the material of melodrama and thus trivializing it, yet Fast's critical perspective, in some respects, goes farther: *Spielberg's List* thinks through the problematic consequences of restaging the past. It is specifically concerned with what Spielberg gets wrong when he plays with the past and renders historical atrocities as contemporary and comprehensible representations.

Many themes are in play in Fast's production, but its centerpiece is its array of interviews with persons who had roles as extras in Spielberg's film. His Polish subjects, who are interviewed as they might have been in the case of a typical expository documentary, describe their experiences, and as they do so, the lines begin to blur: are we listening to actual testimonies of people who were deported to the ghettos and camps, or are these the voices of people who were cast in the roles of Jews, and who performed deportation for the sake of Spielberg's film? Fast plays a game of uncertainties, and the power of his work lies in its moments of convergence, or with the idea that the leveling effect of the medium makes the types of testimonies in question difficult to distinguish from one another.

Although he prefers to simply say that he makes short films, Fast, who was born in Israel and educated in the United States, is certainly more a video artist than he is a filmmaker.[45] He has received a number of prizes for his art including the Preis der Nationalgalerie für Junge Kunst in 2009 and the Bucksbaum Award at the Whitney Museum in 2008. He works primarily with film, video, and television footage, but he critiques their uses, focusing mainly on processes of popular and mediated image reception, as in, for example, his eerie and hypnotic work *CNN Concatenated* (2002), which strings together an enormous number of words and phrases spoken by CNN's anchors such that they form a visual and aural tapestry that seems to speak directly to the viewer. The longer speech into which the statements are edited comprises a series of alarmingly personal comments (for example: "You're afraid of dying alone but you're even more afraid of dying in public"), and *CNN Concatenated* thus highlights the invisible affective connections viewers have with news reporting, as well as viewers' personal stake in hearing anchors' voices, which are designed to alternately calm and alarm us.

To make *Spielberg's List*, Fast went to Kraków and Płaszów, where Spielberg filmed. He inspected and toured Polish sites that have since been turned into tourist attractions. Fast spoke to people who were cast in small roles in the film, and in many cases, the persons interviewed speak about their experiences with Spielberg not as though they were speaking about the making of the film, but rather as though they were speaking about having witnessed or survived the Holocaust itself. The witnesses do not appear to have been coached; they are simply speaking of events that were part of the production, including the roll calls, the deportations by train, the entrance to the showers, and other activities one frequently hears about when one listens to Holocaust testimony. They are not pretending to have been survivors, but are instead speaking about something they lived through, and their testimonies, as a result, ring true. Fast's work is thus a reality-based work of video art about the making of a historical feature film. It is a nonfiction work about the production of a Hollywood fabrication, and it is, in this way, a hall of mirrors: it is a reflection on the vexed project of reconstructing concentration and death camps for the sake of a film, and on the problematic bridging of the real and the fake where something as un-simulateable as the Holocaust is concerned. Fast's installation also concerns how our experience of watching video, and specifically how our reception of video testimony, is contingent on certain presuppositions about truth and authenticity. We bring expectations to the form, and we impose meaning on that type of testimony long before we have heard or seen it.

There is precedent for this type of work, including the many installations that were part of the "Mirroring Evil" exhibit at the Jewish Museum in New York City in 2002. In Boaz Arad's *Hebrew Lesson* (2002), for example, Arad spliced together portions from Hitler's propaganda speeches so that Hitler could be heard saying in Hebrew, "Shalom Jerusalem! I apologize." In its technique and concept the piece is similar to *CNN Concatenated*. For a much earlier example, however, one might look to Beryl Korot's *Dachau 1974* (1974/75), a four-channel, 23-minute long video installation. On its four channels Korot presented black-and-white images as she saw and filmed them in 1974, with the aim of communicating how she viewed the camp memorial site as a tourist attraction. Some of the same issues about whether these are appropriate sites for tourist excursions had already been raised by others, but here, because of its status as installation art, the question of the artist's form is central: Korot's four channels show the same footage—somewhat ordinary sequences filmed at the Dachau memorial site, taken with a camera mounted on a tripod—yet the channels depict the scenes from the camp at varied paces. These formal characteristics of the work resonate with Fast's piece and provide insight into why a video artist would choose to do a multichannel installation. Repetition can be extremely important in such pieces, and in *Dachau 1974* each of the four separate channels "inflects different viewers' encounters with the subject . . . in different ways, and can even affect the same viewer's encounter in different ways over the 24-minute course of the work."[46] The temporal variations in the multichannel presentation underscore the subjective nature of the visitor's perceptions: although the camera is static, the gaps between the images relative to their sameness—the fact that they are staggered views of the same object, and that one is required to view the same objects numerous times, so that it is at once the same and yet different—recall the extent to which experiences are shaped by the standpoints of individual observers.

In itself the claim is hardly radical: one can always assert that standpoints are subjective. In the case of *Dachau 1974*, however, some of the images, such as, for example, Dachau's watchtower, are iconic and are taken to have certain ineluctable, irreducible meanings. Some of these images are "secular icons" in the sense explored by Cornelia Brink, who argues that some Holocaust images, and particularly certain photographs of the Nazi concentration camps, have special status, in part owing to how they circulate: they seem authentic because photographs appear to capture reality and they appear to lose nothing of that authenticity regardless of how often they are reproduced.[47] More important, perhaps, is that these images are taken to stand for the whole, they seem to provide access to the entirety of the crime, an effect that is amplified because the crime is so monstrous that it cannot be known in its entirely. People tend to not see the images for what they are, but instead turn them into myths as a response to this monstrosity, and in order to deal with feeling overwhelmed. The images in *Dachau 1974* are hardly atrocity images; they are mainly watchtowers and barracks, yet they are well known and they are presumed to have an established meaning. Showing us the images again and again is an attempt to decompose their iconicity. The gesture is meant to make the viewer aware of the differences between standpoints, as one side effect of their repetition on multiple screens. According to Mark Godfrey, the gesture "deliberately destabilizes what would otherwise be too facile a presentation of the camp." Godfrey adds, "The broken structure of *Dachau 1974* . . . renders impossible any viewer's attempt to treat the concentration camp as a tourist location that they can visit and consume vicariously."[48] Relying on near simultaneous iteration, the installation is meant to challenge and oppose the notion of a singular standpoint.

Three decades later, Fast enacted a similar interruption. *Spielberg's List*'s use of multiple channels, its staggered temporality, and its repetitions bring it into dialogue with feature films, which seem, by contrast, monological. With rare exceptions, feature films are presented as a single projection on a single screen, and as long as the illusion is preserved that one is seeing through a window into reality, that is, the nearly universally held claim on mimesis that is part and parcel of most Hollywood filmmaking, such monological films present themselves as the sole window onto the world they depict. The single "channel" of feature films serves to underscore the image's authenticity precisely because it restricts our gaze. It naturalizes and even insists on the singularity of its perspective, averring that the events shown happened at a particular time and that there was only one perspective from which those events could be seen. From this perspective even *Rashômon* (1950), because it tells its stories one after the next, does little to undermine the process of orderly, monological narration. Kurosawa's film, although it tells several stories, presents them one at a time. In contrast with a multichannel installation, cinema's single channel, with its conventions of indivisibility, insists upon its singular viewpoint. Cinema is a monologue, and that monological character is highlighted when seen in relation to Fast's multichannel video art (Figure 2.6).

But this criticism of cinema as monological and restrictive applies especially profoundly to *Schindler's List*, which has been subject to criticism for its apparent aspiration to offer a monolithic account that purports to be *the* account of an event that was either too unwieldy to be depicted, or too incoherent to be comprehensible. The critiques of Spielberg's film as totalizing or monological include the assertion that he made straightforward sense of something that historians, theologians, and others have struggled to comprehend, and that by embodying the evil of the Third Reich in the person of Amon Göth, difficult questions about the human capacity for evil were made too easily understandable.[49] Göth was a villain in a history of cinematic villains, and Spielberg's film makes neither of the more difficult charges—it engages with neither of the debates—concerning whether group dynamics played a role in anti-Semitic violence, or whether the Holocaust was a chiefly German problem,

Figure 2.6 One of Fast's interview subjects next to The Legions of Marshal Józef Piłsudski Bridge in the two channels of Omer Fast's *Spielberg's List*. Courtesy the artist and gb agency, Paris. © Omer Fast.

a result of a long history of anti-Semitism. Omer Bartov finds the presentation of anti-Semitic violence in *Schindler's List* reductive, and he writes that the evil in Spielberg's film, "is an evil we can live with, made in Hollywood, one that can be defeated by skill and perseverance, willpower and determination." He explains, "This is troubling because so many of the millions who perished had no less will, no fewer skills, were in no way inferior to the survivors, and yet they drowned."[50] Objecting, along similar lines, that the film makes too much sense of events, that it is simplistic and presented in facile terms to its audience, Bartov also observes that the film's ending, which places the formation of Israel as a logical and proper conclusion to the story, "giv[es] (retrospective) sense and meaning to an event which for its victims had neither."[51]

Every one of Bartov's objections is correct. However, Fast approaches the film from another perspective, appearing more concerned with how Spielberg's film tries to depict a singular version of events, too preoccupied with making memory within the narrow logic of cinema history to be concerned with historical nuance, or with specific questions of representation. According to some, Spielberg's film either deliberately or inadvertently showed that the Holocaust was indeed representable: there was no point in arguing over whether this is a story that is too difficult, too tragic, or too atrocious to be depicted. It thereby provided closure, particularly in Germany, for those who did not like to feel as though German horrors were unique.[52] Others asserted that Spielberg was more concerned with filmmaking than with fidelity to the facts, and that his main intention was to offer a paragon of Hollywood storytelling (again, in the spirit of *Citizen Kane*). Spielberg thus used black and white—or particular multi-tonal variants of black and white with lots of silvers and grays—not only because he was trying to make his images appear like those seen in newsreels, which are memories for some, and memories of memories for most, but also because he was citing cinema history, a history that included German expressionism, films noir, and, in certain cases, even vérité documentaries, as in the case of the film's grainier, handheld sequences.[53] The film is consistently preoccupied with citation. Yosefa Loshitzky adds: "the memory recaptured and 'relived' through *Schindler's List* is not an 'authentic,' 'reexperienced' memory but a cinema memory produced and recycled by the movie industry."[54] The film is, of course, responsible for a great deal of discussion and Holocaust education, and it is likely that, in terms of the expansion of widespread knowledge about the Holocaust, it accomplished what many years of filmmaking, both documentaries and features, had not. Fast's work seeks, however, to highlight not only the film's monolithic claim, but also how deviating from history, and how getting matters slightly wrong or changing facts to suit the narrative can entirely alter a work's meaning.

Small alterations make all the difference. Fixing history to suit one's purposes, even a little, changes everything. Many of the testimonies in Fast's work are presented simultaneously on both of the two channels, but here, as in Korot's work, they are not entirely synchronized. It frequently seems to be the case that we are seeing the same testimony from two slightly different angles, but, upon reflection, it becomes evident that they are different portions of testimony, and the temporal relationship in which the two stand becomes unclear. This deliberate muddling self-consciously undermines the testimonies' authenticity, recalling for the viewers that even testimonies can be reedited and that their claim to authenticity can be undermined in the moment that they, as recorded content, loosed from their point of origin, are divorced from their speakers. No matter what the content, no matter how intimate testimony is, it is always manipulated and reframed by the filmmaker.

A still more profound alteration is how Fast deliberately mistranslates the spoken words of the testimonies themselves. A single word will frequently be changed in the English subtitles and shown in two forms. When the original language of the testimony is in Polish, the titles are not marked so as to indicate which is the more accurate translation. At one point, Fast shows the testimony of an older woman draped in a dark headscarf who describes the wages they were paid to work on the film, as well as the fact that there was corruption involved. She talks about Spielberg and her words are translated on the left channel such that they exonerate the director, who did not participate in the corruption ("I am not acclaiming him as a hero"). The translation on the right channel, however, implicates him in it ("I am not accusing him of ill intentions"). She continues, and the left channel then shows the translation, "Even though he is a little bigger than life, as I said," while the right channel has her saying, "Even though he is a little child, as I said." Such variations in the translation have to be read as representations of a larger phenomenon. If it changes the meaning entirely to mistranslate one word—to go from, say, "acclaiming" to "accusing"—then how much information is lost when one takes liberties with narratives of whole lives, synthesizing biographies of multiple characters into one storyline for the sake of linearity. What truths are elided when one invents scenes from whole cloth, and what is lost in the "translation" of historical atrocities into Hollywood film? Small changes and transformations of single words here stand in relative terms to the transgression entailed in Hollywood's attempt to shape history. Seen in this way, Spielberg's project was flawed from the start.

The mistranslations in *Spielberg's List* are not confined to the testimonies. At one point in the video, a tour guide is asked a question that appears in the left channel's titles as "Did they develop this area after they deported the Jews?" The question appears on the right channel as, "Did they destroy this area after they deported the Jews?" The two forms of the question reveal an interesting distinction: only a single word is changed. It is *develop* on the one side, and *destroy* on the other. But with the transformation, the whole meaning shifts. In the one case the question would have to do with the extent of Nazi crimes—whether, after the deportations, the Ghetto was completely leveled—while, in the other case, it would concern the process of rebuilding after the war. The proximity of the two terms, "development" and "destruction," which are linked to one another yet distinct, reveals the degree to which taking small liberties with a story thoroughly undercuts a director's ability to tell a story accurately. If one is prepared to admit that Spielberg cannot have gotten the story of Oskar Schindler and Itzhak Stern completely right and that he took liberties with it, subordinating details in the service of narrative, the mistranslations in *Spielberg's List*, each of which entirely change a statement's meaning, can be seen as symptomatic or exemplary. As some letters are shifted slightly, entire meanings are reversed and revised.

By playing with these testimonies, Fast straddles the key poles of what have become historical positions in the reception of Spielberg's film. The earliest of these controversies around *Schindler's List* offers insight into the ethical issues posed by reconstructing the Holocaust for the sake of a film. Near the time of the film's release Claude Lanzmann criticized Spielberg in *Le Monde*.[55] It was there he made the self-centered argument that there was "a time before *Shoah*, and a time after *Shoah*, and that after *Shoah* certain things could no longer be done," adding, "Spielberg did them anyway."[56] More important, however, was his overall argument that fiction trivializes the Holocaust. Lanzmann asserted that fiction is a transgression and there should be a prohibition on that sort of representation. Seeing *Schindler's List*, he said, he reexperienced the same impressions he had watching NBC's TV miniseries *Holocaust*. "Transgression or trivialization, it is the same: soap operas or Hollywood films transgress because they 'trivialize,' eradicating the uniqueness of the Holocaust."[57] Lanzmann's thinking on this point is connected to Jean-Luc Godard's, who also objected to *Schindler's List*. When Godard was offered an honorary award from the New York Film Critics' Circle in 1995, he turned down the prize, and the first of his itemized reasons was that he had been unable to prevent Steven Spielberg from reconstructing Auschwitz. (He also reproached himself for failing to beg Diane Keaton to read Bugsy Siegel's biography, and failing to shoot *Contempt*, his most famous film, with Frank Sinatra and Kim Novak.) Although some of the failings he cited are more enigmatic than others, it is clear that the central question for both him and Lanzmann is one of "re-creation." Should one be permitted to re-create historical scenes of Holocaust history, and does too much get lost in translation?

Unlike Lanzmann, Godard has no problem with including images of Holocaust atrocity in his films. He includes them in his *Histoire(s) du cinema* (1988–98).[58] According to Libby Saxton, Godard wants to criticize cinema for being part of the rise of fascism, and he asserted that cinema should own up to its responsibility for Hitler. "Hitler the movie-star," she writes, "can only be removed from under the sweeping beams of the Twentieth Century Fox klieg lights by a penitent cinema wiling to retrace its steps and renew its documentary charge in a long-overdue communion with history."[59] Saxton links this to Adorno's concerns about whether one can write poetry after Auschwitz: if poetry is so compromised that it cannot continue, then cinema should, unless it subjects itself to similar scrutiny, also not continue.[60] Cinema can represent the horror, indeed it must do so in order to dissect itself and its role in not anticipating or not doing enough to prevent fascism. The problem with Spielberg, Saxton argues, is that he streamlines in order to accommodate a Hollywood narrative. In Godard's view, to explain is to mislead, and here—in terms of the discourse of understanding, in terms of *comprehension*—Godard and Lanzmann would surely see eye-to-eye. To make things comprehensible is to distort them. Saxton writes about the obscenity of dominant representational forms, or the fact that Hollywood itself is obscene, and, drawing on Colin MacCabe, she summarizes that Godard objects to Spielberg's approach

> in terms which hint at the proximity of his concerns to Lanzmann's: "Spielberg's *Schindler's List* is, for Godard's aesthetic, a genuine obscenity. It is impossible to film the camps now, because it is impossible to starve actors to the point of death. It is impossible to film the camps because the narratives we impose on them, which 'explain' them, are necessarily misleading and actually prevent understanding." Godard's hostile reaction to *Schindler's List* is grounded, like Lanzmann's, in a conviction that the reality of the camps can neither be

reconstructed nor accommodated within conventional narrative frameworks. What unites *Histoire(s) du cinéma* with *Shoah* is not only a critique of Spielberg's presumption to trademark the subject of Auschwitz, but also a wider call for a systematic questioning of the obscenity of dominant representational forms.[61]

Key in this account is the idea that Spielberg's version is "necessarily misleading," and that it "actually prevent[s] understanding." *Schindler's List* is a fabrication that inhibits comprehension, diverting us, and pretending to provide answers where there are none. Godard, like Fast, always remains conscious of representation *as* representation, as mediation and fabrication. Although film can document, it can and should not re-create; it should not provide the illusion that one was there, or, as one of Fast's interviewees says, that one can live through an event such as the Holocaust "on a mini scale."

Along precisely these lines Fast intervenes. In a broader sense, Hollywood historical films are foils for *Spielberg's List* because those re-representations change matters; they change things in order to impose marketable narratives upon them, in order that they fit into comprehensible terms. Fast wants to disrupt all of this by drawing our attention to the act of translation, to the multiple possible perspectives on events, and to the distortions of meaning. With this in mind Fast undermines Spielberg's frames, showing how singular shot compositions entail assumptions: their singularity insists upon a specific viewpoint. The single frame is a type of monologue, particularly when viewed relative to the dual channels of Fast's video. In order to be disruptive Fast, as the first order of business, integrates images from Spielberg's film into his two channels. Each time he does so, he disrupts the voice that speaks monologically through the feature film's frames.

Fast uses Spielberg's own images to reflect critically on *Schindler's List*. At the very beginning of Fast's installation piece—assuming that one can even speak of a beginning when referring to a work meant to continuously loop and repeat—we see the famous candle from the start of Spielberg's film. This candle is a well-known transition in *Schindler's List* because it is freighted with symbolic meaning: the light obviously stands for life (in more than only the Jewish tradition), and the candle is extinguished in a wisp of smoke. That wisp, in Spielberg's film, then transitions to the smoke produced by the engines of the trains that will ultimately take the deported Jews to the camps. The transition highlights the machinery of destruction, underscoring the technological roots of the industrial horror that awaited the victims. In part, through his dual channel approach, Fast disassembles this cinematic production of meanings. The cut from the candle to the train has now become a canonically famous moment of montage; it echoes other famous montages such as the transition from the bone to the spacecraft in Stanley Kubrick's *2001* (1969). The dual channel installation, owing to its bifurcation, undermines the image's didacticism; Fast's images can be shown simultaneously—a candle on the left side, a train leaving the station on the right. It is not montage: one image can persist uninterrupted while the next one appears. A viewer can choose to link these images in a meaningful way or not to; attention can focus on one image or another. The pairing of the images highlights the didacticism inherent in the film's form, and viewing the work from this perspective, as a video art installation that comments on film, one learns from Fast's deconstructive reframing.

Another concern of Fast's is insisting on the present-ness of his own production in relation to Spielberg's historical re-creations. Spielberg's train, in black and white, reappears within Fast's frames, and Fast responds to Spielberg's imagery by lingering on his own footage of a contemporary European train. He juxtaposes images from Spielberg's simulation of the past with his own contemporary color images. In *Night and Fog*, Resnais had alternated between black and white and color, and although he was highlighting the difference between "yesterday," when the camps were in operation, and "today," which was 10 years afterward, his intention was to play with the possible dedifferentiation. Resnais could not make yesterday present with his camera, yet the sites of the past remained and persisted, as ruins, threatening to return. Fast likewise aims to dedifferentiate; yet his intention is to highlight the fact that we are looking at two interdependent simulations: Spielberg's black and white is a simulacrum, while the "today" of Fast's film is a static image of a train at a platform. In Fast's color footage, in contrast with images from *Schindler's List*, nothing happens. Spielberg's film continues on the left channel, but it fades in and out of focus and is constrained by the confines of a small screen such that one cannot fully read the expository titles. Fast lets the footage, the excerpt from Spielberg's film, fade in and out of focus, showing us all the while, on the other channel, color footage of an inert train. The stationary train is meaningful only as a reference to Spielberg's simulation of the past. Spielberg's footage is, in contrast with Fast's, an enframed fantasy.

A central theme of Fast's video is Spielberg's didacticism. Fast includes yet another image from *Schindler's List*, but this time it is the famous depiction of Jews crossing the Legions of Marshal Józef Piłsudski Bridge over the Vistula, heading into the Kraków Ghetto. Fast first shows the shot as it appears in the film, although it is now differently enframed and restricted by its smaller aspect ratio. He again cuts Spielberg's text off at the margins, which signals a disruption, making plain that Fast is interrupting Spielberg's expository prose. His choice, however, also must be seen in terms of the larger question of how Spielberg treats information and how he is reacting to Spielberg's reframing of the truth. Spielberg excludes material, pushing it to the side, and Fast, doing to Spielberg what Spielberg does to history, reflects back upon that gesture, excluding portions of Spielberg's exposition from the frame. He dismisses it at its margins, but only enough to make it nearly incomprehensible. He then shows the bridge as it is today, but with no exposition. The gesture denaturalizes *Schindler's List*, undermining its deceptive appearance of authenticity. Acting *as if* these were images from yesterday and today, Fast draws our attention to the extent to which Spielberg's "yesterday" is entirely simulated.

Another vista made famous by Spielberg makes an appearance at a later point in *Spielberg's List*. Fast includes a shot of a small cityscape that was featured in *Schindler's List*, the vantage point high on a hilltop from which Oskar Schindler observes the girl in the red coat. The building on the corner, seen from above, here serves as a projection surface. Fast superimposes the shot from the feature film onto his contemporary scene; it is a frame within a frame. This girl, a small colorful figure, thus appears in a black-and-white shot, which is, in turn, embedded in a color image. On the right side, the image of the street corner can be seen in proportions akin to that of widescreen (in what is approximately a 1.85 aspect ratio, the common US widescreen standard), while the left side is presented in something closer to standard television ratio. The right channel accommodates titles, while the left channel shows the black-and-white inset. Reframing Spielberg yet again, Fast shows the corner, adopting Oskar Schindler's imperious gaze. We now stand where Schindler stood in Spielberg's film. We are later told that the standpoint was itself a fabrication: there was no vista from which Schindler could have seen that girl on that corner and in that way. The presence of the girl in the feature film's narrative was also an invention, inspired by an image in testimony given at the Eichmann Trial. Here, this Kraków street is rendered visible as another surface onto which the fictive embellishments, or the fantasies of witnessing associated with *Schindler's List* were projected.

Viewers of Spielberg's film have come to know about Kraków and about the Holocaust through Spielberg's images, yet the knowledge is story-bound; it is based on the truth, but removed from it. Fast's work underscores an argument made at some length by Tobias Ebbrecht about the reception and transmission of such images. Writing about *Schindler's List,* Ebbrecht argues that the film has itself become an archive because Spielberg has taken unprecedented numbers of prior images of the Holocaust and reordered and resignified them. He adds that the film assumes, in this way, a position prototypical for subsequent films about the Holocaust.[62] Spielberg aggregated documentary images for use in his film, and they then migrated into other works. Fast is certainly aware of how cultural memory is produced through transmitted images, as well as of the problems associated with reducing the Holocaust to the status of quotation or citation. His critique thus involves engaging in citation, or playing a game with indirect references. He redoubles *Schindler's List*'s indirect relation to reality: every image in Fast's video is made meaningful by virtue of the fact that it is an image of an image, yet the same can be said of Spielberg's film. It is also a series of images of images. The film and the dual channel video are both caught up in the same self-referential media-specific system. These images speak mainly to one another, and because few of us have reference points in reality for the Holocaust (few viewers have their own Holocaust memories to which to refer), we are reliant on this archive of filmed memories. The language of film is our adopted memory language, because most of us have no other language on which to draw.

Two more examples come to mind: early on in *Spielberg's List,* Fast shows us an image of a woman in a fairly typical red winter coat waiting to cross the street at a crosswalk. The image is more than merely uneventful; it is banal. She does not, however, seem to be a little girl, but is rather a woman, and so the image resists the girlishness associated with Spielberg's child. She is not an infantilized Hollywood victim. Moreover, the image, in its banality, returns as parody. In Spielberg's version the image is poignant and threatening, but here it is mundane. The woman would go unnoticed if no one pointed her out. In yet another reference, Fast includes images of the "camp," but does not make clear whether this is the site of the Kraków-Płaszów concentration camp or if this was Spielberg's set (Figure 2.7). No didactic exposition informs us. We know only that it too appears as a reference to a reference: the snow recalls one of Spielberg's most famous sequences, the one in which ashes from cremated bodies, fall like snowflakes from the sky.

Spielberg's metonymies thus reappear in *Spielberg's List*. Fast and Spielberg are not, of course, the first directors to operate in this way. Metonymy is a key part of the language of Holocaust representation. Where death and atrocity cannot be

Figure 2.7 A snow-covered landscape with barbed wire projected in the two-channels of Omer Fast's *Spielberg's List*. Courtesy the artist and gb agency, Paris. © Omer Fast.

shown, filmmakers rely on a helpful language of signs. Even Lanzmann relies on snow as a major part of the mise-en-scène when he films the former camps in *Shoah*, specifically where he includes images of Auschwitz-Birkenau. Snow is one among the many metonymies in his film, and what Gertrud Koch writes about *Shoah* goes for many Holocaust films: "the mountains of eyeglasses, suitcases and hair take the place of the dead; they represent the dead in a cultural symbolic system."[63] Where he plays with this mode of association, Fast is not commenting on so called "Holocaust sublimity," or the idea that certain things cannot be shown, a point about which there has been nearly universal agreement. In showing a commonplace commuter in a red coat, or a snow-covered landscape that may or may not be the site of an actual camp, he is rather responding to an opportunistic employment of such metonyms. Spielberg's reliance on them is inconsistent: he uses metonymies when they are powerful, and includes atrocity images when he feels it is appropriate. His film is, of course, not *Shoah*, and one should not suggest that it ought to have been *Shoah*. As Miriam Hansen rightly pointed out, it need not be judged in light of the ban on images (the *Bilderverbot*). One can, however, surely hold the film responsible for the choices it does make. As Omer Bartov writes: "We cannot blame [*Schindler's List*] for not showing people actually being gassed, but only for showing them *not* being gassed; we cannot blame it for not showing the emaciated bodies of concentration camp inmates, but only for showing us the attractive, healthy naked bodies of young actresses whose shorn hair strangely resembles current fashions. It is precisely because of the inability of cinematic representation authentically to re-create a distorted reality that the claim of authenticity, and the sense of the viewers that they are seeing things as they 'actually were,' is so troubling."[64] It veers toward the depiction of atrocities, yet at times it veers away from them, translating atrocious history into a palatable Hollywood language.

When Fast brings his crew to Amon Göth's actual villa, he engages even more directly with Spielberg's choices. He here highlights the feature film's manipulations of history. During this sequence the two channels are nearly, but not quite synchronized with one another. We hear from a woman traveling with the filmmaker in a car who may be a tour guide, but we receive no exposition that would establish this clearly. She is speaking accented English and she is thus transmitting or translating her culture for the sake of the tourists. She notes that what we are seeing is indeed Göth's villa, but she points out that some things were changed for the film (Figure 2.8). She continues, and the left channel renders her words: "Because in the 'Schindler's List' by Spielberg his house was inside the camp." On the right channel however, the titles read: "his house was outside the camp." She is speaking in English, and she says "inside." The fact that English-speaking viewers hear her—that she has spoken in English and has said "inside"—reflects the brazenness of Fast's mistranslations. His decision says: despite everything we know to be true, I am retranslating for the sake of the installation, bending the truth without concern for the consequences, perhaps as Spielberg has done for the sake of his film.

As the tour continues, the tour guide appeals to her passengers' knowledge of the film. The left channel, once again, contains an accurate transcription: "Remember? On the hill? He was shooting from this villa." On the right channel, however, the title reads: "Remember? In the film? He was shooting from

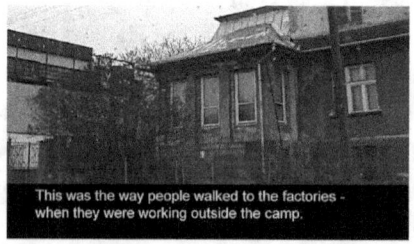 

Figure 2.8 Amon Göth's villa, with two different subtitles. As projected in Omer Fast's *Spielberg's List*. Courtesy the artist and gb agency, Paris. © Omer Fast.

this villa." In substituting "on the hill" for "in the film," a falsehood is brought to light: Göth, the character in the film, was shooting from a nonexistent place, a balcony originally located elsewhere and then later reconceptualized for the sake of the film. A unique aspect of this particular translational error is that the word "shooting" has, in this context, a double meaning: Göth *shot* people and Spielberg *shot* his film. The sense of the double entendre comes to the fore when the guide speaks the words that the left channel represents as: "he would be shooting from behind the curtains," while at the same moment the right channel reads, "he would be shooting from behind the camera." Owing to the double meaning, the pronoun "he" is exchanged and refers, on the one hand, to Spielberg, and on the other, to his villain. Marianne Hirsch writes about the double meaning of shooting (with a gun and with a camera), and asks how postmemorial viewers are meant to look at an image such as the one of Göth executing Jews. She writes, "Unbearably, the viewer is positioned in the place identical with the weapon of destruction: our look, like the photographer's, is in the place of the executioner. Steven Spielberg makes that utterly plain when he photographs Amon Göth's random executions through the viewfinder of his gun in *Schindler's List*. Is it possible to escape the touch of death and the implication of murder that these images perform? To repeat a form of witnessing that is not so radically tainted?"[65] In that sequence, Spielberg is surely aware of what he is doing, but adopting the perpetrator's gaze can be problematic. *Schindler's List* already diminishes the story of Stern and other Jews' stories, subordinating them to those of Schindler and Göth.[66] Hirsch suggests there is additional, even greater risk in seeing the Jewish characters through the telescopic eyepiece of the perpetrator's rifle.

Times, places, and events are reordered in the spaces between Fast's two channels. He willfully decontextualizes in order to undermine the mimetic tendencies associated with accepting the "here" and "now" of feature film representation. Although Spielberg's film offers a great deal of exposition, it is not required to because viewers take for granted that the director is transporting them back in time, and that the realistic representations are depictions of things as they "actually were." In Fast's film, however, it is frequently unclear whether we are at the former site of a concentration camp or on the film's set, the site that Spielberg had built to look like the concentration camp. According to Gideon Lewis-Kraus, Fast asserts that the slippage between the real and the fake camps is an "objective correlative" to the misperception that the film extras are survivors. Lewis-Kraus notes that the confusion about the status of speakers can be connected to the condition of the two camps, outside Kraków. "The real, original camp is in full disrepair, while the staged camp is beginning to accelerate into disrepair, thus increasingly resembling its original."[67] The camp is decaying, and the set of the camp is also decaying; Holocaust survivors are aging, and the extras of *Schindler's List* are aging as well. The point is not that there is no reality to which one can point, but rather that Holocaust feature films such as Spielberg's are part of a self-referential system of filmed memories; the cinematic images are allusions to one another.

The testimonials of those who played the roles of victims are thus akin to a hall of mirrors: these interview subjects are testifying, yet Fast's treatment of the testimony is an exploration of the extent to which testimony acts as a guarantor of veracity. By virtue of its form, we are made to feel that the testimony is authentic. This, too, is an engagement with Spielberg's approach to relying on the presence of the real-life Schindler Jews who authenticate his story by appearing at the very end of his film. Their appearance is, as Duncan Wheeler writes, "intended to function as a guarantee of historical veracity." Wheeler adds, "By making a serious movie, in opposition to his traditionally fantastical fare, Spielberg envisages a film that uses 'reality' as both its justification and its source material. Though he admits certain changes were made to the source material for various reasons such as dramatic coherence, or moral propriety, he never doubts the objectivity of the source material itself."[68] In inverting Spielberg's formula by having his interviewees authentically testify to real experiences of a simulated situation, Fast also uses testimony to authenticate his account. It authenticates because it is the truth, yet it does not give the film authenticity. It is rather the opposite: the confusion of the real and the fictional is the hallmark of a calculated inauthenticity at the film's center.[69]

Most remarkable is that the persons testifying in Fast's work—Fast's witnesses—exhibit a profound awareness about the use of racial stereotypes in *Schindler's List*, something about which Lanzmann once expressed concern. Responding to the use of Jewish stereotypes in Spielberg's film, Lanzmann once noted that when Spielberg depicts Schindler asking the Jews for money, the scene takes place in a car with "old bearded stereotypical Jews from the Judenrat," who produce their money to give to Schindler. He objects to what he views as "identification by stereotype."[70] The artist and graphic novelist Art Spiegelman responded to this stereotyping, pointing to similar moments in the film, particularly to the councilmen who are shown dealing with Schindler. Spiegelman asserts: "These Jews are slightly gentrified versions of Julius Streicher's *Der Stürmer* caricatures: the juiceless Jewish accountant, the Jewish seductress, and, most egregiously, the Jews bargaining and doing business inside a church. It's one of the few scenes where the Jews become vivid, a scene that wasn't even borrowed from the novel."[71] Both Lanzmann's and Spiegelman's concerns have to do with the problematic way film reproduces the past. These two have each famously attempted to circumvent mimesis, creating new forms, in one case a nine-and-a-half-hour-long testimonial film that Lanzmann calls "a fiction of the real," and in the other case *Maus*, a Holocaust graphic novel, in order to circumvent the problem of showing the Jews of that era as they were seen by the Germans.[72] It is difficult to reproduce the past, a past we know largely from film, without bringing in the baggage of stereotypes and thus according them even a small measure of veracity.

This problem of mimesis appears most acutely when it came to casting *Schindler's List*. The perception of the interviewees is that the film needed extras who resembled Jews, and that many were chosen for their Jewish features. The rhetoric that persons might have been selected because they looked more Jewish intersects embarrassingly with the Nazis' rhetoric about biologism. In *Spielberg's List*, the witnesses provide an account: "Suddenly, some men started walking around through the crowd," "A few people at a time went inside," "And in there was a jury that made selection. They would choose or they sent away." "They were looking for Semitic types, you know?" "Well, they were simply looking on the basis of certain features," "Those similar to Semitic features," "Simply facial structure and, well, such things." One woman describes how she was chosen because "her hair was black for a time." Another woman goes on at length, explaining: "one can assume that many people had a fairer complexion. . . . I had a dark complexion," adding "maybe that was important." In several cases, the interviewees seem to have had their own stereotypes affirmed by the situation, and watching contemporary Poles testify about what they think it means to have looked Jewish is particularly disconcerting.

These sequences suggest that the Hollywood casting call may have been racializing.[73] In one case, a woman explains, "they were selecting people with dark features," and she then speaks about her husband: "he had dark hair and maybe characteristic features." When her discourse takes this turn, the right channel goes completely dark so that our attention is focused entirely on what she is saying. Here the witnesses speak about embodying Jews and one man remembers, "There were those who were assigned roles as Jews but wanted more to be Germans." He adds, "And I think I also wanted to be a German more." As he says this, the right channel, the one on which he had been speaking, goes away, leaving an emptiness, and we see him only on the left channel, sitting uncomfortably. After an audible sigh, he continues his story, "Well, I didn't pay any special attention to this then. But, from what I can remember, there was this feeling that. . . . I don't know . . . that I. . . . That I preferred not to. . . . I preferred not to be a victim." Perhaps he has inadvertently expressed the truth: why would anyone choose to be a victim?

None of the actors, either in *Schindler's List* or in *Spielberg's List*, were truly victimized, and it is certainly no serious hardship to be an extra in a Hollywood film. However, their negotiation of victimhood and its performance sheds light on the connection between testimony and reenactment. Testimonies are reenactments. One woman in Fast's production describes having filmed a sequence in which the SS men capture her. She looks old enough, or potentially old enough, that one might mistake her for a Holocaust survivor recounting her own story. At one point her enthusiasm gets the best of her and she rises to her feet, proclaiming, "I ran out of the crowd. . . . And. . . . And I'm simply . . . running. . . . Wait! Wait! There is something more. . . . And I'm facing the crowd. . . . And I run. . . . And I fling my arms apart . . . what's going on? . . . They're pulling me by my hands and I'm yelling, 'No! No! No!'. . . . And that's the end." She laughs at this point, having once again given a bravura performance, and having enjoyed reenacting the staging of trauma. Lanzmann's *Shoah* is most famous for its depiction of survivor testimony as a physical reenactment of violent trauma. Its accounts are based on the notion that the same physical body, the one that endured the trauma, is telling a particular story. Its testimonies are not wholly verbal. One relives an experience as one testifies, and Lanzmann expertly permitted the "signs of bodily distress," including the grimacing and the tears, to bring the testimony forth and to make it real for the observer.[74] In Fast's work, subjects play-act the infliction of trauma and it appears as authentic as any testimony. They are, after all, speaking about their own experience. *Spielberg's List* picks up on a truth about testimony: it is a re-performance of the past.

Fast's subjects raise the key ethical issues themselves. One interviewee remembers asking, "should I be doing this?" and recalls wondering whether that question occurred to Spielberg. Another speaks about how, when reenacting the deportation of Jews, he was provided with actual lists—or rather, photocopies of lists—of the Jews from Kazimierz and elsewhere who died in the ghetto. The props, he realized, were lists of real names, or the real dead. What is the point of striving for this level of veracity in play-acting an attempted genocide? Everyone knows that it cannot be done: black-and-white footage and photocopies of lists cannot transport one back to the past, and even if they could, no one would want to go there. The extras were aware that they were cooperating with a misguided project, and that same interviewee wonders aloud what he was doing holding this prop. He concludes that it was, maybe, "just so we would all look serious," and he then adds, "it still made an awful impression on me."

As I indicated at this chapter's beginning, *Schindler's List* doubtlessly expanded most viewers' knowledge about the Holocaust, and it has promoted a great deal of discussion. Lawrence Baron responds to those who feared that *Schindler's List* would be a hindrance to knowledge because people would be exposed to a Hollywood film and nothing else, by arguing that "reading a book or article and watching a movie [about the Holocaust] are not mutually exclusive activities."[75] He is right. Of primary importance is not whether there should have been this film at all, but whether Fast's two-channel production, made in response to Spielberg's monologic one, helps us reflect on the interaction between feature films and testimony, and on the expectations we bring to both. Toward the end of *Spielberg's List* one of Fast's interview subjects talks about watching Jews being tortured, and everything sounds very real. Until this point, we might not have been unnerved by these differences, but at this moment, things become quite murky. The story is related with such detail—he is, after all, speaking from experience—that it is no longer clear whether these stories stem from the Holocaust or from Spielberg's reenactment. Then, a woman's voice from behind the camera interrupts, voicing our concern: "when was this?" His answer is that it was when they were making the film, and viewers may feel relief in knowing that we have not in fact ventured into testimony of historical violence without knowing it. The woman behind the camera also seems reassured that she is not hearing first hand Holocaust testimony, but the interviewee is, in this case, hardly attuned to the significance of the distinction; he is only proud to have his own form of authenticity to put on display.

The point is neither that testimony can be falsified, nor is it that testimony should be doubted. One can raise those issues, but neither is among Fast's concerns. The point is rather that the installation, like *Schindler's List* itself, refers mainly to a system of references; it consists of images that refer to other images. Film and video are not experience; they are media. Many viewers, however, encountered Spielberg's film as reality, and in this way it succeeded in destabilizing the relationship between the real and the fictional.[76] Whether this confusion is deliberate or inadvertent on Spielberg's part, whether it is an indication of the film's success or failure, it is evidently transformative. It is difficult to think of any other feature film that interacts with documentaries to the same degree. Moll's *Inheritance*, unlike Fast's video installation, did not take a critical position in relation to Spielberg's film, but it shared a common point of reference: the extent to which *Schindler's List* shapes twenty-first century knowledge of the Holocaust. The film was an event in the history of the Holocaust film, and the destabilization it occasioned brings it into dialogue with cultural memory, shaping the subsequent discussions about the cinematic migration of Holocaust images, and about how we encounter history and testimony.

3

Forgiveness on Film: Resentment and Reconciliation in *Forgiving Dr. Mengele* and *Landscapes of Memory: The Life of Ruth Klüger*

In Chanoch Ze'evi's documentary *Hitler's Children* (2011), Rainer Höss, the grandson of the murderous Auschwitz commandant Rudolf Höss, visits the site of the former Auschwitz camp. Accompanied by the Israeli journalist Eldad Beck, Höss tours the villa that had been occupied by his family during the Holocaust, the place where his father had spent part of his childhood. After examining a number of black and white photographs, Höss wanted to know what his father, as a child, had been able to see from the standpoint of the villa's gate. Could he have simply looked out through the villa's entryway and seen the adjacent death camp? Was it possible that his father lived on those grounds without having known exactly what was going on?

After standing where his father once stood and establishing that he must have perceived quite a lot, even as a child, Höss and Beck walk onto the grounds of the camp memorial and museum. Ze'evi foreshadows an imminent encounter: we see Israeli flags approaching in the distance. The next shot is of a hall filled with young Israeli students. Höss is in the room with them and he volunteers to come to the front and answer questions. They ask, "Why are you here?" and "do you feel guilty?" Each one of his answers is reasonable and indicates only contrition. One student begins a question about the tortures that took place at that very site, but she is unable to keep herself together. Overwhelmed by emotion, she can barely speak. A Holocaust survivor in the room then comes up to shake Höss's hand. The two embrace and Höss begins to cry. The Holocaust survivor absolves him ("You weren't there. You didn't do it"). It is an extraordinary encounter to have caught on camera. The emotions seem genuine, and it is difficult to watch the scene without being moved.

In the following sequence, the filmmaker debriefs Beck about these events. Beck notes that the meeting offered the students "a happy ending at the end of this terrible journey," but he is concerned that "it lacked depth" and was perhaps "too quick." In print, he also revealed that he came to feel that Höss should not have received forgiveness. Beck found out that Höss had contacted Yad Vashem with an offer to sell some of his grandfather's personal belongings. He was, Beck maintained, trying to profit from his father's crimes, and the "obscene business offers" were "motivated by pure opportunism." Beck writes about the scene at Auschwitz: "In front of the camera, [Höss] says what is expected of him to say. But a person who cannot take responsibility for small sins he committed himself, cannot take responsibility for the much worse crime his grandfather committed."[1] If what Beck says is true, then one has to wonder: did the Israeli students and the survivor forgive the wrong man?

I could not and would not begin to pass judgment about any of this. Rainer Höss's remorse seems quite genuine. It is, after all, not the perpetrator himself that the students and the survivor are dealing with, but rather the grandson, a person who is surely not responsible for crimes against Nazi victims committed decades before he was born. Feeling responsible for one's grandparents is a simple matter; words can be easily offered. Taking responsibility is something altogether different. It may be a matter for courts, prosecutors, or commissions, none of whom would hold this man responsible. Legal accountability—sentencing the grandson, for example, for crimes committed by his grandfather—would be perverse. What we are witnessing on camera is a matter of sentiment and fellow feeling, not an issue of law.

When separated from the sphere of law, forgiveness and absolution are more or less irrational responses to a situation. Discussions of forgiveness resemble wishes: all parties involved would like to undo what has been done, which of course cannot be the case. During Rainer Höss's encounter at Auschwitz the moderator, perhaps repeating a question posed by a student, asks what he would do were he to meet his grandfather. "I would kill him myself" is Höss's immediate and certain reply. No one feels the need to embellish on this counterfactual question. Does Höss mean he would kill his grandfather now, long after the fact, as a form of capital punishment? If so, isn't his grandfather also entitled to a measure of forgiveness? Or does he mean that he would like to have had the opportunity to kill his grandfather in advance, in order to prevent the crime, precisely as people have wished to go back in time and kill Hitler? The details, perhaps, do not matter. All of this is pure sentiment; these desires cannot be fulfilled in reality. Every one of us agrees that if we could undo that part of the past, we would.

But the past cannot be undone. If it could be, then forgiveness would not be required. We would build time machines and make it all better. Perhaps forgiveness should be treated differently, as more than a shared agreement that we would like to see the past changed. If the past could be erased, then forgiveness would mean nothing. The term could then be reserved for use in cases where there is a permanent loss or a wound, where things cannot be made better. "If," as Jacques Derrida points out, "one is only prepared to forgive what appears forgivable... then the very idea of forgiveness would disappear."[2] Forgiveness, if it is to be worthy of the name, acknowledges that the slate cannot be wiped clean. It must, in other words, be separated from reconciliation, which is shared sentiment. As a personal matter, rather than as a matter of law, forgiveness is, by contrast with reconciliation, internal and private.

Where the Holocaust is concerned, the gravest personal losses are ones that survivors have to live with. The loss of immediate family members may be open wounds of this type. Losing parents, children, and siblings to senseless violence or hatred is not usually food for counter-factual thought. One lives with the loss as long as one lives, and making it good through reconciliation only redoubles violence; family members are lost again if and when the wounds are closed. In the cases of the survivors Eva Kor, who lost her twin sister as a long-term result of Josef Mengele's cruel experiments, and Ruth Klüger, whose half-brother Schorschi was deported to Riga and shot, the memory of the sibling is a persistent injury, it haunts them yesterday as well as today. Forgiveness is a struggle because the losses cannot be made good. In *Forgiving Dr. Mengele* (2005) and *Landscapes of Memory: The Life of Ruth Klüger* (2011), documentaries about these two survivors, forgiveness is the central issue. How does one act when confronted with the perpetrators or even the perpetrator nation (in Klüger's case, Austria, which she maintains is still today anti-Semitic)? If forgiveness is simply about sentiment, whom does it help, and need one even involve the perpetrator in the process?

The Austrian born Holocaust survivor Simon Wiesenthal, who after the war became a famous tracker of Nazis, wrote a story entitled *The Sunflower*, which is apparently based on true events. When Wiesenthal was a prisoner at Lwów, he was taken to meet an SS man, who is later identified as Karl Seidl, although that name is not mentioned in the story. The man, at that point on his deathbed suffering from painful injuries, confessed to having participated in a particularly cruel murder of 300 Jews. He wanted to confess to a Jew, and Wiesenthal was arbitrarily chosen for the task. After hearing the man's confession, including a biographical account of how he came to join the SS, Wiesenthal leaves the room, saying nothing. Seidl asked for forgiveness, but received only silence. Wiesenthal's story ends by posing the explicit question as to whether his silence was right or wrong. In the published responses that followed, most concurred that he had been under no obligation to forgive, particularly in those circumstances. On the one hand, guilt is a legal matter, best left to commissions and prosecutors; on the other hand, Wiesenthal had a right, even an obligation, to resist being instrumentalized by his tormentors. Primo Levi's response to the story is along exactly these lines: "once again, the Nazi was using the Jew as a tool, unaware of the danger and the shock his request must have constituted for the prisoner: his action, examined in depth, is tinged with egoism, since one detects in it an attempt to load onto another one's own anguish."[3]

Forgiveness can take place in many registers, but the SS man in Wiesenthal's story was seeking reconciliation or comfort. The wounded parties, particularly survivors and victims' families, have no obligation to perform sentimental scenes. Such moments are only happy endings tacked onto painful journeys. In the cases of Klüger and Kor, each of them considers forgiveness in internal terms. It is a decision made without regard to the perpetrators' interests. Kor's attitude is that she forgives the Nazi doctors who harmed her and killed her sister, but she has no concern for their stake in it. The decision is for her; she has no control over them. Klüger, for her part, avoids scenes of reconciliation, because she is disinclined to indulge her tormentors. In the following chapter, I examine these two stories of forgiveness and resentment, particularly in terms of how these themes impact the shape of the films' narratives, and how, in both cases, the subject's attitude toward the question contributes to dictating the tone. They each deal with women of a certain age, now in the position of deciding, in light of the knowledge that what is done cannot be undone, whether to hold on to or let go of their resentments.

Liberation from resentment: *Forgiving Dr. Mengele*

Bob Hercules and Cheri Pugh's documentary *Forgiving Dr. Mengele* begins with a sequence drawn from an NBC News broadcast from 1985 featuring Eva Mozes Kor and her twin sister Miriam during their liberation from Auschwitz 40 years earlier. They were 10-year-old survivors of Mengele's medical experiments, and they only survived the camps because of Mengele's fascination with twins. The footage is from Soviet film taken during the liberation, footage taken over a period of several months starting from the end of January 1945, and released to the public in May of that year.[4] The sequence is surely familiar to most viewers: it depicts the two young girls along with other victims of Mengele's experiments leaving a barracks through a corridor of wire. NBC News altered the footage, images that to some extent made Eva and her sister famous insofar as they have by now become often-seen icons of the camp's liberation, slowing it down in order to focus the viewer's attention on the victims' faces. Hercules and Pugh's film then shows the images from that same sequence a second time, now no longer explicitly framed by the telecast. They remove the framing conceit, rescreening the footage for us. The directors' stylization calls to mind the fact that the past is being screened and rescreened in this documentary. The images are triply filtered: Soviet footage becomes NBC footage, which then becomes Hercules and Pugh's footage; the past is, again and again, folded into the present.

One would not describe Hercules and Pugh's documentary as over-produced. The film was shot on an extremely low budget, and to some it reads as amateur. It is willing to use the array of expressive means such as archival footage and non-diegetic music in order to convey its story. The film neither adheres to dogmatic assertions such as those that guided the decisions of a filmmaker like Lanzmann, nor is it meant to be an explicitly political provocation. It is less concerned with unearthing new information about the past than it is with its Romanian-born survivor's life in America. It spends actually very little time sorting through the details of the past, and it does not retrace its survivor's steps. *Forgiving Dr. Mengele* is, akin to HBO's widely acclaimed documentary *Paper Clips* (2003), much more centered on questions relating to the contemporary American point of view on the Holocaust.

The bulk of the documentary's narrative is centered nearly 5,000 miles away from Auschwitz in Terre Haute, Indiana, where Eva Kor resides, and where she has established a museum. Kor has placed herself at the center of what can be described as a self-generated controversy: she openly and insistently proclaims that she forgives Josef Mengele and other Nazis. The documentary, which follows her from place to place, was shot mainly between 2001 and 2004, and its present, the film's "here and now," is contemporary Middle America. Contemporaneously, that is, in the moment of the film's production, Kor is in her late 60s, and she is working as a real estate agent who sometimes wears a red, white, and blue American flag silk scarf around her neck. The scarf in part offsets for her clientele the foreignness of her Romanian accent, but for viewers it also bespeaks the Americanness of her project, that is, that forgiveness might be a distinctively American phenomenon: it corresponds to a culturally specific fascination with a survivor who seeks to put the past behind her and announce to the world that she is moving forward.

Forgiving Dr. Mengele is concerned with Kor's here and now, and its mise-en-scène directly links its subject's past and present. This enables the film to focus on the individual survivor's trauma. Much more than other films, it is about the encroachment of the past on a survivor's daily life. When we are initially introduced to Kor, she is securing a realtor's sign in a lawn with the help of a sledgehammer (Figure 3.1), and the directors, Hercules and Pugh, slow down and digitally manipulate the footage, dissolving the contemporaneous shots into images of concentration camps. Kor's hammering is repetitive, forceful, and resonant, and it is calculated to recall the continual presence of concentration camp violence in her psychic life. The film's *then* and *now* are linked in a moment of associative editing, one that is meant to reflect her consciousness, particularly the extent to which she lives with the past. The sound of a hammer hitting a surface may make memories resurface, and that return may happen unpredictably. The film takes the structure of individual traumatic memories and how they recur in everyday life for granted. At another point in Hercules and Pugh's documentary, when we first see a swimming pool in a home for sale in Terre Haute, the shot is followed by an image of barbed wires reflected in what appears to be pooled up rainwater at Auschwitz. Finally, a choo-choo train circling a children's playground is crosscut with images of deportation. On the one hand, these shots recall gestures such as that canonical opening image of *Schindler's List* in which the smoke of an extinguished candle becomes the smoke venting from a train on which deported Jews are being transported to the ghettos. On the other hand, there is something different at work: Spielberg attempted to tell a story wherein the Holocaust impacted the whole of postwar Jewry. Here, the focus is on a single survivor's trauma, and on how the past is always imposing itself on her.

The modesty of the film's ambitions actually enables something that a film with more sweeping historical scope cannot achieve: the exploration of individual trauma. Crosscutting and cross dissolving—as with, for example, the playground train—are important parts of the film's stylization. They routinely intertwine the past with the present as when Kor explains how, on her first return trip to German speaking countries, the voice of the uniformed Lufthansa

Figure 3.1 Eva Kor hammers a sign into the ground in *Forgiving Dr. Mengele* (2005).

flight attendant threw her back emotionally onto the selection platform. Kor is aware that the trauma is still a part of her daily life, and because the film is focalized through her, it adopts this position formally and axiomatically. How is she supposed to move forward, when she still lives every day with the pain of the past? The film follows her logic: forgiveness would be an act of healing. Kor is depicted as a quintessentially tough survivor, and despite the obvious need to show restraint in drawing such conclusions viewers will likely be inclined to connect the dots between her resilience and her survival. She is intrepid, and she cavalierly claims that there is "more to life than just Auschwitz," yet the film itself makes a competing claim insofar as it is preoccupied with the inexorability of the past.

Without explicitly undermining assertions made by the protagonist, her aim of getting beyond her resentment competes with the film's formal choices, which set into question the extent to which their survivor-subject has moved on. To this end Hercules and Pugh include a sequence in which Kor, in present day Indiana, undergoes an ordinary optometrist's exam. After being instructed to sit in a room and wait for the eye doctor, she recalls in voice-over how she was made to stand naked at Auschwitz for 6 to 8 hours, and how the Nazi doctors would compare the size of her eye to that of her twin sister and then "compare it to charts . . . for hours and hours."[5] The scene is similar to one in *Kitty: Return to Auschwitz*, another documentary that was likewise focalized through a single subject. When that film was made in 1979, Kitty Hart was working as a radiographer and the images of her at work recall medical experiments. They are indirect echoes; they suggest but cannot guarantee that viewers will make the appropriate association. The image of the evil medical experiment was well known at that time: *Marathon Man* with its fearsome Nazi dentist was released in

1976 and *Boys from Brazil*, a successful feature film about Mengele's manias was released in 1978. The intrusiveness of medical practices and the idea of testing and experimenting on subjects are, especially with respect to Kor's biography, linked to the Nazi objectification of their Jewish victims. These types of mise-en-scène are of course calculated: at some point the filmmakers surely decided that following Kor to the eye-doctor's office would create a setting that suggests that as long as she leads a normal life, including going to the doctor or flying on Lufthansa, her memories will resurface.

The documentary follows Kor to the location of Auschwitz, or contemporary Oświęcim. We hear from her in voice-over that she grew up in Transylvania, and that when she was 10 she was sent to Auschwitz. Her story is narrated with the help of fragmented, deteriorating photos from before the deportation, followed by a number of perpetrator photographs that tell the story of the ensuing horrors. She explains how she was separated from her father and her older sisters and never saw them again, how the twins were called for at the platform, and how she and Miriam were taken for experiments. Subsequent to the liberation of Auschwitz, Kor and her sister returned to Romania for 5 years. In 1950, they moved to Israel, both joining the Israeli Army in 1952. The film, which includes a number of archival images, presents photos of Kor and her sister looking relatively happy during that time. Problems came later. Eva's miscarriages and a cancer that her son developed may have been legacies of the experiments.[6] Her sister Miriam's problems—that her kidneys never fully developed, which led to an organ transplant and later to her death in 1993—are clearly presented as consequences of what was done to them.

In June 1960, Eva met Michael Kor, who was also a Holocaust survivor, and the two moved to Terre Haute. As charming as Michael Kor is, he provides one of the film's counter-examples: he has not worked through the past, and he explains that he never talks about it. "I have forgiven the Germans," he says, "but not the stockade, not the wires. And the shouting and the yelling—I don't want to see 'em again." As he utters the word "wires," his voice breaks, he loses composure, and despite his otherwise evident happiness, his emotions, whether they find their source in depression or in anger, are shown to be precariously close to the surface. From the perspective of his psyche, little time seems to have passed; it takes barely an instant for him to bridge a gap of 60 years. Michael and Eva Kor represent two responses to the past: his prolonged victimhood is set against her resilience. In this same spirit, the film also includes a story told by the Kor children about how their parents reacted when their house was vandalized at Halloween. While their father counseled that they should simply keep a low profile, their mother, always the tough one, ran around chasing the vandals through the yard. Kor's actions read as an overreaction conditioned by a biographical connection to persecution, yet one of the children also mentions that swastikas had been scrawled on the family home, which suggests that her strong reaction to a hate crime, however young the perpetrators, may have been appropriate.

In February of 1985 in Jerusalem—marking the 40th anniversary of the liberation of Auschwitz—twins who were experimented upon held a mock trial for Mengele, who it was believed at the time was living in Paraguay.[7] Wiesenthal, the famous Nazi hunter, and Gideon Hausner, who prosecuted Adolf Eichmann, participated in the trial. Hercules and Pugh's film includes footage of Kor from around this time, in the 1980s, and her rage is palpable. She is shown addressing an audience in 1988, angrily explaining that she and Mengele's other victims are still suffering. The turning point comes shortly afterward, in June 1993 when she receives the news that her sister has died. Kor explains, "And that was it." She does not say what "it" was, but we may conclude that "it" was the moment at which she began her process of forgiveness. Once her sister's suffering ended, she made the decision either to live differently with her anger or to dispense with it.

Miriam Mozes's death is a turning point that prompts Eva Kor to seek out Hans Münch, a Nazi doctor who worked with Mengele but was acquitted of crimes. Münch is said to have refused to take part in the selections at Auschwitz. It has also been said that Münch did bogus, less harmful human experiments in order to protect inmates. After the war he was tried as part of the 1947 Auschwitz Trial in Poland, and he was the only one of 40 defendants to be acquitted. His acquittal explains that he was favorably inclined toward the camp inmates and that he was not ideologically connected with the SS.[8] He died in 2001. The story of Kor's initial contact with Münch is not spelled out in the film, leaving the timeline of their conversations somewhat unclear. Kor elsewhere describes the situation leading up to July 1993.[9] She had acquired Münch's name from the German public television company ZDF. She, her sister Miriam, and Münch had all appeared in the same program for ZDF, although they had not appeared together. She asked for the doctor's address and phone number, as she says, "in the memory of my sister," who had died a month earlier.[10] The link is clear: her sister's death spurred her on. The rest happened very quickly, and in August she was on the way to meet him and to set her project of forgiveness in motion.

In "Resentments," a now famous chapter of his 1966 book *At the Mind's Limits: Contemplations by a Survivor of Auschwitz and Its Realities*, Jean Améry writes about the anger he carried with him after the war. Writing as a Jewish survivor, Améry describes why he continues to carry these feelings and refuses to absolve the Germans. The problem is temporal: it is rooted in the wish that the irreversible be turned around, that the event be undone. He writes, "the time-sense of the person trapped in resentment is twisted around, dis-ordered, if you wish, for it desires two impossible things: regression into the past and nullification of what happened."[11] In part, the survivor, like Kor in the years in which her twin sister was suffering, wants to reverse the past, even though he or she acknowledges that the fantasy is not rational. Drawing on a Christian metaphor Améry writes, "resentment is not only an unnatural but also a logically inconsistent condition. It nails every one of us onto the cross of his ruined past."[12]

Améry's explicitly stated wish was to bring the perpetrator into a moment of isolation identical to the perpetually repeated one—the traumatic moment—as it was experienced by the victim. In this regard, and despite his assertion that, "it is not a matter of revenge," Améry provides a paradigmatic rationale for vengeance. He writes: "The experience of persecution was, at the very bottom, that of an extreme *loneliness*. At stake for me is the release from the abandonment that has persisted from that time until today. When [my tormentor] SS man Wajs stood before the firing squad, he experienced the moral truth of his crimes. At that moment, he was with *me*—and I was no longer alone with [his] shovel handle."[13] Describing a scene with similarities to the one described by Wiesenthal in *The Sunflower* in which a dying SS man wishes that things had been different, Améry surmises: "I would like to believe that at the instant of his execution he wanted exactly as much as I to turn back time, to undo what had been done. When they led him to the place of execution, the antiman had once again become a fellow man."[14] Here Améry makes it explicit: he wants to "turn back time" because his own wound remains open; his abandonment has "persisted from that time until today."

Is a new beginning even possible? For Hannah Arendt forgiveness is a political concept, and she wrote more optimistically about new beginnings.[15] Améry's book appeared not long after Hannah Arendt's 1958 publication *The Human Condition*, and some of Améry's writing reads as a response to Arendt.[16] Forgiveness was not a legal consideration for him, as it was for Arendt, for whom legal and institutional forgiveness open new possibilities of action. From this perspective, a new beginning would indeed be possible, but only that which can be punished can be forgiven; forgiveness cannot remain abstract. Forgiving enables us to come to terms with the past and liberates us to some extent from the burden of irreversibility. In order to forgive, however, one has to understand criminals as criminals, not as satanic and irredeemable images of radical evil. Through this lens one can better understand Arendt's own desire to render Adolf Eichmann "banal." The Israeli prosecutors who demonized him removed him from the sphere of punishment in the moment they began to mythologize his evil.

In this respect Arendt, at least the Arendt of *The Human Condition*, is less existential than Améry: forgiveness is something more along the lines of exoneration. It is perhaps the many approaches to forgiveness that creates controversy. It is not clear that Kor's intention is to exonerate Nazi doctors, and there could surely be forgiveness beyond an institutional framework such that one forgives without surrendering the right to prosecution.[17] Many, however, believe that persons should no longer be prosecuted for crimes committed during this period. A German court convicted John Demjanjuk in 2011, when he was over 90 years old, of being an accessory to the murder of thousands of Jews. Kor does not seem interested in pursuing policy at this level and her public addresses proclaiming forgiveness are much more geared toward bringing her own subjective resentment (along the lines described by Améry) to an end. She no longer wishes to force her own isolation on the perpetrator. To use Améry's language, her desire to impose upon Mengele and others the experiences of isolation and doom had dissipated. Her forgiveness is less political than it is intimate and personal.

Initially, however, Kor approached her encounter with Münch in terms of an exchange. When she spoke with Münch, according to her, she invited him to commemorate the 50th anniversary of the liberation of Auschwitz in her company, and, in the presence of witnesses, "on the ruins of the gas chambers," she would ask him to sign a document affirming that the gas chambers had existed. Münch agreed, and, as she tells it, "I went home completely confident that I would receive a document about the gas chambers—a document that would help me combat the revisionists, who assert that there were no such things."[18] For her, it was about countering historical lies. In exchange, she offered Münch a letter of forgiveness. Kor reiterates many times that forgiveness was about freeing herself, yet the initial impetus for her arrangement with the former Nazi doctor came from a desire to respond to arguments of Holocaust deniers.

Deborah Lipstadt's *Denying the Holocaust: The Growing Assault on Truth and Memory* was published in 1993 and its publication led to a British libel suit in 1996.[19] It is likely that Kor's interests were motivated historically by those same forces that motivated Lipstadt: the idea that Holocaust denial was getting worse. Kor wanted to enlist Münch as a witness.

Kor thus broke from the other twins, many of whom raised questions about her right to forgive. In Berlin in 2001 when the Kaiser Wilhelm Institute invited surviving representatives of the Mengele twin experiments in order to apologize to them, Kor went her own way. In the film one survivor, Ephraim Reichenberg, counters Kor's position, arguing, "We do not have the right to forgive on behalf of the victims who have died." Kor, however, asserts: "Forgiveness has nothing to do with the perpetrator, has nothing to do with any religion, [it] has only to do with the victim." In indirect dialogue with the survivor Jona Laks, an exchange communicated largely through crosscutting, Kor asks rhetorically: "does she think that living without pain would betray the memory of [her] loved ones?" From the perspective of those who hold onto their resentments Kor is compounding the act of violence. She is abandoning her sister's ghost, closing the wound in the moment her anger ceases. If she no longer holds onto her rage, then she is guilty of forgetting.

Kor took a different path, making a statement at Auschwitz in Münch's presence. She invites him to stand with her not only because of her philosophy of forgiveness, but also because Münch, as she notes, will be there as an eyewitness to verify the existence of the gas chambers as well as to admit to guilt. Münch, of course, went unpunished at the Auschwitz Trial, and is thus not admitting guilt in a legal sense so much as he is admitting to having feelings of guilt, which is a different matter. Regardless, at the ceremony for the fiftieth anniversary of the liberation of the camps, he reads a document that includes the words: "I am so sorry that in some way I was part of it. . . . Joining the SS was a mistake. I was young. I was an opportunist. And once I joined, there was no way out." As Münch's companion at the event, Kor also reads a statement, one that enrages her fellow survivors: "50 years after liberation, I, Eva Mozes Kor, in my name only, hereby give amnesty to all Nazis who participated directly or indirectly in the murder of my family and millions of others. Because it's time to forgive, but not forget. It's time to heal our souls."

The film then explains that representatives of the Mengele Twins organization were furious with Kor, and Laks tells the filmmakers that bringing Münch and reading the statement "was not tactful." In this way Kor's behavior runs counter to Améry's position. Writing about resentment Améry raises the issue of tact, noting that it is "no amusing enterprise" to speak as a victim. He continues:

> [P]erhaps I would do well to excuse myself . . . for the lack of tact. . . . Tact is something good and important. . . . But no matter how important it may be, it is not suited for . . . radical analysis . . ., and so I will have to disregard it—at the risk of cutting a poor figure. It may be that many of us victims have lost the feeling for tact altogether.

Again, the terms, as Améry lays them out, are inverted: in *Forgiving Dr. Mengele*, the forgiver becomes the tactless one. Kor ultimately gets little information out of Münch. When she looks for details—exactly what was it with which her sister's kidney was injected?—he has nothing enlightening to say. His ignorance is also an alibi; he claims Mengele never spoke with him about his methods.

Kor's primary goal was an exchange: her forgiveness for his testimony. By her account, however, she also wanted to break a cycle. She writes about how we have seen in Bosnia, Kosovo, and Rwanda how the victims become perpetrators and vice versa. "Let us," she adds, "try something new, to break through the vicious cycle of violence."[20] The idea is also expressed in Berel Lang's writing about the Holocaust and revenge. Lang writes that revenge, "seems in principle contradictory of forgiveness," and notes: "Unlike forgiveness which erases the past, revenge preserves it; rather than seeing individual acts as (at least sometimes) finite and redeemable, revenge sounds an indefinite echo. What has made the English expression 'forgive and forget' a cliché is not only its linguistic chime; forgiving brings a release from the past, a deliberate forgetting, as opposed to the impulse for revenge which reinscribes the past, entering it into a potentially endless chain. Even when someone has 'had' what he believes to be his revenge, he cannot assume that the person with whom (from his own point of view) he has evened the score will agree that the score is even or, if he does, will agree to settle for that."[21] Forgiveness, by contrast, should erase and leave no remainder. In this respect, her actions can be understood in opposition to revenge.

Based on what we see of Münch (Figure 3.2), this appears to make sense. Why would anyone want to take revenge on him, either by juridical or vindictive means, after all these years? A court, after all, exonerated him, and he is elderly. As we see him in *Forgiving Dr. Mengele*, he plausibly presents himself as a victim. Kor remarks that to her great surprise he treated her with kindness and respect. At the meeting, captured on camera several years before Hercules and

Figure 3.2 The Nazi experimenter Hans Münch in 1945 and later, in the company of Eva Kor, in *Forgiving Dr. Mengele*.

Pugh started filming in Terre Haute, but included in the film, Münch talks about Mengele, describing him as dilettantish and, mirroring the discourse of survivors, he explains how he himself "hasn't had any joy following the liberation." In a description that makes it sound as though he suffers from some manner of perpetrator trauma, he adds: "this is the nightmare that I live with."[22] At this encounter, the two are no longer perpetrator and victim; here they both appear to be survivors, united by Auschwitz. However, Münch comes off much differently, and far worse, in the Holocaust documentary *The Last Days* (1998), directed by James Moll, who also directed *Inheritance*. In *The Last Days* Münch is chiefly concerned with exonerating himself, not with anyone else's healing. He plays a similar role, speaking to a survivor about what happened at Auschwitz, yet he is of little assistance. He frustrates a Hungarian survivor named Renée Firestone by replying to her direct inquiries with evasions and useless platitudes.

Münch may have experimented on Firestone's sister, Klara, who died in Auschwitz. In *The Last Days* his assertions tend to exonerate him, though

Moll, the director, explains that he does not know whether these self-interested comments can be considered trustworthy, and that the viewer has to decide.[23] Münch explains that the only way to avoid sending victims to the gas chambers was to make them undergo more tests: "To save them, we had to keep conducting harmless tests on them. That is what we planned to do, and somehow it worked. And that is why I was acquitted." Firestone comes to see him with newly found documentation about her sister's death. She says: "I would like you to explain these papers." Münch, the ostensibly "good" Nazi doctor, replies with unhelpful comments about the documents including "nothing important" and "it's nothing, everything is good," as though it were reassurance instead of actual information that Firestone was seeking. It is possible, and has been asserted, that Münch was already suffering from senile dementia at the time of filmmaking, which would account for the fact that he is not in the least bit helpful. Following this brief interview, Firestone explains: "I tried to be civilized, but he was very evasive and I became very angry. I kept thinking that thousands and thousands of people died in his clinic."

The former Nazi seems nearly "banal," as Arendt might have used the term. One critic, Geoffrey Macnab, notes that, "the encounter between Firestone and Münch . . . is the one instant in which Hannah Arendt's weary old saw about the 'banality of evil' makes sense."[24] This is, however, misleading. Both films make him seem more harmless than he appears to be in *The Meeting: An Auschwitz Survivor Confronts an SS Physician*, a book-length interview with the Austrian Holocaust survivor Dagmar Ostermann. In that conversation from 1994, from around the same time Münch came into contact with Kor, he comes across as obstinate and unrepentant. His interlocutor's background places her not that far apart from Ruth Klüger: Ostermann was born in Vienna in 1920, and was interned in Ravensbrück and Auschwitz. Münch, responding to her questions, both defends Mengele and perpetuates stereotypes of Jews.[25] He even airs his far-fetched conviction that it was because of a Jew, who was implausibly posing as an SS man, that he was recruited to practice in Auschwitz.[26]

In interviews during the mid-1990s in his stately home in Roßhaupten in Bavaria (in Eastern Allgäu), Münch talked with journalist Bruno Schirra. That interview is horrendous, even worse than his interview with Ostermann. Münch not only describes Mengele in sympathetic terms, but he also has rude and insulting words for Eva Kor in spite of the fact he had not long before reconciled with her at Auschwitz. He maligns her as a "pathological case" who had a "mother-child relationship to the SS."[27] Harsher still were his words about the survivor Vera Kriegel, another one of the Mengele twins (who also appears in *Forgiving Dr. Mengele*). If Schirra's account is to be believed, Münch said, "Frau Kriegel is one of these very rotten (*ganz miesen*) prisoners.... This repulsive little Jew. She had it good then; she stepped over others and threw herself at Mengele just to save her little life."[28] Throughout the interview his anti-Semitism is blatant, particularly where he describes the SS "doctor" Carl Clauberg, who sterilized hundreds of women: "A disgusting person," Münch says, "He looked like a Jew" ("hat ausgeschaut wie ein Jud").[29]

Sounding like Franz Suchomel, the death technocrat from Treblinka who Lanzmann interviewed with a hidden camera in *Shoah*, Münch describes the disposal of bodies in terms of the difficulties it presented when Jews were piled in heaps and did not easily burn. Münch adds, that it was a "technical problem" that had to be solved. Schirra here adds detail that makes Münch seem particularly villainous: "Sitting in his leather chair under a crucified Jesus nailed to the cross, Münch rubs the scruff of his cat Peter's neck, and describes how the prisoners dug ditches around the pyre to collect the fat. They then collected it up with trowels and poured it over the bodies, which then burned better."[30] The entire interview incriminates Münch. He always averred that he had nothing to do with the selection process, but Schirra gets him to indicate that he saw more than he had previously admitted by—of all things—watching *Schindler's List* with him. Schirra describes how Münch dissects the film and notes that the selection, as shown, is "absolutely authentic" (*absolut authentisch*) down to the details. Schirra adds: "He would know. He was on the ramp at Auschwitz-Birkenau."[31]

If, at that point, there were not enough evidence to force one to rethink Münch's complicity, Schirra then describes what Münch says he witnessed at the gas chamber. Münch mimics the gestures of the dying: "His face contorts, he opens his mouth, gasping, clasps his arms together above his head, and clutches his hands around his throat. Then, he imitates their sounds. A hum emerges slowly and deeply from his chest, muffled and subdued, 'like the buzz of a beehive.' Then the gassing is over, the doors are opened, and 'sometimes they were all huddled there, sometimes they lay on each other like a pyramid, the children always at the bottom, trodden. And sometimes they were standing. Like basalt pillars.'"[32] The unapologetic tone of his descriptions, and the revelations about how much he had seen, cast doubt on his innocence. He was, it turned out, likely more criminal than the 1947 Auschwitz Trial in Kraków had concluded. In 1998 the Bavarian Justice Ministry, in part as a result of Schirra's interview, reinstated charges against Münch, but the charges were not pursued owing to his progressed dementia. He died in 2001.

In light of the revelations, one can say that Kor has chosen the wrong person to forgive. But she was unaware of all of this when she invited Münch to come as her invited guest to the commemoration at Auschwitz in 1995. From a legal standpoint, Münch was the wrong person because he was, based on Schirra's reporting, probably far guiltier than was initially supposed, despite the claims that he had not done anything wrong. But there is no need to regret the decision if the forgiver suspends any and all questions about of the state of mind of the person who is absolved. Münch's legal guilt, even his feelings of guilt, are hardly relevant to Kor. He is a cipher, meant to stand in for others. Only the survivor's state of mind is pertinent. Part of Kor's statement at Auschwitz read, "It is time to go on; it is time to heal our souls; it is time to forgive," and in that sense, the forgiveness has little to do with the object of her forgiveness. Münch's awful postwar persona, a legacy of his wartime behavior, was irrelevant. It is only the act of forgiveness that matters.

At an academic meeting depicted in the film, at the Spertus Institute in Chicago, a number of participants and interlocutors try to figure out what Kor really means when she forgives. They disentangle the term "forgiveness," separating it from "justice," "empathy," and "understanding," yet little of this makes a difference to Kor insofar as she is not a particularly rigorous academic thinker. Her aim is not to come to terms with the psychic condition of resentment as Jean Améry sought to do. Her approach does not reward attempts at systemization. Her self-healing is connected to empowerment, and for this reason, conscious of mise-en-scène, Hercules and Pugh depict Kor working out in a gym. Kor explains: "Most of my fellow survivors are so hurting . . . so many of them will die without ever feeling free from their pain." She adds: it is a "life-changing experience, to be free of that pain . . . as a victim, all of us feel extremely helpless. . . . I had no idea that I had the power to forgive a Nazi . . . no one could give me that power and no one could take it away." This discourse of empowerment is why Harald Welzer, the German social-psychologist and co-editor of the well-known book *Opa war kein Nazi* (*Grandpa Was No Nazi*; 2002), affirms Kor's project. Welzer observes: "A central element of survivor trauma was precisely that the survivor's harrowing experience, and the destruction of the prospect of a 'normal' life after their experience, has not been recognized. The praxis of truth commissions and the agonizing encounters between perpetrators and victims have this as their goal. Forgiveness has a direct relation to restoring the victim's autonomy, which is something justice and reparation cannot accomplish alone. Forgiveness as a political concept is meant to recover exactly what was taken from the victims of totalitarian violence: subjectivity, agency, and autonomy."[33] This attitude, with its discourse of empowerment, has its appeal, but it is not without problems. As it removes forgiveness from the legal sphere, it also suggests that those who refuse to forgive are expressing a preference to remain weak and disempowered. It makes forgiveness normative. Along these lines Micha Brumlik and Lena Inowlocki criticized Welzer: "By transforming the real victims' experience into a more or less arbitrarily redefined 'victim role,' [Welzer] pathologizes . . . precisely those survivors who are neither able nor willing to acquire the magic formula of forgiveness."[34]

Hercules and Pugh are sympathetic with Kor's project, and, like Welzer, they are inclined to view forgiveness as a choice in favor of empowerment. They are most sympathetic to Kor where they depict a hate crime perpetrated against her small, independent museum. We are told that in 1995, between the meeting with Münch and the start of Hercules and Pugh's film, Kor established the C.A.N.D.L.E.S. Holocaust Museum, an unlikely Holocaust memorial museum situated in an Indiana strip mall. Seamlessly integrated footage from an Action News report from November 2003 explains that her museum was burned to the ground, and that there is evidence of arson. Someone has scrawled "Remember Timothy McVeigh" on the wall, and the museum's interior resembles a war ruin. Kor is thrown back into the past, now holding a tin drinking cup, which is the same as or similar to the one she kept at Auschwitz. Speaking to the camera, she maintains that she is without hate, and that she again hopes to forgive.

The film eventually turns its attention to the Arab-Israeli conflict. Near to its conclusion, the directors bring Kor to Israel's West Bank in 2003 during the second intifada. While in Israel, Kor has an awkward dialogue with Palestinian teachers and an Israeli peace activist. She meets with a professor, who, along with other Palestinians, tells stories of his victimization at the hands of the Israeli secret service. In these situations, Kor becomes uncomfortable and resists engaging in productive exchange. She rationalizes the difference—the fact that she can forgive Nazis but is unwilling to warm up to Palestinians—by claiming that, "the idea of forgiveness cannot really happen while people are fighting for their lives." The filmmakers pursue the analogy between Kor's attitude about the Holocaust and her attitude about the Israeli-Palestinian conflict. They avoid, however, making the terms of the analogy explicit. The sequence does not neatly map the discourses of perpetration and forgiveness onto one another, and this is perhaps its strength. As a documentary about redemption, it resists redemption. The trip to Israel depicts Kor as having a history she cannot get beyond. There are, it seems to suggest, limits on her ability to forgive.

It should not come as a surprise that the film's focalization diverges at points from Kor, particularly where the question of Israel arises. From start to finish, the filmmakers have been unprogrammatic. They follow Kor, acknowledging her contradictions without defending her. It is hardly the filmmakers' goal to declare Kor superior to someone like Améry, who wrote in and for a different time. One need not be persuaded by Kor's position on healing, which is fundamentally anti-psychoanalytic insofar as it suggests that one can willfully leave their strong feelings about the past behind, a position that might be described as "new age." This unprogrammatic film veers away from making a strong statement for or against its subject, which reflects its mode; it attempts to be an observational documentary. To some viewers Kor's attitude might resemble a very American marketing campaign, but, watching Hercules and Pugh's work, it is difficult to fault this survivor for enjoying the power she has granted herself.

Born in the house of the hangman: Renata Schmidtkunz's *Landscapes of Memory: The Life of Ruth Klüger*

The nonfiction television production *Landscapes of Memory: The Life of Ruth Klüger* opens with an on-screen epigraph written by Klüger herself: "Vienna's wound, which I am, and my wound, which is Vienna, are not healable" (*Wiens Wunde, die ich bin, und meine Wunde, die Wien ist, sind unheilbar*).[35] The sentiment, far removed from Eva Kor's positivity, is emblematic of Klüger's writings. She generally underscores the extent to which wounding and healing are processes with two largely irreconcilable sides. On the one hand there is the survivor, and on the other there is Vienna, the city in which she was born and away from which she was deported. Whether Vienna knows it or cares to know it, the two remain one another's open wounds. Unlike Kor, Klüger would rather that these wounds persist and that her readers remain conscious of them. It may, of course, be unfair to think in terms of what Klüger would "rather" do insofar as the decisive events of her past were by and large not matters of choice, but where her postwar and contemporary emotions are concerned, she prefers to articulate her continued antipathy. The metaphor is deliberately graphic. The traumas did not only leave a mark, but they made incisions that refuse to close up and go away. Her writings, for this reason, take the form of a continued provocation: she forbids herself and others from papering over the past.

Klüger's position, the sometimes implicit and sometimes explicit assertion that her wounds are unlikely to heal, is a major engine of her autobiographical writing, and her resentment can be compared to Améry's, who, like Klüger, was born in Vienna and survived Auschwitz. In "Resentment," Améry explains why he bears a grudge. In the German in which he wrote, "grudge" is the onomatopoetic word *Groll*, which originates with the sound of plaintive moaning. Améry acknowledges that his writing is, in other words, a possibly irritating noise that most, but particularly the Germans, did not wish to hear. As a survivor who famously changed his name in order to leave his German origins behind, Améry continued, after the war, to hold a grudge against his persecutors. He draws on the concept of resentment (*ressentiment*) as articulated by Nietzsche, referring to the concept's appearance in *The Genealogy of Morals* and echoing Nietzsche's *Beyond Good and Evil* in his own work's German title *Jenseits von Schuld und Sühne*, which means, "Beyond Guilt and Atonement."[36] In contrast to Nietzsche, who held resentful persons in contempt, Améry chooses to avow or claim his bitterness. He willingly proclaims his resentment, the very weakness that Nietzsche abhors, and for him, like Klüger, it is an engine. Germans, by contrast, had no reason or desire to look backward, and, in their opinion, if he could not find it within himself to look forward to a common future, then that was *his* failing. His feelings were, in turn, pathologized as something akin to "concentration camp syndrome," a concept widely discussed by psychologists in the early to mid-1960s.[37]

In Améry's essay, he relates the story of his 1958 encounter with a southern German businessman, who kindly explained to him that the German people bear no ill will against the Jews ("das deutsche Volk trage dem jüdischen nichts nach").[38] The phenomenon he describes, whereby the Germans alternately blame and forgive the Jews for the Holocaust, is something generally referred to as "secondary anti-Semitism."[39] This particular German's comment is surely thoughtless, but Améry here is pointing more to the difference between himself, who still suffers, and this man, whose disposition appeared to him to be on an even keel.[40] The difference, or rather the man's indifference, redoubled Améry's victimization: already once tortured, he, in holding onto his past, was now made to feel like Shylock demanding a pound of flesh.[41] Améry's irritation had still other dimensions: not only was there a confusion about who at the table was the victim (how kind it was of the Germans, after all *they* had been through, not to resent the Jews), but his interlocutor is also distressingly content. The phrase, "his mind was at ease" indicates that Améry longs to upset him; he wanted to provoke.

But why would one not merely walk away? Eva Kor would certainly assert that one forgives in one's own interest; you might do it because it is good for you. Améry, writing many decades earlier and expressing the sentiments he felt immediately after the war, couches his reflections on resentment in terms of time. When his wounds were inflicted he was left feeling isolated and alone, and his resentment corresponds to the continued pain of that isolation. He had been physically tortured and he lost many loved ones. At what point, however, is that isolation meant to end? When is he supposed to admit that he no longer feels the pain of the torture, or that he no longer notes the absence of the dead? His resentment is meant to force the perpetrator into his psychic space. Améry is aware that his position contains the irrational demand that time be reversed, yet for the victim of torture (for the survivor) the past is never truly in the past. There may come a moment when Améry has caught up with his tormentors, a time when both can share the pleasure of a calm, collected disposition and be done with the past, but that moment has not yet arrived. In this sense, Améry's resentment is utopian: it looks to another point, another moment, one that may never come, and it preserves an understanding of the persistent difference between him and his persecutors. Even though the businessman with whom he spoke in 1958 was likely not among his actual tormentors, Améry holds the fact of his indifference against him. This indifference seemed to have been enough of an invitation to call attention to himself as a walking wound. He concludes his chapter: "We victims must finish with our retroactive rancor, in the sense that the KZ argot once gave to the word 'finish'; it meant as much as 'to kill.' Soon we must and will be finished." Améry anticipates his own death as the final endpoint of his resentment. Until that time has come, he concludes, "we request of those whose peace is disturbed by our grudge that they be patient."[42]

Klüger's challenge to the rhetoric of forgiveness is quite similar to Améry's. The Germans, and the Austrians as well, as far as she is concerned, are preoccupied either with self-serving narratives or with their own rhetoric of victimization. Such discourses leave little room for others' suffering. Her position appears as a corrective to Kor's, which announces itself as forward looking. Kor and Klüger are, obviously, two very distinct women with vastly different sets of experiences, yet these two documentaries, *Forgiving Dr. Mengele* and *Landscapes of Memory*, can be seen in connection with one another. Kor, on the one hand, explicitly gears her actions toward smoothing over the frictions produced by her traumatic memories. She found relief in publically forgiving her tormentors. The film that documents her acts of forgiveness, regardless of any distance that film takes from its subject, is suffused with Kor's language of healing. Klüger tends toward a different set of truths about human psychology, specifically toward the truths of psychoanalysis: psychic energy created by the impact of traumatic incidents and the inner conflicts they produce has to go somewhere; it cannot be disregarded. Angers that are repressed, in other words, return. A major motif of Klüger's autobiographical work *Still Alive* is the reiteration of the difficult fact that being wounded has consequences, and that survivors and their families might not necessarily heal, no matter how great their conscious efforts, not even over the course of their lifetimes.

In a 2002 essay entitled "Forgiving and Remembering," Klüger describes how, after publishing her autobiography, German audiences often asked her whether she could forgive.[43] Many Germans at the time, between four and five decades after the end of the war, wondered at what point they would no longer be held responsible for the decisions made and the atrocities committed by their parents and grandparents. Many hoped that the past could be squared away, and they aimed to enlist the victims' endorsement. The German idiom "*einen Schlussstrich unter etwas zu ziehen*," which means "to draw a final line (*Strich*) beneath something" and which may be equivalent to the English phrase "to wipe the slate clean," was often mentioned in German considerations of the Holocaust, especially by Germans who wanted to stop examining their culpability for Auschwitz.[44] Whether this kind of dismissal of the past was possible—whether it was indeed time to render the past the past—was debated toward the end of the 1990s, especially in connection with the German writer Martin Walser's well publicized 1998 speech (discussed in Chapter 1), wherein he expressed the sentiment that references to Auschwitz were now being used for short-term political ends, and that he had started looking away when confronted with Germany's Auschwitz memorial culture.[45] Walser even went so far as to criticize the plan for Berlin's major new Holocaust memorial, calling it a "soccer field-sized nightmare" (*fußballfeldgroßen Albtraum*) built into the heart of the capital city.[46]

Klüger writes about contemporary Germans' desires to be forgiven, but also about the problems that complicate the act of forgiving from her end. The most complicating factor is mourning: among other relatives, Klüger's half-brother

Schorschi died in the Holocaust. He was deported first to Theresienstadt and then to Riga, where he was murdered.[47] She was able to live out the remainder of her life, and has, she writes, neither the capacity nor the right to forgive in his name: "a person may forgive an insult or even a slap in the face if the other party apologizes, but how can I 'forgive' the murder of my teenage brother when I have had my life and he didn't get to have his?"[48] The standpoint that says that she cannot speak on behalf of her brother echoes that of Primo Levi, who describes himself as not being a true witness to Auschwitz, precisely because he survived. She thus feels compelled to leave the wound open on her brother's behalf, and along these lines she makes a telling remark, which may have been calculated, when she comments that, "remembering and resenting are, or may be, siblings, like their opposites, forgiving and forgetting."[49] Her brother, that is, her sibling, is a figure for remembrance and resentment. He *is*, in this sense, her grudge; as long as she remembers him—and she will likely always remember him—resentment *is* her sibling.

The request that she forgive perpetrators, Klüger continues, "irritated" her, and her essay on the subject is one among several attempts in her body of work to explain why she rejects the premise. It is a response to Germans who look to her for an absolution she has no interest in providing.[50] Klüger writes that taking on the guilt of others, as younger Germans attempted to do, "smacks of sainthood," and doing so in public "can be a kind of sentimental self-castigation, the flip side of moral self-congratulation." She asks whether alleviating another's guilt feelings was a pious way for one generation to take on another one's sins. Absolution is among a number of Christian motifs here, and she is concerned about the drive to recast Jewish history in a Christian framework.[51] The forgiveness that Kor offers is thus called into question from several perspectives: it is neither something that the survivor can offer, nor does it bring about appropriate "penitence" for the perpetrators. Klüger does not want to be mistaken for a cleric or a saint, offering absolution and forgiveness.

Survival is, according to Klüger, not an accomplishment that puts her in a position to forgive others. The point is underscored where she writes in *Still Alive* that nothing, really, was learned in Auschwitz, adding that such lessons are typically "sentimental rubbish" and that they depend upon "a false concept of suffering as a source of moral education."[52] Statements of this sort are, I do not believe, to be taken at face value: survivors such as Klüger and Levi surely learned a great deal from their experiences and have a lot to teach. Klüger, however, does not want to be in the position of absolving Germans or Austrians because more truth is produced by disputation and discord, or at least by provocation, than by reconciliation and by smoothing things over. There is nothing that stands in the way of her telling former perpetrators or contemporary Germans that she no longer holds them responsible for her brother's death and that she bears them no ill will. She could certainly say that she forgives Germans of the past or the present, which is probably what many Germans and others would like to hear, yet nearly all of her autobiographical writing (and some of her literary critical writing as well) calls into question whether that affirmation would be productive.

The wound remains open, and Schmidtkunz's documentary, taking cues from its subject and allowing her to speak for herself, avoids conciliatory gestures. Although the film's director surely has a hand in shaping the information we are given about Klüger (in choosing to begin, for example, with Klüger's epigraph about the open wound), presenting Klüger in a more conciliatory light would have gone against her subject's grain. In a 1992 essay entitled "Writing Fiction about the Shoah" ("Dichten über die Shoah") Klüger relates what she describes as a bad joke in which Jews, after Kristallnacht, whisper to avoid having their prayers heard by their own god, whom they believe has turned against them. The joke certainly is structured like a joke, but its content is disquieting. She refers to the discomfort it produces and the need for a "confrontation with that discomfort" ("Auseinandersetzung mit diesem Unbehagen").[53] In this respect her desire for wounds to remain open, especially where Germany and Austria are concerned, is akin to Améry's. Where she writes about works of Holocaust literature by Polish authors such as Jerzy Kosiński and Tadeusz Borowski, and about Cordelia Edvardson's autobiographical Swedish language book *Burned Child Seeks the Fire* (1984), Klüger points out that there is a lack of serious Holocaust books coming from Germany, where it has become not much of a topic.[54] The books that are published there, she asserts, remain little read.[55] To some extent this is ascribable to the diminished Jewish population in Germany, which continues to hover at around one-fifth of what it was in 1933. In Austria those numbers are much lower.[56]

Schmidtkunz is a German-born journalist working for the public television station Österreichischer Rundfunk (ORF) in Vienna. Her documentary is, in part, connected to the Austrian attempt to alter their own national unresponsiveness to Holocaust writing: in 2008 the city of Vienna distributed 100,000 copies of Klüger's memoir for its "One City, One Book" project, and this accounts for Klüger's celebrity status when she returns to the city of her birth.[57] It deals with the impact that Holocaust survival had on her family and with questions of national belonging. It takes up the question of whether Klüger can ever feel that she is Austrian in addition to being American.[58]

As a film made by Schmidtkunz, an Austrian television personality, and funded in part by ORF, it can be seen as Austria's attempt to ingratiate itself to Klüger. If one, however, sees the film as Klüger's film, that is, as the profile of a female survivor, it begins to resemble *Kitty: Return to Auschwitz* and *Forgiving Dr. Mengele*. All three films are expository documentaries focalized through a woman who was a child or young adult when she was interned in Auschwitz (Hart was born in 1926, Klüger in 1931, and Kor in 1934), and the documentaries all depict these women's lives long after Auschwitz, filling out their portraits with interviews of family members. Klüger's case is, however, unique because she has contributed as much as any major scholar to contemporary critical thinking about the representation and repercussions of the Holocaust, so depictions of her experience are over-shadowed and to some extent determined by what she would likely say about those representations. She is the subject of the documentary, but because she has said and written so much about the Holocaust, she also contributes to giving the film shape. Her disinterest, for example, in revisiting the camps in which she was tormented has been documented, and that likely played a role in the documentarian's decision not to cajole her into staging or performing onsite memories for the purposes of her film.

In *Landscapes of Memory* Klüger explains that she is more interested in the distinction between victims and free persons (or "free beings"), referring to the German words *Opfer* and *Freisein*, respectively, than she is in the traditional distinction between victims and perpetrators. The difference is the basis of an existential question: when does a prisoner, especially a traumatized prisoner, stop being one? If trauma involves the loss of family members, then at what point should a survivor such as Klüger declare herself free of the past? Her programmatic statement can, on the one hand, be seen in terms of what does *not* interest her: she excludes the perpetrator from her equation. The perpetrator's frame of mind and their comfort, then as now, are of little concern to her, and her position corresponds to Lanzmann's willful lack of comprehension about the perpetrators, or his famous statement that the one purpose he had in mind the entire time he worked on *Shoah* was "not to comprehend."[59] To take one example: the former Nazi tormentor Hans Münch was, despite Kor's superficial assessment of his motives and her willingness to absolve him, largely unreconstructed insofar as he remained an anti-Semite throughout his life.

But his comment, published in 1998, that he knows no "freilebende" (or "free-living") Jews, he knows only "Auschwitz Jews," alights inadvertently on a truth about the past.[60] Most of the Jews with whom he interacted were still living with, and to some extent defined by, their nightmares. Klüger explains, "We have always known that the Holocaust was our nightmare, not theirs."[61] She contrasts postwar dispositions of perpetrators with their victims: "The perpetrators have innocent minds and are fond of fresh mountain air. . . . The ex-Nazis act like people who once worked in a slaughterhouse, no more. Sad and terrible, to be sure, but what was one to do?"[62] Why should she or we be interested in the frame of mind of persons who remain comparatively unperturbed by the horrors they inflicted or the messes they made? As Klüger writes elsewhere, one cannot count on the victors to understand the victory; that is for the defeated. Although the Germans were not victorious in the traditional sense, they nearly succeeded in eliminating Jewry from Europe. About that experience one is sure to learn more by talking to those who had been nearest to the true witnesses: the survivors.

Writing about Lanzmann's *Shoah*, when she first saw it in 1985, Klüger describes how the perpetrators generally adopt a condescending tone, and her response to that tone seems central to her resentment. Klüger watches Lanzmann's exchange with Franz Suchomel, the SS squad leader who participated in Operation Reinhard and who was convicted of war crimes in 1965. She describes the condescending voice with which Suchomel deals with Lanzmann, who, as Klüger points out, is a French Jew with "unpolished" German language skills. When he talks, "to a Jew who doesn't speak German correctly," he "condescend[s] to him."[63] When he and Lanzmann discuss the number of Jews liquidated each day at Treblinka, Suchomel "set[s] him straight": "'Believe me, Mr. Lanzmann, 18,000 [murders] a day is too high a figure, 15,000 at the most.'"[64] In another sequence, Lanzmann asks Martha Michelsohn, the wife of a Nazi schoolteacher from Chlemno about having seen Jews tormented and murdered in mobile gas vans. Michelsohn describes having been exposed to the screams of terror, and then, after misstating the number of Jews murdered at Chelmno by a factor of 10, she concludes: "Sad, sad, sad!" In response to the scene, Klüger writes, "I feel a twinge of envy for these people, including Mrs. Michelsohn . . . to whom 400,000 murdered in her backyard are like 40,000. (She knew it was something with a four in it.) Essentially the interviews with the ex-Nazis show us minds at peace."[65] The perpetrators are untroubled; it was indeed sad and terrible, but "what was one to do?"

Echoing Améry's writing, particularly where he describes the even disposition of that German with whom he spoke in 1958, Klüger adds, "They harbor no grudges." Presumably the persons she has in mind believe others are interested in what they have to say; they are experts on crimes committed either by them or by those around them. They are people relating the facts of the matter, rather than those making a noise of discontentment, those with a grudge, or people making sounds that no one wants to hear. One should not be unfair to Michelsohn, who surely had some bad memories and is entitled to complain of the nightmares she describes to Lanzmann, but Klüger's point is worth examining: the grudge, the complaint, or the gripe is the manifestation of an open wound, a wound associated with loss, and, in Klüger's case, it comes from not having had her brother's and father's bodies to bury, a loss that hardly went away.

Schmidtkunz's film opens in Austria, on the Memorial Day against Violence and Racism in Memory of the Victims of National Socialism, which takes place annually on May 5, the day of the liberation of Mauthausen concentration camp. Klüger is giving a celebrated public address. From there *Landscapes of Memory* transitions and spends most of its first 30 minutes depicting aspects of Klüger's present-day life in southern California. This part of the documentary is quite straightforward: it features a number of talking heads, testimonials from her two sons, and from her colleagues at UC Irvine. Students, generally college-aged women, occasionally request to have her sign their books. Klüger helps fill out the portrait of herself, describing things such as her politics—that, for example, she was initially enthusiastic about Barack Obama's presidency, but she then found herself a little disillusioned. Positions such as these are presented less as consequences of her having survived the Holocaust than as evidence that she is now a typical Californian. They serve to frame assertions later in the film that Austria, where Klüger was persecuted and nearly murdered, is, despite her intentions, also her *Heimat*, or homeland.

The film eventually extracts itself from California, and Klüger, accompanied by Schmidtkunz, goes to the memorial site at the former camp Bergen-Belsen. This is a modification of the concept of the "return documentary," because Klüger was never a prisoner at that camp and is thus not returning to it.[66] It is where she would have ended up at the conclusion of her final death march, had she not escaped. Bergen-Belsen is where Anne Frank died at nearly that same time, in March of 1945. Because the visit to the camp is not a recounting of Klüger's experiences, the production of the documentary is different from that to which Kitty Hart had subjected herself in *Kitty: Return to Auschwitz*, and it is probably in everyone's interest that Klüger not be made to relive horrific incidents. Klüger's accounts, both in her autobiographical work *Still Alive* and here, are preceded and informed by *Shoah* or by stories such as Hart's, but they seek another register. The film is a product of a different generation, and it incorporates additional skepticism about Holocaust tourism and memorial culture.

Klüger, like Levi before her, prefers not to cast her story of survival in a heroic light. One reads a memoir such as Levi's *The Drowned and the Saved*, which was published only a few years prior to the first edition of Klüger's memoir, and walks away with the impression that survival was mainly a question of fortune, much more so than it was a question of strength, ingenuity, or faith. Klüger says something similar at this point in the film, asserting that her survival seems to her to have been the most outlandish of accidents ("der lächerlichste Zufall"). As she looks at a memorial grave marker for the 5,000 dead, she points out that nothing makes her superior to those who are buried here; she could just as well have been among them. At the same time, however, we know from Klüger's writings that she was remarkably bold, that she made choices to survive, and that, for example, it required courage to organize food, to lie about her age, and to elude her keepers at key moments. One can be sympathetic to Levi's famous assertion that it was not the best among the prisoners who survived, yet at the same time acknowledge that Klüger has a story to tell, one that no one else can recount. She resists the clichés associated with survival and would reject them, in particular the idealization of survivors, even at the expense of the truth that she herself acted bravely. At Bergen-Belsen she stands before the memorial wall next to the obelisk erected by the British and describes the platitudes inscribed there as so much sentimental nonsense.

In a 2006 interview with the German weekly *Der Spiegel*, one in which Klüger proclaims that the city of Vienna still "reeks" of anti-Semitism, she explains that she prefers not to visit camp memorial sites such as Bergen-Belsen.[67] This follows comments in *Still Alive* in which she famously expresses critical sentiments about memorial sites, asserting that they are "formed by the vagaries and neuroses of our unsorted, collective memory," and that they are sentimental places, where one looks, "into a mirror instead of reality."[68] Perhaps for this reason the visit to the camp is only a brief interlude in the film, which, consistent with Klüger's own writing, is less interested in examining the mechanisms of killing. *Landscapes of Memory* is more concerned with Klüger's life after the Holocaust and with her subsequent attitudes about all that happened. Writing about Lanzmann's *Shoah*, Klüger observes that, "the museum culture that has sprung up around the concentration camps is based on a sense of *spiritus loci* which I lack. What was done there could be repeated elsewhere, I have argued, conceived as it was by human minds, carried out by human hands, somewhere on earth, the place irrelevant, so why single out the sites that now look like so many others?"[69] The idea of traveling to the scene of the crime is unimportant because the scene itself has nothing to offer; no particular landscape, no terrain, can be held responsible for creating killers.

The central question for Lanzmann concerns what happened at the site. The site is the trigger of memory. Like a detective, Lanzmann finds that it is generally best to start with the crime scenes and the witnesses, if one wants to answer questions. Moreover, the contemporary silence of the camp often implies that there is little residue of the past. He goes back to Auschwitz, for example, in order to show the absence of traces: a horrible thing happened, and now the silence suggests that no one cares. For Klüger the space itself is less important. Her memories, as she relates the story in her memoir, and as is recounted in *Landscapes of Memory*, came back to her not while visiting a camp, but at the moment a passing bicycle struck her in Göttingen. In *Still Alive*, she describes the 1988 accident in vivid, nearly violent terms: "I want to push him away with both arms outstretched, but he is on top of me, bike and all. Germany, Deutschland, a moment like hand-to-hand combat."[70] The collision left her hospitalized and paralyzed, and it was at this point, she says, that the memories and the need to write them down came to her. She describes her efforts to speak as having been like those of Gregor Samsa in Franz Kafka's *Metamorphosis*. When one looks at the other incidents of violence in her childhood—the memory, for example, of the time that she tried to get a little extra food at Christianstadt concentration camp and a German SS man hit her[71]—it is little wonder that having been hit hard served as a trigger for her memories.

In this way, the title *Landscapes of Memory*, which was also the UK title of her memoir *Still Alive*, potentially misleads. It is not that the landscapes contain memories, but rather that memory itself *is* a landscape. Klüger prefers the metaphor of inner furniture (*inneres Mobiliar*), which has to be rearranged. In Schmidtkunz's film Klüger's son, Dan Angress, travels with her to Vienna and he participates in the project of trying to trigger memories of the past. The consequences are embarrassing. Angress encourages his mother to go back to the building where she grew up, clearly with the hope that the encounter with the place will, as in Lanzmann's films, produce something new, revelatory, or epiphanic. Although Klüger goes through the motions, she appears irked by the exercise and is reluctant to indulge him. He attempts to coax her into thinking from her own mindset as a young girl, asking her to remember what it was like, and how it felt to push at the door. Unlike Kitty Hart, to whom all the memories return, Klüger grows impatient. She does not want to make a return documentary and nothing is going to happen here because she does not believe in *spiritus loci*. Also, she has already testified for the world at length. Her demeanor suggests that if her son really wants to know what happened here, he might be better served by rereading her book.

Lost siblings form a central part of these stories of resentment. Klüger has that loss in common with Eva Kor. There are, of course, distinctions between the two stories: Kor's sister died decades after the war, even though it was as a consequence of Nazi medical experimentation. Klüger, by contrast, never saw her brother after he was first taken away. As Freud points out, both mourning and melancholia are triggered by loss, but the latter condition is one for which the loss remains unacknowledged and the subject struggles internally, having incorporated the image of the lost loved one. The subject thus turns the anger that results from the loss upon him or herself. Melancholia is typically associated with depression, and in general clinical depression is now taken as the term for what was once called by that name. One might, however, consciously choose to leave one's wounds open, that is, to refuse to work through a loss. The conscious decision-making process is at the heart of the difference between Kor and Klüger: as documented in *Forgiving Dr. Mengele*, Kor opts to begin the work of letting go, which is difficult in light of the loss of her twin, and because of the atrocities the two had suffered through together. Several factors impede Klüger's mourning, particularly that the bodies of her father and brother will never be buried in a proper grave.[72] Deprived of a proper farewell with them, she chooses not to pretend her mourning process is typical.

Holding a wound open and asserting the presence of the ghosts of the dead can also be a means of processing loss. Based only on the two films, one cannot say whether Kor or Klüger has done a "better" job of working through the death of their loved ones. It is not a determination anyone should care to make. Moreover, as viewers we know neither of them; we know only what we see and hear, so any assertion would be speculation. Their different modes of mourning, however, provide insight into how and whether survivors hold onto the past. Klüger, for example, speaks about her father, how happy they were in Vienna before he disappeared, was deported to Drancy, and then killed in the East. In *Still Alive*, she recalls that a childhood disputation with him, one that led to punishment, was among their last interactions, and she explains, "The problem is that there was nothing more to come. It's as if I resent his death because it deprived me of a chance for reconciliation. As if his uncompleted life had no other purpose than to be patient with the demands of an eight-year-old, or to listen to the carefully prepared explanations and apologies of the teenager or the adult she turned into."[73] Their relationship never had a chance to mature. She mourns him as the child he knew, and as the teenager and the woman she became. In another onscreen epigraph, Klüger describes him as the "unredeemed ghost" who haunts her.

For this reason, Klüger takes a position that is deliberately provocative. By all rights, the ghost that haunts her should plague Vienna, a city that still reeks of anti-Semitism. In this sense, her memoir's American title "Still Alive" has multiple meanings. Not only does it refer to her survival, but to the continued survival of her brother and father: the ghosts are still alive, and the title thus cuts both ways. If these ghosts haunt her, should they not, for the reasons described by Améry, also haunt others? What, one has to ask, is "still alive?" In his famous essay on working out the past, Adorno referred to Nazism as a ghost (*Gespenst*), writing, "National Socialism lives on, and even today we still do not know whether it is merely the ghost of what was so monstrous that it lingers on after its own death or whether it has not yet died at all, whether the willingness to commit the unspeakable survives in people as well as in the conditions that enclose them."[74] The postwar story can be seen as a clash of ghosts: the ghost of fascism and the ghosts of the dead. After the Holocaust Klüger is "still alive," yet so are her half-brother and her father, and so is anti-Semitism.

Klüger's resentment and her decision to declare that she cannot properly mourn her loved ones are entangled, and the decision not to forgive in their names contains twin mandates: to remember and to resent. Catherine Smale ties the appearances of Klüger's ghosts less to Freud's "Mourning and Melancholia," than to his "Totem and Taboo," particularly where he writes that the apparition of ghosts is directly connected to a sense of guilt. "The return of the dead," she writes, "is facilitated by a sense of not having treated them properly, or rather by a fear that the spirits of slain men will return to seek revenge."[75] Smale continues, "Klüger's individual and collective engagement with the Holocaust through the figure of the ghost is fraught with ambivalence. She longs to be free of the dead, yet simultaneously clings to their presence; she realizes that she cannot speak on their behalf, yet continues to emphasize the ongoing need to consider what their experiences might have been."[76] In "Forgiving and Remembering" Klüger's rhetoric stems from the close proximity of the words "guilt" and "debt," both represented in German by the word *Schuld*. Klüger writes: "My brother was a mere boy when he was shot, and I visualize him healthy and alive at his own graveside. My father was a young man. Their ghosts are unforgiving. I can't give them some of my years to buy back, to redeem, theirs. So I remain in their debt, for a family is obligated to share, isn't it?"[77] If her grief does not seem curable—if it is not likely to go away—then it may also be because she does not want to be cured of it. Her feeling of guilt and her debt to her family prevent her from most attempts to leave the past in the past.

There do, however, seem to be moments when Klüger describes letting go of the past. In one of the film's sequences, she speaks in voice-over about having had her tattooed number removed. We hear her say this as we see her gazing directly into the camera. The film does not explore this point further; Klüger simply alludes to an essay she has written about it. That essay, published in the collection *unterwegs verloren*, begins with the ghost of her half-brother reproaching her, making again the point that he is deprived of the long life she has been able to lead. Here, however, she acknowledges that her time has grown shorter. The tattooed numbers, she explains, are "a symbol of absolute evil," but the numbers in themselves were neither evil nor were they anything special.[78] Her mother had had hers removed in the 1950s and a scar remained, but, Klüger writes, the scar healed over, and, as she died, it was hardly even visible.[79] She recounts a story about seeing her own image in a photograph and being surprised at how shocking the number was, as if seeking a confrontation with the viewer. After public readings from her memoir, she recounts, the paper would run headlines like, "Not Hiding the Auschwitz Number" (*Die Auschwitznummer nicht verdecken*).[80] The position she had taken earlier now seems to have softened, and in reading the essay, it seems as though Klüger was tired of being the permanent provocateuse. She adds that she no longer wanted to feel like the condemned man in Kafka's "In the Penal Colony": "That was enough for me. No longer did I want . . . to have a law that was unjust, absolute, incomprehensible and inaccessible to reason etched into my body."[81] The essay ends positively, with a gesture toward a farewell to the brother, an acknowledgment that she won't be able to remember him forever; soon she will no longer recognize him.[82] It suggests the possibility that the wound, like the trace of a tattoo, might almost entirely fade away before she dies.

One of the sequences that sheds the most light on Klüger's feelings about Germany and Austria is a filmed conversation with Herbert Lehnert, a former colleague who was a German literary scholar, specializing in Thomas Mann. Lehnert was born in 1925, and he was thus in his mid- to late teens during the war. He was in the Hitler Youth and then, when he was older, in the German military (the *Wehrmacht*). Klüger explains dispassionately: "Herbert is a friend of mine, and he hired me; [he is] a professor of German, who valued my work and wanted to have me here. He was in the Hitler Youth, and, as he himself says, he was a convinced Nazi, who served in the *Wehrmacht*, and then changed, as did, hopefully, most of the Germans." Lehnert's story is not all that unusual. There were many German professors, as well as Germans of that age group in general, who were in the Hitler Youth; it was not uncommon. Many subsequently drew an analogy to the Boy Scouts insofar as participation was conventional for young men at the time. These sorts of analogies normalized that part of the past, for those who participated in the Hitler Youth, if not for others.

In the film, Lehnert and Klüger walk on the beach and reflect on their long friendship. The conversation touches on the question of how one should view the Holocaust. Lehnert remarks that one shouldn't render the Nazi period in absolute terms ("verabsolutieren"), explaining that it was "only one episode" ("nur eine Episode"), which minimizes it. Klüger responds that he is trivializing her childhood, which is an understatement. The remark trivializes a great deal. Améry points out the problem with remarks like that in "Resentments," arguing that the Third Reich will "continue to be regarded as an operational accident of history," and that position will ultimately extinguish the moral demands of resentment.[83] Améry then quotes from none other than Thomas Mann: "For as long as the German nation, including its young and youngest age groups, does not decide to live entirely without history . . . then it must continue to bear the responsibility for those twelve years."[84] Thinking of it as an operational accident of history or as an isolated episode trivializes by normalizing. One should not have to point out, but one somehow still needs to, that it was not merely one episode among others, where the lives it destroyed are concerned.

Lehnert asserts that working on German-Jewish thinkers is a way of undoing or patching over the past. He advances a model of cultural symbiosis as an antithesis of Nazism. It was, for cultured persons and intellectuals, the never-to-be-recovered loss associated with the Holocaust: no one can restore what German-Jewish culture from Moses Mendelssohn to Walter Benjamin and Hannah Arendt was becoming. Klüger is, however, contrarian, and she expresses an overall lack of affinity for—as Lehnert puts it, questionably—"Jews who wanted nothing more than to be German." The two appear to be close friends, and it is a friendship that has gone on for years, yet his obliviousness is painful to observe, particularly for those who have read Klüger's autobiography, and who are familiar with the encounters Klüger has had with colleagues and their spouses, those who either claimed that the Germans had it tougher than the Jews after the war—those who competed on the field of suffering—or asserted that they knew better than she did what went on in the camps. [85] Lehnert is, however, a friend, as the author Martin Walser had once been her friend: these men of a particular generation are important foils for her, especially owing to their clumsy attempts to close off the past. As this is a documentary, one that takes its cues from its subject, one can here detect Klüger's fleeting, cynical glance into the camera lens (Figure 3.3). The look suggests she is with the viewer more than she is with her conversation partner. She has allies, but they are not next to her on the screen.

Every bit of this resentment comes forward clearly where Klüger speaks from Vienna, a city that is familiar and uncanny to her like no other city, but which

Figure 3.3 Ruth Klüger speaks with Herbert Lehnert in *Landscapes of Memory: The Life of Ruth Klüger* (2011).

she also describes as her Heimat. She notes that the crimes committed here remain to her unforgiven and unforgotten, adding "this too is Heimat: these old resentments." [86] In *Still Alive*, she writes about her attitude toward Austrians:

> There was a joke current in postwar Vienna about two people to whom Jews had entrusted their things before deportation. One says to the other: "You are lucky your Jew didn't return. Mine did." . . . Vienna was awash in self-pity. . . . Everyone felt they had been victims of the Nazis, whereas to me, *they* had been the arch-Nazis. Statistics bear me out. Percentage-wise more Austrians than Germans were involved in the more gruesome tasks performed by the Nazis, in guarding concentration camps, for example.[87]

In a stunning use of mise-en-scène Schmidtkunz's *Landscapes of Memory* has Klüger speak from the Heldenplatz, the plaza near Vienna's city center where Hitler was welcomed in March 1938, and where he declared the *Anschluss*. In voice-over, we hear Klüger's poem, which has been published under the titles "Wien, Mai '97" or "Wiener Neurose."[88] The poem has as its starting point the adage: "In the house of the hangman, one should not speak of the noose" (*Im Hause des Henkers spricht man nicht von dem Strick*). The turn of phrase originates with Cervantes's *Don Quixote*, where it is said that in the house of the *hanged* man, one should not speak of the noose. Klüger picks up on a play on the phrase, one that slips back and forth as easily in English as it does in German, between the hangman and the hanged man. (*Es heißt:/ Im Hause des Henkers/ sprich nicht/ vom Strick* [They say:/ In the house of the hangman/ don't speak/ of the noose]). The punning is attributed to Adorno and found in a letter defending his own 1955 study *Guilt and Defense*, where he explains that despair was for the victims, not for the surviving Germans, but it is difficult to point this out insofar as one should not mention the noose in the house of the hangmen, lest, he adds, one be "suspected of harboring resentment."[89] Klüger's poem explains that she knows not to speak of the noose in the hangman's house, but she does, because her thoughts run contrary to good manners. In keeping with the theme that she is Vienna's wound, she writes that she seeks out the noose where it hides, and that a fiber of it remained in her neck (*Mir blieb eine Faser davon im Genick*). Her tenacity, she adds, was her good fortune.

In this sequence in the film, present experience is layered over the faded past. A person becomes part of the palimpsest. She stands in the heart of Austria, making herself visible; not an undetectable ghost, but a wound. A neurosis, as referred to in her poem's title, is, of course, an invisible injury; there is no lesion. Here, she displays herself at the happy, tourist friendly Heldenplatz, directly in front of the monument to Archduke Charles of Austria, the pride of the nation, the field marshal who was considered one of Napoleon's most formidable opponents. The positioning is hardly accidental. It recalls Anselm Kiefer's photographic work *Occupations* (*Besetzungen*) from 1969 for which the German artist photographed himself giving the Hitler salute at several sites in Europe, in front of famous landmarks. One of the best-known images in that work is on a plaza such as this. Although the act of giving the Hitler salute was controversial and provocative, most interpreters are inclined to see it in terms similar to those articulated by Andreas Huyssen, who remarks that in Kiefer's photographs, "There are no jubilant masses, marching soldiers, nor any of the other emblems of power and imperialism that we know from historical footage from the Nazi era. The artist does not identify with the gesture of Nazi occupation, he ridicules it, satirizes it."[90] Klüger is not giving the Hitler salute. She is simply standing quietly in a white coat, among tourists (Figure 3.4), yet she, similar to Kiefer, steps into the public space and forces a reckoning with her presence. The resemblance to *Occupations* shown in the images here is striking. She stands stoically and no one notices her, yet she has no intention of quietly going away. As a mortal and ultimately a vanishing counterpoint to Archduke Charles, Klüger objectifies the desire that reminders such as herself, in contrast to seemingly permanent and monumental Austrian landmarks, would "just hurry up and disappear."[91]

To borrow a term from the cultural historian James Young, Klüger is a living "countermonument."[92] After she vanishes, the city will have to choose whether to remember or reject her. She reads the entirety of her poem "Wiener Neurose" into the film along with its conclusion that the hangman is dead and lilacs now bloom where the gallows were. The word *Galgenplatz*, or place of the gallows, is meant to resonate with the word *Heldenplatz* (the "Plaza of Heroes"), and the wordplay inscribes Klüger into the tradition of Ernst Jandl, whose 1962 poem *wien: heldenplatz* took Austria similarly to task. This is, of course, not the only wordplay: as indicated earlier, "einen Schlussstrich unter etwas zu ziehen" is to draw a final line under something, or to be done with it, particularly the past. Klüger might also have been tired of hearing about the desire for the clean slate, especially on the part of Walser, whom she had known for many years, and to whom the position was attributed.[93] In order to replace the call for the *Strich*—the decisive line that would close the discussion and render the past the past—she reintroduces Adorno's pun and turns a *Strich* into a *Strick*, or a noose,

Figure 3.4 Ruth Klüger positions herself, like Anselm Kiefer, before a heroic memorial in *Landscapes of Memory: The Life of Ruth Klüger*.

which is a reminder of the past and a provocation. With the smallest stroke of the pen she calls for those around her to deal with the past, even and especially in the house of the hangman.

Both *Landscapes of Memory* and *Forgiving Dr. Mengele* follow their subjects and show how they interact with the world, as survivors. They share one additional common characteristic: both films take their protagonists to Israel. In *Landscapes of Memory*, the film travels to Jerusalem for a reading of Klüger's work. There, Klüger talks about how she might have been at home in Israel, perhaps even more than in America. We see her at Yad Vashem, and at the Ghetto Fighters Memorial, and Klüger critically examines the idea of memorializing Jewish resistance, noting that the war was really won by the Allies. As in *Forgiving Dr. Mengele*, this film sets up a constellation between its model of forgiveness and the Arab-Israeli conflict, and Klüger, unlike Eva Kor, talks about how reconciliation seems possible, and how the Arabs seem to belong there as well. Despite the fact that Klüger is the one who holds onto her resentment toward the Germans, she comes across as more open and accommodating toward the Palestinians. She meets with a peace activist and they talk about whether Israel can be a just land. Israel is often an endpoint of the argument where the Holocaust is concerned, though in their interactions with it, these two films contrast sharply with one another. Both documentaries follow the leads of their subjects, who wonder what it would mean, in the time they have left and in the service of forgiveness, were they to attempt to put the past entirely in the past.

4

Family Issues: Oedipal Confrontations in *2 or 3 Things I Know about Him* and *The Flat*

Although Claude Lanzmann can hardly be said to have invented the investigative documentary interview, and impactful interviews had already appeared earlier, in films by Jean Rouch and Marcel Ophüls, among others, *Shoah* is remarkable for the extent to which it makes its interview subjects truly central. One after another Lanzmann's subjects' voices, with what Erin McGlothlin describes as an "extraordinary multivocality that characterizes [*Shoah*'s] soundtrack," coalesce such that they unfold on an unprecedented scale the story of a pan-European catastrophe.[1] Diverse witnesses, a triumvirate identified by Raul Hilberg as being divided into victims, bystanders, and perpetrators, recount events on screen, one after the next.[2] Lanzmann's film attempts to show all three groups, and in general it is easy to tell who is who, in part because the interviewer himself carries his resentments into the film: he is a Jew, and he was a member of the French resistance. As a young man, he bore a good deal of anger, and one cannot fail to see this on screen. Alternately, when he speaks with survivors, he empathizes with them, eliciting some of the most compelling conversations in cinema history. His highly emotional dialogue in a barbershop with Abraham Bomba, who cut victims' hair before they were gassed at Treblinka, is cited in countless studies of documentary film not only for its ground-breaking and revolutionary use of mise-en-scène, but also with respect to the question of whether Bomba is working through his trauma on camera, before our eyes.[3]

In the interest of providing a fuller portrait, Lanzmann also confronts the perpetrators, and here the documentarian hones his peerless style of interrogation. He elicits testimony where there would otherwise be silence, and he brings his subjects to speak, which is often a thorny issue where the Holocaust is concerned. The film's perpetrators were disinclined to speak of what they had done, and they were in many cases more reticent than the survivors. Using, in one case, a hidden camera, Lanzmann acquired the historically important testimony of Franz Suchomel, the SS Sergeant who participated in the Action T4 euthanasia program in Operation Reinhard. Suchomel, under the impression he was not being recorded, gave a candid account of his role in an industrial murder that was unlike any other, one that included not only his repugnant personal opinions, but also eyewitness details about "the funnel," or the uphill path lined with barbed wire that led directly to the gas chambers. McGlothlin points out that, "although Suchomel appears to be in control in these scenes as Lanzmann's teacher and mentor, it is ultimately of course Lanzmann who manipulates the interaction between them."[4] Most critics absolve Lanzmann of the charge that he behaved unethically when he filmed Suchomel without his knowledge, owing to the import of the historical information he elicited. Florence Jacobowitz writes, "The means are justified, exposed as an act of resistance to the masking of a crime."[5] Justifying his decision in a way that refers to the mode of documentary he was making, Jacobowitz adds that Lanzmann's stance is, "an expression of the idea that the director makes his personal voice, his mark, felt. The film is not an objective work; Lanzmann's position is presented with a forthright intensity (as is the filmmaker's right)."[6] The director's strong, emotionally intense involvement in eliciting the truth, especially because that involvement is at all times transparent to the viewer, explains what would otherwise be a questionable decision.

Lanzmann's interview with the perpetrator Josef Oberhauser is somewhat different. It is directly and explicitly confrontational. Oberhauser committed war crimes at the killing center Bełżec and was charged with 450,000 counts of accessory to murder, yet he was only sentenced to four and one-half years of imprisonment. Lanzmann finds Oberhauser where he is working, decades after the war, at a beer hall in Munich. We enter the hall with Lanzmann: we do not see him on screen, not right away, but we follow his gaze, and we are intruding into the space alongside him. The camera spies Oberhauser behind the taps off to the left of the frame, separated from us by a counter, which here acts as a barrier. The prolonged silence ratchets up the tension. After a pause Lanzmann inquires coyly about how many liters of beer are sold there each day, which is then followed by an awkward exchange, one that reveals only that Oberhauser would prefer not to be caught on camera. Lanzmann then presents him with a picture of Christian Wirth, an architect of the exterminations at Bełżec and Treblinka. The questions then become tougher: referring to the difficulties the Nazis had in disposing of the bodies, he asks whether Oberhauser does not recall Bełżec and its overflowing graves. The scene is instructive with respect to documentary technique and what an aggressive, performative style can accomplish. There is little new information provided by this interview, and yet we learn a great deal about the retired mass executioner. Oberhauser does not speak, but everything about how he avoids the camera makes matters plain: even at this point, decades later, he is dodging his past and going about his business. The specter of his crimes, presented to him by a determined French Jew, is a disruption from which he is forced to flee.

The scene also tells us a good deal about the filmmaker himself: Lanzmann is willing to make everyone uncomfortable in his attempt to get at the truth, and to provoke speech where there is mostly silence. Lanzmann, however, was dealing chiefly with witnesses, those who had experienced the Holocaust first hand, and Lanzmann himself can be included among that number. In the twenty-first century, a new figure enters the equation: the postmemorial subject. And although the persons in these equations have changed, that is, the children of survivors and perpetrators are now included in the frame, the problems and questions associated with documentary filmmaking pick up where older films left off: what role does a filmmaker play and how dogged must he or she be in an effort to elicit the truth?

Documentaries about families and their entanglement with the wartime past can be particularly thorny, and familial interviews can be among the most difficult. Confronting family members can be trickier than confronting strangers. Michael Renov examines these types of films under the rubric of "domestic ethnography," which, he writes,

> play[s] at the boundaries of inside and outside in a unique way. This work engages in the documentation of family members or, less literally, of people with whom the maker has maintained long-standing everyday relations and has thus achieved a level of casual intimacy. Because the lives of artist and subject are interlaced through communal or blood ties, the documentation of the one tends to implicate the other in complicated ways; indeed consanguinity and co(i)mplication are domestic ethnography's defining features.[7]

Renov adds, "In all instances of domestic ethnography, the familial other helps to flesh out the very contours of the enunciating self, offering itself as a precursor, alter ego, double instigator, spiritual guide, or perpetrator of trauma."[8] The documentarian is, in such films, both an observer and a participant; the interviews reveal as much about them as they do about the subjects. Where these documentaries become participatory, they consist of approaching filmmakers' friends and families, those linked to them "through communal or blood ties," and they run the risk of ruining their relationships and of personally exposing themselves.

Both of the participatory documentaries examined in this chapter can be called domestic ethnographies, and both of them are explorations of the familial legacy of the Holocaust; they are documentary versions of "Holocaust family memoirs."[9] The German film *2 or 3 Things I Know about Him* (2004) about a perpetrator and his legacy, and *The Flat* (2011), a film by an Israeli director about a Jewish family and the silence surrounding their past are closely linked with one another. The films share not only commonalities of content, each featuring a family damaged by silence and each thematizing the obstacles in the way of the truth, but they share a number of formal commonalities as well. The interviews—in particular, the confrontations—in these films run the risk of creating major rifts in the two filmmakers' families: they document closely knit groups, linked with one another in an economy of guilt and silence.

Cutting into the past: Malte Ludin's *2 or 3 Things I Know about Him*

Malte Ludin's family was deeply embroiled in the history of Holocaust perpetrators. Ludin was born in 1942 in Bratislava, which at the time was known to the Germans as Preßburg. He was the son of Hanns Ludin, a successful Nazi diplomat whose family "aryanized" a villa in 1941, legally but unethically taking it from the Slovakian Jews who were living there. Ludin examines his upbringing in the shadow of his father's war crimes, as well as his family's guilt by implication in his 2004 documentary *2 or 3 Things I Know about Him*. The film is his means of dealing with the past, of rewriting its terms and engaging it in dialogue. But how does a filmmaker confront both his family and German history at the same time? Ludin uses filmic strategies to cut into the past, turning the ostensibly complete and closed narrative into which he was thrown and with which he was presented into a tendentious debate. He transforms his own memories and unanswered questions into newly opened wounds.

From 1970 to 1974 Ludin studied at the German Film and Television Academy in Berlin (the Deutsche Film- und Fernsehakademie Berlin, or the dffb), and since that time he has been an independent author, filmmaker, and producer. By 1979 he had already begun to write about how film should engage the past, publishing a critical essay on Joachim Fest and Christian Herrendoerfer's film *Hitler, A Career* (1977), which had been released 2 years earlier. Fest and Herrendoerfer's film was a composite: it consisted mainly of footage filmed by the Nazis, thus reproducing and redistributing a large amount of wartime material with the intention of examining why ordinary Germans had been so enamored of Hitler. In their film, Hitler is depicted as having been widely idolized and as having enjoyed the popularity of a rock star. The film itself drew on and imitated National Socialist propaganda films and its directors even added enhanced sound effects to amplify the impressions made by the images. Some of their choices could have been interpreted as ironic or as an attempt at what Eric Santner affirmatively describes as a homeopathic remedy for Germany's past ills, but there was little evidence, either in the comments made by the producers or in the film's reception, that would have made such claims convincing.[10]

Remarking on the editing of *Hitler, A Career* Anton Kaes observes: "By using shot/countershot, [Fest and Herrendoerfer] established the union between the Führer and the people as both pseudoreligious and erotic: masses of women listen raptly at the dictator's feet as he exhausts himself, fulfilling their libidinous, ecstatic desire to submit themselves."[11] Through their editing the filmmakers aimed to re-create the erotic and quasi-erotic attachments many held for the Führer. Objections to the deliberate awakening of those problematic erotic investments were widespread, and numerous critiques reiterated this position vis-à-vis the film's harmonizing depiction of its subject and his spectators, of Hitler and the German public. The editing was not intended to be dialectical, but it instead emphasized the process of identification and the feeling of adulation, all of which made their work little different, in the eyes of critics, from Leni Riefenstahl's Nazi-era films. Ludin added his voice to the critiques, asserting that despite the passage of three decades, the film advanced Nazi lies. His essay takes Fest and Herrendoerfer to task on many fronts. He asks, for example, why the filmmakers didn't include other material or information that might have been retrieved in the course of their film-archival research. If one depicts a speech by the Führer, shouldn't one show, using captions or other types of commentary, the violence that underlies such a speech? And, instead of enhancing the images with special effects, shouldn't one try to rend those images from their sounds, sundering the false impressions created by Joseph Goebbels?[12]

Malte Ludin's analysis of the film squares with that of his contemporary Wim Wenders. The two filmmakers are of the same generation: Ludin was born in 1942 and Wenders in 1945. In a critical essay on the film titled "That's Entertainment: Hitler," Wenders writes, "in no other country have images and language been abused so unscrupulously as here, never before and nowhere else have they been debased so deeply as vehicles to transmit lies. And now a film comes along which, with an incomprehensible thoughtlessness, wants to sell exactly those images as the heart of the matter and as 'documentary footage.'"[13] Wenders offsets the term "documentary footage" (*Dokumentaraufnahmen*) with quotation marks, already indicating his awareness that documentary is a contested category, that is, that Nazi propaganda films such as *Triumph of the Will* (1935) and *The Eternal Jew* (1940) had already done much to undermine the form's privileged claim on representing reality. More important, perhaps, was that the film was, from Wenders's perspective, a monologue; it was one-sided, and it depicted the Führer from the standpoint of his visionary manipulation of the masses. It should instead have been turned into a dialogue, one in which the filmmakers disrupt rather than reproduce the legacy of the Nazi past. Wenders asserts that a filmmaker has a responsibility to "stop the flow of these images" and a film of this sort should sit across the table from that era's self-understanding and reject its authority.[14] Why, as a filmmaker, would one permit his or her film to remain subordinate to the Nazis' vision? Wenders's language of interruption is a valuable tool for thinking about Ludin's essay. Ludin likewise views *Hitler, A Career* as doctrinaire, asking why it depicts Hitler as a star and a superman who, with a bit more luck and without having been caught unawares by the unfortunate Russian winter, might have succeeded? Why, he wonders, do these directors show the German ecstasy but not the subsequent hangover, sublimity without debasement, dominance without resistance, and order without injustice?[15]

The major metaphor that guides Ludin's critique has to do with the process of cutting into documentary material. Behind his argument is a vision regarding the work and meaning of film editing. The central question running throughout both his and Wenders's critical essays is how one turns monologic footage such as that of the Führer's famous speeches, which were always intended to function as hermetically sealed showcases of sound and image, into dialogical depictions? How does a filmmaker tear into an esthetic whole and permit a contemporary, critical perspective to enter into dialogue with history? Parallel questions arise for Ludin when he confronts his personal, familial past in *2 or 3 Things I Know about Him*. He seeks to become a filmic interlocutor, intervening into both the cinema-historical images and into his family's self-understanding of their father's wartime deeds. The past is a wound that his film aims to reopen.

The facts of the matter could be more or less agreed upon: Hanns Ludin, Malte's father, was the highest-ranking representative of Germany in Slovakia from 1941 to 1945. He was a diplomat "first class" (*Gesandter I. Klasse*) who oversaw the deportation of large numbers of Slovakian Jews. Raul Hilberg documents that over 57,000 Jewish prisoners were deported on Ludin's authority during the period from March to October of 1942.[16] Ultimately he was executed for his crimes, and this history, from his father's involvement with the Nazi party, through the Night of the Long Knives, his service in Slovakia, and his postwar execution, becomes Malte Ludin's cinematic subject. Seen from a filmic perspective and in light of his remarks about Fest and Herrendoerfer's film, the need to take control by editing together—or by cutting into—his family's narrative was analogous to the project of disrupting the Führer's self-serving orations. Carrying both a cinematic legacy as well as a number of familial conflicts specific to the second generation into his film necessitated a varied approach; the many voices that echo throughout the documentary, specifically those of his mother, his siblings, and even the ghostly, reverberating words of his late father form a polyphonic narrative. These multiple voices call for multiple modes of intrusion, and the choices he makes in cutting his film reflect the diverse wounds Hanns Ludin imposed on members of his family. When Malte Ludin asserted that *Hitler, A Career* was a "surrogate film" that failed to sunder the past, or to draw attention to debasement, resistance, and injustice, he was likely thinking in Oedipal terms about his own history. Even his choice of the word "surrogate" (*Surrogat*) is revealing: *Hitler, A Career* is not a false film, but it is rather one that stands in for another film and for another filmmaker as though it were that earlier project's deputy. The film's real director was Goebbels, who had, after all, been responsible for the original footage. Fest and Herrendoerfer's work serves as a deputy, representing Goebbels's aims, and Ludin criticizes it as though it had been the story of his own father, who was himself a deputy, or a surrogate of the Third Reich.

The concepts of cutting into the past and of conceiving of film editing in terms of divisive incisions are particularly significant insofar as German wartime crimes are frequently understood as inheritable wounds. Erin McGlothlin writes about legacies of perpetration as "a brand of perpetually present guilt that eludes resolution," and her description is extraordinarily apt where *2 or 3 Things I Know about Him* is concerned.[17] She observes that the inheritance of perpetrator guilt, akin to the mark of Cain ("the sign of an unresolved criminal past"), may be bequeathed to the children of perpetrators. The legacy of German perpetration, however, "does not, as with Cain, take the form of an external stigma that immediately distinguishes [perpetrators'] children visually. Rather, their inherited mark is figured as hereditary, an internal genetic flaw that is passed down from perpetrator parent to child, an identification that signifies how the child is bound to the parent's criminal legacy."[18] Alexandra Senfft, Hanns Ludin's granddaughter, describing the impact her grandfather's crimes had on her mother, Erika, alights, similar to McGlothlin, on the image of a "mark" or "sign." Senfft writes: "My grandfather is actively implicated in an industrial mass murder, the greatest of all crimes against humanity, and it happened in an environment and at a time when the extermination of the Jews was taken for granted. My mother, not yet ten years old and completely innocent, was already marked by these developments for life."[19] In attempting to render the invisible past visible, Malte Ludin uses his film to engage in a familial archaeology.

Many Germans were already familiar with Malte Ludin's father, Hanns, from his appearance in Ernst von Salomon's *Der Fragebogen* (*The Questionnaire*, 1951).[20] Von Salomon's book, which became a bestseller, was a response to denazification, and its framework is based on a denazification questionnaire distributed by the Allied military government. Von Salomon answers the inquiries in an overly elaborate way that, through its excesses, parodies the naïve perspective on culpability adopted by the Allies. It pokes fun at the process, but it also provides a detailed account of how von Salomon saw his own Nazi ideology develop over the course of his career, including the time he spent as a filmmaker during the war and as a prisoner afterward. As an unusually nuanced narrative concerning its author's somewhat marginal complicity, the story avoids assigning guilt in black and white terms, which may have been the basis for its warm German reception. Toward the end of *The Questionnaire*, von Salomon finds himself in POW camps, first at Natternberg and then at Plattling, where he encounters and becomes friends with his fellow prisoner Hanns Ludin. Throughout this last section of von Salomon's book, the internment is depicted as an act of vindictiveness guided by contempt. The Germans, in particular Ludin, come off as more cultured than their captors. Richard Herzinger describes the dignified, even noble figure cut by Ludin in von Salomon's account: Although he was seduced by the Nazis, he was "a thoroughly honest man of conviction," one who "rejects any trite expression of remorse." Ludin never admits guilt, but, in von Salomon's depiction, he bears his responsibility with dignity.[21]

Hanns Ludin was executed in 1947 in Bratislava as a war criminal. He had been a lieutenant general (an *Obergruppenführer*) in the SA, but in von

Salomon's book he is depicted more as a committed representative of the Reich and Führer than as a committed anti-Semite. Von Salomon reports, for example, that when Ludin, while working as an ambassador, received the message that the Slovakian Jews were not settled elsewhere as arranged but instead were deported to extermination camps he exclaimed: "That is an abysmal mess!" ("Das ischt [sic] eine bodenlose Sauerei!")[22] He also provides insight into Ludin's commitment to Hitler. Although one should treat the words of von Salomon's book with appropriate skepticism, Ludin is purported to have maintained that what he had done was in the interest of the German people and in the service of a greater ideal. In *The Questionnaire*, Ludin is quoted explaining himself: "I submitted to them, not because I feared [Hitler's] power, but because I really believed that he was right.... I wanted to contribute for the sake of things, and for matters that were greater than myself."[23] Germans, in other words, may have known Hanns Ludin as someone who purportedly acted freely, and as someone who was unapologetically willing to defend his actions to the end. He is not presented as an anti-Semite, but instead as a paragon of stalwart German masculinity, who chose not to recant. Unlike Amon Göth, whose last words were purportedly "Heil Hitler," Ludin's last words were "Long live Germany!" (*Es lebe Deutschland!*).[24]

All of this clearly had consequences for his children, not only because of the sense of responsibility they might have had toward the victims—their familial mark of Cain—but also because of the space that had been taken up by nationalism in their father's heart. Ludin's statements about his fealty to Germany during and after the war seem predicated on an affective relationship that may have, in the minds of his family, eclipsed his bond with them. According to von Salomon, Hanns Ludin praised the German people for all their faults and weaknesses: "If I was guilty, if we were all guilty, then we were guilty out of love."[25] He was, in this way, a believer, and he was not afraid to stand up for his actions. He even passed up an opportunity to escape the POW camp and avoid his inevitable sentence. As von Salomon, together with other POWs, was working on a stage production of *Faust* in Plattling, von Salomon offered Ludin a way out: the two men looked similar enough that Ludin could be released with von Salomon's papers in hand, and von Salomon, who wanted in any event to stay and complete the production, would later indicate that there had been a mix-up and, according to plan, would protest that he himself had been not released at the proper time.[26] Ludin declined von Salomon's offer. It must have been difficult for Malte Ludin and the other siblings to read this widespread, bestselling account of their father declining a last chance to see his children again. And although *The Questionnaire* depicts Hanns Ludin as longing now and then to be reunited with his family, he is, in von Salomon's story, far more preoccupied with speaking about and assessing his postwar convictions about his homeland.

Hanns Ludin's attachment to Hitler and Germany cast a long shadow over his family. At one point in *2 or 3 Things I Know about Him*, Malte Ludin includes original sound recordings of his father speaking of the "good fortune of his life" ("Glück [s]eines Lebens") as his devotion to the cause of Germany's freedom. When he subsequently refers to "the happiness of our children" ("Das Glück unserer Kinder") in his political speeches, he speaks not about his family, but rather in general terms about Germany's impending glory. Malte Ludin underscores how alienating this was to him and his siblings by cutting from his father's orations to testimonials in which his sisters detail their conflicted childhood memories. Hanns Ludin's love for Germany had, as a young man, driven him into the Reich's Defense—the *Reichswehr*, which later merged with the *Wehrmacht*—and earned him a prison sentence for aiding Hitler in 1930. Moreover, he felt that Hitler had, with a godlike grace, saved his life after the Night of the Long Knives in 1934; although many party members were executed, Ludin recalled that Hitler had "sentenced" (*verurteilte*) him to continue living.[27] Ludin owed his survival to Hitler's mercy, and his strong investment in the Führer and the fatherland take the form of a preoccupation that appears to have exceeded his attachment to his family.

Early on in *2 or 3 Things I Know about Him*, Malte Ludin informs the viewer that he had long wanted to make this film, but that he could not do so while his mother Erla (née Erla von Jordan), who died in 1997, was still alive; the archaeological unearthing of incriminating material would have been too divisive, too painful. Alexandra Tacke sums up that in the course of the film, "Sixty years after the war, Malte Ludin finally opens the lid, gathering his relatives, his sisters, his brother, his nephews and his nieces around the 'grief chest' (*Kummerkiste*) and confronting them with its contents. He breaks the silence and thus violates a family taboo."[28] The Ludin family is large: Malte was the second youngest of six children. Relying on earlier interview footage for his mother's contribution, Ludin begins, subsequent to her death, to explore the dimensions of familial guilt and responsibility. He interviews his surviving sisters Ellen and Andrea, as well as his father's most ardent defender, Barbara, who was born in 1935. Barbara is the oldest living sister. Malte's brother, Tilman, passed away in 1999, a year after Erika, the eldest sibling, died by her own hand. Arguably, Malte's disputation with his father is not only on behalf of the murdered Jews, but also on behalf of Erika, who can, owing to feelings of guilt and a legacy of perpetration, be counted among his father's victims. She apparently suffered from depression, abused alcohol, and spoke frequently of suicide, now and again burdening her own children with threats that she would harm herself. At age 65, in 1998, she finally succeeded, nearly boiling herself to death in the bathtub, and subsequently dying of self-inflicted burns in the hospital.[29]

Akin to many Holocaust documentaries, this one begins in an archive. Immediately following a short clip of a conversation between Malte and his sister, in which Barbara Ludin defends, in front of Malte and the camera, her right to remember her father as she wants to, the film opens onto a corridor full of records and files, a signal that things are about to be unearthed. We are then shown color photographs of a Nazi party rally (a *Reichsparteitag*) in 1937, and the strangeness of the color photographs is matched by the strangeness of the trombone sounds that Malte Ludin has chosen to accompany those images in which his father appears, sounds that do not ramp up the drama, but which can be said to undermine it insofar as they can be described as comic. The color in the photographs has a double edge: it inspires a sensation of heightened reality and the images appear to leap out at the viewer, but that same color also makes these images seem unreal. Because the preponderance of images from World War II are in black and white, the color images strike us as otherworldly, and this is likely why Ludin opens with them. It is as if he knew his father—a criminal who was executed when he was a toddler—only in the unreal space of a dream. The black and white or sepia pictures that are later integrated into the film create a sense of normalcy, even of nostalgia, but these color images signal one of the film's chief dilemmas: how does the filmmaker come to terms with a remembrance that hardly seems real? His exploration of his father's culpability begins with "archival" images—that is, images of archives—intercut with images of his father that recall *Triumph of the Will*. Then, the words that make up Ludin's title pop out from the base of a shelving unit in the form of graphic text (Figure 4.1); the words emerge, as if by their own will, from their hiding place. They are text that refuses to be contained.

Figure 4.1 The film's title appears, slipping out from under the shelves of the archives in *2 or 3 Things I Know about Him* (2004).

Ludin's title speaks volumes. It will be generally recognized as a reference to Godard's 1967 new wave film *2 or 3 Things I Know about Her*. Despite the fact that Godard's film is famously known as an essay film, and is thus by implication directly associated with the voice of its cinematic *auteur*, it is a conscious attempt to be anti-monological: Godard's film has a hybrid form, and the self-conscious legacy of the cinema essay, or the essay film, which developed and expanded throughout the 1950s and 1960s, underscores a coupling of elements essential to documentary, autobiography, and fiction, which produces something synthetic, or a polyphony. Timothy Corrigan observes that Godard's film was made, "just after the period when Godard begins consistently to describe himself as a film essayist."[30] The form and its history are particularly appropriate to a film that cannot establish certain knowledge of its subject. An essay film such as this might be disputed as a documentary; it is not objective and is closer in style to probing investigative journalism than it is to the purely observational style associated with archetypes of documentary filmmaking such as films made by Frederick Wiseman. Ludin's self-positioning can be viewed as a deliberately deconstructive stance in relation to a genre that is, owing to Leni Riefenstahl and others, extraordinarily contested in the German tradition. In Godard's film, the director approaches his subject, who is a French woman who makes her living doing childcare for prostitutes, just as Ludin approaches the memory of his father: in imaginative bits and pieces, and through the eyes of others. Godard's film explored a woman's life in contemporary Paris, examining how it was bound together with the city's economy and even with the contemporaneous war in Vietnam. Corrigan remarks: "In Godard's fictional documentary..., the Paris of *2 or 3 Things I Know about Her* becomes the doubled 'her' of the city and the character Juliette Janson."[31] Along similar lines, in Ludin's film familial and national histories are wrapped up in one another, and the same observation can be applied to its titular pronoun "him" (*ihm*), which in the German language refers as much to the director's father as it does to the German nation and to its history of perpetration.

As a director and a son, Malte Ludin sets out to determine what kind of person his father was, and his pursuit of an enigmatic patriarch recalls a passage from von Salomon's *The Questionnaire* in which Hanns Ludin recollects his impression of Hitler: "I have not yet found the proper measure for [Hitler].... Sometimes I have thought of him as a genius, sometimes I thought we were being led by a madman. Sometimes I considered him demonic, sometimes pathological. But none of this is right, and neither was your expression, 'lemur-like' (*lemurenhaft*)."[32] Hanns Ludin, however, protests too much: he proceeds to describe Hitler in terms that are truly lemur-like, adding, "When I try to find the correct word for him, I come up with 'remote' (*abseitig*): a man who could not stand the light, a man in the shadows, who comes out of the shadows and speaks from the shadows, and who pushes everything that wants to come to light back into the shadows."[33] In Roman myth, the lemurs were shades or spirits of the restless and malignant dead, and they may have been on Ludin's mind at the time of his internment in Plattling because in the second installment of Goethe's *Faust* drama, a version or portion of which the POWs were in the process of producing, a chorus of lemurs in the service of Mephistopheles dig Faust's grave. The scene is climactic; it is bound up with the final fate of Goethe's most famous character, who, not incidentally, has committed to a pact with the devil. Hanns Ludin, grappling with the debt he owed to Hitler and his lingering investment in the idea of the fatherland, now saw Hitler as someone who spoke to him from out of the shadows. How different is all this from the opaque, elusive image Malte Ludin had of his own father? More important, perhaps, than the influence of the French new wave, which has indeed had a longstanding impact on filmmaking at the Film and Television Academy, is the reference in Ludin's title to this uncertain knowledge. Owing to the many obscurities and willful occlusions—the parts of the past that remain in the shadows—his access to the truth about his father remains so obstructed that he cannot positively lay claim to having even two or three pieces of information.

And what are these two or three "things"? Perhaps that part of the title refers to the key family members confronted in the film including his mother and his siblings, particularly Barbara Ludin, generally referred to as "Barbel." Most discussions of *2 or 3 Things I Know about Him* begin with her. Nearly every account starts with Barbel's slip of the tongue during the first interview, the shots with which Ludin begins. In the film's initial moments, she is being questioned by her younger brother about her attitude toward her father, and she remarks: "It is my right . . . to see my father as I want to see him, or as I see him; not as I want to see him, but as I see him." She appears conscious that there is, or rather that there ought to be, no difference between seeing something and seeing something as one wants to see it. If I truly believe, in other words, that the sky is blue, then it makes no sense to speak of the matter in terms of my beliefs; it *is* blue. Similarly, Barbel recognizes that to want to see Hanns Ludin one way rather than another admits the possibility that things could be otherwise—it suggests doubt. Barbel thus catches herself, and Ludin begins his film with a slip of the tongue and a self-correction (an "or" followed by a "not"). She seems to be in dialogue with herself, and no effort is required on her brother's part to contradict or undermine her.

At a later point in the film, Malte visits Barbel in what may be her own art studio (Figure 4.2). The two of them have a set-to in front of a bulletin board on which a page has been clipped from the newspaper, one that features a reproduction of Caravaggio's *Love Conquers All* (*Amor Vincit Omnia*, 1601–02). The painting depicts a winged personification of Amor treading over items associated with a variety of mortal undertakings including a violin, armor, compasses, and manuscripts. Amor, with his eagle-like wings, tramples them all just as Barbel's loving devotion to her father allows her to run roughshod over historical fact. Her niece Alexandra summarizes Barbel's devotion to her father and her assumption of the role of the eldest sibling in her memoir, writing that after the deaths of Erla and Erika, "Barbel took hold of the role of the family elder, and she plays it with natural elegance and determination. She stepped into Erla's footsteps and fights for her parents' memories."[34] Barbel strongly believes that her father did not know what was happening to the deported Jews, which is a claim the film roundly rejects. Malte Ludin juxtaposes any claims of this sort with footage of written documentation, typically bearing his father's signature, containing words such as "total solution" and "liquidation." He does not let Barbel's claims stand, and the conversation between them is edited into a relatively fast-paced struggle, recorded with a handheld camera. Short exchanges are separated by jump cuts, which indicate the director's openness about the fact that his film is a construction; the sequence would not be mistaken for unedited

Figure 4.2 Barbel Ludin speaks with her brother in *2 or 3 Things I Know about Him.*

footage. Malte, because he cannot look at the matter objectively, exhibits no pretense of objectivity.

A number of Barbel's responses to Malte's questions are shocking: she normalizes the fact that the Jews were shot in large numbers (*massenhaft getötet*) by referring to them as "partisans," and saying "well, that's war" ("Das ist eben Krieg, Maltechen"). Her diminutive use of her brother's name, "little Malte," makes light of his overall project as well. She condescends, as would a derisive older sister, mocking him when he asks whether she feels any shame. She describes his question as "silly" ("albern") and then ventriloquizes what is apparently the position of a foolish person who would engage in her brother's project of self-flagellation. In a sarcastic singsong voice, she mockingly intones, "I'm so ashamed" ("Ich schäme mich so . . ."). Her defenses are overwhelming: she diminishes her brother's excavation of the past, and she engages in a soft form of Holocaust denial insofar as she describes the murdered Jews as partisans. The sequence reveals the many mechanisms by which she has come to regard her father's choices as normal and to defend herself against the painful incursion of the truth. As a consequence, and as a means of disrupting her otherwise coherent story of the past, Malte Ludin edits rapidly. The result is a somewhat frenetic portrait of an older sister who would do anything not to tarnish her father.

In certain respects, Ludin is engaged in an act of deliberate cinematic de-composition where the women in this film are concerned. Erla, Ellen, Barbara, and Andrea are all quite composed, and Ludin sometimes depicts these women, particularly his mother Erla and his sister Barbara, as they would not want to be seen. For viewers familiar with the probing interviews in Ray Müller's 1993 documentary *The Wonderful, Horrible Life of Leni Riefenstahl*, Erla's appearance, diction, and self-control may recall Riefenstahl's, who was only 3 years older. In old photographs, Erla can be seen at the beach in an athletic posture and with an outfit that recalls Riefenstahl's signature style in *The Holy Mountain* (*Der heilige Berg*, 1926). In Müller's documentary Riefenstahl, controlled and elegant, is confronted, sometimes indirectly, through editing that puts her in dialogue with earlier statements, diary entries, and undisputed facts. Erla seems similarly composed, and her son had to strategize to undercut the control she asserts. In order to do this, he relies on the integration of older footage taken from an interview with Erla conducted for a television film entitled *Die Frau seines Führers* (The Wife of His Führer, 1978) with more recent footage: an interview the director himself filmed in the 1990s, when Erla was 91 years old.

In the 1978 interview, Malte's mother looks dignified. She conforms to the image of an officer's widow, one that is still more or less impressed with her husband. She explains that Hanns Ludin made his choices out of conviction and never for the sake of his career. She speaks candidly, but seems disconcertingly unrepentant. She says that after the Night of the Long Knives, her husband despaired, having just seen his friends executed, and she adds that if she had it to do over again, she would have encouraged him to hang in there (*durchhalten*), indicating that she would have used the idiom, "let the chips fall where they may" ("wo gehobelt wird, fallen Späne").[35] Oddly enough, this is precisely the expression reportedly used by her husband in *The Questionnaire* when he explains to von Salomon that the idea for which he fought was right, but that many sacrifices had to be made. Hanns Ludin uses the phrase with some reservations, calling it "an accursed sentence" ("ein verfluchter Satz").[36] The fact that his wife uses it in a similar context over 30 years later might indicate either that her husband has residual influence upon her—she was, most likely, a reader of *The Questionnaire*—or that her worldview, shared with her husband, remains largely unaltered, petrified since those days. Senfft writes about her grandmother Erla's attitude: "My grandmother raised her six children to believe in a good National Socialist; she taught them only to see his good side, and a good man cannot commit crimes. Anything that did not fit the pristine picture did not exist. It was concealed, explained away, or glossed over. The perpetrators, those were vulgar Nazis, not us. We couldn't be those, because of our education and sophistication."[37] In the older interview, Erla also recounts meeting a woman who told her, for the first time, about Auschwitz, and how the Jews were being gassed there. She remembers not really understanding what was meant, and when she later inquired about it she was told that Auschwitz was an armaments factory (*Rüstungsbetrieb*). She and her husband believed this and considered the matter settled. With the addition of an audio effect—one that was presumably applied by Ludin, rather than by Christian Geissler, who was responsible for the 1978 film—her comment, "it was settled" ([*es*] *war erledigt*) echoes in postmemorial repetition. It indicates that phrases of this sort resonated for Ludin and his family insofar as he was stuck, for his lifetime, with dubious explanations.

As Ludin indicated, he waited for his mother to die before making this film, and his later interview with her is shot with what appears to be a hidden camera. She no longer looks as she once did, now wrinkled and blemished with age. He surrounds the image with a wide black margin (Figure 4.3), which has

Figure 4.3 The director's mother, Erla Ludin, interviewed in *2 or 3 Things I Know about Him*.

the effect of placing her at the end of a long tunnel, effectively taking some distance from her. It also recalls the mediation involved in preparing this image; it denaturalizes the shot. In the space of the portrait's wide margin, he asserts the truth. It was a year before her death, he explains, that his mother told him something she apparently hadn't before: a story about a thug from the SA, whom Hanns Ludin protected. This is, Malte Ludin makes clear, the story of the manslaughter of Hermann Stern, which his father helped to conceal. It happened on March 25, 1933 in Creglingen. During the course of a Pogrom, Stern was beaten and died. Ludin's mother places the event during *Kristallnacht*, which she does not call by that name, rather preferring to say that it took place on November 9, 1938. Ludin corrects her errors in the image's margins, in what may be his own handwriting. Shown in fragments, she is at times only a talking and somewhat aged mouth at the top of the screen. Depicting her in this unflattering way is a means of exerting authority, as a director, over his mother. She appears here neither whole, nor as she would have wanted to appear. He fills in the information for her, undercutting that which he believes to be lies and self-deceptions with the facts of the matter.

Malte Ludin's willingness to subject his mother to scrutiny and to undermine her worldview corresponds, to some extent, with a well-known conversation between Rainer Werner Fassbinder and his mother in the 1978 film *Germany in Autumn* (*Deutschland im Herbst*). Ludin was clearly impacted by the French new wave, but because he was, like Fassbinder, a member of the generation of filmmakers born during or near the end of the war, his decision can also be understood in terms of New German Cinema and its specific, critical disposition toward the past. In Fassbinder's sequence, the most well known in that omnibus film, the director can be seen yelling at his own mother across the table, accusing her of not having reconstructed her views, even decades after the war. Following a fair amount of give and take, some of which was likely prepared in advance insofar as his mother comes off as a very game participant, she remarks that, given the turbulence of the times and particularly the actions of the Red Army Faction (RAF), it would be best to have an authoritarian ruler, one who is good, kind, and orderly. With his fist pounding the table, Fassbinder looks Germany's past, in the person of his mother, in the eye and says "no." It is in this way tempting to see the common threads as based in generational conflict, and to look at matters in terms of how German filmmakers born in the 1940s see their parents' generation. On the other hand, Ludin's camera angle, which suggests a hidden camera, also finds a parallel in *Shoah*, specifically in Claude Lanzmann's famous hidden camera interview with the notorious SS squad leader and Treblinka perpetrator Suchomel.[38] In that interview, akin to Ludin's interview with his mother, Lanzmann makes clear that he is presenting the testimony of someone who is reluctant to provide it, and that only through concealing the camera could the interviewer elicit new information. Attending to the two different possible modes of reading Ludin's stylized interruption, whether it is in the mode of New German Cinema and thus about German generational conflict, or in that of Lanzmann's *Shoah* and thus specifically about perpetrators, highlights an ambivalence in the filmmaker's own orientation. Malte Ludin, on the one hand, sees his mother as a passive participant, perhaps as Fassbinder saw his mother, yet he is, on the other hand, also willing to entertain the possibility that she could be presented as a true accomplice.

The sequences that involve Barbel and Erla constitute two attempts to know something about Hanns Ludin, but where, one wonders, is Hanns's own voice in all this? He appears in photographs throughout the film, in both color and black and white, and his voice is heard several times in original recordings, ones in which he orates about the fate of Germany. At one point, however, the son takes the opportunity to deliberately disrupt his father's sentences, using the occasion to intervene and thereby recast the past. The filmmaker himself reads aloud from a document, written by his father shortly before his execution, and Malte, in ventriloquizing his father's voice, provides a testimonial performance: he enacts, stages, and appropriates the persona of the perpetrator in order to re-contextualize it for purposes of his documentary. Strictly speaking, this is not true "testimonial performance" insofar as it is not Hanns speaking his personal testimony, but it is instead something along the lines of "testimonial re-performance."[39] Obviously, there is a simple explanation for Malte's decision: his father cannot read his own letter for the camera because he is dead.

The decision, however, to perform his father's sentences himself provides Malte Ludin with an opening to engage in indirect dialogue with his father. His tone is somewhat languid as he reads the opening sentence: "The prosecution will allow me to prove that I can die respectably. If necessary I will certainly provide this proof." The camera then, in the following sentence, cuts to a corridor, presumably the one down which Hanns Ludin strode to his death, and, as it progresses along the hall, we hear Malte speaking his father's words, saying that what he did was in the name of his children and "in the interest of the Slovakian people." Here, at his father's egregious exclusion of his true victims, Malte Ludin draws air in through his teeth and interjects a distressed and despondent, "Ay, ay, ay!" ("ui, ui, ui"). He then stumbles over his father's denial of his own guilt, "No, I cannot declare myself guilty" ("Nein, ich kann mich nicht schuldig erklären").

Ludin's father engages in a rationalization, similar to many of those made by Adolf Eichmann, that he acted according to orders, and Ludin attempts a number of different emphases to give the sentence a sense he can comprehend. He stresses the words "nicht schuldig" and then the word "kann," but neither seems to enable him to make real sense of what he is reading. His staged interruption is a disruption in his father's speaking body—first through dissolving his father's speech into non-language ("ui, ui, ui"), and then by breaking off and rejecting it. The performance is only a half-embodiment along the lines of Manfred Zapatka's performance in *The Himmler Project* (2000), in which the actor reads the text of a speech by a perpetrator but is unwilling, perhaps for reasons of good taste, to create the illusion that he *is* that perpetrator.[40] Zapatka and the film's director, Romuald Karmakar, prefer to leave those illusions to Hollywood-style films. Here, Malte Ludin does not want to create the illusion of his father's presence; he is much more concerned with his personal relationship to his father's words and the extent to which his re-articulation of them can be an opportunity for reassessment and reconstruction.

A final editorial interruption comes when Ludin puts two of his subjects into confrontation with one another, at the point at which Ludin closely examines his family's aryanization of a Jewish home. The villa in which the family lived had been appropriated from the Jewish family of a Slovakian brewer named Stein. Juraj Štern, who had lived as a child in a neighboring household, is interviewed as surrogate for the Stein family. Štern's account of those times is edited in parallel with Barbel's testimony. When he was a 3- or 4-year-old child, Štern explains, his family home was also taken, and he had to hide in a stable to avoid arrest and deportation. He concealed himself in a feeding trough, and, covered in hay, he was entirely alone apart from the brief visits of a farmer, who came to bring him food and to reprimand him not to cry or scream.[41] Following this period of torment, Štern explains to Ludin, he developed a substantial stutter that he did not overcome until he was 18 years old. He lost the power of speech and, quite deliberately, Ludin at that moment cuts to Barbel, who is recounting her joyful memories of singing in the Ludin household. She and her siblings had a voice, which was, for so long and as a consequence of trauma, denied to Štern. Ludin's intercutting undermines Barbel's self-satisfied account, and indicates his willingness to use editing to turn his family's testimony against them. Barbel, at a later point, says that she is participating in the film, which she was reluctant to do, on behalf of Erla, her father, and their deceased siblings. Conspicuously absent from her explanation are the victims, and for this reason Malte is sure to include in his film Štern, along with the poet Tuvia Rübner, whose family were among those deported from Bratislava. The victims' voices cut through, interrupt, and contradict the family's coherent story.

Each one of these interruptions—the jump cutting in his sister's interviews, the juxtaposition of older and newer testimony from his mother, the re-performance of his father's letter, and the indirect interactions between Barbel and Juraj Štern—constitutes a filmic strategy deliberately meant to cut into the past. Malte Ludin obstructs and revises in order to weave his own, new narrative, disregarding his family's desire to keep matters neat and tidy. But there is yet another means of viewing Ludin's work as that of a self-reflexive filmmaker, whose project stands in a history of German disputations with the past. The final shot of the film lands upon Hanns Ludin's grave marker in a cemetery in Bratislava on which the initials "H.E.L." are written (Figure 4.4). Ending in this way surely echoes Wolfgang Staudte's 1946 *The Murderers Are Among Us* (*Die Mörder sind unter uns*), the DEFA film meant to confront the problem of perpetrators who seamlessly reintegrated themselves as industrialists in postwar Germany. By fighting back and weeding them out, ordinary Germans, particularly eastern Germans in the Soviet occupied zone, who, for the most part, understood themselves as victims of the war, were meant to move forward and rebuild. Staudte's film ends with an image similar to the final one in Ludin's film, a single cross marking a grave and meant to demand the remembrance of the martyred dead.[42]

Malte Ludin was familiar with Staudte's film. He had written about Staudte, and his book-length biography, *Wolfgang Staudte*, details, one after the next,

Figure 4.4 The director's father's grave-marker in *2 or 3 Things I Know about Him*.

Staudte's films. The connection between the final images is thus hard to overlook. The cross over Hanns Ludin's grave bears his initials, and the Old Norse name it resembles, "Hel," is related to the word Hell (*Hölle*) as well as to the verb *verhehlen*, referring to that which is concealed. It cannot remain so: the restless dead have done their work and the past has been unearthed. In writing about *The Murderers Are Among Us*, Ludin observes that the psychically wounded doctor at that film's center, Hans Mertens, shares "exactly the state of mind of the majority of Germans after the war," whose numbers include the disappointed or betrayed supporters of Hitler, those who fled or were driven away (the *Flüchtlinge* and *Vertriebene*), or the soldiers returning to civil society. For them, he writes, "Hitler and the war were not a disaster that was brought about by people, but rather a catastrophe caused by evil forces, and they were its victims. They avoided looking to the past, they were silent and secretive." To this description, which could have been a sketch of his family dynamics, Ludin adds, "feelings of remorse or shame, such as they were, were suppressed. They knew no compassion for the millions of dead, for which they, through electing Hitler, tolerating his reign, and participating in his war were responsible."[43] How awful it must have been for Ludin to read in von Salomon's book about his father's lack of repentance and about his stubborn "Long live Germany!" at the very end. In his description of Staudte's film, one readily discerns the urge to awaken feelings of remorse or shame (*Reue oder Beschämung*). Here, in *2 or 3 Things I Know about Him*, he gets to present his own adaptation of *The Murderers Are Among Us*, not as a feature film with closure and a satisfying ending, but rather as a personal story, with all the messiness such stories entail. From start to finish, the author-filmmaker struggles against the tendency to deliberately or inadvertently make yet another surrogate film about the past. He attempts instead to tear apart a familial narrative and to enact a cinema-historical interruption.

Searching for the plot: Arnon Goldfinger's *The Flat*

2 or 3 Things I Know about Him presents the problem of intergenerational communication through its examination of silence as a means of covering over a history of Holocaust perpetration. Silence, however, cuts both ways: not only did the families of perpetrators refuse to articulate memories and feelings about the past, but the families of victims were silent about the past as well. There are, for this reason, uncanny similarities between Ludin's German film about a German family and its silences and *The Flat* (2011), a film by an Israeli director about a Jewish family and its silences. In both films, performative documentaries that Michael Renov might describe as domestic ethnographies, the filmmaker is present in body and voice throughout. The documentarian is part of the action because it is his story as well. Each film is an encounter with the parents' generation in which the introduction of a camera affords the filmmaker an opportunity to stage an intrusion into and an interrogation of the most difficult parts of his family history.

The Flat, directed by Arnon Goldfinger, deals with a grandson's excavation of his grandparents' Tel Aviv apartment. In the apartment and in the wake of their deaths, he uncovers evidence of his grandparents' longstanding friendship with a member of the Nazi Party, and he explores how that relationship could have stayed hidden for so long. For English language viewers, the title, *The Flat*, contains a double meaning: it refers to the apartment at the center of the film, but in English it also resonates with the flatness of the filmmaker's mother's affect. The filmmaker is, throughout, disappointed that his mother does not appear to have deeper, more pained feelings about the family's history and losses, and he asks her at the film's climax, once important information has been uncovered: "does it bother you that you aren't moved?" The film is, in a way, about revealing whether and why his mother should care about the past as much as he does, and tracing the path by which she came not to care.

The deaths of the filmmaker's grandparents, Gerda and Kurt Tuchler, reveals a great deal of information. Their deaths evacuate the space of the apartment, but they also yield an opening through which Goldfinger can go and reconstruct the

Figure 4.5 The stairwell at the Tuchler's apartment in *The Flat* (2011).

past; he can play the part of filmmaker *as* detective. The apartment itself is thus the staging area for the film, but it can also be understood as a crime scene: what happened here, and how can the objects be made to speak, when the witnesses will not? Goldfinger interviews several family members, asking them what they know about their grandfather. The answer is uniform: they know nothing. As sources of information, they are nearly worthless, communicating only known facts such as that Kurt Tuchler once had been a judge. Goldfinger, looking at a photograph of his extended family, concludes that if he wants answers, he will have to begin with the apartment itself. The film thus returns repeatedly to the stairwell just outside of the Tuchler's apartment (Figure 4.5). It is a deep stairwell with a cavernous center and it signifies the story's unknowable core. There appears to be a hole into which the past has vanished, and unless Goldfinger can illuminate the space, he may never find out about the past. The family is taking apart the objects in the apartment, which one by one are being taken down that staircase and out.

The apartment is a world of objects, a family history that is being disassembled, and it gives the film a sense of urgency insofar as Goldfinger sees it as his job to prevent everything from being cast into the abyss. Its ordinary household items speak differently from the witnesses. When his grandparents were alive, they refused to speak, and now the remaining witnesses cannot speak on the subject because they believe they have nothing to say. Goldfinger's camera lingers on the various objects: a house key, assorted Hummel figurines that preserve a link to the German bourgeoisie, and an old German bicycle license from 1911, which Kurt Tuchler may have kept due to sentimental value. Among these things, Goldfinger finds copies of the Nazi newspaper *Der Angriff* (The Attack) from 1934, which included an installment of the journalistic travelogue "A Nazi Travels to Palestine" (*Ein Nazi fährt nach Palästina*).

While sorting through the material Goldfinger also finds what appears to be a racy fashion or men's magazine, which contains an article about Leopold von Mildenstein, the Nazi who traveled to Palestine for *Der Angriff*, and who concluded that the Jews should all move there.[44] The story also mentions his grandmother. Goldfinger tracks down the authors of the article, one of whom reports remembering how surprised he was that Gerda Tuchler met with them at all, because "people don't usually like to talk about such things." He then makes a major discovery: these people still have a set of photos she had given them, taken during a trip the Tuchlers went on with the von Mildensteins. These pictures reveal, "a friendship that continued after the war," and the director becomes absorbed with the question of how his grandparents could have remained friends with these people given what had happened to his great grandmother Susanne, who died in Theresienstadt. How were his grandparents not bitter—how were they not too bitter—to continue a friendship with Nazis? Wouldn't the loss have gotten in the way? How could his grandparents have mourned Susanne, but not resented or even hated the von Mildensteins?

But the Tuchlers viewed it as worthwhile to retain their connection to the von Mildensteins and to Germany, and this was the balancing act in which the Tuchlers were engaged. As Goldfinger looks around the flat, he notes that his grandmother lived there for 70 years, "as if she had never left Germany." He explains that she "never mastered Hebrew," and that he didn't want to learn German, "so we'd sit and chat in English, over Apfelstrudel and Swiss chocolate." The apartment appears to have been a preserved German cultural space. Goldfinger makes some of these observations as his camera surveys the books on his grandparents' shelves, including a fine collection of works by Heinrich Heine, the nineteenth-century German-Jewish writer, and by Goethe, the best known of all German authors. Goldfinger is particularly interested in the fate of the books, because they indicate so much about his grandparents' cultural investment. Some of these books were brought with them, and the Heine edition might not otherwise have survived the war. Many of the books were purchased afterward. They were still buying German books, which seem to be predominantly what the Tuchlers read. Michael Adler, a book dealer who comes to cart these volumes away, declares uninteresting, both for resale and as a matter of opinion, the Tuchlers' copy of Werner Keller's 1966 "postbiblical" history of the Jews entitled *Und wurden zerstreut unter alle Völker: Die nachbiblische Geschichte des jüdischen Volkes*.

As part of the Tuchlers' library this book, which was published in English under the title *Diaspora: The Post-Biblical History of the Jews*, is indeed of interest. It is about the relocation of the Jews from Europe to Palestine. The section of Keller's book that deals with the Holocaust is tough on the Germans, arguing that they set back what had been a long struggle for Jewish emancipation and that "cultured Germany remained silent. The middle class displayed no signs of outrage; the university professors raised no storm of protest when their Jewish colleagues were driven from their teaching posts overnight. Nowhere was there open protest against the violation of justice, against measures that were a disgrace to a civilized nation."[45] Keller concludes, "the history of Germany will remain tainted for all time by the most atrocious crimes that human beings have ever inflicted upon helpless human beings, by the extirpation of millions of innocent Jewish souls." Then, in a passage that sharply reflects the contents of the Tuchlers' own shelves, especially their own strong identification with Germany's cultural heritage, Keller adds, "No one will ever be able to describe Germany as the land of Goethe and Bach, Kant and Lessing, and cathedrals. It was also and remains henceforth the land of Hitler, Himmler, and the death camps."[46] This historical duality embodies the dilemma faced by the Tuchlers: were they going to view Germany in connection with Goethe or with Hitler? Against Keller, they seem, so the film contends, to have chosen the former, and for Goldfinger that continued attachment is a mystery. Keller's diasporic story ends differently than that of the Tuchlers, who were, at least according to the film, never quite at home in Israel. Keller writes: "In 1950 the Law of Return was passed, which gave to every Jew the right to immigrate into Israel. After two thousand years the circle had come round to its beginning again. From Mount Zion in Jerusalem the Star of David waved. The dispersed throughout the world had their ancient homeland again—Eretz Israel, the Promised Land that had been the cradle of the Jewish people."[47] The story, as Keller tells it, has a happy ending, one in which the atrocities ultimately helped a people find their way home to Israel. The portrait painted by *The Flat*, however, is of two people who did not see it that way, and who were never quite at home in the Jewish homeland. Goldfinger goes through a number of their documents, ones that express his grandparents' conflicted relationship to Germany, including Kurt Tuchler's delegate card to the meeting of the nineteenth Zionist congress in Lucerne, while he, at the same time, was a German patriot who had served honorably in World War I. Germany, where they were raised, remained the Tuchlers' home.

At a later point in *The Flat*, Goldfinger is directed to an article about the Tuchlers' friend von Mildenstein, which appeared in *Der Spiegel* in 1966.[48] In the article, von Mildenstein is not referred to as a "journalist," as his daughter Edda, at that point in the film, contends, but rather as "Eichmann's first boss." The article, "Der Orden unter dem Totenkopf" ("The Order of the Death's Head"), written by Heinz Höhne does not hold von Mildenstein responsible for crimes. Höhne reports that von Mildenstein was, like Eichmann and Reinhard Höhn, the famous Nazi administrative lawyer, not particularly anti-Semitic, and Höhne points out, referring indirectly to the Tuchlers, that von Mildenstein even became friends with some Zionist leaders. The article says that the emigration to Palestine was, from von Mildenstein's perspective, the best solution to the Jewish problem, and that von Mildenstein had argued that mobilizing National Socialist anti-Semitism was a way to promote that emigration.[49] The Nazis' ideas overlapped here for a period with those of ardent Zionists in that they shared a common goal of encouraging Jewish emigration to Palestine. Historian Jacob Boas asserts that the trip to Palestine was really an idea attributable to Tuchler and the Zionists, noting that, "There were Nazis . . . who appreciated the efforts of the Zionists to make Germany *Judenrein* (free of Jews)."[50] He continues, "Well aware of this particular current in Nazi thought, the Zionist Federation of Germany commissioned Kurt Tuchler to seek out Zionist sympathizers in the Nazi Party and enlist their aid in acquainting the German public with the Zionist cause and the progress of Jewish efforts in Palestine."[51] Tuchler was aware of the various currents in Jewish-German thought. In a document in the archives at Yad Vashem entitled "Observations and Experiences from the First Four Hitler Years" he describes the two prevailing types of National Socialism after Hitler took power: the radical direction, identified with the Nazi Alfred Rosenberg, which advocated the total extermination of the Jews, and the less radical direction, which was willing to consider the emigration to Palestine.[52] If the radical direction had dominated, Tuchler points out, then there would have been no 1933 Haavara Agreement, which allowed the Jews to transfer their own goods to Palestine as German exports, in order to facilitate emigration.[53]

In the article in *Der Spiegel*, Höhne echoes the problem that von Mildenstein likely ran into with his Jewish friends—with the Tuchlers—writing, "von Mildenstein's Palestine-plan concealed a difficulty. Only a minority of German Jews expressed desire to emigrate to Palestine. The bulk of them, in vain and despite terror and defamation, held onto their fatherland."[54] The magazine article, in other words, reflects the questions that dominated the relationship between the Tuchlers and the von Mildensteins: the Tuchlers were German Jews who would likely have preferred to stay in Germany, the land that Kurt Tuchler had served and for which he once fought. How was Leopold von Mildenstein to convince his ambivalent friends, not so much in their interest, but in the interest of Nazi Germany and as part of his job as minister for the party, that they would be better off moving and leaving their homeland behind?

In the film, Goldfinger gets in touch with Höhne, who had done research for his article, and who explains to him that there are no traces of von Mildenstein having been in the SS after 1937. This prompts Goldfinger to head to archives in former East Germany, "to find what Höhne couldn't." He looks through the documents, and into von Mildenstein's party membership application—materials from before the Nazis took power. He examines a curriculum vitae, written in von Mildenstein's own handwriting, which says that from 1935 to 1936, he was the department head in the Sicherheitsdienst des Reichsführers-SS also known as the SD, or the intelligence agency of the SS. The résumé continues: 1937, travels abroad, and since 1938: consultant in the Reich Propaganda Ministry, where, as Goldfinger explains, he spent 7 years as department head. According to the Cold War historian Timothy Naftali, von Mildenstein spent the war working in Goebbels's ministry, where he designed "virulent anti-Allied and anti-Semitic tracts primarily for use among Arabs in the Middle East."[55]

The English historian David Cesarani expands on the relationship between Eichmann and von Mildenstein, and makes it hard to believe that the latter was unaware of the ramifications of the ideological project in which he was participating, He explains that Eichmann was employed by the SD, gathering intelligence on enemies of the Nazi party and the Reich, and that he "was put to work compiling a card index of Freemasons and their organizations in Germany."[56] There Eichmann was later reassigned to the museum, where he "spent five months classifying Masonic seals and medallions, preparing an exhibition to educate the SS about the perils of Freemasonry." Cesarani's account continues: "One visitor was struck by Eichmann's diligence. This was Untersturmführer Edler von Mildenstein, a Bohemian-born Nazi who had been taken on by Heydrich to develop an office specializing in Jewish matters. Mildenstein returned, located Eichmann ... and asked if he was interested in a new job.... Eichmann seized his chance."[57] Cesarani speculates that Eichmann "may have joined Mildenstein's team just to escape the monotony of sorting Masonic bric-à-brac, but he was not deterred by the prospect of working in a secret service department devoted to combating the Jewish 'enemy.' When his decision is set against the background of Nazi attitudes and the existing anti-Jewish legislation it is clear that he cannot have had any illusions about what the work would entail. He was joining the ideological war against the Jews."⁵⁸ Cesarani adds, "In Mildenstein Eichmann, once again, had found a mentor in an older man. . . . Mildenstein gave him several books on Zionism and ordered him to summarize the history, structure and activity of the Zionist movement."⁵⁹

According to Cesarani, von Mildenstein was among those Nazi ideologues whose position on encouraging the Jews to leave Germany made him more sympathetic to Zionism. Von Mildenstein argued that, "the way to 'solve' the Jewish problem *in* Germany was to remove the Jews *from* Germany. But [von Mildenstein] did not propose emigration as a callous measure to be carried out in a vacuum: he was familiar with the Zionist movement and believed that emigration should be directed to Palestine and managed by Jewish organizations whose business it was to settle Jews in their designated homeland."⁶⁰ He continues, "Mildenstein was no philo-semite. He operated within the parameters laid down by Heydrich, who believed in the need for 'ceaseless Jewish emigration' culminating in the total removal of the Jews from Germany. The training he gave to his men . . . rested on the assumption that Jews were alien to Germany and had no long-term future in the Reich."⁶¹ The historian Jacob Boas's assessment is similar: von Mildenstein was

> no friend of the Jews. . . . His sympathy went out only to that segment of Jewry that called itself Zionist. For the so-called assimilated Jew, the Jew who claimed to be a German first and a Jew second, or denied his Jewishness altogether, and for the Jew who eschewed all racial feeling, he held no brief, his view of them being close to the official party position. The Baron's support of the Zionist cause was not, however, grounded in expediency alone; rather it stemmed from a liberal application of Nazi racial theories. . . . [A] race was the product of a union . . . between a people and the soil in which it was historically rooted. And because the Jews were said to lack this vital relationship to the German soil, Nazis considered them an alien force in their midst, branding them as a rootless, decadent, parasitical and inferior species of mankind. . . . In Palestine, on the other hand, von Mildenstein encountered a Jew that he liked, a Jew who cultivated his own soil.⁶²

This perspective is borne out in von Mildenstein's later travel writings, where he idealizes the Jews who have been living in Palestine for a long time, over and above the émigré Jews from Europe, who had, as far as he was concerned, no relationship to the Middle Eastern soil.⁶³

Eichmann was also involved in hatching the so-called Madagascar Plan, which would have created a "reservation" for Jews on the island of Madagascar.

The plan was conceptualized in 1938, but it fell apart in late 1940, owing to the complications involved in transporting the Jews overseas while the Germans were at war with the British.[64] Lucy Dawidowicz sees this as a plan that was never likely to have been taken seriously, arguing, "everything we know of National Socialist ideology precludes our accepting the idea of a Jewish reservation as the last stage of the Final Solution." Because of the extent to which the Nazis viewed the Jews as lesser, unworthy people (as *Untermenschen*), they were not seen as a people who could or should be self-governing. Thus, "a reservation, whether in Lublin or Madagascar, could have been conceived of only as a transitional stage, comparable to ghettos as a means of concentration."[65] One might bear Dawidowicz's assessment in mind when trying to assess von Mildenstein's ostensibly well-intentioned approach to Zionism and Palestine. The people with whom he was working generally understood their ideological mission, and likely did not imagine a functioning Jewish state as feasible.

Von Mildenstein traveled in the late 1930s, as indicated on the curriculum vitae Goldfinger located, and he published two books about his travels that provide insight into his developing understanding of the Jewish relationship with Palestine. *Rings um das brennende Land am Jordan: Eine Fahrt bis zu den Quellen des flüssigen Goldes* (Around the burning land on the Jordan: A journey to the sources of liquid gold) was published in 1938 and includes much of the material from the articles in *Der Angriff*. The second book, *Naher Osten—vom Straßenrand erlebt* (The Middle East—Experienced from the Roadside), was published in 1941. The two travel books deal with excursions around similar terrain, but the routes over which he traveled are different. In the earlier of the two, von Mildenstein recounts his departure on a steamship from Brindisi, in the bootheel of Italy, how he then heads for Corinth and Athens, and eventually arrives at the land around the Jordan, including Palestine. In the later of the two books, von Mildenstein starts off in Austria, passing through Graz on his way to Hungary and Bulgaria, eventually making his way over to Palestine and Egypt.

These travel writings offer insight into what von Mildenstein must have been thinking as he traveled with the Tuchlers. He indulges in mild forms of anti-Semitism, including, for example, a joke he has heard about real estate purchases in Tel Aviv, one that involves an emigrated Jew and a native Israeli (referred to in the text as "one of his indigenous race-relations" [*seiner eingesessenen Rassegenossen*]). The émigré inspects a contract with extreme care and finally decides to rent a building only to find out that the building he's rented for a year is to be torn down in a month.⁶⁶ This same anti-Semitic humor is mirrored in the later publication in which, at the very beginning of his travels, he and his wife have a conversation about Gypsies (*Zigeunern*) with a pretty nasty Hungarian, a conversation that had apparently been prompted by his wife's own remark that the Gypsies playing music in an elegant evening room were, so she had thought, "just fat, black Jews in tuxedos!" (*doch nur fette schwarze Juden im Smoking!*). Von Mildenstein gives their companion full room to express his nasty views, particularly that the Gypsies can never be made to work, that they know how to play music but have none of their own, and that they are "a degenerate people" (*ein degeneriertes Volk*). Von Mildenstein reports the Hungarian's comments in full.⁶⁷

More revealing, however, especially where *The Flat* is concerned, is its material about the society and culture of Israel, because this material illustrates the dilemmas faced by the Tuchlers as they were forced to acculturate. The earlier travel memoir describes the phenomenon whereby the émigré Jew is particularly unwelcome in Israel. The Jews of Europe are depicted as a disruptive foreign body (*störender Fremdkörper*), and von Mildenstein uses the pejorative nickname "die Jekes," where he refers to German Jews who had moved out of Germany and Austria since 1933. He claims that no one is interested in these "January Zionists," who have earned that name because January 1933 was when the Nazis took over, and that these recent settlers do not get close to anyone, preferring to stick with their own kind. On the one hand, he provides a sympathetic account of Jews that would be part of organizations such as Olej Germania, ones who would want to retain their German identity. On the other hand, the portrait is extremely unflattering. "They brought in their money," he writes, "and want it to work for them."⁶⁸ But it is their fault that the local economy is now a house of cards: he notes that even though these Jews were major benefactors, they were a great source of uncertainty, specifically the possibility that they would withdraw their capital. They did not come, "to help build the land with work or with their own hands, but rather because Palestine seemed to be the only economic opportunity for them and their money."⁶⁹

In the 1941 book, von Mildenstein repeats a number of his descriptions, including his account of the economics of the immigration to Palestine, the influx of money, and the fact that the Israeli economy is, owing to these January Zionists (a term he uses here as well), now unstable.⁷⁰ Most poignant, however, especially when one knows the story about his relationship with the Tuchlers, is von Mildenstein's description of a trip down Herzl Street in Haifa. He again describes the clash of cultures between the European Jews and those that were there before. "The farther we proceed down the street," he writes, "the more modern, the more European the buildings and businesses become." He continues, "This is the modern Haifa of the immigrants who came after 1933.... They had no intention of living worse or even differently than they lived in their homeland." Von Mildenstein describes the new society they built with modern shops, cinemas, and elegant cafés, all of which are the hallmark of this new part of Herzl Street. "There, they speak German or English, the former fluently, the latter spottily, just not Hebrew, as is spoken in the old part of the street, because they cannot."[71] Today, after the fact, one can read a reproach of the Tuchlers into passages such as these. It is an unkind image of people who lived in Haifa with no intention of becoming part of their new culture, and with no intention of working. The passages are written neither with concern for the degree of stereotyping, nor with consideration for the difficult lot of the immigrants.

Von Mildenstein describes Tel Aviv as having notoriety as a center for business and trade, and his description of German Jews who miss the Kurfürstendamm, the famously fashionable shopping street in Berlin, might have been a description of his friends the Tuchlers: "In the large beach cafés they meet up with the old regulars from the 'good old days' on Berlin's Kurfürstendamm, to make sure they do not belong among the downtrodden, in shirts, shorts and plimsolls at the many dirty food stalls in the old downtown . . . consuming their very modest food and being happy if they can earn something as porters or newspaper vendors. They have still not learned Hebrew, because they silently hope to make a connection to the 'outside.' Their dream is to go to America."[72] Von Mildenstein's description is evidence of the thought he had given to the question of German Jews who miss their homeland, and he may have understood things this way because of his contact with the Tuchlers. His description, however, shows next to nothing in the way of compassion.

These writings complete the picture in a variety of ways. They provide, on the one hand, a glimpse into von Mildenstein's anti-Semitism into the 1940s, such that it is difficult to suggest that he was completely out of step, even at that late date, with his party's thinking on the subject of the Jews. It provides simultaneously an interesting window into the degree of understanding he had of the cultural situation, specifically the vexed and contradictory relationship that his acquaintances the Tuchlers had to their homeland. However unempathetic his conclusions were, his years of looking for ways of solving Germany's Jewish problems, and his conclusion that the Palestine solution was the best possible one, led him to a deeper psychological assessment of the frame of mind of "January Jews" such as his friends.

In this way, von Mildenstein's connection with Eichmann is of particular importance, and it is a connection of which Goldfinger is well aware. The job that Eichmann ultimately had as the key overseer of the solution to the Jewish problem was a logical extension of the work he performed in von Mildenstein's office. The German project that started with the possibility of shipping the Jews first to Palestine, and then to Madagascar, was from its beginnings headed toward the final solution, and Dawidowicz is correct to point out that, with hindsight, plans such as the Madagascar Plan were never likely to be fulfilled. This kind of thinking had a logical endpoint, a process that was triggered as soon as the Nuremberg laws were enacted. Goldfinger underscores all of these connections where he includes footage from the Eichmann trial in his film. Eichmann had been tried in Israel, and at that trial he more or less declared himself to have been respectful of Jews, reiterating that he had applied to learn Hebrew. Von Mildenstein, owing to his interest in Zionism, would have made the same point, yet he administrated an SD office and hand-picked Eichmann for a job, both of which were steps on the road to mass deportations and mass murders. Had there not been a von Mildenstein, there might not have been an Eichmann.

The relevant sequence in Goldfinger's film starts with images of headlines from Israeli newspapers that indicate that Eichmann has been caught. Goldfinger may have been asking himself what his grandparents would have been thinking as the news broke, and the news report to which Goldfinger then cuts is in German, which is to say, it is a report to which the Tuchlers would have been paying attention. The news anchor says that when Eichmann was asked who was responsible for the expulsion of the Jews from Germany between 1933 and 1939, "the following dialogue developed." In the scene, we watch Eichmann communicate with the Israeli prosecutor, Gideon Hausner, but through an interpreter. The viewer of *The Flat* has to ask: would Kurt and Gerda, had they been watching, been listening to the translation, or to Eichmann's own voice, speaking German, the language they preferred to speak? And would they have been listening when Eichmann said at trial, from the witness stand, that the man who was the initiator of the idea, the father of the idea, was von Mildenstein, their German friend, the one with whom they had continued contact? The anchor then mentions that von Mildenstein is today the German representative of a major US beverage company, and adds "But this ladies and gentlemen, is just an incidental remark" (*aber dies, Meine Damen und Herren, nur nebenbei*).

Following the grandparents' trail takes Goldfinger back to Germany more than once in the course of the film. On what is presented as his second excursion, he brings his mother along, and it seems as though part of the excitement of the trip is seeing his mother clash with a culture that is only partly her own. She grew up in a household of German Jews, yet she feels no close attachment to Germany. One of the film's major themes begins to emerge at this point, which is that Goldfinger views his mother as the weak link in the chain of memory: she is unwilling to think about the past and feels unconnected to it.

The two of them pay a visit to the von Mildensteins' daughter Edda Milz von Mildenstein, who lives in Wuppertal. Edda is proud of the past and she appears to be a quite decent person, which makes Goldfinger's position as an interrogator awkward. She is the filmmaker's foil: she does not want to know anything problematic about the past, and the archive of press clippings she keeps is all meant to confirm her father's virtuousness. Whether she does not want to know more, or thinks that she knows all that there is to know, these amount to the same thing. In this respect, the people around her are enablers, nodding their heads in agreement that if there were more to know then they would surely know it. On Goldfinger's second trip to Wuppertal, he and his mother Hannah have an interesting discussion with people close to Edda about how people in their generation discuss the past, and what in general they believed. Impressively, as an indication, perhaps, of her desire to share in her son's provocative project, Hannah Goldfinger asks Edda's close friend and neighbor directly what von Mildenstein did during the war. He claims that he hasn't found anything about him in the books, and that he was "spotless" (*unbescholten*, translated in the English subtitles as "clean as a whistle").

Although Edda Milz von Mildenstein is sympathetic, she is also unaware of key aspects of her father's past, including the mention of his name at the Eichmann trial. For some it may be hard to watch, as Edda, unbidden and proud, retrieves her family tree to exhibit it for Goldfinger. With its many noble crests, going from 372 AD to 1940, all the way up to Edda herself, it contrasts with the makeshift sketch of a Jewish family tree that Goldfinger's German relative, at another point in the film, produces in order to explain to Hannah Goldfinger how he and she are related. For all of the official knowledge Edda has of her family, she obscures major parts of twentieth-century history. At the filmmaker's prompting, she begins to sort through pictures and winds up digging through the past, eventually uncovering a 1956 article from the *Daily Mail*, which concerned whether Von Mildenstein, among others, had been employed by the Egyptian government of Gamal Abdul Nasser to work for its Voice of the Arabs radio station.[73] The report, however, only serves to confirm Edda's sense that her father has been libeled over the years. *The Daily Mail*, she explains, had to pay damages.

Her archive, in other words, consists mainly of the history she finds suitable. Documents such as the transcript of Eichmann's interrogation in which Eichmann implicates von Mildenstein in his activities remain unseen or unpreserved. Insofar as the film is a project of assembling and making sense of mislaid fragments of the past, many of which are scraps of paper, the film asks why anyone, the Tuchlers included, would keep around evidence of a difficult past. Von Mildenstein's daughter's attitude toward this difficult past comes most plainly to the foreground when Goldfinger finally confronts her with the information that her father worked in the Reich's Security Service through 1938 and beyond (Figure 4.6). She responds that this may be true, but the fact is little more than a "skeleton," and there's nothing to hang on it. Yes, one would have to know more, but it is also clear that she does not want to. The interview concludes at a moment when she appears fatigued with Goldfinger's questions, and she wearily asks him: "anything else?"

It seems as though Goldfinger could have offered up more information, more evidence, and perhaps if he had shown her Eichmann's testimony combined with, for example, some of the anti-Semitic remarks in the travel writing, then Edda would have been compelled to admit that her father had truly shown poor judgment, that he was hardly "spotless," and that his type of thinking had deportation of the Jews as a logical consequence. But Goldfinger does not seem to want to do this. The film is less about establishing the facts of the matter than

Figure 4.6 The director, Arnon Goldfinger, confronts Edda Milz von Mildenstein in *The Flat*.

it is about how one approaches matters about which no one wants to speak. Edda's lack of desire to go over the facts of the past reflects less on any German lack of desire to deal with the past—although it does reflect on that—than it does on the filmmaker's relationship with his mother Hannah, whose silence meant that the family history was to remain shrouded in mystery. Being polite to someone while conducting an interview can be an obstacle to the truth, and in this way, the conversation that Goldfinger and his mother have about how to approach Edda is extraordinarily revealing: while riding on the train to Wuppertal, Arnon says, "My question is, should we actually say the word 'Nazi?'" Goldfinger continues, "On one hand, we know [von Mildenstein] was a Nazi. On the other hand, I don't know whether it would be nice to verbalize it." Hannah makes the decision for them: "we won't verbalize the actual word."

The visit with Edda Milz von Mildenstein ultimately has productive consequences: she mentions Susanne Lehmann's name to Goldfinger and his mother, and this, the filmmaker's great grandmother's story, is the key to the film insofar as it is a film about mourning. It is about a mourning that never took place because no one wanted to speak about the past. Susanne Lehmann was deported to Riga, and we are shown a photo, taken in Tel Aviv, of three generations of women, unaware that this is the last photo in which they will ever be seen together. We do not know for certain why Susanne did not leave Germany, only that she stayed too long and was eventually deported. She may have been, like those many Jewish Germans referred to in the article in *Der Spiegel*, someone who, in vain and despite terror and defamation, held onto their fatherland.

The project of the film is, in a way, about convincing Hannah to mourn, or trying to figure out why she will not. When family members introduce her to the Stolperstein Project, a German commemorative project to mark the homes of deported Jews, and offer to place a marker in front of Susanne's home, Hannah shows only the least bit of perfunctory interest. From what Goldfinger captures on film, it could not be plainer that she has no intention of doing this. Goldfinger, however, wants his mother to know more, and if there is an Oedipal conflict in the film it is between Arnon and Hannah: when Arnon reveals that he has found the transcription of Eichmann's testimony, his mother declares that this is interesting, but that she does not intend to look into it, which prompts Arnon to reflect on how "the past never made it into [his] mother's home," and that she taught them only to be interested in the here and now.

Goldfinger is thematizing not only his desire to do things differently from his mother, but also the fact that he needs her to know how her silence affected him. He is troubled by not knowing whether and how he is connected to his grandfather. He has been told he resembles him, but he knows nothing more, and he feels resentment over growing up without a common language with his grandparents. His efforts to convince his mother that she should feel more—more sorrow, more curiosity—are visible in the moment that he reads a letter from his great-grandmother Susanne. Writing about this scene, Odeya Kohen-Raz notes:

> Goldfinger ... does not resign from his efforts to resurrect his great grandmother's voice (he makes his mother read the end of Susanne's letter in German), nor does he abandon his efforts to connect this voice with its original addressee (his mother). The entire letter constitutes both literally and metaphorically Susanne's "last words," her testimony and testament: "Do not forget me." Formally, Goldfinger starts out by rendering the reading of the letters in his own voice (employing voice-over); then the reading continues through his mother's voice in Hebrew; and finally through his mother's voice in German, thus "resurrecting" Goldfinger's mother tongue. This tactic allows for a gradual transition from one language to the other, whose task it is to bring Susanne's words (almost gone and forgotten) from the past into his mother's present existence.[74]

The sequence recalls Malte Ludin's declamation of his father's last letter in *2 or 3 Things I Know about Him*. Goldfinger seems to hope here that by getting Hannah to read the words—to get her to engage in a degree of testimonial performance—he can stir some feelings in her. His willingness to work with her is expressed in the effort, as Kohen-Raz points out, to make this a joint performance. Her obtuseness, on the other hand, is made clear in her unwillingness to even recognize that she is the "her" being referred to in the letter.

For this reason, in order to find a way to mourn properly, the film's two protagonists travel together to the Jewish cemetery in Berlin. This sequence, more than others, is about the mother's absent affect. Yet it is also about the affect expressed throughout the film itself. The two of them go in search of Heinrich Lehmann's grave. Because of how Susanne Lehmann died, either in Theresienstadt or in Riga, there is no gravesite for her. When they visit the cemetery it is raining and the oppressively low cloud cover helps turn this graveyard into a labyrinth, a symbol akin to the spiral staircase. Some of this labyrinthine structure owes itself to the assumption that there is an unsolvable mystery at the heart of the film, and that is why it is an abyss. On the one hand, there are the circumstances of the deaths of loved ones in places like Theresienstadt and in camps that were far worse; on the other hand, there is the mystery of why the Tuchlers stayed in contact with the von Mildensteins, whether they had been open and honest with one another, and whether, when they were together, they discussed the past. Like the abyssal well of the staircase, this cemetery also conceals the facts of the matter, and it is fitting that Goldfinger and his mother are unable to find the gravesite in question. Had this documentary been a feature film, he could not have scripted it better.

As the two of them search around, Goldfinger continues their ongoing discussion, and his mother now agrees that she should have asked more questions of her own mother. She says, "I should have done that more often. I should've disregarded her 'no-nos' much more often." But at this point she says that "it"—the search for Heinrich Lehmann's grave perhaps—does not really move her, and Goldfinger replies with that question, the one that is emblematic for their entire relationship: "does it bother you that you aren't moved?" Goldfinger reproaches her, "It bothers me that you aren't moved by what we're seeing here," and it is an interesting meta-observation in that it includes the viewers; it implicates us, asking whether we are moved by what we are seeing. The film is meant to cut into, explore, and create ruptures in the director's relationship with his mother. As important as uncovering knowledge about the past is, his scrutiny of his mother's somewhat inscrutable indifference toward the family's history of victimization and displacement now, at the end, becomes paramount.

And, as in *2 or 3 Things I Know about Him*, the film's denouement takes place in a cemetery. In Ludin's film, the grave of the perpetrator has been located and the image of the grave marker recalls that this body (the past) has been unearthed so that it could be properly placed, once again, in the ground. One can conclude that the two films, insofar as one is about a family of a perpetrator who chose not to speak of the past, and the other one is about a family of victims and forced émigrés, who also chose not to speak of the past, are most distinguished from one another in that the perpetrators' have a body to mourn. For their part, Goldfinger and his mother remain lost in the cemetery: he is holding flowers, much as he has done throughout the film. In most cases, he was hoping to use the flowers to observe norms for a ritual for which there are no norms, but in this case they are flowers for the dead, and he has no place to put them. The two of them are looking for a plot, in both senses of that word. The search grows frustrating, and Hannah says, "I didn't think we wouldn't find it." Goldfinger then responds: "neither did I. It must be here somewhere."

5

Rescreening Perpetrator Images: Witnessing the Past in *A Film Unfinished* and *Photographer*

At Adolf Eichmann's trial in Jerusalem, Resnais's *Night and Fog* was entered into evidence. The court screened the film on June 8, 1961, and the Israeli journalist Haim Gouri describes the scene: "The sound is not played ('so that the narration will not influence the court'). We are back in the age of the silent movies. And it is a good thing for us too, because it allows us to supply our own narration or to experience on a preverbal level what is being shown."[1] Gouri's observation is misleading when it comes to *Night and Fog* because it played for the court with English language subtitles. A version of the spoken text was there; viewers hardly had to supply their own narration. Although the subtitling was imprecise, the main thread of the argument, specifically that such violence can potentially reoccur, would have been clear enough.

As Eichmann is depicted in the trial footage filmed by Leo Hurwitz, he simply stared at Resnais's work, hardly reacting.[2] Watching Eichmann watch the film, however, it is hardly possible to know what is on his mind. Gouri writes: "some reporters thought the films would 'break' Eichmann. They thought, for some reason, that 'seeing things with his own eyes' would affect him more than witnesses had."[3] The idea that he was only now "seeing things with his own eyes" is confirmation that Resnais had succeeded, in Gouri's mind, in making the violence visible. Based on what we see when we look at Eichmann today, these atrocities were not unsettling to him. No one would look at his reactions, captured here on film, and think that the footage's "visibility" had broken him.

But we know, of course, only what we see. As far as we can tell from Hurwitz's footage, there is no reaction. Sometimes Eichmann's brow furrows, and one could certainly imagine that at those moments he is struggling to comprehend. He supports his head with his index and middle finger, and sometimes he feels the need to adjust his glasses. Not one of these reactions tells us what is in his mind. The viewing screen is only a surface, and the person depicted upon it is a cipher. We want to draw conclusions about Eichmann's state of mind, but we cannot. Even when the Germans protest their innocence at the end of Resnais's film, saying, "I am not responsible," one after the next, Eichmann, to whom this scene should have directly spoken, looks entirely unmoved.

Hurwitz's footage cuts back and forth between the sequences from *Night and Fog* being entered into evidence and Eichmann's face. We are likely seeing the images as Eichmann is seeing them. Hurwitz was making a document of the proceedings, not a poetic or polemic documentary, so it is improbable that he willfully manipulated the timeframe.[4] Although it is framed and edited, his trial footage was meant to show things as they occurred. As such, Hurwitz's document differs from Eyal Sivan and Rony Brauman's *The Specialist* (1999), which, when it shows the screening of films at the trial, chooses to show Eichmann watching films from the galley, from a distance and at an angle, perhaps to make the point, as Darcy Buerkle notes, that spectators knew what they expected to see and that they were likely to "insert the footage for themselves."[5] This is, of course, the theme of *The Specialist*: the court projected absolute evil onto Eichmann, but in order to do that the prosecution had to frame him in a particular way, starting with the theatrical setting of the glass booth. Sivan's film thematizes how Eichmann was himself a projection surface; we watch him watch and we watch him listen, hoping to glean meaning.

There have been other documentaries in which perpetrators have been made to look at evidence, and in which viewers watch them in the act of observation. In *The Act of Killing* (2012), Joshua Oppenheimer interviews extensively Anwar Congo, a self-styled Indonesian "gangster" who killed large numbers of ethnic Chinese and persons who were designated communists in the purge of 1965–66. Oppenheimer had Congo act out executions with the intent of showing audiences how proud these killers remain, but also to open up the possibility that they might reckon psychologically with the past. Congo initially enjoys restaging his murders, and he then watches his own reenactments on video. We watch him watch, and at times he seems to be watching with, one might say, the wrong eyes: he is unaffected by the violence and fixates on minor details. These re-creations are accurate, he notes, but he adds that he would never have worn white pants. Here as elsewhere, these images are less about anything the perpetrators say, than they are about how they respond to what they are seeing. More than anything Congo *says* about what he sees, it is his nonchalance that is striking.

Watching people watch footage always involves speculation. Our response is reflexive. In twenty-first century Holocaust documentaries, the act of watching another person watching redoubles an existing second order observation; we are all always already aware of how we consume these images. We approach the footage, these familiar scenes, with presumptions. What does it mean, in turn, when we project these presumptions onto the faces of those who were contemporary witnesses, but who are now seeing particular film or photographs for the first time.

In the films examined in this chapter, Yael Hersonski's *A Film Unfinished* (2010) and Dariusz Jablonski's *Photographer* (1998), we do not see perpetrators watching, yet the phenomenon is similar: the films draw attention to the witnesses' faces as projection surfaces. In *A Film Unfinished*, we are in the unique position of watching survivors watch footage of living victims. As Hersonski shows the footage, she also shows the images reflecting off their faces and the light playing in the space of the screening room, and she asks us to consider what the Nazis were seeing as they looked at the Jews. In *Photographer*, a former doctor in the Łódź Ghetto looks at photographs from that ghetto. The director depicts him in high contrast black and white in order to highlight a difference between him and those at whom he is looking. He sees the other prisoners, the dead, who are all part of a life he used to know, but he cannot place himself in the scene. His vexed reaction tells us about the context of these images. They were taken, in one case, by a Nazi film crew with a propagandistic intent, and, in the other, by a Nazi accountant who was testing out his color film stock.[6] It is not simply because the directors want us to recall who took these pictures or who made these films, but because the entirety of the intricate and difficult circumstances under which they were made is too rarely understood and brought to light.

Inside the screening room: *A Film Unfinished*

The documentary *A Film Unfinished* by the Israeli filmmaker Yael Hersonski examines footage produced in 1942 for a propaganda film. The Nazis shot much of the now archival film in the Warsaw Ghetto from May 2 to June 2 of that year, 2 months before the major liquidation, the "Grossaktion Warsaw." They intended their film for German consumption, and it may have been slated for release under the title "Asia in Central Europe" ("Asien in Mitteleuropa"). This was perhaps a working title for the film—it appears in postwar scholarship and in memoirs but does not appear as a title on the filmed material itself.[7] The Nazis left their production incomplete, and its fragmentary remnants are the unfinished film to which Hersonski's title refers.

A Film Unfinished includes spoken diary excerpts in voice-over taken from the writings of ghetto prisoners including Rachel Auerbach, Adam Czerniakow, Chaim Kaplan, Abraham Lewin, Emmanuel Ringelblum, Jonas Turkow, and others. The narration accompanies scenes from the 1942 footage, which are, in turn, intercut with sequences in which twenty-first century viewers, all of whom were once prisoners in the Warsaw Ghetto, watch the original propaganda film. The credits refer to these ghetto survivors as "witnesses." *A Film Unfinished* thus presents a suggestive paradigm of redoubled spectatorship: it is an Israeli film about the production of a German propaganda film, but it is also a film about the experience of encountering scenes from one's own past in such a film. Contemporary viewers of Hersonski's documentary observe witnesses determining whether they happen to see themselves or someone they knew on screen. We see witnesses positioned before archival moving images, and the earlier footage is thus reframed. Hersonski's film centers on scenes of encounter mediated by nearly 70 intervening years, but it is also about analyzing the German footage and the formal and intertextual strategies that Hersonski has to call on to find footing alongside the Nazi perpetrators' cinematic gaze. As a Holocaust film that revisits a propaganda film, it attempts to speak with multiple voices. The older film, the history of its reception, and the voices of survivors interact and speak to one another, fashioning an echo chamber of cinema historical contexts.

On May 5, 1942 Czerniakow, who committed suicide less than 3 months later, noted in his diary that an SS camera crew had been filming "both extreme poverty and the luxury (coffee houses)" in the ghetto.[8] Scenes had been staged and the Jewish prisoners were enacting fictions loosely based on the facts of their daily lives. They had to perform ordinariness. In keeping with what has long been a vexing contradiction for those who study documentary film, one must simultaneously maintain that the footage is genuine—it is "real" insofar as it depicts the faces, the objects, and some aspects of daily existence that constituted life in the ghetto—but it is also very much staged. The film is a distorted performance of life, yet it also remains a source of information about those lives, unlike any other. What we see is connected to the truth, but it is false; it is at once a genuine document and a counterfeit one. In *Notes from the Warsaw Ghetto*, Emmanuel Ringelblum describes the staged aspects of the film's production: "On Smocza Street they rounded up a Jewish crowd and then ordered the Jewish police to disperse them. In another place, they filmed a sequence in which a Jewish policeman wants to beat up a Jew and a German comes to help the assaulted Jew and doesn't let him be beaten." Ringelblum's subsequent diary entry refers explicitly to the staging required for the production: "Yesterday they instructed a child to leap over the ghetto wall . . . and buy potatoes there. A Polish policeman caught the boy and raised a hand to beat him. At that moment a German hastened up, stopped the Pole's arm: one shouldn't beat a child."[9]

The intention of the Nazis' propaganda film was two-fold. It was meant to communicate conflicting positions: although conditions in the ghetto as the Germans provided them were meant to appear acceptable, the Jewish people, according to the film, comported themselves horrendously, turning a livable place into an unlivable one. The film's supposed aims contrast with those of the famous 1944 Theresienstadt film, which was, like the Warsaw Ghetto film, known by two titles: its purported one, *The Führer Gives the Jews a City*, and its genuine one, *Theresienstadt: A Documentary about the Jewish Settlement*. In both that film and the one produced in Warsaw, Jewish prisoners were made to perform in front of the camera, and some of the footage communicates, in a partial, fragmentary way, how the prisoners worked, consumed, and socialized. The Theresienstadt film had a less conflicted agenda than the Warsaw one. In that film, the pain and duress is largely, though never entirely, bracketed out. It was intended primarily to convince neutral nations and the Red Cross that living conditions in Theresienstadt were agreeable.[10] The Warsaw film, by contrast, includes scenes of Jewish destitution and misery "to prove the decadent habits of the ghetto Jews."[11]

The majority of the fragmentary Warsaw Ghetto footage surfaced in 1954. Ursula Böser explains that the 1954 find included "eight rolls of film that were sent to Berlin, developed, edited into a rough cut and never released."[12] Building on Anja Horstmann's research, Böser adds, "In 1998 two additional reels of approximately 34 minutes duration bearing the title *Warsaw Ghetto* were identified by the British film researcher Adrian Wood as having been taken contemporaneously with the 1942 footage. They had been part of the Library of Congress holdings in the Motion Picture Conservation Center on the Wright-Patterson American Air Force base."[13] The additional material shows the footage being filmed. It includes outtakes that provide additional evidence of staging, as well as alterations in the camera position, all of which underscores the extent to which information was being shaped and reshaped. Böser also describes a "third type" of footage incorporated into Hersonski's film, which is amateur footage, some in color, taken around the same time as the propaganda film.[14] These various archaeological details are somewhat obscured by Hersonski. She briefly mentions the original discovery and then explains that 45 years later, in 1998, two researchers, an American and an Englishman, were looking for film of the 1936 Olympic Games in a vault at an Air Force base in Ohio and they happened across film canisters with "Das Ghetto" written on them. The historian Dirk Rupnow disputes Hersonski's shorthand version of events. He is chagrined that the location of the 1998 find is given incorrectly (we are told that it turned up on a US Air Force base even though it was really at the Motion Picture Conservation Center of the Library of Congress, which, because nitrate film is highly flammable, is housed on the property of an Air Force base), and he also takes issue with how "the majority of the sources that accompany and comment on the original film, including the surviving witnesses, are, with few exceptions, not situated or described." He adds, "We are exposed neither to the names, the backgrounds, nor to their life stories beyond the remarks made about the film."[15]

This disputation was, to some extent, foreseeable. In Hersonski's film, memory is given priority over history, and historians have treated her apparent lack of factual fervor as a provocation. Although *A Film Unfinished* contains some new historical information, Hersonski is more concerned with documenting the subjective responses of those who were there at the time. She provides some background and some additional details, yet she excludes quite a bit, such as historical context that expert talking heads might have provided. Stuart Liebman raises an objection similar to Rupnow's: "Why did [Hersonski] not include more information from authoritative historians—such as Raul Hilberg in *Shoah* ... who might have been able to place the unfinished 'Das Ghetto' in the spectrum of ... films about ghetto conditions like the ones produced at Theresienstadt in Czechoslovakia and at Westerbork in Holland?"[16] The question is worth asking: given the subject matter—that is, given the key role of the terms truth and propaganda, which attend any discussion of the original footage—why does Hersonski give short shrift to historical detail? She rarely makes it known whether the voice-over commentaries are drawn from writings by Czerniakow, Ringelblum, or Kaplan, nor does she name or provide context that would illuminate the present and past histories of her witnesses. Much like *Respite* (2007), Harun Farocki's film in which the director reframes footage taken at the Nazis' behest at the Westerbork transit camp, Hersonski prefers to narrate her film through inference and suggestion rather than informative exposition.[17]

But filmed testimony should perhaps be held to other standards. Dominick LaCapra notes that testimony often serves a contested function:

> In historiography the attempt at, or effect of, bearing witness to or even "emulating" trauma... in an extremely exposed and experimental style would be questionable to the extent that it overwhelmed the demands of accurate reconstruction and critical analysis instead of... interacting with and, to some extent, raising questions for those demands.

LaCapra argues in favor of testimony's distinctive potential, noting that, "in history there is a crucial role for empathic unsettlement as an aspect of understanding which stylistically upsets the narrative voice and counteracts harmonizing narration or unqualified objectification yet allows for a tense interplay between critical, necessarily objectifying reconstruction and affective response to the voices of victims."[18] His focus on "empathic unsettlement" is central to any reading of *A Film Unfinished*. Both words in LaCapra's designation are important: Hersonski's approach can be described as *empathic* insofar as it puts the victims' affective responses at its center, while the *unsettlement* of our contemporary relationship to the source material aims to disrupt a bounty of presuppositions about its propagandistic intertext.

The Nazis produced the "Ghetto Film" to convey specific impressions about Jewish life: in many of the frames, we see images that objectify the Jews and contain evidence meant to support racializing stereotypes. It was a motion picture made by the perpetrators and the film was part of their genocidal project. Whether or not one considers cameramen to have been perpetrators, there is no denying that German film from Leni Riefenstahl's *Victory of the Faith* (1933) to Fritz Hippler's *The Eternal Jew* (1940) and beyond deserves its share of culpability for the project of extermination, and the Warsaw Ghetto film, which records Jews who had been forced into extreme poverty being compelled to act out quasifictional versions of their daily lives, is more blameworthy than most. This Nazi film is undoubtedly composed of perpetrator images that would fit Marianne Hirsch's definition in which, "the camera is in the exact same position as the gun and the photographer in the place of the executioner who remains unseen."[19] Hirsch's classification characterizes the overall approach of Hersonski's film, especially where Hirsch inquires into what "postmemorial" or contemporary viewers are supposed to do with pictures of this sort. She writes that perpetrator images position the viewer: "in the place identical with the weapon of destruction," and she asks, "Is it possible to escape the touch of death and the implication in murder that these images perform?"[20]

The power of the source text appears overwhelming, and it is hard to imagine counteracting the authority of a narrative that so many found intractable. It is true that the least bit of knowledge would allow today's viewers to understand that the Jews did not choose to live this way, and that they were not what the Nazi filmmakers made them out to be—but it is hard to get around some of the overpowering images. For this reason, among others, Lanzmann resisted integrating wartime footage into *Shoah*: the vast majority of Holocaust-related film and photography from the 1930s and the first half of the 1940s, particularly images of Jewish suffering, were produced by the Nazis, and to include their images in a film requires a filmmaker to assume, even if only temporarily, the perpetrators' viewpoint.[21] The Nazi will, owing to the power of the images, occupies center stage. Hersonski's film seems to flout Lanzmann's concern in that it contains a multiplicity of images from the archives, marked as the past. Every frame of that older footage can be described as a perpetrator image, or film and footage taken by the perpetrator of the victim. And despite the important historical information that older document conveys about life in the Warsaw Ghetto—because it captures some portion of the truth and because little or no other footage exists of these Jewish prisoners' final days—these images cannot be watched without remaining attentive to the question of who was standing behind the camera. However, in addition to the propaganda images from the past, Hersonski also includes ones that take place in the film's "present," that is, images of persons viewing the older footage, and those images are meant to cut through or subvert the Nazi discourse. The contemporary testimony provides an alternative voice to that of the propaganda footage, or a competing point of narrative focalization. Facilitated by Hersonski's editing, the testimonies are intended to usurp the earlier film's authority.

Raising a concern about whether that usurpation is possible, Rupnow asserts that the Nazi images overwhelm the director's attempts to undermine them. He writes: "The problem of Hersonski's movie is that she does not break through the circuit (*Zirkulation*) of perpetrator images, even if she insists on their propagandistic nature. The strategy of counteracting the moving pictures through the voices of victims and surviving witnesses does not work: the images remain dominant. They produce the strongest and most lasting impressions. The film is driven by the footage made by perpetrators, and it turns itself over to their structure and imagery."[22] Rupnow is not the first to register a complaint along these lines, and the older debate sheds light on the recent one. The historian Lucy Dawidowicz expressed similar disapproval several decades earlier when she reviewed the 1968 BBC documentary *The Warsaw Ghetto*.[23] At that time Dawidowicz argued:

> Many viewers will come away . . . with unpleasant feelings with regard to the Jewish victims. For the images of the Jews which persist in our minds long after the spoken words of the BBC narrator have been forgotten are the very images which the Nazi propagandists originally wished to impress on the minds of *their* viewers. . . . These were the images of Jews which the Nazis wanted to convey to their audiences. Even though the BBC film has taken these sequences out of their original anti-Semitic context, even though these and many other sequences have been embellished with a narrative text sympathetic to the plight of the Jews, the photographic images remain what they were intended to be—pictures that elicit disgust and revulsion.

Then, in a calculated and somewhat facetious gesture, Dawidowicz turns to Joseph Goebbels's rhetoric to support her argument about the power of the photographic image. She observes that, "at one of his ministerial conferences in 1942, [Goebbels] severely criticized a Nazi publishing house for a brochure it had issued that was intended to be anti-American but whose effect was pro-American. The photographs themselves, Goebbels said, produce a favorable impression, despite their unfavorable captions: 'Captions, generally speaking, could never undo the publicity value of a picture.'"[24] Criticism from this perspective could surely be leveled at several Holocaust documentaries similar to the BBC's, including Erwin Leiser's *Mein Kampf* (1960), Frédéric Rossif's *The Time of the Ghetto* (1961), and Dieter Hildebrandt's Academy Award nominated *The Yellow Star: The Persecution of the Jews in Europe, 1933–1945* (1981). Each film uses the same Warsaw Ghetto footage with little or no reflection on the conditions of its production.[25] Hersonski's film critiques and revises the perspective of those films, which share a similarly uncritical orientation toward the older material. Even with a surfeit of historical information, they each adopt the perpetrators' perspective in the moment that they seamlessly integrate the ghetto footage.

The disputation is not new, yet Hersonski's film, especially when seen in connection with those other films, suggests new terms. It aims to provide iconic images with new frames and to counteract their propagandistic weight. The contemporary accounts are used to de-center the impression made by the propaganda images, those that Rupnow believes define the experience of watching Hersonski's film. Alongside other stylizations—the employment of slow motion, the recurring use of non-diegetic music, and the application of periodic, ambient street sounds—the witnesses' subvert the centrality of the older film and turn the documented scenes of witnessing into the primary text. Viewing *A Film Unfinished* not as a historical document but with an eye to how it "stylistically upsets the narrative voice and counteracts harmonizing narration [and] unqualified objectification" underscores the film's transformation of what would otherwise be central or dominant into an ornament or *parergon*. It supplements the earlier footage, shifting and destabilizing the frame.

Hersonski's film begins with a self-consciously subjective angle. The camera moves down the corridor of what appears to be the German archive in which the propaganda footage was first found. The tracking shot, which moves along a lengthy concrete hall with exposed pipes, resonates with other postwar documentary depictions of passageways leading to gas chambers (Figure 5.1). Guido Vitiello refers to this signature style—that is, "the ghost-like gaze of the camera exploring the remnants of a disaster"—as a "nobody point-of-view shot," which "recurs in Holocaust documentaries and feature films since Alain Resnais first resorted to it for filming the gas chambers in *Night and Fog* (1955)."[26] The "nobody point-of-view" adopted here is the standpoint of those ghosts whose images are being disclosed, some for the first time in many years; the haunted perspective of the camera that seemingly tracks through the hall of its own volition indicates that the film aims to speak for those who cannot speak for themselves and, although it cannot bring them back, it will retrieve for them a trace of their presence from beyond the terminus of the gas chamber. The filmmaker's reference, however, is not purely thanatographic; it is also film historical. In citing *Night and Fog* and films like it, Hersonski reveals her own film's intent to unsettle the viewer temporally: we see an industrial corridor today, but it could also be from the past. Just as Resnais and Jean Cayrol noted at the onset of their 1955 film that any road, any serene field could lead to a concentration camp, this ordinary, functional walkway could, by implication, also lead to a gas chamber. After these shots, Hersonski introduces the older images in their fragmented and decaying pastness; we see archival shots of streets in the ghetto, and the images crumble and decompose before our eyes. The narrator, the voice of Israeli singer-songwriter Rona Kenan, explains that these black-and-white images, which have been seen many times in other films, "were engraved in memory, as historical truth."[27] The observation, presumably scripted by Hersonski, is revealing: it indicates the film's

Figure 5.1 A nobody point-of-view shot in *Night and Fog* (1955) and the corridor of an archive as depicted in *A Film Unfinished* (2010).

consciously held goal of troubling the relationship between historical truths and the individual lives led by the propaganda film's imprisoned subjects.

Roman Polanski, himself a survivor of the Kraków Ghetto, has spoken about watching footage of the Warsaw Ghetto to prepare for the production of his Academy Award winning film *The Pianist* (2002). He may be have been referring to these shots in particular when he remarked: "It is unimaginable. People in rags that were once clothing, on tattered mattresses; they hardly grasp that the Germans are filming them. When you see that footage, you are so affected that you don't ask yourself who was standing on the other side of the camera."[28] A cursory glance at Hersonski's film, however, coupled with even the smallest amount of background knowledge, indicates that Polanski's assessment that Jewish victims "hardly grasp that the Germans are filming them" falls wide of the mark. Without context it may seem that these images were part of some purely observational documentary, yet the presence of the perpetrators today seems written across the victims' faces, and their reactions to the German cameras are certainly discernible. Polanski's interpretation served his own interests, since he used much of the footage to construct his feature film's mise-en-scène. From that footage he derived insights into daily life in the ghetto, and in *The Pianist* he restages scenes to present something audiences are meant to treat as accurate.[29] *A Film Unfinished* can be seen to provide a counter text to *The Pianist* in that it instructs viewers explicitly in the extent to which the images before them have been calculated and staged; the images from ghetto life are not seamlessly incorporated, as they would be in re-creations made for ostensibly realistic feature films.

Yet Hersonski's film also relies on mise-en-scène, which is anathema to documentarians. Lanzmann has, for his part, frequently been criticized for the use of mise-en-scène—less for his reliance on it, than for his denial that he relies on it—and critics refer to emblematic moments such as the famous sequence in *Shoah* where Lanzmann encourages the survivor Abraham Bomba to cut a man's hair to convey his difficult memories of cutting women's hair shortly before they were murdered by gas at Treblinka.[30] In Lanzmann's filmmaking, choices of this sort are constitutive of the director's vision that he is creating a new kind of text, staging and filming moments in which survivors relive the past such that the central event is their bodily response—the distress or, occasionally, the eerie detachment connected with recalling trauma. During the hair-cutting sequence Bomba struggles with his tears, and Libby Saxton observes that Lanzmann's identification of Bomba's physical gestures as "privileged moments of revelation attests to an investment in mimesis as a vector of memory and vehicle of truth." Saxton continues, "Rather than his words, it is the witness's body, and in particular his hands, that become the locus of representation and testimony; the manual imitation of miming past actions in the present precipitates the 'incarnation' of truth. . . . When the witness begins to act, past and present are no longer distinct moments in a temporal continuum but become simultaneous, at which point the image becomes truthful." In those moments, the "actor-witnesses" can be seen to "incarnate" their traumas.[31] Lanzmann means to show viewers that the divide between past and present is hardly clear-cut. His film is about the past, but in the process of its incarnation—in the subjects' moments of mimesis—the past enters into the present; it is relived by those traumatized subjects who recall it, and it is thus made, in Lanzmann's view, more present than it would be had it been represented through a flood of historical documentation.

Hersonski's present-day scenarios involve clear instances of staging as well. And although most of the film is composed of perpetrator images—the type eschewed by Lanzmann—the camera's gaze, as in *Shoah*, frequently turns toward the response of the victims. We see the witnesses watch the propaganda footage from shortly after the film's onset, and the recurring motif of empty seats in a small screening room contrasts sharply with staged propaganda scenes that the Germans filmed in Warsaw's crowded Nowy Azazel Theater. At one point during filming, the Nowy Azazel was filled beyond capacity, and the filmmakers insisted that the Jews remain in their seats for endless hours. As it is explained in the film, "the audience in the theater was held in isolation . . . until filming was completed, without food, and without being able to take care of their physical needs." In the present of Hersonski's film, an older woman sits alone in the screening room, and we hear a male voice, reading from a diary, explaining that the date is May 7, 1942. We are not told whose diary is being excerpted or that the street scenes we see before us were filmed on that day. Here Hersonski's film deliberately captions its images indirectly, allowing a constellation to emerge of witnesses' testimony in the form of diary excerpts and the expressions of survivors who, decades later, watch the film and react. The present day witness's first words are "*Oi Elohim*" (Oh God), and she then asks, "What if I see someone I know?" Her slip is noteworthy: Hersonski's witness uses the present tense ("I know"), even though almost everyone she is seeing is now dead. Her response indicates the extent to which she has been returned to the moment of the propaganda film's production and is re-experiencing events even if only indirectly, and in a mediated form, much as Bomba's affect was a symptom of the vivid recollection of his traumatic past in *Shoah*.

In these sequences, Hersonski's editor plays a game: we assume that the images we see—intercut with contemporary images of witnesses watching—are the images that they are seeing, but we have no way to be sure. It is also unlikely that they are hearing the same narration we hear, because it was not part of the original footage. When a witness gasps because something shocks or surprises, we have no assurance that his or her gasp coincides with the sequences that subsequently appear and take up the whole of the frame. The editing intimates that the witnesses are seeing the images at the same moment, so to speak, that we are seeing them. At those points, however, we see only the flicker of the image, and the play of light and shadow on their faces and on the adjacent seats in the small screening room can be described as an anamorphosis, which for some viewers will recall the projection of evidentiary footage of camp liberations seen from the side and at a distance in *The Specialist*.³² In Hersonski's film, the images being back-projected onto the theater seats and sometimes onto witnesses' eyeglasses are so fragmentary that their content cannot be reconstructed; our information is intentionally limited, and the documentary is turning its back ostentatiously on the original material. In obscuring the content, the filmmakers—Hersonski as well as Sivan and Brauman—take issue with the tacit presumptions created by our familiarity with the images. The formal choice serves as a provocation against uncritically evaluating the documentary evidence *as* evidence.

After our initial encounter with the propaganda images in Hersonski's film, we see footage of pedestrians moving over the newly constructed overpass that crossed Chlodna Street and allowed Jewish prisoners to travel without setting foot on an avenue designated for Aryans.³³ Some of the figures ascending and descending the steps briefly peer directly into the camera, now connecting, through the logic of shot and reverse shot, with the gaze of Hersonski's contemporary witnesses (Figure 5.2). It is disquieting. Because they are looking into German cameras, most neither smile nor wave, and although Hersonski cuts from black and white images of passersby to present-day witnesses, seated in a darkened screening room—in a *camera obscura* of their own—there is no redemptive reconnection; we are not sutured into a reunion between survivors and their kin. The witnesses look to recall the past, seeking a point of contact with an image, a *punctum*. In Roland Barthes's terms, the *punctum* is connected

Figure 5.2 A prisoner of the ghetto returns the gaze in *A Film Unfinished*.

to the force of a photograph insofar as it is evidence that persons or things were in fact "there," but it is not a response to the evidentiary attribution of historical context (specifically the when and the where). We anticipate seeing the impact of a revelatory moment at which a particular point has shot out from the image, like an illuminating arrow, piercing the witness's memory, but no such encounter is depicted. In an echo of the major theme of Barthes's *Camera Lucida*, one witness conspicuously remarks on how she keeps thinking that among all these people she might see her mother.[34] To our knowledge, she does not.

The film remains unspecific in such details, choosing, for example, not to seek out the witness's mother, and it likewise steers clear of protracted expositions. In one sequence, we see footage accompanied by a voice-over declamation of an entry from Czerniakow's diary. Czerniakow refers directly to the film's production, explaining how the Nazis staged a scene in the office where he served as head of the Jewish Council. While we see what must be the corresponding images—what is surely the footage filmed on that day—the voice reading the diary entry explains how rabbis and petitioners were directed to go upstairs, and a candelabrum was lit and placed on Czerniakow's desk.[35] Other filmmakers might have, at this moment, corrected this Nazi propagated misperception about Jewish life: viewers might not understand that a menorah is hardly likely to have been used in such a setting. Hersonski, however, engages in no such exposition, choosing instead to let the intermittent remarks from the diary and a few non-diegetic piano chords speak to the prisoners' mistreatment. Her point has more to do with empathic unsettlement than with correcting the record. The film does not deliberately mislead, but it suspends discussions of the facts to distinguish itself from films like *Mein Kampf*, *The Time of the Ghetto*, and *The Yellow Star*, for which historical narratives, whether they were employed accurately or inaccurately, fashioned the central theme.

In those major Holocaust documentaries, the footage from the Warsaw Ghetto is freely incorporated, as if it were purely observational; it is as though daily life were being captured transparently, without acknowledgment that the act of filming was part of the persecution. Even from their initial uses some of the images seemed so iconic—an impoverished child dancing, overcrowded apartments, throngs of workers crossing the footbridge—that they were included in nearly every depiction. Among the sequences from the footage found in 1954 that made their way into nearly all of these documentaries was one in which prisoner-pedestrians parade past a corpse on the sidewalk, ostensibly indifferent to its presence, and two Jews in dark uniforms come to collect the body with a cart, as though it were the time of the plague. The workmen load the body into a wooden coffin and take it away as refuse. This sequence has been integrated time and again into films. In Leiser's *Mein Kampf*, for example, the narrator explains that "Goebbels's own cameramen had taken these pictures," yet that accurate remark leads to no further critical reflection on the images' genuineness. The narrator simply treats the sequence as a window onto the truth, explaining that, "the inhabitants of the ghetto must live and die like rats." When it comes to the sequence involving the disposal of the corpse, the narrator repeats the propagandists' message wholesale: "The dead and dying lie in the streets, but the living no longer see them." Hildebrandt's *The Yellow Star* combines the same Warsaw Ghetto footage with diary entries, but when it comes to sequences such as the removal of the body, the voice-over once again treats the footage uncritically. The narrator intones: "Dead, dead, and more dead, impede the way of the living. Those still alive make their way among the bodies. The clatter of the death carts never seems to stop." Finally, in Rossif's *The Time of the Ghetto*, the director adds music composed by Maurice Jarre to the sequence and simply informs the viewer that death has arrived in the city. Hersonski handles the footage differently: in her film a witness explains that the Germans were attempting to depict the Jews' indifference to their own people's suffering by compelling ghetto prisoners to walk by corpses as though they were unconcerned by their presence. People were, she explains, "kindly asked" to walk by the dead with their heads held high. Hersonski elaborates on the performative aspect—that people were made to walk past the body more than once—and she then imposes an intertitle on the iconic scene: "Take 1." Not only are separate moments indexed this way (as "Take 1" and "Take 2"), but Hersonski also intercuts the shot with footage from another reel, taken at the same time, in which a German cameraman, off to the side, can be seen furtively ducking out of the camera's way. In her reiteration of this and other sequences, Hersonski rewrites key moments in the history of the Holocaust documentary.

But to note this is also to note how exceptional and telling the German film's use of mise-en-scène is: not only are the recently deceased being used boldly as props, but the description of what the prisoner-performers were asked to do bespeaks an attempted mimesis between perpetrator and victim. The request that the victims conceal any empathy—that they, in fact, perform its absence—suggests something of what the film can tell us about its producers; they stage their own cruelty through the victims, displacing it on them and thus imagining the extent to which others could be enveloped in complicity. Hersonski's witness, who is not individually named until the end credits, narrates that when a car pulled up and Germans stepped out with their camera, she hid. At that point the footage depicts a young girl hovering by a wall and Hersonski highlights her presence, unabashedly manipulating the original footage, slowing it down and superimposing a bright halo around the child's face. The presence of camera-wielding Germans in the footage indicates that we are watching a sequence not intended for the final cut. In marking the young girl's presence by the wall, Hersonski indicates that the girl *may* have lived to be the woman now speaking, but rather than explicitly identify her in a caption, the director offers only inference. There is no redemptive moment ("there, that is me!"), to enable the audience to meaningfully assemble the memory—no clear narrative trajectory such as that of the red jacketed child in *Schindler's List* (1993)—nor does Hersonski allow her witness to come to terms with the past, to observe herself on screen and put her feelings about it into words.

In avoiding such scenes of closure and highlighting moments of uncertainty, *A Film Unfinished* activates its archival footage as a troubled memorial surface. Hersonski's film, however, handles differently its encounters with perpetrators. At several points, we see the faces or forms of the propaganda film's own cinematographers, and here one could arguably assert that the culprits—or even "criminals"—make an appearance.[36] The witnesses' stories are intercut with those of one cameraman, Willy Wist, who, it is explained, was the only cameraman identified as being involved in making the film.[37] Wist was called on to testify in 1970 and 1972, and he died in 1999.[38] As the film explains, court transcripts record what he was asked and what he replied. But the film does not make clear that the voice we are hearing is not Wist's, and Hersonski goes so far as to include images of a decades-old tape recorder, a prop that deliberately leads some viewers to conclude that they are being exposed to recorded testimony. Our attention is drawn only to the fact that this is an illusion when we recognize the performer's mature face—shown in fragments—as that of the famous German actor Rüdiger Vogler, a readily identifiable member of Wim Wenders's ensemble. As an important and revered actor, Vogler was a star of the New German Cinema, and he brings his own cachet of German cinema history to the role. From his participation in this Israeli film, one might infer a direct connection to German film's culpability. Vogler's face speaks recognizably to German audiences—and to some international ones as well—and it may be taken as a suggestion that Wist's complicity in the production of filmed propaganda should be tied, however marginally, with the history of German cinema, a history that would also include Riefenstahl and Hippler.

Vogler declaims Wist's transcribed testimony, engaging in its reconstruction. It is a re-performance of a testimonial performance, and it thereby undercuts a form commonly employed in documentaries.[39] Hersonski does not explicitly mark the text as being read by an actor or provide even minimal expository background about Wist's trials, which is consistent with the hedging and uncertainty, or inference and implication of the cameraman's own testimony. When his entry pass to the ghetto is presented to him, he says only that he was probably in the ghetto at that time, but the evidence mounts. The interview and the presentation of the material, specifically Wist's denials, recall the similarly disingenuous tone struck by Riefenstahl in the exposé interview-documentary *The Wonderful, Horrible Life of Leni Riefenstahl* (1993). Over time Wist, owing to his evasions, comes across as less and less sympathetic. Czerniakow's diary entry from May 12, 1942—coincidentally, 2 days before the actor Vogler was born in Warthausen—explains how the Nazis filmed a rite of circumcision (a *bris*) on a newborn in a private apartment.[40] Here Hersonski includes the propaganda film's extremely invasive images. They are difficult to watch, and Czerniakow's diary explains that because the child's birth-weight is so low, there is a chance that he will not live long. Speaking Wist's words Vogler denies that he was the one who filmed it. These private images are followed by even more intimate images of a "ritual Jewish bath" (a *mikveh*), yet another filmed compulsory performance. The cameraman confirms details of the torturous conditions under which these images were made, and the wording in Chaim Kaplan's diary conveys the brutality: "This week they have invented a new torture.... First they captured a few dozen young and beautiful women and transported them to a certain Jewish ritual bathhouse; afterward they captured some strong, powerful, virile men and brought them to the same bathhouse. Both sexes were forced by means of intimidation and whiplashes to remove their clothes and remain naked; afterward they were forced into lewd and obscene acts.... There is no limit to the obscene imagination."[41] Embodied by Vogler, Wist admits that he was there and that he was instructed to film inside the bathhouse. The cinematographer's calm recounting of events is intercut with the corresponding images, now accompanied by music, perhaps to counteract or mitigate what would otherwise be an unbearable silence. About this experience, Vogler's Wist adds dispassionately that it was difficult for him to film in the bathhouse because of improper lighting.[42] The testimonial performance is irreverent in that it substitutes—nearly unmarked—an actor's embodiment where it sees fit to do so. Offering only Vogler's performance, Hersonski takes a position on Wist's degree of remorse.

A Film Unfinished then provides us with a striking series of color images that were part of the later or "third category" of footage as described by Böser. Wist's colleague had apparently filmed some footage with his own camera as a "personal memento of ghetto life." These images constitute a sort of meta-film insofar as his colleague was filming the filming. As the color images appear the narrator says "*here* is the funeral procession" and "*here* the market." The emphasis on the word "here" suggests that, whether it is because they are in color or because Hersonski, as voiced by Rona Kenan, is under the impression that they are less staged, we are, from the perspective of the narrative voice, coming closer to seeing things as they were. This is an illusion, but perhaps this break, or self-conscious gesture toward disjunctive layering whereby the original document is overwritten by another effect or context (specifically, the fact that we are re-seeing these people and places in color), is why we now get a caption of the kind that we have not had before.[43] "For a brief second," the narrator informs us, "one of the cameramen can be seen caught in the frame." Wist's name appears onscreen beneath his youthful image (Figure 5.3), and it is as though the film were finally acting as a witness to something that could be understood as the evidentiary truth. Wist is the only personage named onscreen in this way; his is the only name put directly with a face.

The actor playing Wist then recounts some particularly gruesome memories: a cart with bodies and limbs hanging over the side. He notes that at the entrance to the Jewish cemetery there was a shack with 40 or 50 bodies piled up waiting to be burned. Again we see the shots for which this cameraman was likely

Figure 5.3 The cameraman, identified by name, in *A Film Unfinished*.

responsible, and they are among the film's more brutal images. One present day witness, watching the film, covers her eyes, and in a moment geared to the type of empathic unsettlement described by LaCapra, she emotes: "Today I cannot look at this." Her isolation is underscored by the emptiness of the theater where only ghosts have joined her. Writing about Lanzmann's *Shoah*, Sue Vice notes a similar use of mise-en-scène, when the former resistance movement fighter Jan Karski breaks down. Karski had heroically smuggled out to the Allies microfilm with detailed information about the Warsaw Ghetto. He visited the ghetto in 1942, sneaking in to gather intelligence; when questioned decades later by Lanzmann, he has difficulty describing what he saw. His sentiment is that his experience cannot be represented, which conveniently echoes Lanzmann's chief cinematographic tenet. Karski tells Lanzmann: "I don't go back in my memory. . . . It was not a world. It was not a part of humanity. I was not part of it. I did not belong there. I never saw such things . . . nobody wrote about this kind of reality. I never saw any theater, I never saw any movie . . . this was not the world."[44] Of course, Karski's meaning, "I never saw such things," is plain enough. He means neither before nor after had he encountered atrocities of this sort. But looking back on his experience as an outsider to the ghetto, he was also asserting that he could not perceive or comprehend what he saw. The images were not seeable. The problem is hermeneutic, and it echoes Lanzmann's own statement about observing footage of Jews dying en masse in gas chambers, specifically, his sentiment that if he were to come into possession of such footage, he "would have preferred to destroy it." He adds to this observation: "It is not visible. *You cannot look at this.*"[45] Even though Hersonski's film uses archival footage—a decision to which Lanzmann would, in general, object—it relies on its paradigm of redoubled spectatorship to introduce issues of representation. To not see something ("Today I cannot look at this") recalls the overall problem of comprehension: how much of this footage is visible to us now?

In the incorporated testimony—in Vogler's voice—Wist recalls that he was instructed to film a mass grave. The witnesses watch the bodies being disposed of in large numbers and the shadow play of images is mapped across their faces. Wist then speaks about the unreliability of his own memory, that is, that he cannot recall much more than disjointed details. He knows only that the people were skin and bones; he claims that he convinced himself that they simply died of starvation. After triangulating between Vogler, the propaganda film, and the witnesses, Hersonski then pauses on a black and white freeze frame in which a cameraman can be seen scrambling to find his bearings, climbing out from a pit of bodies. This could be Wist, having just filmed a close up of the corpses, and if so, his culpability, or at least his certain knowledge of mass death would be undeniable. Were it Wist, then his statement "I can only say that at the time, I definitely knew nothing of the horrible fate that awaited the Jews of Warsaw" would be difficult to accept. Even if he had not known that Treblinka awaited them, it would have been impossible, in that pit, to overlook the scope of the devastation. However, in this black and white frame, the film does not unambiguously identify Wist—there is no title testifying to the facts. Hersonski chooses to conclude the inquiry with implication and inference.

After this difficult scene, Hersonski transitions into a series of portraits included among the propaganda footage. The camera in these portraits lingers on Jewish faces, and its style recalls the racializing exploration of Jewish physiognomy in Hippler's *The Eternal Jew*, particularly the sequence in which that film's narrator explains how Jews try to hide their origins when they are among non-Jews, and how one requires sharp eyes to recognize them. The sequence in the Warsaw Ghetto film is eerily similar. Hippler's famous dissolves, which revealed the transformations between visible and camouflaged Jewry have here been replaced by simultaneous, side-by-side comparisons; impoverished subjects pose next to well-to-do ones.[46] Some hateful exposition might have been yet to come, but it is difficult to imagine what precisely was intended without inadvertently sharing in the complicity. The similarity between the propaganda films can hardly be surprising. Goebbels was involved in both projects, and *The Eternal Jew*, although it was not a major commercial success, had received official ratings (*Prädikate*) indicating that it was politically and artistically meritorious; despite not being a major financial hit, it had been well received. In 1939, Hippler had already filmed in the ghettos of Łódz and Warsaw at Goebbels's request. According to Hippler's memoir, Goebbels told him that they had to capture those sites on film because the Jews would soon be gone. Goebbels apparently added: "The Führer wants to resettle all of them, to Madagascar or other places. For that reason we need these film-documents for our archive."[47] The history of German film, in other words, bears liability for the genocide, and as images that could have come from *The Eternal Jew* appear, Hersonski allows Vogler's performance of Wist's testimony to continue. His voice intones that he did not know that the Jews were going to be systematically killed, which is now, looking at these objectifying and somber portraits, even harder to accept. He also mentions—despite all evidence to the contrary—how he had confidence that the Jews were hopeful, expecting that they would be resettled in Madagascar or somewhere else. His rationalization echoes the quotation attributed to Goebbels. After the Madagascar plan had revealed itself to be militarily unfeasible in late 1940, the term "Madagascar" was sometimes used as a euphemism for the Final Solution. These films—both Hippler's *The Eternal Jew* and the Warsaw Ghetto film—were steps in the same direction, from resettlement to annihilation. For those that recognize the similarity between the films, they appear to be of one piece.

In *A Film Unfinished*, Hersonski's tone seems consciously imprecise, and it aims to unsettle where it leaves certain matters unsettled. Its truths are impressionistic. In suspending the evidentiary question, the film undermines the aims and the authority of the propaganda images, which, as Goebbels himself made plain, were meant to document history. By reading and re-reading them, by showing the same sequences from more than one perspective, and by letting multiple victims' voices respond to the past, the film undercuts the images' otherwise monologic tone of conviction. Her reliance on self-conscious moments of spectatorship, as well as her varied ellipses and her uses of anamorphosis, all point to her awareness that one should never base a reconstruction of the past on the Warsaw Ghetto footage. Yet her film is best understood in the context of other films: while it plainly connects "the Ghetto Film" to propagandistic German works, it is also a riposte to staged Hollywood-style films such as *The Pianist*, and to didactic and ostensibly authoritative films such as *The Yellow Star* and *Mein Kampf*. She constructs her film not as a univocal address, but as a highly mediated cinematic space in which German propaganda and a lengthy history of Holocaust films reflect, reveal, and expose one another.

Shades of gray: Dariusz Jablonski's *Photographer*

As the first intertitle of *Photographer* explains to the viewer, its subject is a collection of photographs, or, more specifically, color slides taken in the Łódź Ghetto by the Austrian bookkeeper and Nazi party member Walter Genewein (spelled Gennewein in some documents). The collection was privately held by his companion after his death, and it was transferred to a second-hand bookstore in Vienna in 1987. The collection is unique not only because it depicts life in the Łódź Ghetto on film, something that is otherwise rarely seen, but also, and most striking, because it is in vivid color. When we imagine the ghetto it is typically in black and white because that is how we have grown accustomed to seeing images of it. As a result, color photos seem unreal. Whether they are images of prisoners in the ghetto or of Nazi perpetrators, as with Malte Ludin's photos of his father at a party rally in *2 or 3 Things I Know about Him,* color images from the period seem unnatural and oversaturated, and we suspect that their color must owe itself to an artificial intervention, one that must have been made long after the war.

    The very first shots in Jablonski's film are of an archive—the location where the images are held in Frankfurt—and this image, taken by a camera that is surveying the shelves of an official collection, is thoroughly familiar from other films, especially from the beginnings of Ludin's film and also from *A Film Unfinished,* where we see the archived stacks of metal canisters in which the Warsaw Ghetto footage was held. They highlight the ongoing process of discovery. The first voice we hear turns out to be that of Arnold Mostowicz, a doctor, a Jew, and a Łódź Ghetto survivor, who explains to the viewer that the pictures, which emerged somewhat suddenly after so many decades, provoked a feeling of unease: what he sees in them both is the ghetto and is not the ghetto that he knew. His remark is the first suggestion that he is looking at the images while we are looking at them; he is describing the immediate experience of viewing the slides, and, as in *A Film Unfinished,* we as viewers become involved in the process of watching a survivor encounter images out of his or her past. These images are uncanny, or even paradoxical (they are and are not the ghetto) because while they depict the places and bodies with which he was familiar at that time, they show these people in positions and with expressions that would have been unfamiliar to him. Mostowicz's vision could never have been comparable to that of the man behind the camera, Walter Genewein, who should arguably be regarded as a perpetrator. Because Mostowicz was a Jew and a fellow prisoner, no one posed for him; no one looked up from their work and performed normalcy for him. These are people he could have known, yet he would have met their gazes differently. For this reason, the images and the standpoint from which they were taken all seem strange to him.

    The film is thus engaged with the issue of photography's limited ability to record history: simply because one has photographs, one does not know what happened. Only the most literal minded interpreter—and in this context, one might think of such a person as an "accountant"—would take stock of what is in the image without considering its context; who would believe that such images, taken by such a person, show the truth? The contradiction, however, is that they also do, in some measure, show the truth: the photographs capture the physical impressions made by light, as a process of photographic emulsion, and one has to agree that a part of Jewish life that would otherwise remain unseen is depicted here. While the people in the photographs are largely performing for the camera—they are posing, in order to present themselves to the photographer as relatively contented and productive subjects, and they were perhaps chosen instead of those who were suffering more than they, precisely because they could be depicted in that way—their bodies, their clothes, their gazes, and the streets on which they walked are captured on film. These images are thus a major part of the otherwise limited archive of visual evidence that captures how life was lived in that ghetto. However skewed and transformed these photographs are by the gaze of the man who took them, they represent the last days of tens of thousands of Jews, who were never seen again. The question is not *whether* these images, like the extant footage of Westerbork Camp seen in Harun Farocki's *Respite* or the Theresienstadt propaganda film shot by Kurt Gerron, parts of which are included in *The Last of the Unjust*, should be treated as evidence of how they lived, but rather *to what extent* they should be treated that way.

Those depicted in these images do not seem to move, yet because they are placed in this moving picture, and because the camera surveys them, the photographs seem less like still images and more like images that are gradually being set in motion. The process reflects the photographs' animation in Mostowicz's memory. One should, of course, not go so far as to say they are "brought to life." We cannot experience the victims' horrible living conditions via photographs. In speaking of the experience of being in the ghetto, Mostowicz explains that one had to get used to the smell, the odor of unwashed bodies, un-aired rooms, and unremoved feces, yet this description only serves to highlight the extent to which our virtual experience of the conditions is limited. Jablonski adds sound to these images, as Hersonski does in *A Film Unfinished*, including multiple background noises such as the sounds of phones and typewriters. Financial documents are read aloud, onto the soundtrack, and the words, along with images of factory work, are accompanied by orchestral music, much of which sounds like marching music. In those depictions, the film highlights the deluded self-images of ghetto administrators who deceived themselves into believing that they were top-level businessmen running efficient businesses, without ever realizing the extent to which their apparent successes owed themselves to stolen capital and to a vast pool of slave labor. As in Harun Farocki's *Respite* in which the newsreel-style footage of Westerbork seemed to show something akin to a city on the move, the additional sounds buttress the impression of prodigious industry. The car horns, street noises, and the sounds of commerce are all ways that the director self-consciously plays with the effect of reality. The sounds are superfluous and only highlight the all-too-vivid appearance of the color images, and thus the extent to which our images of the past are not reality so much as its construction. The sounds make the images more realistic, but they cannot make them real.

In Jablonski's film, many of Genewein's photographs are subjected to something like the Ken Burns effect, a technique named after the famous American documentarian in which still photographs are set in motion by panning across their surfaces or by zooming in on particular persons. Ulrich Baer, in his discussion of Jablonski's film and Genewein's photographs, acknowledges that photographs such these, and by extension other similar perpetrator photographs, may be read differently than atrocity photographs. There are, however, questions raised by Baer's interpretation. His interest in Genewein's images turns on how they function as a tool to write history against the grain of the Nazis' intentions. In order to see through different eyes than the perpetrators, Baer wants us to look, not only beyond what the Nazis meant us to see, but also beyond "the thanatographic and principally melancholic perspective adopted by many theorists."[48] Baer wishes to make the victims' voices part of the discussion of Genewein's record, and to this end, he notes: "Except for his own family members and his German colleagues, everything and everyone Genewein photographed in the ghetto was not only governed and imprisoned by, but literally owned by and absolutely controlled by his employer, the Nazi state. It is this apparently total correspondence between photographer's perspective and incontestable authority that we must investigate, resist, and tear apart."[49] In asserting that one must challenge the total identity of Genewein and Nazi authority, Baer rightly identifies a phenomenon whereby the Nazis are understood to have conditioned and determined the rules of a game all were forced to play. He writes that one of the effects of a historical trauma such as this is "precisely the replacement of the normal life-world with a suffocatingly hermetic violent universe—a constricting web of forces that ensnares everything with senselessness, contingency, fear."[50]

According to Baer, prior interpreters of Genewein's and other similar photographs have been inclined to let their readings be wholly determined by the perpetrators' intentions and thus potentially thrust those represented in the images back into that same fearful and constricting web. Such interpreters are given to argue that Genewein's slides "record nothing but the 'ruination' and death of the Jews captured in them, while they reveal a complex 'mental' stance and even the overall 'existential attitude' of the German behind the camera." As a consequence, the Jews in these images are effectively "robbed of any interior life and self-directed means of expression, while the Nazi photographer is endowed by the historians with motives, feelings, and a rationale for his actions."[51] Baer takes issue with the approaches of theorists who would dismiss the images based on the perspective from which they were created, asserting that Genewein's slides should not be disregarded "because their meaning is wholly determined by a particular aesthetic," or "in claiming, as Lanzmann does, that Nazi-created images deprive viewers of the possibility of seeing anything the Nazis did not want them to see."[52] Baer's overall aim is to acknowledge that such photographs may contain the seeds or hints of other possible futures and must therefore be wrested from deterministic readings. There are, he maintains, events depicted in those photographs that have not been comfortably assimilated into history or memory, and for this reason they must be read against the grain, counter to the photographer's intentions. Examining the manner in which Jablonski surveys Genewein's still images, Baer concludes that the addition of the camera's movement gives the mute and imprisoned subjects the right to appeal to us; the camera's motion restores something that had been taken from them by the perpetrator.

Looking at one of Genwein's photographs of a necktie vendor on the street (Figure 5.4), one might not notice that there is a face in the image's edge, at the far left, looking through the fence, hardly part of the frame at all. This is obviously the face of a person Genewein neither wanted nor expected to catch on camera. When the image appears in Jablonski's film, the soundtrack features a reading of a request from the ghetto administration to Chaim Rumkowski: does he perhaps have an electrical or manual bone-grinder, because the Sonderkommando in Kulmhof (at Chełmno) needs one? As we hear this macabre request conveyed, Jablonski surveys the image and finds the face at the margin with its curious expression, neither evidently male nor female. He lingers on this face, caught by accident and peering through the chain links in the fence. There is hardly enough of an image there to know a story, and it is difficult to imagine that the person in the photograph would be recognized today. The face is in fragments, and yet the intimation is that if one looks long enough, one may still see something as yet unseen. The partial image, unlike the quite legible profile of Hans Biebow, who is examining the ties, is a reminder of the untold stories of the photographs' vanished subjects. Jablonski, after surveying the photograph, then pointedly cuts to Mostowicz talking about a child, a little girl whom he, in his capacity as emergency doctor, found in a little

Figure 5.4 Ghetto administrator, Hans Biebow examines some ties for sale in the outdoor market of the Łódź Ghetto. Slide Łódź A037. Courtesy Jüdisches Museum Frankfurt. Frankfurt am Main.

room, next to a dead mother and son. The girl, who was crawling with lice, did not live long; she was taken to Chełmno in 1942 and was killed.[53]

Jablonski's film accomplishes much of its temporal layering, its bringing together of past and present, in a style that is in part inspired by Lanzmann's approach to the subject. Rather than recreating or dramatizing scenes from the past (as in, for example, *No Place on Earth*), Jablonski relies on the contemporary testimony of the Łódź survivor Arnold Mostowicz. Mostowicz's first-person account undercuts Genewein's administrative correspondence, which is provided in the form of his extensive record of letters, notes, and billing statements. The survivor's voice asserts itself over Genewein's pictures, and Mostowicz's memory is, in the end, far more compelling and sympathetic than those bureaucratic traces of Genewein that have been put before us. The accountant's documents are saturated with punctilious office rhetoric, which, if it does nothing else, evokes a comparison with Adolf Eichmann. By contrast, Mostowicz's detailed accounts speak on behalf of Jewish experience. In Genewein's letters, which either seek to justify the expense associated with using bullets against Jewish victims or complain to the company that supplied him with the film that his images are, uncannily enough, bleeding too much red, he comes across as diabolical.

As it relates to other films, Lanzmann's stance is that it is important to keep focused on the contemporaneousness of victims' present-day testimony in order to avoid the common and dangerous illusion that one can come into contact with the irretrievable past. For him, it is always too late; the victims' right of appeal can never be returned, not even in fantasy. Even if one considers Lanzmann's earlier objections to including these types of images, one has to agree that in this case the photos are used in a way that counters the illusion of collapsing time and space. As Frances Guerin writes: "The film does not simply challenge the authenticity of Genewein's perspective on the past; it casts its own vision in 1998 as only one version of the past we must continue to seek out."[54] Mostowicz's contemporary testimony is introduced precisely to show us that the photographic evidence on its own is not evidence per se. Janina Struk points out, when describing Jablonski's film, that the survivor's commentary, in its undermining of the apparent evidence conveyed through the photographs, "define[s] the problem of using photographs as records of reality and truth."[55] The truth of Genewein's photographs is challenged and diminished by the more convincing truth of Mostowicz's testimony. This too, however, is imperfect and mediated by time. It is not, therefore, Jablonski's contention that testimony is always superior to photographic evidence, which is hardly the case, but that both are flawed and insufficient, and one can be called upon to question and undercut the other.

Who was the bookkeeper Genewein when he took these photographs? As a Nazi bureaucrat he was surely iniquitous, yet in taking these photos he also becomes a businessman documenting the productivity of his vast workshop, something of which he was proud, as well as a tourist, similar to Heinrich Jöst, the German sergeant who took photographs of the Warsaw Ghetto to fill spare time, experimenting with a camera and viewing a culture with which he was unfamiliar, one that he might have understood as drawing its last breaths.[56] Genewein's photos are thus less interested in documenting things he would have been capable of identifying as brutality, like SS men with trained weapons, or photographs of crater-sized death pits. At first glance, his images seem to occupy an ambiguous space somewhere between the perspective of the perpetrator, who wields the camera like a weapon, and the cold gaze of a bystander. The brutality he documents, that which is associated with forced labor, may not have been entirely recognizable to him as such. For most contemporary viewers, those not trained to look for signs of brutality and torture in these intense images of poverty, the scenes depicted seem neither "graphic," nor do they fit with those images we are trained to see as violent perpetrator images. They might resemble the images of Depression-era poverty seen in, for example, photographs by the Danish-American photojournalist Jacob Riis.

Without the knowledge that the conditions inside their homes were unlivable and that most of the persons depicted would end up murdered at Auschwitz and Chełmno, they simply tell a story of meager conditions, and readers would not be likely to respond to their reproduction in texts with indignation about their opportunistic use.

Yet as Marianne Hirsch has pointed out, photographs analogous to those taken by Genewein present victims who were shot by the camera not long before they were shot and killed, and though these are not the same thing, the two actions cannot be so readily disjoined.[57] Despite the understanding that the camera is linked to the weaponry, and that images of this sort, because of the people who took them, support the narratives or express the voices of the perpetrator, they indeed circulate. Perpetrator photographs constitute a large part, perhaps even the overwhelming majority, of the visual archive of the Holocaust. Many historical texts unabashedly reproduce these photographs in the interest of educating readers about the extent of Nazi horrors, and Janina Struk's *Photographing the Holocaust* reproduces many such images with the intent of reflecting upon these very questions. Is Jablonski's film doing the very same thing? He calls attention to the fact that we and Mostowicz are looking at images, all of us in the screening room, forced to look through the eyes and the camera lens of the perpetrator. He not only shows the images in their frames, either as slides or as part of Genewein's scrapbook, but he includes the sound of a clicking shutter as well, lest we forget. Is the function didactic? Is he teaching us, with the help of testimony, to correct and change the way we view perpetrator images?

Hirsch explores the contradictory dimensions of historical fact and esthetic play using the example of the well-known photograph of a young boy in the "Stroop Report" whose arms are raised in surrender during the liquidation of the Warsaw Ghetto. As Hirsch points out, this photograph has been reproduced many times, and it is not hyperbolic to state, as she does, that this boy has become "the poster child of the Holocaust."[58] Hirsch points out that the proper context of this perpetrator photograph is too rarely explained in the texts that accompany this image's many appearances. She notes:

> The power of th[is] photograph derives from the effort . . . to reanimate the past by undoing the finality of the photographic "take." . . . As we look at photographic images, we hope nothing less than to undo the very progress of time. But in the context of the "total death" of Nazi genocide and its destruction not only of individuals but also of an entire culture, such an act of undoing seems doomed

and the photograph's finality utterly, hopelessly irrevocable. No retrospective irony can redeem or humanize the images produced in the context of Nazi genocide. These images can signify nothing less than the lethal intent that caused them and that they helped to carry out.[59]

The statement is bold, yet Hirsch is only voicing one possible attitude toward the images, one that is shared by Lanzmann, who in general chose to avoid including any such images in his films. This thinking, however, may need to change: viewers are capable of placing them in context and understanding them as images of subjects under duress. They may tell us something about the living conditions of Jews and the difficulties they faced, something more than only about the lethal gaze that captured them.[60] *Photographer* does not only show a view of the ghetto and the lives of its inhabitants, but by constellating Mostowicz's retrospective gaze with that of Genewein's camera, it becomes a film about the decisions these people faced, particularly the decisions made by the German and Austrian ghetto administrators, by the members of the Jewish Council, and by Mostowicz, the doctor whose voice is, more than any other, at the film's center. These people acted in ways that may be truly incomprehensible; owing to the extreme conditions, we cannot put ourselves in their shoes, and this comes into sharp relief as we watch and listen to a survivor gaze back at that past, 54 years later. *Photographer* is thus about photographs—what they tell us, and what they fail to tell us—but it is also about the lack of clarity with which the events of that time can be viewed.

Because the film is concerned with an overall lack of moral certitude, specifically with the decisions made by compromised members of the Jewish Council in an extreme situation in which the traditional moral codes do not apply, the film's use of color is exceptionally suggestive. Its images alternate between the saturated color photographs taken by Genewein on AGFA film, and moving images, both of Polish streets and of Mostowicz himself, which are projected in black and white. The black-and-white images were filmed in the late 1990s and they appear odd because of their artificially heightened contrast. Although Jablonski concerns himself with the expectations we bring to black-and-white images as opposed to color and thus with the iconic place occupied by such images in our cultural memory (as evinced by Spielberg's reliance on them in *Schindler's List*), the film's inversion between the grayish hues of the present and the robust colors of the past suggests something about the behavior of those represented, and especially about Mostowicz himself. As a doctor in the ghetto, he was also responsible for keeping track of the dead. Mostowicz was far from being a perpetrator, and at first pass it may appear that the film is starkly contrasting his position with Genewein's in that it is putting a perpetrator and a victim in dialogue. Listening more closely to Mostowicz's account, however, reveals that his position as a survivor and, at times, as a privileged prisoner placed him between two realms. He occupied a neither-nor space associated with both healing and harming, with perpetration and victimhood, and with life and death. The black and white in which he is filmed, therefore, has to be read as an indication of the shades of gray with which he lived.

When we first meet Mostowicz, he is trying to "place himself" in this reality, but he is finding it difficult. We then hear other voices, among them Genewein's. As in *A Film Unfinished*, an actor has been engaged to perform the part of the departed cameraman. The actor voicing Genewein's role tells us, in the first-person, that he is an Austrian and a Roman Catholic, and he explains that Łódź was not a concentration camp, but rather a closed district, or a small Jewish town. These claims, particularly the first of them, are Nazi euphemisms—that is: lies—although it is likely that Genewein believed in their truth when he wrote such things down. A "closed district" is an odd way of expressing the fact that he oversaw a prison, and the idea that it was akin to a small Jewish town perpetuates the myth that these prisons were like other communities, because much of the self-regulation within their walls was left to Jews themselves. The idea that it was a self-determining community, an idea that Mostowicz's testimony contradicts in the film, recalls similar confusion about Theresienstadt. Ruth Klüger argues that in this case, even the commonly used term ghetto is itself a euphemism, especially where Theresienstadt is concerned (because the word ghetto does not typically mean a prison). The same logic can be applied to Łódź. Even calling it a ghetto misleads. Klüger described Theresienstadt in terms one might use for Łódź as well: it was an adjunct to the concentration camp system, or, in harsher terms, it was "the stable that supplied the slaughterhouse."[61]

Throughout *Photographer*, viewers are likely to perceive Genewein as a murderous bureaucrat. As the film's Polish title *Fotoamator* reminds us, he is an *amateur* photographer, but by the film's end we have also come to think of him as an amateur killer. The image among his own slides in which he appears seated at his writing desk highlights the extent to which he can be seen as a desk-murderer, and because he was a Nazi and because he was clearly, owing to his role in the administration of the ghetto, complicit in deaths by shooting and starvation, it is difficult not to think of his camera as a metonymic extension of

Nazi weaponry. Between the many hours he spent justifying the exploitation of Jewish labor and studying the proper number of German bullets that may be expended in order to punish the most minor of ghetto offenses, Genewein took his pictures. Though he did not pull a trigger, it would not seem that there is all that much space for him in the realm of moral ambiguity Primo Levi referred to as "the gray zone."

Where Levi describes the gray zone in his famous memoir *The Drowned and the Saved*, he first, after discussing the morally tainted Kapos, describes the dilemmas faced by Miklós Nyiszli, a Jewish prisoner at Auschwitz, who, like Mostowicz in Łódź, survived by plying what he could of his craft. In Nyiszli's case, in part to protect his family members, he worked under Mengele's supervision, and thus was in the position of aiding the most sadistic of Nazi tormentors. For his part, Levi tries to understand the difficult position in which the doctor was placed, which was akin to that of the members of the Sonderkommando, who, under duress, burned and otherwise disposed of the bodies of seemingly innumerable Jews. Levi summarizes that the Nazi gesture—co-opting those who would be their blameless victims and making them complicit in their crimes—is an act that says: "We have embraced you, corrupted you, dragged you to the bottom with us. You are like us, you proud people: dirtied with your own blood, as we are. You too, like us and like Cain, have killed the brother. Come, we can play together."[62] Because it was a crime of such long duration—because the torments of the ghetto lasted from its opening in the early months of 1940 until its near total liquidation in the summer of 1944—there were many opportunities for Jews to be made complicit in crimes against one another, for some Jews to be forced to make decisions and choices concerning which ones would be deported and which ones would be saved, and for acts of self-preservation, only some of which would ever be comprehensible in retrospective analysis.

The most notorious and perhaps most paradigmatic case of co-opted Jewish leadership was that of Chaim Rumkowski, the Jewish businessman who headed the Council of Elders in the Łódź Ghetto, and whose name is synonymous with what is today viewed as its corrupt leadership. Rumkowski appears in Genewein's photographs and in one image in particular, one that is included in *Photographer*: he appears in a coach with a driver (Figure 5.5) and the soundtrack features Rumokwski's words in Yiddish—communicating thus not with the Germans but with the Jewish prisoners—explaining about the necessity of ridding the ghetto of undesirables. The image along with the soundtrack confirms suspicions that he had mistaken himself for a monarch. In Dawid Sierakowiak's diaries from

Figure 5.5 Mordechai Chaim Rumkowski is driven in a horse-drawn carriage through a street of the Łódź Ghetto. Slide Łódź A172. Courtesy Jüdisches Museum Frankfurt. Frankfurt am Main.

that time, Rumkowski makes frequent appearances as a tormentor. Sierakowiak describes him as a sadistic moron who was intent on squeezing the last bits of productivity out of the workshops.[63] Hannah Arendt also had harsh words about him, recalling that he was called "Chaim I," that he "issued currency notes bearing his signature and postage stamps engraved with his portrait," and she noted that he "rode around in a broken-down horse-drawn carriage."[64] Levi, who could write quite sympathetically about even the worst human beings, describes how Rumkowski tried to bargain with the Germans, who "kept exacting more and more cloth from Łódź and from him ever more numerous contingents of useless mouths (children, old and sick people) to send to the gas chamber in Treblinka and, later on, Auschwitz."[65] Levi writes generously that Rumkowski was neither "a monster, nor a common man" and that in such circumstances "the intoxication with power is so powerful as to prevail even under conditions seemingly designed to extinguish all individual will."[66] He concludes, "We are all mirrored in Rumkowski, his ambiguity is ours, it is our second nature, we hybrids molded from clay and spirit."[67] In *Photographer*, the central figures, Mostowicz, Rumkowski, Genewein, and Hans Biebow, the leader of the NS administration in the ghetto, are all subjected to (and in the case of the first two, one might dare to say, victimized by) the unusual and unprecedented conditions. One should not lose sight of the extent to which men such as Genewein and Biebow were perpetrators, yet, to apply Levi's metaphor: their decisions, like the others, were molded after the harshness of the circumstances.

Biebow, the Nazi whose bureaucratic instructions can be heard throughout the film, was most directly associated with starving the ghetto's population, and Rumkowski, by most accounts, was his accomplice. Biebow is said to have profited from the work done by the forced laborers in the ghetto and to have skimped on their sustenance, keeping the difference for himself. From this perspective, he and Rumkowski were involved in conspiracy and theft. The historian Saul Friedländer writes about the Warsaw and Łódź ghettos:

> From the outset the ghettos were considered temporary means of segregating the Jewish population before its expulsion. Once they acquired a measure of permanence, however, one of their functions became the ruthless and systematic exploitation of part of the imprisoned Jewish population for the benefit of the Reich (mainly for the needs of the Wehrmacht) at as low a cost as possible. Moreover, by squeezing the food supply and, in Łódź, by replacing regular money with a special ghetto currency, the Germans put their hands on most of the cash and valuables the Jews had taken along when driven into their miserable quarters.[68]

In Henia and Nochem Reinhartz's introduction to Mostowicz's memoir, they note that the ghetto paid for its own food "with the valuables that Rumkowski had extracted from Ghetto inmates with the help of the German authorities." When that source of revenue began to run out, Rumkowski came up with a plan "to transform the ghetto into a labor camp that worked for the Germans. He was helped in his plan by Biebow, who saw in the ghetto a skilled labor force that could be both a source of profit for himself and of benefit for Germany."[69] Levi summarizes that Biebow was "a small jackal too cynical to take race demonology seriously," and that he, "would have liked to put off forever the dismantling of the ghetto, which, for him, was an excellent business deal."[70]

From Rumkowski's own self-serving perspective, business and industry were a means of keeping the Jews alive, and his famous motto, "work is our only path" (*Unser einziger Weg ist Arbeit*), can be treated as a bold call to action. Labor, however, also meant the end for many, particularly those who were dying of fatigue and malnourishment. Rumkowski's phrase is thus no more historically credible or decent than the Nazis' own inscription on the gate at Auschwitz: "Work will set you free" (*Arbeit macht Frei*). In *Photographer*, documents concerning the work habits and amounts of work materials acquired are made audible and visible, and they all underscore the efficient forward progress of Genewein's operation. Genewein's documents count up the numbers of prisoners who were dying of tuberculosis, malnutrition, and heart failure, and Rumkowski was on the wrong side of this fiasco, taking responsibility for the ghetto's courts and the prisons.

The administrators' widespread theft became a numbers game. Balancing books legitimized the robbery. All of it surely felt legal, and the attitude is underscored in the film's constant return to issues of weights and measures: a letter from Josef Hämmerle, the administrator of the ghetto's main supply warehouse, to Rumkowski details how much precisely was collected from the Jews, and Rumkowski informs Himmler: "we're creating a city of labor" ("wir bauen eine Stadt der Arbeit auf"). We hear, in German, how the ghetto administrators were preparing to transport silver and to fill Biebow's orders for porcelain and silver-plated cutlery, and we hear how people of merit, especially Genewein, whose name is underlined in a relevant document, will benefit from the redistribution of property. The cut following this particular itemization is pointed: Rumkowski says in Yiddish that, "crime is the ghetto's grim page," and we hear charges leveled against a Jewish prisoner for dragging four potatoes from beyond the fence into the ghetto area. This, perversely enough, is an act of theft. The man is sentenced to 4 weeks in prison and the steel wire used in the crime was confiscated, but Jablonski makes it obvious who the criminals were. A desk covered in gold coins documents the administrators' success, and the portrait shown here of Genewein seated at this desk shows a man hard at work (Figure 5.6). In his apparently diligent commitment to industry he resembles a figure out of Dutch Baroque painting, but it is no surprise that Jablonski returns to that image at the film's end, when Genewein is quoted asking the court for mercy. The evidence is clear: every coin in front of him is further proof of his misdeeds.

From a distance of half a century, and while he is seated in a Warsaw living room, Mostowicz observes all of this. When he speaks, it is without the support of an orchestral, or any other, soundtrack, and he appears in a particularly high contrast black and white. He feels caught up in the corruption, not superior to it, and throughout the film he points to his own implication in the machinery of death; he either *felt* implicated or *was* implicated in decisions concerning life and death. Like Levi, he talks about how survival is often purely an accident, one that no one can account for. He explains that when he arrived in Auschwitz, having been deported there from the ghetto, he had only a pair of shoes and someone stole them. He cried like a child, he says, because a barefoot man was condemned to die. Someone then told him about how a prisoner in a neighboring block-house had a very nice pair of shoes, and that he was one of five or six persons

Figure 5.6 The Ghetto of Łódź—Head of The Finance Committee: See: Slide Łódź A033. Courtesy Jüdisches Museum Frankfurt. Frankfurt am Main.

who waited for the prisoner to die in order to be first to grab the shoes. Today he has blocked out the trauma of having to survive: "I still don't remember how it happened, but I got those shoes." Levi tells stories quite similar to this one, specifically about how his survival was predicated on taking water, bread, or shoes from others who were dying around him.[71] There was simply not enough to go around, and Levi uses it to explain the sense of shame that he and others felt upon their liberation from the camps—a shame that came of having been brought down to the level of the wretchedness around them.

Mostowicz may have experienced his implication more than others: as a doctor, he participated in deciding the fate of Jewish prisoners, and determining who was to live and who was to die. In his memoir, he describes a situation, one that he also narrates in Jablonski's film, in which he was forced to participate in the selection process—to say who was healthy enough to continue working, and who was to be deported. In the memoir, he reflects philosophically on whether he will, until the end of his life, wonder if he had not made a mistake by saving some at the expense of others.[72] He is told, by a man whom he is about to send to his death, that it is not incumbent upon the other victims to forgive him—to relieve him of the burden of responsibility for what he has done—and that he should have to come to terms with what he was doing regardless of whether the Germans were going to liquidate the ghetto, that is, regardless of whether everyone's impending death was equally inevitable.[73]

Genewein is, of course, the accountant of Łódź, but the fact that Mostowicz issued death certificates and was responsible for keeping track of the dead made him a sort of accountant as well. Mostowicz's Polish story thus has its parallels with Genewein's German and Rumkowski's Yiddish one. The doctor explains that all death "had to be treated in the accurate German manner," and he "considered it his duty to verify each reported death."[74] He was also implicated in Rumkowski's famous bargain with the Germans in which he called for the deportation of 20,000 Jews including 13,000 children and elderly victims in order to spare the remainder of the ghetto. Rumkowski made a horrible decision and it was a horrendous deal to have to have made. He pled, in Yiddish, with those listening, "put yourself in my position and think logically and you yourself will come to the conclusion that you cannot act differently, because the number of the portion that can be saved is much larger than the part that must be surrendered."[75] In *Photographer*, Mostowicz reveals that he was behind the scenes at that infamous moment, but that he did nothing to prevent it. He explains to the camera that he had no children, no elderly or sick relatives, and that he was personally under no threat. "There was no alternative," he says, "it was an utter disgrace."

In a critical reading of the film, Tomasz Łysak notes that at a key point, when Mostowicz admits to not having uttered a word against Rumkowski's plan, "he points to the camera operator, searching for an audience willing to take pains to comprehend his position in the Ghetto at the time."[76] If he had not, up to that point, been caught up in the machinery of complicity, then here he makes it clear: he was party to the most difficult and controversial decision made by any Jewish council during the war, and his position—the position of a man we can understand, and whose voice is in dialogue with the perpetrator Genewein—is now suddenly shared with Rumkowski.[77] Does Mostowicz mean to exonerate Rumkowski? Does his sense of inner conflict, his ambivalence and guilt, wash away the distinctions between the world of the color photographs and the shades of gray with which memory now surrounds him? Much as Jablonski has surprised us with color slides, images that we are used to seeing in black and white, alongside black and white images of today, he has also succeeded in throwing our certain moral footing into disarray.

Although *Photographer* concerns itself with difficult subjects such as Genewein, Rumkowski, and the question of whether one can judge another's guilt and complicity in these circumstances, the film's most compelling subjects are the voiceless victims whose faces peer out from these slides. Even though an encounter with a photo or with an image set in motion by Jablonski's surveying camera cannot collapse time and undo the Holocaust, the film encourages us to excavate these images, examining them in terms of what those in them may or may not have known at the time. It is tricky to look at pictures from the past, particularly at these perpetrator images, because we can never truly understand the anxieties or expectations of those depicted, and, if we are circumspect, we may find it unjust to attribute our own thoughts and desires to them. We hope to reassure ourselves when we encounter these images, and imagining a hopeful or sorrowful address rising from the surface of a photo may be comforting. Yet Jablonski, by reversing our expectations, and by telling a story that is difficult to hear, forces us to examine how we see, and he, in this way, reminds us of the limitations on our own interpretive horizons.

Conclusion

In one particularly fascinating sequence in Lanzmann's documentary *Sobibor* (2001), survivor Yehuda Lerner, who participated in a prisoners' uprising at the Sobibor extermination camp, tells a memorable story about the moments immediately after his arrival there. Lanzmann first depicts the Sobibor train depot, and in keeping with his usual tendency, he shows us the station as it appears decades after the war, inconspicuous and overgrown. We hear the voice of Lanzmann's interpreter, translating the survivor's Hebrew into French, and she relates the salient details: the Germans yelled at the prisoners as they stepped from the train. One of the perpetrators came over and called for 60 strong men. Lerner volunteered, believing that if hard labor were involved, there would probably also be food. Once the Germans had settled on their workers, they sent the remaining deportees to their deaths. The sounds of those prisoners' screams, of men being taken away and then dying in gas chambers, were deliberately drowned out by the loud honking of a gaggle of geese that, according to Lerner, the Nazis had cultivated and used for precisely that purpose.

Not content simply to transmit aurally Lerner's vivid account in which human cries are covered over by those of agitated animals, Lanzmann provides us with a series of images that includes the placid portrait of the train station, as well as a gaggle of crying, snow white geese. As Lerner speaks, the director cuts away to a shot of more than a hundred frantically honking birds, and if one listens very closely, attempting to hear past the noise, one can still discern Lerner's voice, quietly recounting his story in Hebrew. The interview with Lerner was conducted in 1979 as part of the filming of *Shoah*, but these other images, specifically those of the station and the geese, were filmed later, around the time Lanzmann was reediting the interview and turning it into *Sobibor*.[1] Why, one might ask, does Lanzmann cut away to a shot of geese? Viewers surely know what geese look like and can picture them. To some the inclusion of the image will seem unnecessary, and, in re-creating a particularly horrible scenario, it might seem gratuitous. But Lanzmann favors complex constellations of sound and image, and when he cuts back to the geese a second time, a minute and a half after their first appearance, he slowly suppresses the sound of honking on the soundtrack until we hear nothing but the gentle hum of the breeze crossing the Polish landscape. Lerner's testimony, which is initially subdued beneath the birds' cries, like the cries of the dying deportees, is, in this second instance, again obscured. The witness's voice, along with all other sounds apart from that of the wind, dies away.

The French film critic Jacques Mandelbaum compares Lanzmann's decision with the filmmaking styles of Ingmar Bergman and Arnaud Desplechin, who are better known for feature films than for documentaries. Mandelbaum argues that Lanzmann's use of sound returns a voice to the victims: "In appropriating this sensory illusion used by the Nazis to mask horror, and then technically altering its function, [Lanzmann] does much more than point out, in his own terms, the 'struggle' between the cries of the geese and the words of Lerner: he turns the subterfuge inside-out like a glove and makes the voiceless cries of the victims literally scream in the mute whiteness of the fowl filling the shot."[2] This may be so, but one might also read the montage differently: owing to Lanzmann's associative edit, we might feel, for a moment, the strange sensation that we are complicit. We listen and watch as Lerner's voice, that of a survivor, one among the few remaining witnesses, who now stands in for the victims, is gradually drowned out, redoubling the crime. Lanzmann opts to use these types of gestures, ones that produce contradictory or contingent sensations, rather than relying on footage from the past. His sound editing draws our attention to the difficulty in understanding that past from today's point of view. The practice highlights the gap between then and now, and the unbridgeable gulf that divides our time and place from that of the victims.

Released a short time later, Guillaume Moscovitz's documentary *Bełżec* (2005) can be viewed in light of Lanzmann's technique, but it is also worthwhile to think of it in relation to other postmillennial films, such as Rex Bloomstein's *KZ*, and it is best understood with an eye to both. The film consists mainly of interviews and testimonials featuring people who live near the site of one of the largest Nazi killing centers, now located in the southeast corner of Poland. It seems strange to call Bełżec a camp, because the Jews who arrived there were ushered directly from the railcars, which brought them only steps from their destination, into the killing rooms, where they were asphyxiated. Their experience did not resemble Primo Levi's or any of the Auschwitz survivors; there was little time to reflect on their imprisonment, and there was no survival. The Nazis' objective was to move the prisoners to the killing machinery as quickly as possible so they neither could make sense of what was happening nor would they have an opportunity to plan their escape. The camp operated over the course of 9 months in 1942 and was disassembled in 1943, whereupon the remaining corpses were burned. At least 550,000 victims died there, possibly many more. The Nazis aspired to leave no trace of what they had done. Of that large number of victims, there were only four survivors. Braha Rauffmann, the only one still alive, spent 20 months hiding in a tiny recess in a barn where she hardly had room to move her limbs. The other survivors' stories are just as dispiriting. Moscovitz's *Bełżec* thus cannot be a return documentary; barely anyone was left to return.

Bełżec transcends the typical talking head documentary in several ways, but one of those is its employment of sound, which is similar to Lanzmann's in *Sobibor*. At one point, a professor of archaeology named Andrzej Kola speaks directly to the camera about the difficulties he has had in locating the sites of mass graves, and he explains that they have located 31, some of which likely contain tens of thousands of victims. As he speaks, the camera cuts away from him and, as in *Sobibor*, the subject's voice now competes with other sounds. His audibility is threatened by the growl of a digging machine engaged in the daunting project of trying to expose another layer of the camp's past. This aural mise-en-scène, which makes it difficult to hear him above the noisy equipment, recalls not only *Sobibor*, but also a similar sequence from *KZ*, which was made in the same year as Moscovitz's film. There, the revving of an automobile engine drowns out the voice of Harald Brachner, Mauthausen's beleaguered tour guide. Moscovitz's decision, akin to Bloomstein's, treats the noise and interference as an allegory for the obstacles in the way of understanding a past that has either been erased, or about which no one wants to hear.

It is unsurprising that Moscovitz's film strongly resembles Lanzmann's because Lanzmann was its executive producer. But it is not Lanzmann's work, and there are substantial differences. In the film's interviews, the director subdues his own voice, barely allowing his French language inquiries to be heard. In this respect, his touch is lighter than Lanzmann's; he is a milder interlocutor. More important, however, is how *Bełżec* also conducts postmemorial interviews with nonwitnesses, ones who were completely unconnected to the event. In this way, the film reveals its interconnection with newer films. Through his interpreter, Moscovitz interviews a crew of Polish teenagers to whom the numbers of the dead are meaningless and abstract. Hanging out at the site of the camp, they seem confident that they know their history, and they demonstrate that they are not completely uninformed. When it comes to numbers, however, they become quickly confused. The main teenaged interview subject says that 150,000 Poles died at this site, but upon being corrected and told that the number was really 1500, he merely shrugs. For him, this was part of someone else's past, and it happened a long time ago.

In what may be an overt citation of *Shoah*'s most famous scene—Lanzmann's powerful barbershop interview with the survivor Abraham Bomba—Moscovitz includes an interview with a local hairstylist. The woman is no survivor or witness, but is rather a sympathetic present-day Pole. In permitting her to speak about how she perceives her community, the film's interviews more closely resemble the conversations with locals in *KZ* than the ones with witnesses in *Shoah*. Moscovitz's film here considers the present state of mind of those who live in the town. We watch the interview subject react to the thoughtless comments of a client who casually relates how his grandmother explained to him that Bełżec's victims arrived with gold and hid it where they could, and that after their deaths the residents went looking for it. He tells the story in a way he can perhaps comfortably live with: his grandmother's acquaintances were simply looking for gold in the woods. The truth is that they were likely rooting around for it in mass graves, digging through bones in the hopes of finding gold teeth and other valuable traces that had not been incinerated. Expressed in that way, the story is less droll. The historian Jan Gross has researched these crass treasure hunts, and he explains that when the Germans found out that nearby residents were digging in Bełżec's graves, they ushered them away, posting a guard for fear that the treasure hunters would unearth the evidence. According to Gross, "As soon as the guard fled before the approaching Red Army, the local people resumed their excavations."[3] In *Bełżec*, we may recognize a look of distaste in the hairstylist's eyes, but she does not articulate her reaction. Moscovitz hints at it and then moves on, letting the story's stench linger in the cinematic air.

At the end of *Bełżec* Moscovitz includes shots of two paintings that were made several years after the war by Wacław Kołodziejczyk, who lived near the camp when he was a child. One depicts a transport arriving and the other depicts a cremation in action. The painter's son, who is interviewed in Moscovitz's film, believes his father actually saw what he painted, because one could see into the camp from a hill in the distance, and because the depiction of the camp's proportions is relatively accurate. In the painting that depicts the bodies being burned, we see, at the far left, a bulldozer, which the painter's son specifically calls a *buldożer*. An industrial machine like that would have been required to move the corpses from the pits to the makeshift grills so that the air could reach them and prevent the fire from extinguishing itself. Claude Lanzmann would have likely discouraged Mocovitz from using archival images had he had them, but none of that matters; no such images exist. If there was a bulldozer at Bełżec, there is no photo of it. Ordinarily paintings in films mean many things, but here, like sketches in the sand, they signify the total absence of photographic evidence. This trace, the painted perpetrators' bulldozer, calls to mind the British one with which *Nazi Concentration Camps* concludes. Bełżec was not Belsen; the camp went unfilmed, there was no liberation. Whether we think of Lanzmann's work, Bloomstein's, or even George Stevens's compilation film, knowing the one helps us understand the other. Newer works are made more interesting when they appear in light of earlier ones. *Bełżec* has an esthetic and cinematic quality, and its wooded landscapes, at first blush, seem to speak for themselves, yet these films also carry others with them, and attending to those pasts enables new constellations of meanings to come into view.

Notes

Introduction

1. The text of the documents appears on screen at the beginning of *Nazi Concentration Camps* and is reproduced in the trial transcript. See *Trial of the Major War Criminals Before the International Military Tribunal. Nuremberg 14 November 1945–1 October 1946*, vol. 2 (Nuremberg: Secretariat of the Tribunal, 1947), 433–4.
2. Lawrence Douglas, *The Memory of Judgment: Making Law and History in the Trials of the Holocaust* (New Haven, CT: Yale University Press, 2001), 29. Ulrike Weckel notes that the affidavits, along with two other affidavits and the film's transcript were turned over to the court as defense exhibits. See Weckel, *Beschämende Bilder: Deutsche Reaktionen auf alliierte Dokumentarfilme über befreite Konzentrationslager* (Stuttgart: Franz Steiner Verlag, 2012), 116 n236.
3. Commander James Britt Donovan, Prosecution Counsel for the United States, told the court, "These motion pictures speak for themselves in evidencing life and death in Nazi concentration camps." See *Trial of the Major War Criminals*, 433.
4. Ibid., 432.
5. Douglas, *The Memory of Judgment*, 21. Weckel asserts that it served the purpose of shaming the defendants in "The Power of Images. Real and Fictional Roles of Atrocity Film Footage at Nuremberg," in *Reassessing the Nuremberg Military Tribunals: Transitional Justice, Trial Narratives, and Historiography*, eds. Kim C. Priemel and Alexa Stiller (New York: Berghahn Books, 2012), 221–48; here, 226. See also Weckel, *Beschämende Bilder*, especially 206. Christian Delage's documentary *Nuremberg: The Nazis Facing their Crimes* (2006), a highly edited compilation of John Ford's trial footage, agrees in part with Weckel's thesis, asserting that the courtroom screening was intended to bring the perpetrators "face to face with their deeds."
6. Raymond Daniell, "War-Crimes Court Sees Horror Films. Motion Pictures of German Concentration Camps are Displayed as Evidence," *The New York Times*, November 30, 1945, 6.
7. I do not mean to give the impression that the first survivor testimonies were heard at the time of the Eichmann Trial, only that they had not been so closely listened to before. On the various attempts to archive survivor testimony in the immediate aftermath of the war, see Laura Jockusch, *Collect and Record! Jewish Holocaust Documentation in Early Postwar Europe* (Oxford: Oxford University Press, 2012).

8 Joshua Hirsch applies the term "newsreel form" in *Afterimage: Film, Trauma, and the Holocaust* (Philadelphia: Temple University Press, 2004), 33–6. In *Beschämende Bilder*, Weckel calls them "compilation films" (*Kompilationsfilme*), 79–177. In writing of these films, I am referring mainly to Allied rather than Soviet ones. On the Soviet world's first encounters with images from the camps, see Jeremy Hicks, *First Films of the Holocaust: Soviet Cinema and the Genocide of the Jews, 1938–1946* (Pittsburgh, PA: University of Pittsburgh Press, 2012), especially 157–85.

9 Weckel's study deals with a number of additional compilation films, including *Deutschland erwache* (1945) and the French production *The Death Camps* (1945).

10 Although the authorship of the 21 minute long *Death Mills* has been contested, it is generally surmised that the theater and film director Hanuš Burger, born in Prague in 1909, was largely responsible for assembling the film, and that he worked with and received some supervision from Billy Wilder. Wilder played down his own role in the production, and Weckel argues convincingly that Burger played the larger role. See Weckel, *Beschämende Bilder*, 152–61. On the role of *Death Mills* in Wilder's body of work, see David Bathrick, "Billy Wilder's Cold War Berlin." *New German Critique* 37, 2 (2010): 31–47.

11 Kay Gladstone explains that attention was paid to the film in 1983 and 1984 even though it had been accessible at the museum for years. See Gladstone, "Memory of the Camps: The Rescue of an Abandoned Film," in *Concentrationary Cinema: Aesthetics as Political Resistance in Alain Resnais's* Night and Fog *(1955)*, eds. Griselda Pollock and Max Silverman (New York: Berghahn Books, 2011), 71–83; here, 71.

12 Gladstone studied the development of this film quite closely, interviewing Peter Tanner, the film's editor, who explains Hitchcock's limited role. See "Separate Intentions: The Allied Screening of Concentration Camp Documentaries in Defeated Germany in 1945–46: *Death Mills* and *Memory of the Camps*," in *Holocaust and the Moving Image: Representations in Film and Television Since 1933*, eds. Toby Haggith and Joanna Newman (London: Wallflower Press, 2005), 50–64; here, 56. Gladstone also makes this point in "Memory of the Camps," noting that Hitchcock was a "treatment advisor" and that he shot none of the camp footage himself (78). See also Steven Jacobs, "Hitchcock, the Holocaust, and the Long Take: *Memory of the Camps*." *arcadia* 45, 2 (2011): 265–76.

13 Gladstone, "Separate Intentions," 56.

14 The narration of *Die Todesmühlen*, originally written by the German Jewish literary scholar Oskar Seidlin, is provided in Weckel's appendix (*Beschämende Bilder*, 611–15).

15 Weckel, *Beschämende Bilder*, 171. My translation. Weckel contests the often-repeated story that watching *Die Todesmühlen* was compulsory for Germans. According to her research, screenings in the American Zone in 1946 were mostly voluntary. See 25 and 505–6.

16 Weckel, *Beschämende Bilder*, especially 18.
17 Gladstone, "Separate Intentions," 61.
18 Ibid.
19 There has been a tremendous amount of research on this film. For a definitive account of the filmmakers' sources and the film's various versions, see Sylvie Lindeperg, *"Night and Fog": A Film in History*, trans. Tom Mes (Minneapolis, MN: University of Minnesota Press, 2014). For a study of the range of responses to the film, see the essays collected in *Uncovering the Holocaust: The International Reception of Night and Fog*, ed. Ewout van der Knaap (London: Wallflower Press, 2006).
20 Libby Saxton, "*Night and Fog* and the Concentrationary Gaze," in *Concentrationary Cinema*, eds. Pollock and Silverman, 140–51, especially 142–45. See also Debarati Sanyal, "Auschwitz as Allegory in *Night and Fog*," in *Concentrationary Cinema*, 152–82. Sanyal writes, "the perspectival shifts of *Night and Fog* periodically position the spectator as a collaborator or accomplice to the Nazi gaze" (153).
21 Griselda Pollock identifies the close-up as a detail from an identity photograph from the Auschwitz museum. See "Death in the Image: The Responsibility of Aesthetics in *Night and Fog* (1955) and *Kapò* (1959)," *Concentrationary Cinema*, eds. Pollock and Silverman, 258–301; here, 283.
22 Sanyal, "Auschwitz as Allegory," 157. Sanyal is paraphrasing Delbo's refrain "Try to look. Just try and see," which can be found in the prose poem "Evening." See Charlotte Delbo, *Auschwitz and After*, trans. Rosette C. Lamont (New Haven: Yale University Press, 1995), 79–86. See also Annette Insdorf, *Indelible Shadows: Film and the Holocaust*, 2nd edn (Cambridge: Cambridge University Press, 1989), 40 and 213.
23 Lanzmann has expressed some antipathy toward *Night and Fog*. He once forced a Parisian theater in 1987 to pull the film when he discovered it was playing back to back with *Shoah*. See Vincent Lowy, *L'histoire infilmable. Les camps d'extermination Nazis à l'écran* (Paris: L'Harmattan, 2001), 85–6.
24 Stuart Liebman puts the issue clearly, noting that Lanzmann's strictures "effectively consign to oblivion countless films about the Holocaust that do not depend on oral testimony, that have used archival footage, or that attempt to re-create or imagine stories about the experience of Jews during the most harrowing period of their existence in modern times." Liebman, "Historiography/Holocaust Cinema: Challenges and Advances," in *Cinema and the Shoah: An Art Confronts the Tragedy of the Twentieth Century*, ed. Jean-Michel Frodon (Albany, NY: State University of New York Press, 2010), 205–16; here, 206.
25 Henry W. Pickford, *The Sense of Semblance: Philosophical Analyses of Holocaust Art* (New York: Fordham University Press, 2013), 177.
26 See Georges Didi-Huberman, *Images in Spite of All: Four Photographs from Auschwitz*, trans. Shane B. Lillis (Chicago: University of Chicago Press, 2008), 100.

27 See Claude Lanzmann, Ruth Larson and David Rodowick, "Seminar with Claude Lanzmann, 11 April 1990." *Yale French Studies* 79 (1991): 82–99; here, 99.
28 This is a paraphrase of Didi-Huberman's conclusion in "The Site, Despite Everything," trans. Stuart Liebman, in *Claude Lanzmann's* Shoah*: Key Essays*, ed. Stuart Liebman (Oxford: Oxford University Press, 2007), 113–23; here, 122. The essay originally appeared in 1995.
29 Cornelia Brink, "Secular Icons: Looking at Photographs from Nazi Concentration Camps." *History & Memory* 12, 1 (2000): 135–50; here, 144.
30 The term "perpetrator images" is from Marianne Hirsch. See *The Generation of Postmemory: Writing and Visual Culture after the Holocaust* (New York: Columbia University Press, 2012), 133–9.
31 For discussions of ben-Menachem and Grossman's ghetto photography, see Janina Struk, *Photographing the Holocaust: Interpretations of the Evidence* (London: I.B. Tauris, 2004), 92–4 and 86–91, respectively.
32 See Didi-Huberman, *Images in Spite of All*, 68–9.
33 Zachary Braiterman explores the term "sublime" as I am using it here in "Against Holocaust-Sublime: Naïve Reference and the Generation of Memory." *History & Memory* 12, 2 (2000): 7–28.
34 Benjamin Murmelstein died in 1989. Theresienstadt is often referred to as a ghetto, but "camp" might be more accurate. Ruth Klüger writes, "a ghetto doesn't normally mean a prison." In her memoir she refers to it as "the so-called ghetto of Theresienstadt." See *Still Alive: A Holocaust Girlhood Remembered* (New York: Feminist Press at the City University of New York, 2003), 70–1.
35 For background on the propaganda film, see Brad Prager, "Interpreting the Visible Traces of Theresienstadt," *Journal of Modern Jewish Studies* 7, 2 (2008): 175–94.
36 Lutz Niethammer addresses the question in "Widerstand des Gesichts? Beobachtungen an dem Filmfragment 'Der Führer schenkt den Juden eine Stadt.'" *Journal Geschichte* 2 (1989): 34–47.
37 Saxton, *Haunted Images*, 2.
38 Ibid.
39 Didi-Huberman, *Images in Spite of All*, 21.
40 Ibid., 26 and 66–7, respectively.
41 Claude Lanzmann, *The Patagonian Hare: A Memoir*, trans. Frank Wynne (New York: Farrar, Straus and Giroux, 2012), 411.
42 Marcel Ophüls praised *Shoah* upon its release in 1985 as "the greatest documentary about contemporary history ever made, bar none, and by far the greatest film I've ever seen about the Holocaust." See Ophüls, "Closely Watched Trains," in *Claude Lanzmann's* Shoah*: Key Essays*, ed. Stuart Liebman, 77–87;

here, 78. Didi-Huberman elaborates on Lanzmann's debt to Ophüls's style, referring to Ophüls as Lanzmann's "true master." *Images in Spite of All*, 132.

43   Axel Bangert, Robert S. C. Gordon and Libby Saxton, "Introduction," *Holocaust Intersections: Genocide and Visual Culture at the New Millennium*, eds. Axel Bangert, Robert S. C. Gordon and Libby Saxton (London: Legenda, 2013), 1–21; here, 5.

44   I have in mind Niklas Luhmann, whose systems are communicative models wherein first-order observations concentrate on what is perceived, while second-order observations look at those first-order perceptions from the outside, viewing them as restrictive sets of choices. Each new order of observation steps outside the last and looks back in. See *Art as a Social System*, trans. Eva M. Knodt (Stanford: Stanford University Press, 2000), 62–3.

45   Michael Rothberg, for example, describes the changing perception of testimony in connection with the development of cinéma vérité in *Multidirectional Memory: Remembering the Holocaust in the Age of Decolonization* (Stanford, CA: Stanford University Press, 2009), 188–98.

46   See the record at the United States Holocaust Memorial Museum (USHMM), under the title "Juden Exekution in Libau 1941." http://www.ushmm.org/online/film/display/detail.php?file_num=556.

47   Reinhard Wiener, "Mr Wiener's Interview Re Libau," Transcribed March 1992. Interview originally held on September 27, 1981. Document available at ushmm.org: http://www.ushmm.org/online/film/display/detail.php?file_num=5507; see especially 7.

48   Hirsch, *Afterimage*, 14. The term "vicarious trauma" comes from Lisa MacCann and Laurie Anne Pearlman, "Vicarious Traumatization: A Framework for Understanding the Psychological Effects of Working with Victims." *Journal of Traumatic Stress* 3, 1 (1990): 130–49.

49   Bill Nichols, *Introduction to Documentary*, Second edn (Bloomington, IN: Indiana University Press, 2010), 14.

50   Lanzmann expresses his belief that *Shoah* is not a documentary. He prefers to call it "a fiction rooted in reality [*fiction du réel*]." Contrary to his contention, I am treating it as a documentary here and throughout. See Marc Chevrie and Hervé Le Roux, "Site and Speech: An Interview with Claude Lanzmann about *Shoah*," trans. Stuart Liebman, in *Claude Lanzmann's* Shoah: *Key Essays*, ed. Stuart Liebman, 37–49; here, 44.

51   See Michael Renov's description of documentary as describable in terms of four central modalities of desire. He specifically mentions *Night and Fog* as a film that desires to "persuade or promote." See Renov, "Toward a Poetics of Documentary," in *Theorizing Documentary*, ed. Michael Renov (New York: Routledge, 1993), 12–36; here, 30.

52 Sylvie Lindeperg, "*Night and Fog*: Inventing a Perspective," in *Cinema & the Shoah*, ed. Jean-Michel Frodon, 71–91; here, 85. See also Weckel, who cites reports of the bulldozer driver's reluctance (*Beschämende Bilder*, 66n82 and 123).

53 Pollock, "Death in the Image," *Concentrationary Cinema*, 287. She offers a gendered reading of subsequent uses of the photo. Lindeperg argues that the critical attacks on the image's placement are "not entirely justified," although she agrees that the film's "somewhat confused narrative" may be "indicative and symptomatic of the hesitations that surfaced during scriptwriting" ("*Night and Fog*: Inventing a Perspective" [81]).

54 Didi-Huberman, *Images in Spite of All*, 67.

55 Thomas Trezise, *Witnessing Witnessing: On the Reception of Holocaust Survivor Testimony* (New York: Fordham University Press, 2013), 1. See also Rothberg, *Multidirectional Memory*, especially 175–9.

56 See Aaron Kerner, *Film and the Holocaust: New Perspectives on Dramas, Documentaries, and Experimental Films* (New York: Continuum, 2011), 15–30.

57 Bhaskar Sarkar and Janet Walker, "Introduction: Moving Testimonies," in *Documentary Testimonies: Global Archives of Suffering*, eds. Bhaskar Sarkar and Janet Walker (New York: Routledge, 2010), 1–34; here, 7.

58 Discussing testimony in Holocaust films, Kerner writes that the documentarian adds content to testimony by incorporating it into a frame. "Transmitting factual events necessitates a degree of deformation in order to make them intelligible—structuring information into a narrative" (*Film and the Holocaust*, 210).

59 Noah Shenker writes about the United States Holocaust Memorial Museum's ways of meeting the challenges of filming talking heads. See Shenker, "Embodied Memory: The Institutional Mediation of Survivor Testimony in the United States Holocaust Memorial Museum," *Documentary Testimonies* 35–58, especially 46–8.

60 Sarkar and Walker, "Introduction," 8.

61 Stuart Liebman writes that Lanzmann's approach "explode[s] certain features of the talking heads genre," and that those who liken it to that earlier form are missing its compositional complexity. See Liebman, "Introduction," *Claude Lanzmann's* Shoah: *Key Essays*, 3–24; here, 16. See also Tim Cole, who examines the importance of visits for Auschwitz as a landscape that awakens memory experiences in "Crematoria, Barracks, Gateway: Survivors' Return Visits to the Memory Landscapes of Auschwitz." *History & Memory* 25, 2 (2013): 102–31.

62 Janet Walker, "Moving Testimonies: 'Unhomed Geography' and the Holocaust Documentary of Return," in *After Testimony: The Ethics and Aesthetics of Holocaust Narrative for the Future*, eds. Jakob Lothe, Susan Rubin Suleiman and James Phelan (Columbus, OH: Ohio State University Press, 2012), 269–88; here, 273.

63 Siegfried Kracauer, "Photography," trans. Thomas Y. Levin, *Critical Inquiry* 19, 3 (1993): 421–36; here, 426.

64 For a more detailed account of these terms, see Nichols, *Introduction to Documentary*, especially Chapter 6 (142–71). Kerner also relies on Nichols's terms to categorize Holocaust documentaries. See 177–80.
65 Siegfried Kracauer, *Theory of Film: The Redemption of Physical Reality* (Oxford: Oxford University Press, 1960), 202–3.
66 Nichols, *Introduction to Documentary*, 148.
67 Ibid., 206–7.
68 Hirsch writes about *Night and Fog*: "The commentary . . . repeatedly breaks away from the traditional chronicling and explanation of historical events, and enters into poetic mediations on the difficulties of historical memory" (*Afterimage*, 42).
69 Eric Kligerman, "Celan's Cinematic: Anxiety of the Gaze in *Night and Fog* and 'Engführung,'" *Visualizing the Holocaust*, eds. David Bathrick, Brad Prager and Michael D. Richardson (Rochester, NY: Camden House, 2008), 185–210; here, 189. Kerner also discusses the resemblance to the Van Gogh painting, noting that Van Gogh shot himself not long after completing it (*Film and the Holocaust*, 235).
70 Jakob Lothe, Susan Rubin Suleiman and James Phelan, "'After' Testimony: Holocaust Representation and Narrative Theory," *After Testimony: The Ethics and Aesthetics of Holocaust Narrative for the Future*, eds. Jakob Lothe, Susan Rubin Suleiman and James Phelan (Columbus, OH: Ohio State University Press, 2012), 1–19; here, 2.
71 Berel Lang, *Act and Idea in the Nazi Genocide* (Syracuse, NY: Syracuse University Press, 2003), 81.
72 Jean-Paul Sartre, *On Genocide* (Boston: Beacon Press, 1968), 57. Quoted in Lang, *Act and Idea*, 10.
73 Didi-Huberman, *Images in Spite of All*, 58.
74 Hirsch, *The Generation of Postmemory*, 7–8.
75 Gary Weissman makes a stronger distinction than filliation and affiliation, referring to "the second generation" and "nonwitnesses." See Weissman, *Fantasies of Witnessing: Postwar Efforts to Experience the Holocaust* (Ithaca: Cornell University Press, 2004), 18.
76 Hirsch, *The Generation of Postmemory*, 5.
77 Andrea Liss, *Trespassing Through Shadows: Memory, Photography, and the Holocaust* (Minneapolis, MN: University of Minnesota Press, 1998), 86.
78 Jean Améry, *At The Mind's Limits: Contemplations by a Survivor on Auschwitz and Its Realities*, trans. Sidney Rosenfeld and Stella P. Rosenfeld (Bloomington, IN: Indiana University Press, 1980), 33.
79 "Fantasies of witnessing" is Weissman's term. On "prosthetic memory," see Alison Landsberg, *Prosthetic Memory: The Transformation of American Remembrance in the Age of Mass Culture* (New York: Columbia University Press, 2004).

80 Philippe Mesnard, "La mémoire cinématographique de la Shoah," *Parler des camps, penser les génocides*, ed. Catherine Coquito (Paris: Éditions Albin Michel, 1999), 473–90; here, 487. Mesnard's number is cited in Didi-Huberman, 214n45.
81 Tobias Ebbrecht, *Geschichtsbilder im medialen Gedächtnis. Filmische Narrationen des Holocaust* (Bielefeld: Transcript Verlag, 2011), especially 25–45.

Chapter 1

1 I am referring to Rex Bloomstein's *KZ* (2005), Ra'anan Alexandrowicz's *Martin* (1999), Romuald Karmakar's *Land of Annihilation* (2004), and Jes Benstock's short film *The Holocaust Tourist* (2005).
2 Ruth Margalit, "Should Auschwitz Be a Site for Selfies?" newyorker.com, June 26, 2014. http://www.newyorker.com/online/blogs/culture/2014/06/should-auschwitz-be-a-site-for-selfies.html.
3 Henryk M. Broder, "Auschwitz ist heute ein Disneyland des Todes," *Die Welt*, January 27, 2014. http://www.welt.de/kultur/article124251623/Auschwitz-ist-heute-ein-Disneyland-des-Todes.html. This is part of the argument Broder makes in his *Vergesst Auschwitz! Der deutsche Erinnerungswahn und die Endlösung der Israel-Frage* (Munich: Albrecht Knaus, 2012). On Broder's anxiety about left wing anti-Semitism, see Roland Dollinger, "Anti-Semitism *Because of* Auschwitz: An Introduction to the Works of Henryk M. Broder," in *Rebirth of a Culture: Jewish Identity and Jewish Writing in Germany and Austria Today*, eds. Hillary Hope Herzog, Todd Herzog and Benjamin Lapp (New York: Berghahn Books, 2008), 67–82.
4 See Tim Cole, *Selling the Holocaust: From Auschwitz to Schindler—How History is Bought, Packaged, and Sold* (New York: Routledge, 1999), 100. His italics. Cole describes pilgrimages to it by Catholics as well as Jews, starting in the 1970s. See 101–2.
5 Originally published as "At Auschwitz, a Discordant Atmosphere of Tourism," *New York Times*, November 3, 1974, 14.
6 The quotation cited by Sontag originally appeared in McLuhan, Marshall and Harley Parker, *Counterblast* (Toronto and Montreal: McClelland Stewart, 1969), 135.
7 The title of the work is *Atlas. Zusammengestellt von deutschen Autoren* (Berlin: Wagenbach, 1965). No author or editor is named.
8 See Peter Weiss's essay "Meine Ortschaft," in his anthology *Rapporte* (Suhrkamp: Frankfurt a.M., 1968), 113–24. Also published as "My Place," trans. from the German by Roger Hillman, in *TRANSIT* 4, 1 (2008): 1–14.
9 F. K. Stanzel, *A Theory of Narrative* (Cambridge: Cambridge University Press Archive, 1986), 232–4. Stanzel borrows the term "camera-eye" from Norman Friedman's "Point of View in Fiction: The Development of a Critical Concept." *PMLA* 70, 5 (1955): 1160–84.

10 Weiss, "My Place," 6.
11 Ibid., 9. Italics added.
12 Stanzel here acknowledges that he is following Christian Paul Casparis. See *A Theory of Narrative*, 234.
13 The connection to *Night and Fog* is made by Hillman as well. See Weiss, "My Place," 1.
14 Ibid., 13.
15 Gary Weissman, *Fantasies of Witnessing: Postwar Efforts to Experience the Holocaust* (Ithaca and London: Cornell University Press, 2004), 2. Weissman is citing Martin H. Lax, *Caraseu: A Holocaust Remembrance*. With Michael B. Lax (Cleveland, OH: Pilgrim Press, 1996).
16 Weissman, *Fantasies of Witnessing*, 192.
17 On how Austrians see themselves as victims, see Karl Stuhlpfarrer, "Österreich," in *Verbrechen erinnern: Die Auseinandersetzung mit Holocaust und Völkermord*, eds. Volkhard Knigge and Norbert Frei (Munich: Beck, 2002), 233–52, especially 235.
18 According to Berel Lang, establishing what *happened* is "the single most important task of all writing about that event." See Lang, *Act and Idea in the Nazi Genocide* (Chicago: University of Chicago Press, 1990), 81. Lang's italics.
19 I am referring here to "trauma culture" as described by Anne Rothe in *Popular Trauma Culture: Selling the Pain of Others in the Mass Media* (New Brunswick, NJ: Rutgers University Press, 2011), see especially 7–8.
20 Writing in 1999 Jay David Bolter and Richard Grusin observe: "all mediation is remediation." They add, "Our culture conceives of each medium or constellation of media as it responds to, redeploys, competes with, and reforms other media. . . . [O]urs is a genealogy of affiliations, not a linear history, and in this genealogy, older media can also remediate newer ones. See Jay David Bolter and Richard Grusin, *Remediation: Understanding New Media* (Cambridge, MA: MIT Press, 1999), 55.
21 See Bill Nichols, *Introduction to Documentary*, 2nd edn (Bloomington, IN: Indiana University Press, 2010), especially Chapter 6, "How Can We Differentiate among Documentaries? Categories, Models, and the Expository and Poetic Modes of Documentary Film," 142–71.
22 We hear this mechanized voice later, as we are observing the tour. It appears to be greeting visitors to the memorial.
23 See David Thomas, *Vertov, Snow, Farocki: Machine Vision and the Posthuman* (New York: Bloomsbury, 2013). Along these lines Thomas describes some of Farocki's preoccupations—similar to those of Dziga Vertov—as "ones that explore the complex equation that exists between automated forms of industrial production, new labor practices, and the types of image recording and processing technologies implicated in these manufacturing processes" (231).

24 During an interview with the tour guides they indicate that some of their grandfathers were in the Waffen-SS or in the Wehrmacht. Panhölzl mentions that it is likely that his grandfather was in the "Viking Division" (the SS Panzer Division "Wiking").

25 I am deliberately recalling Leslie Morris's interpretation of the "hypnotic" images shot through a car window in Thomas Mitscherlich's German documentary *Journey into Life* (1996). See Leslie Morris, "Berlin Elegies: Absence, Postmemory, and Art after Auschwitz," in *Image and Remembrance: Representation and the Holocaust*, eds. Shelley Hornstein and Florence Jacobowitz (Bloomington, IN: Indiana University Press, 2003), 288–304; here, 294–95.

26 See J. Hillis Miller, "Imre Kertész's Fatelessness: Fiction as Testimony," *After Testimony: The Ethics and Aesthetics of Holocaust Narrative for the Future*, eds. Jakob Lothe, Susan Rubin Suleiman and James Phelan (Columbus, OH: Ohio State University Press, 2012), 23–51; here, 35.

27 Thomas Blum editorializes: "The Concentration Camp as a folkloric prop in a bar-song—how ignorant, how self-satisfied, how obtuse, how resistant to any thought must a population be, that they drink their apple cider while listening to such obscenities?" See "Mauthausen is' no' net untaganga!" *Jungle World* 5 (February 1, 2007), http://jungle-world.com/artikel/2007/05/19008.html.

28 Martin Walser, "Erfahrungen beim Verfassen einer Sonntagsrede," in *Die Walser-Bubis-Debatte. Eine Dokumentation*, ed. Frank Schirrmacher (Frankfurt: Suhrkamp, 1999), 7–17; here, 13.

29 Volkhard Knigge, "Gedenkstätten und Museen," in *Verbrechen erinnern. Die Auseinandersetzung mit Holocaust und Völkermord*, eds. Volkhard Knigge and Norbert Frei (Munich: Beck, 2002), 378–89; here, 384–5.

30 Theodor W. Adorno, "Education after Auschwitz," *Can One Live after Auschwitz? A Philosophical Reader*, ed. Rolf Tiedemann (Stanford, CA: Stanford University Press, 2003), 22. The essay is translated by Henry W. Pickford.

31 Ibid., 31.

32 James E. Young, *At Memory's Edge: After-Images of the Holocaust in Contemporary Art and Architecture* (New Haven, CT: Yale University Press, 2000), 122. See also much more about Barbara Distel's discussion of this piece in her essay "Neue Formen der Erinnerung," in *Realität, Metapher, Symbol. Auseinandersetzung mit dem Konzentrationslager*. Dachauer Hefte, vol. 22 (Dachauer Hefte Verlag: Dachau, 2006), 3–10. Distel cites Gerz's work as being from 1972, but she also refers to a Munich exhibition of the work from 1977 (3).

33 Young, *At Memory's Edge*, 123.

34 Ibid., 124.

35 The timeline of Alexandrowicz's film is a little different than what one sees in the film. The timeline presented here—that the director met Zaidenstadt and later

returned to make a film about him—is based on my Skype conversation with Alexandrowicz, conducted on July 16, 2013.
36 Ra'anan Alexandrowicz, in discussion with the filmmaker, July 16, 2013.
37 Ra'anan Alexandrowicz, July 16, 2013. On this Israeli relation to memory, see Eyal Sivan's documentary *Izkor: Slaves of Memory* (1991), which was shot in April 1990 during the single month in which Israel commemorates Passover, the Day of Holocaust Commemoration, the Day of Commemoration of Israeli soldiers, and Israeli Independence Day. Sivan asks, with that film, whether Israel does not suffer beneath the weight of a surfeit of memory.
38 On "empathic unsettlement," see Dominick LaCapra, "Holocaust Testimonies: Attending to the Victim's Voice," in *Catastrophe and Memory: The Holocaust and the Twentieth Century*, eds. Moishe Postone and Eric Santner (Chicago: University of Chicago Press, 2003), 209–31; here, 223.
39 Timothy W. Ryback, *The Last Survivor: Legacies of Dachau* (New York: Vintage, 1999), 33.
40 Ryback, *The Last Survivor*, 118.
41 Ibid., 125.
42 Ra'anan Alexandrowicz, July 16, 2013.
43 Ibid.
44 Harold Marcuse, *Legacies of Dachau: The Uses and Abuses of a Concentration Camp, 1933–2001* (Cambridge: Cambridge University Press, 2001), 175.
45 Marcuse, *Legacies of Dachau*, 193–4.
46 Ibid., 194.
47 Ra'anan Alexandrowicz, July 16, 2013.
48 Peter Thompson's remarkable short documentary *Universal Hotel* (1986) deals with Rascher's experiments at Dachau. On that film, see Gary Weissman, "A Filmmaker in the Holocaust Archives: Photography and Narrative in Peter Thompson's *Universal Hotel*." *Post Script: Essays in Film and the Humanities* 32, 2 (2013): 34–52.
49 Ryback, *The Last Survivor*, 106–7.
50 Dr. Franz Blaha, the former camp inmate, said he had once conducted autopsies on victims in the gas chamber at the request of Rascher, who did not want to enter the chamber himself. Blaha subsequently "broadened his testimony" saying, "Later, many prisoners were killed in this way." See Falk Pingel, "Building X at Dachau: A Special Case," in *Nazi Mass Murder: A Documentary History of the Use of Poison Gas*, eds. Eugen Kogon, Hermann Langbein and Adalbert Rückerl (New Haven, CT: Yale University Press, 1993), 202–4; here, 204.
51 Alexandrowicz, July 16, 2013.
52 Herbert Obenaus, "Das Foto vom Baumhängen—ein Bild geht um die Welt." *Gedenkstättenrundbrief* 68 (October 1995): 3–8; here, 8.

53 See, for example, the photo's use in, Heinz Höhne, "Der Orden unter dem Totenkopf: Die Geschichte der SS." *Der Spiegel* 42 (October 10, 1966): 101.

54 Obenaus, "Das Foto vom Baumhängen," 8.

55 "Pole hanging" was a torture method in interrogation. Josef Seuß testified to it at the first Dachau trial in 1945 and it is detailed in Paul Martin Neurath, *The Society of Terror: Inside the Dachau and Buchenwald Concentration Camps*, eds. Christian Fleck and Nico Stehr (Boulder, CO and London: Paradigm, 2005). Neurath writes, "In my time the 'tree' was a regular punishment, usually given for one hour at a time. In addition, it was used as the most common means of extorting confessions whenever an investigation was underway. In earlier times, the 'tree' was used more irregularly; men were hung on the nearest tree whenever an officer deemed it advisable. They were often left hanging for hours, sometimes until they died" (89).

56 Jean Améry, *At The Mind's Limits: Contemplations by a Survivor on Auschwitz and Its Realities*, trans. Sidney Rosenfeld and Stella P. Rosenfeld (Bloomington, IN: Indiana University Press, 1980), 33.

57 Ulrike Weckel discusses this footage in particular, which purports to be of Dachau's gas chamber. Initial reports of survivors suggested the pile of corpses was the result of gassing, but these reports were later revised. See Weckel, *Beschämende Bilder*, 122 n249 and n250. Where the nearly identical shot is used in *Nazi Concentration Camps*, the floodlight is visible, but where it is used in *Death Mills*, it is mostly concealed.

58 See Ryback, *The Last Survivor*, 123–4.

59 Jenny Edkins, "Authenticity and Memory at Dachau." *Cultural Values* 5, 4 (2001): 405–20; here, 417.

60 Ryback, *The Last Survivor*, 192–3.

61 Document number 9933609. See also the entry on Munich-Allach in *The United States Holocaust Memorial Museum Encyclopedia of Camps and Ghettos, 1933–1945*, ed. Geoffrey P. Megargee (Bloomington, IN: Indiana University Press in association with the United States Holocaust Memorial Museum, 2009), 516–18.

62 ITS documents bearing the numbers 9894554 and 78798900 respectively.

Chapter 2

1 See "Schindler's List Tour Krakow," http://www.krakow-tours.com/tour/Schindlers_List-Krakow

2 Among the most critical readings of *Schindler's List* and its aftereffects are Tim Cole, *Selling the Holocaust: From Auschwitz to Schindler—How History Is Bought, Packaged, and Sold* (New York: Routledge, 1999), 73–94, and Gary Weissman,

Fantasies of Witnessing: Postwar Efforts to Experience the Holocaust (Ithaca, NY: Cornell University Press, 2004), 150–89.

3   Miriam Bratu Hansen, "*Schindler's List* Is Not *Shoah*: Second Commandment, Popular Modernism, and Public Memory," in *Visual Culture and the Holocaust*, ed. Barbie Zelizer (New Brunswick, NJ: Rutgers University Press, 2001), 127–51; here, 144 and 147. Originally published in *Critical Inquiry* 22 (1996): 292–312.

4   Janet Walker, *Trauma Cinema: Documenting Incest and the Holocaust* (Berkeley: University of California Press, 2005), 129.

5   Claude Lanzmann, "Holocauste, la représentation impossible," *Le Monde*, March 3, 1994, "Arts et Spectacles," 1.

6   Miriam Bratu Hansen, "*Schindler's List* Is Not *Shoah*," 143.

7   See Sara R. Horowitz, "But Is It Good for the Jews? Spielberg's Schindler and the Aesthetics of Atrocity," in *Spielberg's Holocaust: Critical Perspectives on Schindler's List*, ed. Yosefa Loshitzky (Bloomington, IN: Indiana University Press), 119–39; here, 123. Joshua Hirsch (in *Afterimage: Film, Trauma and the Holocaust* [Philadelphia: Temple University Press, 2004]) also points to this connection between the films (144 and 147), as does Tobias Ebbrecht (191).

8   See the testimony of Dr. Martin Foeldi from Session No. 53 of the Eichmann Trial, May 25, 1961: "After that I went on walking to the right and I saw how the boy was running. I wondered to myself how would he be able to find his mother there? After all, there were so many women and men, but I caught sight of my wife. How did I recognize her? My little girl was wearing some kind of a red coat. The red spot was a sign that my wife was near there. The red spot was getting smaller and smaller. I walked to the right and never saw them again." The transcript is available online at *The Nizkor Project: The Trial of Adolf Eichmann*, http://www.nizkor.org/hweb/people/e/eichmann-adolf/transcripts/Sessions/. Foeldi's testimony is mentioned in Haim Gouri's *Facing the Glass Booth: The Jerusalem Trial of Adolf Eichmann*, trans. Michael Swirsky (Detroit, MI: Wayne State University Press, 2004), 94, as well as in Deborah E Lipstadt's *The Eichmann Trial* (New York: Nextbook/Schocken, 2011), 98.

9   On *Schindler's List*'s apparent authenticity, particularly its resemblance to German *Wochenschauen* (weekly newsreels), see Karyn Ball, "For and Against the *Bilderverbot*: The Rhetoric of 'Unrepresentability' and Remediated 'Authenticity' in the German Reception of Steven Spielberg's *Schindler's List*," in *Visualizing the Holocaust: Documents, Aesthetics, Memory*, eds. David Bathrick, Brad Prager and Michael D. Richardson (Rochester, NY: Camden House, 2008), 162–84; here, 172–3.

10 Joshua Hirsch, *Afterimage*, 147–8. See also Yosefa Loshitsky, who makes a similar point about pastiche and Spielberg's use of different modes of black and white, in "Holocaust Others: Spielberg's *Schindler's List* versus Lanzmann's *Shoah*," in *Spielberg's Holocaust*, ed. Loshitsky, 109.

11 Omer Bartov explains that this patriotic song was not used in all versions of the film: its Israeli release omitted the song because for some Israelis it "came to symbolize first the euphoria of the Israeli victory of 1967 and then the bitter fruits of conquest, occupation, and repression of others by the young Jewish state." See "Spielberg's Oskar: Hollywood Tries Evil," in *Spielberg's Holocaust*, ed. Loshitsky, 41–60; here, 45.
12 On the idea that it represents a "destabilization," see Michael Rothberg's *Traumatic Realism: The Demands of Holocaust Representation* (Minneapolis, MN: University of Minnesota Press, 2000), 239.
13 Michael Rothberg compares *Schindler's List* to *Shoah*, both of which end in Israel, in *Traumatic Realism*: "Israel, as a presumed site of 'realness'—an originary site of testimony in *Shoah* and the end point or telos for both films—provides the supplement which allows the directors [Lanzmann and Spielberg], in their very different ways, to broach the problem of representing the Holocaust and, particularly in *Schindler's List*, to cross over the breach between aesthetics and reality, and between 'inauthentic' American Jew and survivor" (240).
14 Lanzmann, "Holocauste, la représentation impossible," 1.
15 In *Inheritance* Helen Jonas-Rosenzweig is referred to only as Helen Jonas.
16 See *Inheritance*, Director's Notes: http://www.inheritancedocumentary.com/project.php?p=inheritance.
17 Monika Göth describes in detail going alone to see *Schindler's List* in Nuremberg. See *"Ich muß doch meinen Vater lieben, oder?": Die Lebensgeschichte der Monika Göth, der Tochter des KZ-Kommandanten aus* Schindlers Liste (Frankfurt am Main: Eichborn, 2002), 19–22.
18 Urs Jenny, "Holocaust mit Happy-End?" *Der Spiegel* 21 (May 24, 1993): 208–13; here, 213. The description echoes the description given by Thomas Keneally in *Schindler's List*, "Oskar [Schindler] abominated Göth as a man who went to the work of murder as calmly as a clerk goes to his office," in *Schindler's List* (New York: Scribner, 2000 [orig. 1982]), 171.
19 Monika Knauss geb. Göth, "Rettung durch Schweigen." *Der Spiegel* 11 (March 14, 1983): 12.
20 She repeats statements similar to these in *"Ich muß doch meinen Vater lieben, oder?"* 70.
21 The confessional book, *"Ich muß doch meinen Vater lieben, oder?"* is a series of interviews and recollections assembled by Matthias Kessler. The interview appeared as a 2003 German documentary entitled *Amons Tochter (Amon's Daughter)*, directed by Kessler.
22 Jenny, "Holocaust mit Happy-End?" 210.
23 Hertwig defends her mother against her depiction in *Schindler's List* as "the whore of Płaszów." See *"Ich muß doch meinen Vater lieben, oder?"* (28).

24 Weissman writes, "Keneally met with Hirsch but Sternlicht, approached at the time she was mourning her husband's death, declined to be interviewed. Consequently, Sternlicht is absent from the novel as well as the film" (*Fantasies of Witnessing*, 156). Weissman is drawing on Elinor J. Brecher, *Schindler's Legacy: True Stories of the List Survivors* (New York: Dutton, 1994).

25 On this exaggeration see Weissman, *Fantasies of Witnessing*, 156–7, and Sara R. Horowitz, "But Is It Good for the Jews? Spielberg's Schindler and the Aesthetics of Atrocity," in *Spielberg's Holocaust: Critical Perspectives on Schindler's List*, ed. Yosefa Loshitzky (Bloomington, IN: Indiana University Press), 119–39; especially 126–8.

26 For background on the two, see David M. Crowe, who writes: "[Itzhak] Stern felt that what Helen Hirsch suffered under Amon Göth was 'more than ten lifetimes' worth of pain. This was why Stern thought that 'no one is more entitled to greater, stronger, more ardent admiration than Helen Horowitz.' But the same could be said for Göth's other Jewish maid, Helen Sternlicht Jonas-Rosenzweig, who served Göth almost as long as Helen Hirsch and suffered the same horrible mistreatment." *Oskar Schindler: The Untold Account of his Life, Wartime Activities, and the True Story Behind the List* (New York: Basic Books, 2004), 261–62.

27 Hertwig describes Blair's visit with Ruth Kalder in *Ich muß doch meinen Vater lieben, oder?* She mentions specifically that the discussion of Göth caught her mother off guard (201) and that she herself found Blair very nice (202). In a profile of Steven Spielberg for the UK edition of *Esquire*, Jon Blair wrote about flirting with Hertwig when he was there to film Kalder. He flirted "shamelessly" with this "tall, handsome woman in her mid to late thirties." He daydreams about seducing her, and then afterward revealing his Jewish origins. See Blair, "Spielberg Comes of Age." *Esquire* (London, England) 4, 2 (March 1994): 62–6; here, 64.

28 Kalder needed an affidavit from Göth's father, Franz Amon Göth, after the war, indicating that his son had planned to marry Kalder. With his help, she was able to keep the name. See Kessler, 103. Tom Segev (*Soldiers of Evil: The Commandants of the Nazi Concentration Camps* [New York: McGraw-Hill, 1987]) quotes an interview with Kalder, one that shows how taken she was with Göth, even decades after the war: "'[Göth] was an impressive man, tall, strong, the dream of any secretary,' she said" (153). Kalder continued: "It's true, I slept with many officers, but only until I found Göth, and he brought me a horse. Ah, yes, Göth—what a dream man. . . . 'It was a beautiful time,' his widow said, 'We enjoyed being together. My Göth was the king, and I was the queen. Who wouldn't have traded places with us?' She was only sorry that it all had ended, she said" (155).

29 The last letter exchange between Kalder and Göth is discussed in Johannes Sachslehner, *Der Tod ist ein Meister aus Wien. Leben und Taten des Amon Leopold Göth* (Styria: Wien, 2008), 362–5.
30 See Kessler, "*Ich muß doch meinen Vater lieben, oder?*" 124.
31 Kessler, "*Ich muß doch meinen Vater lieben, oder?*" 94–7.
32 Hertwig adds that she identified with Anne Frank, "because she fought with her mother, and her father was the saintly one, exactly as it was with me." See Kessler, "*Ich muß doch meinen Vater lieben, oder?*" 98.
33 Research has been done on the mother-daughter dynamic especially on the side of survivors, both in terms of postmemorial relations, which is central to Marianne Hirsch's work, particularly in *Family Frames: Photography, Narrative, and Postmemory* (Cambridge, MA: Harvard University Press, 1997), but also in terms of surviving pairs of mothers and daughters. On the latter, see Na'ama Shik, "Mother-Daughter Relationships in Auschwitz-Birkenau, 1942–1945." *Tel Aviver Jahrbuch für Deutsche Geschichte* 36 (2008): 108–27.
34 Crowe, *Oskar Schindler*, 262.
35 Delman says: "My experience going to Plaszow was both healing and traumatic. Hearing about my mother's experiences and actually seeing where it all took place made it more real for me. As a child of Holocaust survivors, I was able to block a lot of feelings growing up because it was too painful to comprehend what they went through and how they survived. My sister had a different experience; she was very affected by what she heard. She had and continues to have a difficult time with it all. I think this is true for many children of survivors—we too are traumatized people." See "A Daughter's Point of View," *POV* interview with Vivian Delman, December 10, 2008. http://www.pbs.org/pov/inheritance/special_survivor.php.
36 Hertwig's grandson, it turns out, also carries the family name. Against her protestations, her daughter Yvette named her son David Amon. See Kessler, 221–2.
37 Teege was born in 1970 in Munich as Jennifer Göth and soon after put up for adoption. In her memoir, *Amon: Mein Grossvater hätte mich erschossen* (written together with Nikola Sellmair [Reinbek: Rowohlt, 2013]), she recounts learning about her past by accidentally coming across her mother's 2002 interview book, and by subsequently watching Moll's *Inheritance* (18–19) and Jon Blair's documentary *Schindler: The Real Story* (120–2).
38 The daughter Hertwig gave up for adoption sees it this way as well. Teege writes about watching Moll's *Inheritance* and says that her biological mother looks "haggard" (*verhärmt*). She adds, "Her posture is strange. Her shoulders are bent as though she were bearing a heavy burden. I feel sorry for her." See Teege and Sellmair, *Amon*, 18 and 127.
39 Crowe, *Oskar Schindler*, 262.

40 These stories are also recounted in Johannes Sachslehner, *Der Tod ist ein Meister aus Wien*. Sachslehner describes the death of Jonas-Rosenzweig's mother (302–3) and the murder of Sztab (333–4).
41 On this torturous activity, see Crowe: "Göth would punish Helen Hirsch by making her run up three flights of stairs until she collapsed from exhaustion" (*Oskar Schindler*, 261).
42 Crowe writes about how Kalder attempted to save "Susanna" (Helen Rosenzweig, whom Göth named "Susanna" for his convenience) from punishment but then her conscience got the better of her such that she eventually betrayed her to Göth (*Oskar Schindler*, 264).
43 The controversy seems to stem from a British National Geographic documentary called *Bloody Tales*, in which it is maintained that "the video was from 1947 and shows Dr. Ludwig Fischer being hanged." See Becky Evans, "Amon Goeth: Did 'Executed' Nazi Criminal in *Schindler's List* Escape Justice?" *Mail Online*, March 21, 2013, http://www.dailymail.co.uk/news/article-2296911/Amon-Goeth-Did-executed-Nazi-murderer-Schindlers-List-escape-justice.html.
44 Crowe, *Oskar Schindler*, 286–7.
45 See Buddy Kite, "The Man Turning the History of Our Time into Art," *Esquire.com*, December 15, 2008, http://www.esquire.com/features/best-and-brightest-2008/video-artist-omer-fast-1208.
46 Mark Godfrey, *Abstraction and the Holocaust* (New Haven, CT: Yale University Press, 2007), 160.
47 See Cornelia Brink, "Secular Icons: Looking at Photographs from Nazi Concentration Camps." *History & Memory* 12, 1 (2000): 135–50. For prior, influential uses of the term "secular icon," Brink cites Vicki Goldberg, *The Power of Photography: How Photographs Changed Our Lives* (New York: Abbeville Press, 1991) and Patrick Maynard, "The Secular Icon: Photography and the Functions of Images." *The Journal of Aesthetics and Art Criticism* 42, 2 (1983): 155–69.
48 Godfrey, *Abstraction and the Holocaust*, 162.
49 Lawrence Baron argues against this position: "While many scholars faulted Spielberg for incarnating Nazi evil in the monstrous villain Amon Göth, they ignored or minimized the recurring scenes of the bureaucratic steps that preceded the Jews' liquidation." See *Projecting the Holocaust into the Present: The Changing Focus of Contemporary Holocaust Cinema* (Lanham, MD: Rowman and Littlefield, 2005), 211.
50 Bartov is using the term "drowned" in Primo Levi's sense, as it was used in *The Drowned and the Saved*, to refer to those who died in the camps. See Omer Bartov, "Spielberg's Oskar: Hollywood Tries Evil," in *Spielberg's Holocaust*, 47.
51 Bartov, "Spielberg's Oskar: Hollywood Tries Evil," 48.

52 The figure of Schindler was received warmly in Germany. The cover of *Der Spiegel* from February 21, 1994 featured a picture of Liam Neeson as Oskar Schindler and read: "The Good German—Spielberg's Holocaust Drama: Jews' Savior Schindler" ("Der gute Deutsche: Spielbergs Holocaust-Drama: Juden-Retter Schindler"). As to the implicit universalization—the de-Germanization—of the crime, Gertrud Koch observes: "On the front page of one of the most important conservative newspapers . . . was an article by one of the editors. . . . In it he wrote that *Schindler's List*, which he praised very highly, finally shows that all this bullshit the intellectuals tell about aesthetics after the Holocaust is just not true, because one can narrate it. What Spielberg has shown the world is there is nothing that can't be narrated. And therefore, it tells us that aesthetics in general has to come back to these kinds of conventional forms, you know, you have to have a nice beginning, you have to have a nice ending, and in between you squeeze a whole epoch and its horrors. And it's very convenient, let's say, for a German audience to see it this way. So, if this is true, that you can make out of the Holocaust a historical film with a proper closure, then probably the events themselves were not so singular in their monstrosity; you just have to package them differently." See Koch's contribution to the roundtable "Schindler's List: Myth, Movie, and Memory," *Village Voice*, March 29, 1994, 24–31; here, 30–1.
53 See Yosefa Loshitzky, "Holocaust Others: Spielberg's *Schindler's List* versus Lanzmann's *Shoah*," in *Spielberg's Holocaust*, 109–10.
54 Loshitzky, "Holocaust Others," 113.
55 Lanzmann, "Holocauste, la représentation impossible," 1.
56 Ibid.
57 On the television miniseries, the "Feuilleton" to which he refers, see Lanzmann, "From the Holocaust to the *Holocaust*." *Telos* 42 (1979/80): 137–43. In this piece he writes, "The Holocaust is unique in that it creates a circle of flames around itself, a limit which cannot be crossed because a certain absolute horror cannot be transmitted" (139). His critique of the television miniseries was originally published in *Les Temps Modernes*, June 1979.
58 For a close reading of Godard's inclusion of Holocaust imagery in his film, see Libby Saxton, *Haunted Images: Film, Ethics, Testimony and the Holocaust* (London and New York: Wallflower, 2008), 46–53.
59 Saxton, *Haunted Images*, 49.
60 Ibid., 49.
61 Ibid., 65. The quotation is from Colin MacCabe, *Godard: A Portrait of the Artist at 70* (London: Bloomsbury, 2004), 327.
62 See Tobias Ebbrecht, *Geschichtsbilder im medialen Gedächtnis. Filmische Narrationen des Holocaust* (Bielefeld: Transcript Verlag, 2011), 184. On this point

he is drawing on Jörg Schweinitz. See *Film and Stereotype: A Challenge for Cinema and Theory*, trans. Laura Schleussner (New York: Columbia University Press, 2011).

63 Gertrud Koch, "The Angel of Forgetfulness and the Black Box of Facticity: Trauma and Memory in Claude Lanzmann's *Shoah*." *History and Memory* 3, 1 (1991): 119–34; here, 123.
64 Bartov, "Spielberg's Oskar," *Spielberg's List*, 50.
65 Marianne Hirsch, *The Generation of Postmemory: Writing and Visual Culture After the Holocaust* (New York: Columbia University Press, 2012), 136.
66 An argument advanced by Bartov. See "Spielberg's Oskar," especially 48–9.
67 Gideon Lewis-Kraus, "Infinite Jetzt," in *In Memory: Omer Fast*, eds. Sabine Schaschl and Kunsthaus Baselland (Berlin: Green Box, 2010), 61.
68 See Duncan Wheeler, "Godard's List: Why Spielberg and Auschwitz Are Number One." *Media History* 15, 2 (2009): 185–203; here, 188–9.
69 I am drawing on an argument about "authentication" made by Andreas Huyssen with regard to Art Spiegelman's *Maus*. Huyssen observes that, "Documentary *authenticity* of representation can therefore not be [Spiegelman's] goal, but *authentication* through the interviews with his father is." See Huyssen. "Of Mice and Mimesis: Reading Spiegelman with Adorno." *New German Critique* 81 (2000): 65–82; here, 76.
70 Lanzmann, "Holocauste, la représentation impossible."
71 "*Schindler's List*: Myth, Movie, and Memory," *Village Voice*, March 29, 1994, 24–31; here, 26.
72 Again, see Lanzmann's reference to *Shoah* as "fiction rooted in reality" (*fiction du réel*) in "Site and Speech: An Interview with Claude Lanzmann about *Shoah*," trans. Stuart Liebman, Claude Lanzmann's *Shoah: Key Essays*, ed. Stuart Liebman, 37–49; here, 44.
73 Fast has explored the question of casting calls elsewhere, in particular in his video installation *The Casting* (2007) in which a US Army sergeant's memories are staged in a series of tableaux vivants. The testimony and staging are then intercut with footage that appears to be derived from the process of auditioning actors to participate in what we are seeing.
74 Here I am referring to Michael Renov's argument, where he notes that "Lanzmann has chosen to interview Bomba as he works, the repetition of the gesture helping to unleash memory." See Renov, *The Subject of Documentary* (Minneapolis, MN: University of Minnesota Press, 2004), 127.
75 Lawrence Baron, *Projecting the Holocaust into the Present*, 215.
76 Michael Rothberg writes about this destabilization in *Traumatic Realism* (239).

Chapter 3

1. See Eldad Beck, "The Nazi's Grandson," May 18, 2011, *ynetnews.com*, http://www.ynetnews.com/articles/0,7340,L-4070115,00.html
2. Jacques Derrida, *On Cosmopolitanism and Forgiveness*, trans. Michael Hughes (New York: Routledge, 2001), 32.
3. Simon Wiesenthal, *The Sunflower: On the Possibilities and Limits of Forgiveness*, rev. edn, eds. Harry J. Cargas and Bonny V. Fetterman (New York: Schocken Books, 1997 [orig. 1969]), 192.
4. For detail on the footage, which was released in 1945 under the title *Auschwitz: Film Documents of the Monstrous Crimes of the German Government in Auschwitz*, see Jeremy Hicks, *First Films of the Holocaust: Soviet Cinema and the Genocide of the Jews, 1938–1946* (Pittsburgh, PA: University of Pittsburgh Press, 2012), 174–85. Hicks describes the footage of the 180 twins whom Josef Mengele spared from the gas chambers as "the film's most memorable image" (177).
5. According to testimony (in Michael A. Grodin, Eva M. Kor, and Susan Benedict, *The Trial That Never Happened: Josef Mengele and the Twins of Auschwitz* [Berkeley, CA: Berkeley Electronic Press, 2011], http://works.bepress.com/michael_grodin/1), Kor was taken for experiments, "where we would stay for 8 hours at a time naked. They would measure and compare. Doctors in white uniforms were continuously writing notes. The experiments were difficult in that they were degrading and made us feel like animals. Because they lasted such a long time, it was impossible to say 'Oh, it will be over in half an hour'. . . . I was photographed continuously. Photographed and compared, always in the nude. The humiliation was the closest thing to making someone feel like a nothing, a piece of garbage, a piece of meat" (81). The mock trial of Mengele at which she testified took place in 1985.
6. See Eva Mozes Kor and Lisa Rojany-Buccieri, *Surviving the Angel of Death: The True Story of a Mengele Twin in Auschwitz* (Terre Haute, IN: Tanglewood Press, 2009).
7. The transcript of the mock trial from 1985 begins: "Frustrated by the inability of various governments to apprehend Mengele and bring him to justice, these survivors sought to record their testimonies while they were still able, to be used in the event Mengele was eventually captured." See Grodin, Kor, and Benedict, *The Trial that never Happened*, 2. Mengele, in fact, died in Brazil in 1979, which was determined in June 1985, only a few months after the trial. See Ralph Blumenthal, "Scientists Decide Brazil Skeleton Is Josef Mengele," *New York Times*, July 22, 1985.
8. For an excerpt from the acquittal, see *The Meeting: An Auschwitz Survivor Confronts an SS Physician*, ed. Bernhard Frankfurter, trans. Susan E. Cernyak-Spatz (Syracuse, NY: Syracuse University Press, 2000), 171.

9   See Eva Kor, "Heilung von Auschwitz und Mengeles Experimenten," in *Die Verbindung nach Auschwitz: Biowissenschaften und Menschenversuche an Kaiser-Wilhelm-Instituten—Dokumentation eines Symposiums*, ed. Carola Sachse (Göttingen: Wallstein Verlag, 2003), 59–70.
10 Eva Kor, "Heilung von Auschwitz," 67.
11 Jean Améry, *At the Mind's Limits: Contemplations by a Survivor on Auschwitz and Its Realities*, trans. Sidney Rosenfeld and Stella P. Rosenfeld (Bloomington, IN: Indiana University Press, 1980), 68.
12 Améry, *At the Mind's Limits*, 68.
13 Ibid., 68. His italics.
14 Ibid., 70.
15 Natan Sznaider (in "Grenzen der Vergebung: Vesöhnung ist ein politischer Prozess," *Frankfurter Rundschau*, June 30, 2003) writes that Hannah Arendt sees forgiveness as a purely political concept, arguing that it liberates political action and opens up new horizons. A new beginning is thus possible. He adds, however, that we have to be careful on this point: "Forgiveness can only be that, which can be punished, according to Arendt. 'Radical evil' is excluded. It is therefore not so simple to derive from forgiveness of the Holocaust a program for post-totalitarian societies."
16 Arendt's book appeared in German in 1960. Arendt also writes about forgiveness in Christian terms: "The freedom contained in Jesus's teachings of forgiveness is the freedom from vengeance, which [e]ncloses both doer and sufferer in the relentless automatism of the action process, which by itself need never come to an end." See Hannah Arendt, *The Human Condition* (Chicago: University of Chicago Press, 1998), 241. When Améry writes that resentment "nails every one of us onto the cross of his ruined past," he is explaining—and rationalizing—the subjective desire for vengeance.
17 This idea is also expressed in Derrida's essay: "We can imagine that someone, a victim of the worst, himself, a member of his family ... demands that justice be done, that the criminals appear before a court, be judged and condemned by a court—yet in his heart forgives." *On Cosmopolitanism and Forgiveness*, 54.
18 Kor, "Heilung von Auschwitz," 67.
19 On the Lipstadt case, see Richard J. Evans, *Lying about Hitler: History, Holocaust, and the David Irving Trial* (New York: Basic Books, 2001).
20 Kor, "Heilung von Auschwitz," 69.
21 Berel Lang, *The Future of the Holocaust: Between History and Memory* (Ithaca, NY: Cornell University Press, 1999), 158.
22 On the term "Perpetrator Trauma," see Raya Morag's analysis of recent Israeli documentaries, "Perpetrator Trauma and Current Israeli Documentary Cinema." *Camera Obscura* 27, 2 (2012): 93–133. See also the essays in *Tätertrauma:*

Nationale Erinnerungen im öffentlichen Diskurs, eds. Bernhard Giesen and Christoph Schneider (Konstanz: UVK-Verlagsgesellschaft, 2004).

23. "It's up to audiences to decide whether or not he's telling the truth." Quoted in Geoffrey Macnab, "Packaging the Holocaust," *The Independent*, August 5, 1999, http://www.independent.co.uk/arts-entertainment/film-packaging-the-holocaust-1110951.html.
24. Macnab, "Packaging the Holocaust."
25. Münch defends Mengele (in Frankfurter, ed., *The Meeting*) arguing that Mengele did not try to change the eye color of twins and that "you will not find one concrete example of what Mengele actually did" (70).
26. Münch claims that a man named Strassburger, who was on Heydrich's staff, recruited him, and he suspects that Strassburger might have been Jewish, a fact that, however unlikely, would conveniently make his fate and all that followed the Jews' own fault. See Bernhard Frankfurter (ed.), *The Meeting*, 18–19.
27. Bruno Schirra, "Die Erinnerung der Täter." *Der Spiegel* 40 (1998): 90–100; here, 97. See also the follow-up: Bruno Schirra, "Erkennen Sie mich noch, Herr Doktor?" *Die Welt*, January 25, 2005.
28. Schirra, "Die Erinnerung der Täter," 97.
29. Ibid., 91.
30. Ibid., 90.
31. Ibid., 90.
32. Ibid., 100.
33. Harald Welzer, "Vergeben ist ein Recht aller Opfer. Rückgewinnung der eigenen Autonomie ist das entscheidende Ziel," *Frankfurter Rundschau*, June 30, 2003.
34. Micha Brumlik and Lena Inowlocki, "Die grundlegende Bedeutung der Vergebung. Antwort auf Harald Welzers Umgang mit der Trauma-Therapie," *Frankfurter Rundschau*, June 23, 2003.
35. The words also appear in Klüger's *unterwegs verloren. Erinnerungen* (Wien: dtv, 2010 [Orig. 2008]), 200. The film's English translation of the German word *Wunde* (wound) is "sore spot."
36. *At the Mind's Limits* was the book's English language title.
37. Améry, *At the Mind's Limits*, 68. An example of the "syndrome" he is describing can be found in William G. Niederland, "Psychiatric Disorders Among Persecution Victims: A Contribution to the Understanding of Concentration Camp Pathology and Its After-effects." *Journal of Nervous and Mental Disease* 139, 5 (1964): 458–74.
38. Améry, *At the Mind's Limits*, 67–8.
39. This is often connected with Zvi Rex's remark: "The Germans will never forgive the Jews for Auschwitz." Cited in Henryk M. Broder's 1986 book *Der ewige Antisemit: Über Sinn und Funktion eines beständigen Gefühls* (Frankfurt am Main: Fischer-Taschenbuch-Verlag, 1986), 130.

40 "Dessen Gemüt [war] im Gleichen." The English translation is "his mind was at ease."
41 Améry, *At the Mind's Limits*, 67.
42 Ibid., 81.
43 *Still Alive* was first published in German as *weiter leben*, in 1992. It was released under the title *Still Alive* in the United States in 2001, with a number of changes. The title of the book in the United Kingdom was *Landscapes of Memory*, the same as Schmidtkunz's film (*Landscapes of Memory: A Holocaust Girlhood Remembered* [London: Bloomsbury, 2004]). On the difference between the US and German versions, see Erin McGlothlin, "Autobiographical Re-vision: Ruth Klüger's *weiter leben* and *Still Alive*." *Gegenwartsliteratur* 3 (2004): 46–70. All references to *Landscapes of Memory* in this chapter are references to Schmidtkunz's film.
44 The theme of the *Schlussstrich* was already mentioned by Adorno in his 1955 publication *Schuld und Abwehr*, an empirical study in which he indicted the Germans for their failure to pay proper attention to their mostly passive but sometimes active complicity with the perpetrators. Adorno entitles a section "draw a line under it" (*Strich darunter*), and he there writes with some degree of sympathy about the "guileless" German youths in his focus group who had more than once used that phrase. He described them as being engaged in a "desperate defense against any feeling of guilt," one that "represents the symptom of an extremely dangerous social-psychological and political potential." See Adorno, *Guilt and Defense*, 138. The German version of these remarks is in Adorno's *Gesammelte Schriften*, vol. 9, no. 2, ed. Rolf Tiedemann (Frankfurt: Suhrkamp, 2003), 263.
45 Martin Walser, "Erfahrungen beim Verfassen einer Sonntagsrede," in *Die Walser-Bubis-Debatte. Eine Dokumentation*, ed. Frank Schirrmacher (Frankfurt: Suhrkamp, 1999), 7–17.
46 Martin Walser, "Erfahrungen beim Verfassen einer Sonntagsrede," 13.
47 Detailed in Ruth Klüger, *Still Alive*, 79–80.
48 Ruth Klüger, "Forgiving and Remembering," 311.
49 Ibid.
50 Ibid.
51 The title of Klüger's autobiography was nearly "Stations," but she did not like the Christian connotation. See *Still Alive*, 68.
52 Ruth Klüger, *Still Alive*, 52.
53 Ruth Klüger, "Dichten über die Shoah. Zum Problem des literarischen Umgangs mit dem Massenmord," in *Spuren der Verfolgung: Seelische Auswirkungen des Holocaust auf die Opfer und ihre Kinder*, ed. Gertrud Hardtmann (Gerlingen: Bleicher, 1992), 203–21; here, 203.
54 Klüger writes, "Der Holocaust ist literarisch kein deutsches Thema geworden." See "Dichten über die Shoah," 211.

55 Ruth Klüger, "Dichten über die Shoah," 219.
56 The Jewish population of Austria was nearly entirely eliminated by the Holocaust. According to the USHMM there were 250,000 Jews in Austria before the war, and 18,000 after, in 1950. The current Jewish population in Austria is under 15,000.
57 Schmidtkunz's first televised interview with Klüger, from 2005, went by the title, "Ich komm' nicht von Auschwitz her, ich stamm' aus Wien" ("I don't come from Auschwitz, I'm from Vienna").
58 The film also includes some sequences in Israel, and it takes up the question of whether Klüger could consider that her *Heimat* as well. Israel is an interest of Schmidtkunz's, and other short nonfiction films of hers include *Lesereise Israel. Junge SchriftstellerInnen in Israel* (2008) for the channel 3sat and *Tel Aviv—eine Stadt und ihre Menschen* (2009) for the channels 3sat and ORF.
59 See Claude Lanzmann, *The Patagonian Hare: A Memoir*, trans. Frank Wynne (New York: Farrar, Straus and Giroux, 2012), 420.
60 Schirra, "Die Erinnerung der Täter," 90.
61 See Klüger's chapter, "Lanzmanns *Shoah* in New York," in her book of essays, *Gelesene Wirklichkeit. Fakten und Fiktionen in der Literatur* (Göttingen: Wallstein, 2006), 25. Translated as Ruth K. Angress, "Lanzmann's *Shoah* and Its Audience," Museum of Tolerance Online Learning Center, http://motlc.wiesenthal.com/site/pp.asp?c=gvKVLcMVIuG&b=395045.
62 Klüger, "Lanzmanns *Shoah* in New York," 25.
63 On this, see Erin McGlothlin, "Listening to the Perpetrators in Claude Lanzmann's *Shoah*." *Colloquia Germanica* 43, 3 (2010): 235–71.
64 Ruth Klüger, "Lanzmanns *Shoah* in New York," 24; English translation from "Lanzmann's *Shoah* and Its Audience," n.p.
65 Ibid.
66 On the "return documentary," see Janet Walker, "Moving Testimonies: 'Unhomed Geography' and the Holocaust Documentary of Return," in *After Testimony: The Ethics and Aesthetics of Holocaust Narrative for the Future*, eds. Jakob Lothe, Susan Rubin Suleiman and James Phelan (Columbus, OH: Ohio State University Press, 2012), 269–88.
67 "Ruth Klüger: 'Wien schreit nach Antisemitismus'" Interview with Ruth Klüger, *Der Spiegel* online, August 31, 2006.
68 Klüger, *Still Alive*, 66.
69 Ruth Klüger, "Lanzmanns *Shoah* in New York," 10; English translation from "Lanzmann's *Shoah* and Its Audience," n.p.
70 Ruth Klüger, *Still Alive*, 206.
71 Ibid., 126.

72 See Catherine Smale, "'Ungelöste Gespenster?': Ghosts in Ruth Klüger's Autobiographical Project." *Modern Language Review* 104, 3 (2009): 777–89, here, 780 and 781. Klüger also notes that, as a woman, Jewish law prohibits her from saying Kaddish, the mourning prayer. See *Still Alive*, 30–1.
73 Ruth Klüger, *Still Alive*, 36.
74 "The Meaning of Working through the Past," trans. Henry W. Pickford, in *Can One Live after Auschwitz? A Philosophical Reader*, ed. Rolf Tiedemann (Stanford, CA: Stanford University Press, 2003), 3–18; here, 3.
75 Smale, "Ungelöste Gespenster?" 784.
76 Ibid., 785.
77 Ruth Klüger, *Still Alive*, 312.
78 Ruth Klüger, *unterwegs verloren. Erinnerungen* (Wien: dtv, 2010 [Orig. 2008]), 13.
79 Ruth Klüger, *unterwegs verloren*, 20.
80 Ibid., 28.
81 Ibid., 28.
82 Ibid., 29.
83 Améry, *At the Mind's Limits*, 79.
84 Ibid., 76. In an essay on the lack of fully developed Jewish characters in Mann's fiction, Klüger cites Lehnert's work affirmatively. See "Thomas Manns jüdische Gestalten," in Klüger's *Katastrophen: Über deutsche Literatur* (Göttingen: Wallstein, 1994), 54. Klüger also mentions her relationship with Lehnert (without naming him) and seems to describe precisely this conversation, or one that is very similar, in "The Future of Holocaust Literature: German Studies Association 2013 Banquet Speech," *German Studies Review* 37, 2 (2014): 391–403; here, 393.
85 Particularly a woman she refers to by the name Gisela. See Klüger, *Still Alive*, 79.
86 I am citing from Ruth Klüger, "Wiener Neurosen. Eine Rede." *Hören: Zeitschrift für Literatur, Kunst und Kritik* 46 (2001): 21–9; here, 23. A revised version of this appeared later in Klüger's *unterwegs verloren*, 195–216.
87 Ruth Klüger, *Still Alive*, p. 59.
88 See "Wiener Neurose," in Ruth Klüger, *unterwegs verloren. Erinnerungen* (Munich: DTV, 2010), 216. The poem appeared earlier under the title "Wien, Mai '97" in "Wiener Neurosen: Eine Rede." *Die Hören: Zeitschrift für Literatur, Kunst und Kritik* 46, 201 (2001): 21–9; here, 23.
89 See Theodor W. Adorno, "Reply to Peter R. Hofstätter's Critique of *Group Experiment*," in *Guilt and Defense: On the Legacies of National Socialism in Postwar Germany*, ed. and trans. by Jeffrey K. Olick and Andrew J. Perrin (Cambridge, MA: Harvard University Press, 2010), 197–209; here, 208. The "Reply" was originally published in German in 1957. Adorno also used the phrase in the first paragraph

of his essay "The Meaning of Working Through the Past," which is reproduced in *Guilt and Defense*, 213–27; here, 213. That essay first appeared in 1959.
90 Andreas Huyssen, *Twilight Memories: Marking Time in a Culture of Amnesia* (New York: Routledge, 1995), 215. On Kiefer's "Occupations," see also Andrea Liss, *Trespassing through Shadows: Memory, Photography, and the Holocaust* (Minneapolis, MN: University of Minnesota Press, 1998), 96–8.
91 James E. Young, *At Memory's Edge: After-Images of the Holocaust in Contemporary Art and Architecture* (New Haven, CT: Yale University Press, 2000), 281.
92 Young, *At Memory's Edge*, 96–7.
93 Walser did not actually use the word in his speech, which has been noted by Ludiger Jansen, among others, in "Alles Schlußstrich – oder was? Eine philosophische Auseinandersetzung mit Martin Walsers Friedenspreisrede." *Theologie und Philosophie* 80 (2005): 412–22, see especially note 2.

Chapter 4

1 Erin McGlothlin, "Listening to the Perpetrators in Claude Lanzmann's *Shoah*." *Colloquia Germanica* 43, 3 (2010): 235–71; here, 235.
2 See Raul Hilberg, *Perpetrators, Victims, Bystanders: The Jewish Catastrophe, 1933–1945* (New York: Harper-Collins, 1992).
3 See Michael Renov, *The Subject of Documentary* (Minneapolis, MN: University of Minnesota Press, 2004), 126–7; see also Dominick LaCapra, *History and Memory After Auschwitz* (Ithaca, NY: Cornell University Press, 1998), 123–4.
4 McGlothlin, "Listening to the Perpetrators," 262.
5 Florence Jacobowitz, "*Shoah* as Cinema," in Shelley Hornstein and Florence. Jacobowitz, eds. *Image and Remembrance: Representation and the Holocaust* (Bloomington, IN: Indiana University Press, 2003), 7–12; here, 18.
6 Florence Jacobowitz, "*Shoah* as Cinema," 18.
7 Renov, *The Subject of Documentary*, 218.
8 Ibid., 228.
9 On the "Holocaust family memoir," see Irene Kacandes, "'When facts are scarce': Authenticating Strategies in Writing by Children of Survivors," *After Testimony: The Ethics and Aesthetics of Holocaust Narrative for the Future*, eds. Jakob Lothe, Susan Rubin Suleiman and James Phelan (Columbus, OH: Ohio State University Press, 2012), 179–97.
10 Santer uses the term "homeopathy" when writing about Hans-Jürgen Syberberg's *Hitler—ein Film aus Deutschland* (1977). See Eric L. Santner, *Stranded Objects, Mourning, Memory and Film in Postwar Germany* (Ithaca, NY: Cornell University Press, 1990), especially 22–6.

11 Anton Kaes, *From 'Hitler' to 'Heimat': The Return of History as Film* (Cambridge, MA: Harvard University Press, 1989), 6.
12 Malte Ludin, "Nazi-Lügen verbreitet: zum Film *Hitler—eine Karriere*," in *Neofaschismus: Die Rechten im Aufwind*, ed. Jan Peters (Berlin: Sozialpolitischer Verlag, 1979), 45–51; here, 48–9.
13 Wim Wenders, "That's Entertainment: Hitler," in *West German Filmmakers on Film: Visions and Voices*, ed. Eric Rentschler (New York: Holmes and Meier, 1988), 126–31; here, 128.
14 Wenders, "That's Entertainment: Hitler," 129.
15 Ludin, "Nazi-Lügen," 50.
16 Raul Hilberg, *The Destruction of the European Jews*, 3rd edn, vol. II (New Haven, CT: Yale University Press, 2003), 785.
17 Erin McGlothlin, *Second-Generation Holocaust Literature: Legacies of Survival and Perpetration* (Rochester, NY: Camden House, 2006), 26. Susanne Luhmann interprets the film along precisely these lines. See "Filming Familial Secrets: Approaching and Avoiding Legacies of Nazi Perpetration." *New German Critique* 112 (2011): 115–34; especially 121–6.
18 McGlothlin, *Second-Generation Holocaust Literature*, 26.
19 Alexandra Senfft, *Schweigen tut weh—Eine deutsche Familiengeschichte* (Berlin: Claassen, 2007), 80–1.
20 Malte Ludin references von Salomon's famous book only once in *2 oder 3 Dinge, die ich von ihm weiß*, referring to it not by its title, but only indirectly as "a much read book in the postwar period" ("in der Nachkriegszeit vielgelesenes Buch").
21 Richard Herzinger, "Ernst von Salomon: Konservativ-revolutionäre Literatur zwischen Tatrhetorik und Resignation." *Zeitschrift für Germanistik*, n.s. 8, 1 (1998): 83–96; here, 92.
22 Ernst von Salomon, *Der Fragebogen* (Reinbek bei Hamburg: Rowohlt, 1969), 635–6. The "ischt" is as it appears in von Salomon's account.
23 von Salomon, *Der Fragebogen*, 661.
24 This is widely repeated and is also mentioned in von Salomon (668). Senfft adds more detail: "Der Anwalt sagt, kurz vor seinem Tod habe Hanns ihm noch zugerufen: 'Doktor, grüßen Sie mir meine liebe Frau.' Der anwesende Bischof indes will gehört haben, dass seine letzten Worte lauteten: 'Es lebe Deutschland.' Wahrscheinlich hat er beides gesagt" (44–5).
25 von Salomon, *Der Fragebogen*, 662.
26 Ibid., 667.
27 Ibid., 661. Additional background is also provided by Senfft (61).
28 Alexandra Tacke, "Zwei oder drei Dinge über Malte Ludins Film *2 oder 3 Dinge, die ich von ihm weiß*," in *Das Böse im Blick: Die Gegenwart des Nationalsozialismus*

29 *im Film*, eds. Margrit Frölich, Christian Schneider and Karsten Visarius (Munich: Text + kritik, 2007), 191–203; here, 192.
29 Senfft's memoir processes her mother's death in relation to the Nazi past. She talks specifically about that incident (9–16) as well as about the impact of her uncle Malte's film (335–6).
30 Timothy Corrigan, *The Essay Film: From Montaigne, after Marker* (Oxford: Oxford University Press, 2011), 52.
31 Corrigan, *The Essay Film*, 52.
32 von Salomon, *Der Fragebogen*, 661.
33 Ibid., 661–2.
34 Senfft, *Schweigen tut weh*, 335.
35 Translated literally, the phrase is "Where wood is chopped, splinters fall." Sometimes people choose to translate the idiom with the English language one, "You can't make an omelet without breaking some eggs."
36 von Salomon, *Der Fragebogen*, 647.
37 Senfft, *Schweigen tut weh*, 14.
38 On this see Erin McGlothlin, "Listening to the Perpetrators in Claude Lanzmann's *Shoah*." *Colloquia Germanica* 43, 3 (2010): 235–71, especially 260–5.
39 Noah Shenker uses the term "testimonial performance," although he applies it to documentary performances in which subjects speak their own testimony, rather than that of another. See Noah Shenker, "Embodied Memory: The Institutional Mediation of Survivor Testimony in the United States Holocaust Memorial Museum," in *Documentary Testimonies: Global Archives of Suffering*, eds. Bhaskar Sarkar and Janet Walker (New York: Routledge, 2010): 35–58; here, 44.
40 On this, see Michael D. Richardson, "Reenacting Evil: Giving Voice to the Perpetrator in *Das Himmler-Projekt* and *Das Goebbels-Experiment*." *Colloquia Germanica* 43, 3 (2010): 175–94.
41 Štern's story is recounted in Mark Kurlansky, *A Chosen Few: The Resurrection of European Jewry* (Reading, MA: Addison-Wesley, 1995), 121.
42 On this film, its management of the past, and its leveling of differences between the victims, see Jennifer M. Kapczynski, *The German Patient: Crisis and Recovery in Postwar Culture* (Ann Arbor, MI: University of Michigan Press, 2008), 75–117.
43 Malte Ludin, *Wolfgang Staudte* (Reinbek bei Hamburg: Rowohlt, 1996), 36.
44 Von Mildenstein's full name is sometimes represented as Leopold Eduard Stephen von Mildenstein. He published his writings in *Der Angriff* under the name "Lim," a name he derived from spelling the first three letters of his last name from right to left, as one reads in Hebrew.
45 Werner Keller, *Diaspora: The Post-Biblical History of the Jews*, trans. Richard and Clara Winston (New York: Harcourt, Brace & World, 1969), 438.

46 Keller, *Diaspora*, 446.
47 Ibid., 454.
48 Heinz Höhne, "Der Orden unter dem Totenkopf. Die Geschichte der SS—10. Fortsetzung: Die antijüdische Politik der SS," *Der Spiegel* 52, December 19, 1966, 66–84.
49 See Heinz Höhne, "Der Orden unter dem Totenkopf," especially 70–1.
50 Jacob Boas, "A Nazi Travels to Palestine." *History Today* 30, 1 (1980): 33–8; here, 34.
51 Boas, "A Nazi Travels to Palestine," 35.
52 See Kurt Tuchler, "Erlebnisse und Beobachtungen in den ersten vier Hitlerjahren," Yad Vashem Archives, Ball-Kaduri Collection, Archive Number 01/24 (1945).
53 The Haavara Agreement was signed on August 25, 1933. For background, Tuchler cites Gustav Krojanker, *The Transfer: A Vital Question of the Zionist Movement*, English edn (Tel Aviv: Publications of the Hitachduth Olei Germania, 1936). Krojanker was in favor of the Haavara Agreement and the move to Palestine.
54 Höhne, "Der Orden unter dem Totenkopf," 72.
55 Timothy Naftali, "The CIA and Eichmann's Associates," *U.S. Intelligence and the Nazis*, written by Richard Breitman, Norman J. W. Goda, Timothy Naftali, and Robert Wolfe (Cambridge: Cambridge University Press, 2005), 337–74; here, 341.
56 David Cesarani, *Becoming Eichmann: Rethinking the Life, Crimes, and Trial of a "Desk Murderer"* (Cambridge, MA: Da Capo Press, 2004), 38–9.
57 Ibid., 43.
58 Ibid., 45.
59 Ibid., 47.
60 Ibid., 46.
61 Ibid., 46.
62 Ibid., 38.
63 See Axel Meier, "'Ein Nazi fährt nach Palästina': Der Bericht eines SS-Offiziers als Beitrag zur 'Lösung der Judenfrage.'" *Jahrbuch für Antisemitismusforschung* 11 (2002): 76–90; here, 85.
64 Cesarani, *Becoming Eichmann*, 86.
65 Lucy S. Dawidowicz, *The War Against the Jews, 1933–1945* (New York: Holt, Rinehart and Winston, 1975), 118.
66 Leopold von Mildenstein, *Rings um das brennende Land am Jordan: Eine Fahrt bis zu den Quellen des flüsigen Goldes* (Berlin: Verlagsanstalt Otto Stollberg, 1938), 50.
67 Leopold von Mildenstein, *Naher Osten—vom Straßenrand erlebt. Ein Reisebreicht mit sechzehn Frabblidern* (Stuttgart: Union Deutsche Verlagsgesellschaft, 1941), 31–2.

68 von Mildenstein, *Rings um das brennende Land*, 51.
69 Ibid., 52.
70 von Mildenstein, *Naher Osten*, especially the section "Kartenhaus," 109.
71 von Mildenstein, *Naher Osten*, 1941, 113–14.
72 Ibid., 118.
73 See "Ralph Izzard Exposes: The Nazis behind the Egyptian Propaganda War—Goebbels Men Help Nasser," *Daily Mail*, December 10, 1956. Naftali draws conclusions that support the assertions about Nasser in "The CIA and Eichmann's Associates" (342).
74 Odeya Kohen-Raz, "Arnon Goldfinger's *The Flat* (2011): Ethics and Aesthetics in Third Generation Holocaust Cinema." *Studies in Documentary Film* 6, 3 (2012): 323–38; here, 332.

Chapter 5

1 Haim Gouri, *Facing the Glass Booth: The Jerusalem Trial of Adolf Eichmann*, trans. Michael Swirsky (Detroit, MI: Wayne State University Press, 2004), 133.
2 The *New York Times* boldly asserted that Eichmann was unmoved by the "eighty minutes of filmed horror" screened at the trial. Writing from Jerusalem, Homer Bigart observes: "The presiding judge, Moshe Landau, appeared ashen and ill as he hurried from the court during a recess called after the movies. The last scene was a vision of apocalyptic horror; it showed bulldozers shoving thousands of corpses into a pit at Belsen. The bulldozers were British. Attorney General Gideon Hausner assured the court that Eichmann was not to blame for this unceremonious handling of the dead." Bigart, "Eichmann is Unmoved in Court as Judges Pale at Death Films," *New York Times*, June 9, 1961, 16. The film was shown during session 70. For the relevant parts of the trial transcript, see: http://www.nizkor.org/hweb/people/e/eichmann-adolf/transcripts/Sessions/Session-070-06.html.
3 Gouri, *Facing the Glass Booth*, 134.
4 Sylvie Lindeperg writes that Hurwitz was very accurate, taking pains to mirror the structure of *Night and Fog* and to "pay tribute to Resnais." He shows long sequences from *Night and Fog* without cutting them, and the number of edits in Hurwitz's version, including the shots of Eichmann watching the film, is 307, precisely the number of shots contained in Resnais's film. See Lindeperg, "*Night and Fog*: A History of Gazes," trans. Pauline Haas Hammel, in *Concentrationary Cinema*, eds. Pollock and Silverman, 55–70; here, 67–8.
5 Darcy C. Buerkle, "Affect in the Archive: Arendt, Eichmann and *The Specialist*," in *Visualizing the Holocaust: Documents—Aesthetics—Memory*, eds. David Bathrick,

Brad Prager, Michael D. Richardson (Rochester, NY: Camden House, 2008), 211–38; here, 225.

6 On the definition of perpetrator images, see especially Marianne Hirsch, "Nazi Photographs in Post-Holocaust Art: Gender as an Idiom of Memorialization," in *Phototextualities: Intersections of Photography and Narrative*, eds. Alex Hughes and Andrea Noble (Albuquerque: University of New Mexico Press, 2003), 19–40, especially 23–6.

7 Janina Struk (in *Photographing the Holocaust* [London and New York: I.B. Tauris, 2004], 81) refers to the title "Asia in Central Europe," and cites the following source: *The Warsaw Ghetto in Photographs*, ed. Ulrich Heller (New York: Dover Publications, 1984). Heller in turn cites, *Martyrs and Fighters, The Epic of the Warsaw Ghetto*, ed. Philip Friedman (Praeger: New York, 1954), 43. The database cine-holocaust.de names Jonas Turkow as the origin of the supposed title, citing his *Azoi iz es gewen. Hurban Warsche* (Buenos Aires: Zentral-Verband fun poilischen Jiden in Argentinien, 1948). Anja Horstmann also believes that Turkow is the original source for the title. See Anja Horstmann, "Ghetto (1942). Unvollendetes dokumentarisches Filmmaterial aus dem Warschauer Ghetto." *Filmblatt* 15, 44 (2010–11): 68–81, here, 69.

8 *The Warsaw Diary of Adam Czerniakow: Prelude to Doom*, eds. Raul Hilberg, Stanislaw Staron and Josef Kermisz, trans. Stanislaw Staron and the staff of Yad Vashem (New York: Stein and Day, 1979), 350.

9 These are from entries from May 7, 1942 and May 12, 1942, respectively. Both can be found in "Inside the Ghetto: Emmanuel Ringelblum," in *The Holocaust: A Reader*, eds. Simone Gigliotti and Berel Lang (Malden, MA: Blackwell, 2005), 313–33, here, 317–19.

10 The intentions behind the Warsaw film—specifically Josef Goebbels's rationale—are further discussed by Horstmann. See Anja Horstmann, "'Judenaufnahmen furs Archiv'—Das dokumentarische Filmmaterial *Asien in Mitteleuropa, 1942.*" *Medaon: Magazin für Jüdisches Leben in Forschung und Bildung* 4 (2009): 1–11, especially 4. On the intention of the Theresienstadt film, see Brad Prager, "Interpreting the Visible Traces of Theresienstadt." *Journal of Modern Jewish Studies* 7, 2 (2008): 175–94.

11 Struk, *Photographing the Holocaust*, 81.

12 Recounted in Ursula Böser, "*A Film Unfinished:* Yael Hersonski's Re-representation of Archival Footage from the Warsaw Ghetto." *Film Criticism* 37, 2 (2013): 38–56; here, 40.

13 Böser, 41.

14 Ibid.

15 See Dirk Rupnow, "Die Spuren nationalsozialistischer Gedächtnispolitik und unser Umgang mit den Bildern der Täter: Ein Beitrag zu Yael Hersonskis *A Film*

Unfinished/ Geheimsache Ghettofilm," October 2010, http://www.zeithistorische-forschungen.de/site/40209029/default.aspx.

16   Stuart Liebman, "The Never-Ending Story: Yael Hersonski's *A Film Unfinished*." *Cineaste* 36, 3 (2011): 15–19; here, 19.

17   Unlike Hersonski's film, *Respite* is silent. Hersonski mentions that difference in Laliv Melamed, "A Film Unraveled: An Interview with Yael Hersonski." *International Journal of Politics, Culture, and Society* 26, 1 (2013): 9–19; here, 12–13.

18   Dominick LaCapra, "Holocaust Testimonies: Attending to the Victim's Voice," in *Catastrophe and Memory: The Holocaust and the Twentieth Century*, eds. Moishe Postone and Eric Santner (Chicago: University of Chicago Press, 2003), 209–31; here, 223.

19   Marianne Hirsch, *The Generation of Postmemory: Writing and Visual Culture after the Holocaust* (New York: Columbia University Press, 2012), 136.

20   Hirsch, *The Generation of Postmemory*, 136.

21   As is widely acknowledged, Lanzmann makes exceptions to his own policies. Preexisting photos of Dachau are used in *Shoah*, and in *The Last of the Unjust* (*Le Dernier des Injustes*, 2013) Lanzmann includes a long sequence from the 1944 Theresienstadt propaganda film. On the use and exclusion of perpetrator images in *Shoah*, see Libby Saxton, *Haunted Images: Film, Ethics, Testimony and the Holocaust* (London and New York: Wallflower, 2008), especially 26–30.

22   See Rupnow, "Die Spuren nationalsozialistischer Gedächtnispolitik."

23   Her review was published in 1978, 10 years after the film was made. See Lucy S. Dawidowicz, "Visualizing the Warsaw Ghetto: Nazi Images of the Jews Refiltered by the BBC. A Critical Review of the BBC Film, *The Warsaw Ghetto*." *Shoah: A Journal of Resources on the Holocaust* 1, 1 (1978): 5–6 and 17.

24   Dawidowicz, "Visualizing the Warsaw Ghetto," 6.

25   Ilan Ziv's *Tango of Slaves* (1993) is an example of a documentary that is highly self-reflective in its use of the Warsaw Ghetto footage. In this respect, it diverges from the earlier documentaries mentioned here.

26   Guido Vitiello, "Portrait of the Chimpanzee as a Metaphysician: Parody and Dehumanization in *Echoes from a Somber Empire*," in *A Companion to Werner Herzog*, ed. Brad Prager (Malden, MA: Blackwell, 2012), 547–65, here, 555. See also Georges Didi-Hubermann, who refers to "tracking shots with no subject" in *Images in Spite of All: Four Photographs from Auschwitz*, trans. Shane B. Lillis (Chicago: University of Chicago Press, 2008), 129.

27   Hersonski narrates the Hebrew language release of the film; Kenan, the English version.

28   See "Wir waren zu viert: Leon de Winter im Gespräch mit Roman Polanski über eine Jugend im Krakauer Getto," *Die Welt*, November 30, 2002, http://www.welt.de/print-welt/article278631/Wir-waren-zu-viert.html.

29 Noting that Germans are depicted filming in the Warsaw Ghetto in *The Pianist*, Tobias Ebbrecht articulates Polanski's avoidance of the images' "ambivalence"— that they are documentary images, but that they are also staged—insofar as the director "recodes them in terms of his own perception.... The audience should *consciously* forget who stood behind the camera. The film makes clear that this is a conscious process in that he conceals the perpetrators' perspective within his recreations, but at the same time he also puts the filming and photographing perpetrators in the image." See Ebbrecht, *Geschichtsbilder im medialen Gedächtnis. Filmische Narrationen des Holocaust* (Bielefeld: Transcript Verlag, 2011), 172–4.

30 See Sue Vice, *Shoah* (London: Palgrave Macmillan/BFI, 2011), especially 50–63. On Lanzmann's *Shoah* and mise-en-scène, see Michael D'Arcy, "Claude Lanzmann's *Shoah* and the Intentionality of the Image," in *Visualizing the Holocaust: Documents—Aesthetics—Memory*, eds. David Bathrick, Brad Prager and Michael D. Richardson (Rochester, NY: Camden House, 2008), 138–61.

31 Saxton, *Haunted Images*, 38.

32 See Darcy C. Buerkle, "Affect in the Archive: Arendt, Eichmann and *The Specialist*," in *Visualizing the Holocaust: Documents—Aesthetics—Memory*, 211–38.

33 For detail, see Barbara Engelking and Jacek Leociak, *The Warsaw Ghetto: A Guide to the Perished City*, trans. Emma Harris (New Haven, CT: Yale University Press, 2009), 129.

34 *Camera Lucida* was in large measure Roland Barthes's discussion of his own relationship with a photograph of his mother, Henriette Barthes, who died in 1977. See Barthes, *Camera Lucida: Reflections on Photography*, trans. Richard Howard (New York: Noonday Press, 1981 [Orig. 1980]). On the *punctum*, see especially 26.

35 See Czerniakow's diary entry from May 3, 1942. They filmed again in his office on June 2, 1942. See *The Warsaw Diary of Adam Czerniakow*, 349 and 361.

36 Hersonski does not go so far as to call the cameramen criminals. She reserves judgment: "I can tell you that the system did not perceive propaganda filmmakers as war criminals and cameramen, reporters, filmmakers were not put on trial for being Nazi propagandists. You know, it was a whole nation involved in this war, so it's historical—it was a point in time in which you really have to understand how the system couldn't deal with a massive quantity of people involved with the crimes and the nature of the genocide. How can you squeeze all of that into judicial terms?" See Leonard Jacobs, "How Yael Hersonski Finished *A Film Unfinished*," in *The Clyde Fitch Report*, September 6, 2010, http://www.clydefitchreport.com/2010/09/how-yael-hersonski-finished-a-film-unfinished/.

37 Hersonski's claim may not be accurate. Horstmann names other cameramen involved in filming these images. See Horstmann, "Ghetto (1942)," 70.

38 Rupnow, in "Die Spuren nationalsozialistischer Gedächtnispolitik," points out that Wist was deposed in Warsaw in 1970 in connection with an investigation of Heinz Auerswald, the SS commissioner for the Jewish residential district in Warsaw, and again in 1972 during an inquiry into Ludwig Hahn, the SS Standartenführer.

39 Noah Shenker refers to "testimonial performance" in "Embodied Memory: The Institutional Mediation of Survivor Testimony in the United States Holocaust Memorial Museum," in *Documentary Testimonies: Global Archives of Suffering*, eds. Bhaskar Sarkar and Janet Walker (New York and London: Routledge, 2010), 35–58; here, 44. Hersonski is doing something different by having Vogler enact a testimonial performance, a decision that challenges a traditional documentary boundary. In an interview, the director explains her motivation to use a stand-in for Wist, noting mainly that it helped her with the film's visual breaks. Remarkably, the interviewer does not realize that Wist is not present in the documentary but has been replaced by an actor. He asks, specifically, how Hersonski coaxed Wist to appear on camera. See Leonard Jacobs, "How Yael Hersonski Finished *A Film Unfinished*."

40 *The Warsaw Diary of Adam Czerniakow*, 352–3.

41 See *The Warsaw Diary of Chaim A. Kaplan*, trans. Abraham I. Katsh (New York: Collier Books, 1973), 331–2. This is not the only time that the Nazis attempted to capture Jews bathing in a prurient way. They tried to capture similarly private scenes in Theresienstadt. See Karel Margry, "The First Theresienstadt Film (1942)." *Historical Journal of Film, Radio and Television* 19, 3 (1999): 309–37.

42 Dawidowicz objects to how these images were included in the BBC documentary, pointing out that the film failed to note the distinction between the ritual bath and the bathhouse, that it tells a story that does not involve the *mikveh*, and that its efforts to "avoid the mendacity of the original film" result in further lies ("Visualizing the Warsaw Ghetto," 6).

43 The term "disjunctive layering" is borrowed from Michael Renov who writes about a similar effect when discussing Rea Tajiri's *History and Memory* (1991) in *The Subject of Documentary* (Minneapolis, MN: University of Minnesota Press, 2004), 64.

44 See Claude Lanzmann, *Shoah: An Oral History of the Holocaust. The Complete Text of the Film* (New York: Pantheon, 1985), 174. On the use of mise-en-scène in the sequence, see Vice, *Shoah*, 62–3.

45 Claude Lanzmann, Ruth Larson, and David Rodowick, "Seminar with Claude Lanzmann." *Yale French Studies* 79 (1991): 82–99; here, 99. Italics added.

46 On Hippler's dissolves, which are meant to make apparent "the real face that lurks behind the mask," and especially how such dissolves can be seen in connection with Veit Harlan's *Jud Süß* (*Jew Süss*, 1940), see Eric Rentschler, *The Ministry of Illusion: Nazi Cinema and Its Afterlife* (Cambridge, MA: Harvard University Press, 1996), 159–60.

47 See Fritz Hippler, *Die Verstrickung: Einstellungen und Rückblenden* (Düsseldorf: Verlag Mehr Wissen, 1981), 187. Two days later, on October 10, Hippler went with a half dozen cameramen to film in the Łódź Ghetto. The exchange is also cited by Horstmann in "Judenaufnahmen furs Archiv," 4.
48 Ulrich Baer, *Spectral Evidence: The Photography of Trauma* (Cambridge, MA: MIT Press, 2002), 129.
49 Baer, *Spectral Evidence*, 130–1.
50 Ibid., 21.
51 Ibid., 136.
52 Ibid., 138.
53 See Mostowicz's memoir (*With a Yellow Star and a Red Cross: A Doctor in the Łódź Ghetto* [Portland, OR: Vallentine Mitchell, 2005]) in which he also tells this story (33–5).
54 Frances Guerin, *Through Amateur Eyes: Film and Photography in Nazi Germany* (Minneapolis, MN: University of Minnesota Press, 2012), 154–5.
55 Janina Struk, *Photographing the Holocaust: Interpretations of the Evidence*, 96.
56 See Daniel H. Magilow, "The Interpreter's Dilemma: Heinrich Jöst's Warsaw Ghetto Photographs," in *Visualizing the Holocaust: Documents—Aesthetics—Memory*, eds. David Bathrick, Brad Prager, and Michael D. Richardson (Rochester, NY: Camden House, 2008), 38–61.
57 Marianne Hirsch, *The Generation of Postmemory: Writing and Visual Culture After the Holocaust* (New York: Columbia University Press, 2012), 136.
58 Hirsch, *The Generation of Postmemory*, 129.
59 Marianne Hirsch, "Nazi Photographs in Post-Holocaust Art: Gender as an Idiom of Memorialization," in *Phototextualities: Intersections of Photography and Narrative*, eds. Alex Hughes and Andrea Noble (Albuquerque: University of New Mexico Press, 2003), 19–40; here, 26.
60 Magilow examines Jöst's photographs in a similar way. See also Brad Prager, "Leben heißt Posieren: Bilder aus dem Warschauer Ghetto—mit Susan Sontag betrachtet." *Fotogeschichte* 126 (2012): 37–48.
61 Ruth Klüger, *Still Alive*, 70.
62 Primo Levi, *The Drowned and the Saved*, 55.
63 *Diary of Dawid Sierakowiak: Five Notebooks from the Lodz Ghetto*, trans. Kamil Turowski (New York: Oxford University Press, 1996), 102–3 and 172 respectively.
64 Hannah Arendt, *Eichmann in Jerusalem: A Report on the Banality of Evil* (New York: Penguin Books, 1994), 119.
65 Primo Levi, *The Drowned and the Saved*, 64.
66 Ibid., 67.
67 Ibid., 69.

68 Saul Friedländer, *The Years of Extermination: Nazi Germany and the Jews, 1939–1945* (New York: Harper Perennial, 2008), 38.
69 Arnold Mostowicz, *With a Yellow Star and a Red Cross*, xxvii. Originally in Polish.
70 Levi, *The Drowned and the Saved*, 66.
71 Ibid., 79–80.
72 Mostowicz, *With a Yellow Star and a Red Cross*, 105.
73 Ibid., 106.
74 Ibid., 52.
75 Isaiah Trunk, *Łodz Ghetto: A History*, trans. and ed. Robert Moses Shapiro (Bloomington, IN: Indiana University Press, 2006), 275. Rumkowski's speech of September 4, 1942 is on 272–5.
76 Tomasz Łysak, "On the Impossibility of Believing in the Documentary: Dariusz Jabłoński's *Photographer*," *Kwartalnik Filmowy*, special issue (no number) 2013: 128–39; here, 135.
77 In Mostowicz's memoir, he is more critical of Rumkowski then would seem to be the case here, noting that Czerniakow (of Warsaw) committed suicide, but that Rumkowski, "had not mustered such courage." See Mostowicz, *With a Yellow Star and a Red Cross*, 113.

Conclusion

1 On positioning *Sobibor* in Lanzmann's body of work, see Manuel Köppen, "Erinnerungslandschaften. Claude Lanzmanns *Sobibor* (2001) und Romuald Karmakars *Land der Vernichtung* (2004)," in *NachBilder des Holocaust*, eds. Inge Stephan and Alexandra Tacke (Cologne: Böhlau Verlag, 2007), 77–90.
2 Jacques Mandelbaum, "Recovery," trans. Anna Harrison, *Cinema & the Shoah: An Art Confronts the Tragedy of the Twentieth Century*, ed. Jean-Michel Frodon (Albany, NY: SUNY Press, 2010), 25–41; here, 33.
3 Jan Tomasz Gross, with Irena Grudzińska-Gross, *Golden Harvest: Events at the Periphery of the Holocaust* (New York: Oxford University Press, 2012), 23.

Selected Filmography

2 or 3 Things I Know about Him (*2 oder 3 Dinge, die ich von ihm weiß*; 2004). Dir: Malte Ludin. Prod: Iva Svarcová/ National Center for Jewish Film. 85 minutes. Documentary.

The Act of Killing (2012). Dir: Joshua Oppenheimer. Prod: Final Cut for Real/ Piraya Film A/S/ Novaya Zemlya/ Spring Films. 115 minutes. Documentary.

Amon's Daughter (*Amons Tochter*; 2003). Dir: Matthias Kessler. Prod: N.E.F. Filmproduktion. 83 minutes. Documentary.

Auschwitz: Film Documents of the Monstrous Crimes of the German Government in Auschwitz (1945). Prod: Central Studio for Documentary Film, Moscow. 21 minutes. Documentary.

Bełżec (2005). Dir: Guillaume Moscovitz. Prod: VLR Productions. 100 minutes. Documentary.

Blind Spot: Hitler's Secretary (*Im toten Winkel—Hitlers Sekretärin*; 2002). Dir: André Heller and Othmar Schmiderer. Prod: Dor Film Productiongesellschaft. 87 minutes. Documentary.

Branko: Return to Auschwitz (2013). Dir: Topaz Adizes. Prod: New York Times/ Op-Docs. 10 minutes. Documentary.

Dachau 1974 (1974/75). Artist: Beryl Korot. New Art Trust, San Francisco. 23 minutes. Video installation.

The Death Camps (*Les camps de la mort*; 1945). Prod: Les Actualités Françaises. 19 minutes. Documentary.

Death Mills (1945). Dir: Hanuš Burger. Office of Military Government, United States (OMGUS). 22 minutes. (German version: *Todesmühlen*). Documentary.

Deutschland erwache (1945). Prod: USA War Department. 24 minutes. Documentary.

The Eighty-First Blow (*Ha-Makah Hashmonim V'Echad*; 1974). Dir: Haim Gouri. Prod: Ghetto Fighters' Museum. 92 minutes. Documentary.

"Execution of Jews in Liepaja" ("Juden Exekution in Libau 1941"; 1941). Camera: Reinhard Wiener. 1 minute 39 seconds. Amateur film.

A Film Unfinished (*Shtikat Haarchion*; 2010). Dir: Yael Hersonski. Prod: Itay Ken-Tor and Noemi Schory/ Belfilms, Ltd. 92 minutes. Documentary.

The Flat (*Ha-dira*; 2011). Dir: Arnon Goldfinger. Prod: ARTE/ Arnon Goldfinger Productions/ Noga Communications/ Südwestrundfunk (SWR)/ Zero One Film/ Zweites Deutsches Fernsehen (ZDF). 97 minutes. Documentary.

Forgiving Dr. Mengele (2005). Dir: Bob Hercules and Cheri Pugh. Prod: Media Process Group. 80 minutes. Documentary.

Hebrew Lesson (2002). Artist: Boaz Arad. Featured in "Mirroring Evil" at Jewish Museum, New York. Video installation. 17 seconds (loop).

The Himmler Project (*Das Himmler-Projekt*; 2000). Dir: Romuald Karmakar. Prod: Pantera Film. 182 minutes. Documentary.

Histoire(s) du cinema (1988–98). Dir: Jean-Luc Godard. Prod: Canal+/ La Sept/ France 3 (FR 3)/ Gaumont/ JLG Films/ Centre National de la Cinématographie (CNC)/ Télévision Suisse-Romande (TSR)/ Vega Film. 266 minutes. Eight-part video project.

Hitler, A Career (*Hitler—eine Karriere*; 1977). Dir: Joachim Fest and Christian Herrendoerfer. Prod: Interart/ Werner Rieb Produktion. 150 minutes. Documentary.

Hitler's Children (2011). Dir: Chanoch Ze'evi. Prod: Maya Productions/ Saxonia Entertainment. 83 minutes. Documentary.

Holocaust (1978). Dir: Marvin J. Chomsky. Prod: Titus Productions. 475 minutes. Television miniseries.

The Holocaust Tourist (2006). Dir: Jes Benstock. Prod: Technobabble/ Skyline Production. 10 minutes. Documentary.

Inheritance (2006). Dir: James Moll. Prod: Allentown Productions. 75 minutes. Documentary.

Izkor: Slaves of Memory (1991). Dir: Eyal Sivan. Prod: IMA Productions/ Rhea Films/ Zweites Deutsches Fernsehen (ZDF). 98 minutes. Documentary.

The Joel Files (2000). Dir: Beate Thalberg. Prod: DoRo Produktion. 60 minutes. Documentary.

Journey into Life (*Reisen ins Leben*; 1996). Dir: Thomas Mitscherlich. Prod: Bremer Institut Film & Fernsehen/ Hamburger Filmbüro/ Norddeutscher Rundfunk (NDR). 131 minutes. Documentary.

The Karski Report (*Le Rapport Karski*; 2010). Dir: Claude Lanzmann. Prod: Les Films Aleph. 49 minutes. Documentary.

Kitty: Return to Auschwitz (1979). Dir: Peter Morley. Prod: Yorkshire Television (YTV). 82 minutes. Documentary.

KZ (2005). Dir: Rex Bloomstein. Prod: Rex Entertainment/ Shooting People Films Ltd. 97 minutes. Documentary.

Land of Annihilation (*Land der Vernichtnug*; 2004). Dir: Romuald Karmakar. Prod: Pantera Film. 140 minutes. Documentary.

Landscapes of Memory: The Life of Ruth Klüger (*Das Weiterleben der Ruth Klüger*; 2011). Dir: Renata Schmidtkunz. Prod: Navigator Film/ Renata Schmidtkunz/ Westdeutscher Rundfunk (WDR)/ Österreichisscher Rundfunk (ORF). 84 minutes. Documentary.

The Last Days (1998). Dir: James Moll. Prod: Ken Lipper/ June Beallor Production/ Shoah Foundation/ Survivors of the Shoah Visual History Foundation. 87 minutes. Documentary.

The Last of the Unjust (*Le Dernier des Injustes*; 2013). Dir: Claude Lanzmann. Prod: Synecdoche/ Le Pacte/ Dor Film Produktionsgesellschaft. 220 minutes. Documentary.

The Last Stage (*Ostatni etap*; 1948). Dir: Wanda Jakubowska. Prod: Przedsiębiorstwo Państwowe Film Polski. 105 minutes. Feature film.

Martin (1999). Dir: Ra'anan Alexandrowicz. With Artemis Chalkidou and Florian Rohdenburg. Prod: Ra'anan Alexandrowicz/ David Ofek Productions. 50 minutes. Documentary.

Mein Kampf (*Den blodiga tiden;* 1960). Dir: Erwin Leiser. Prod: Minerva International Films. 117 minutes. Documentary.

Nazi Concentration Camps (1945). Compiled by George Stevens. Prod: U.S. Army Signal Corps. 59 minutes. Documentary.

Night and Fog (*Nuit et brouillard*; 1955). Dir: Alain Resnais. Prod: Argos Films/ Como Films/ Cocinor. 31 minutes. Documentary.

No Place on Earth (2012). Dir: Janet Tobias. Prod: A List Films/ Delirio Films/ PPM Film Productions/ Sierra Tango Productions. 83 minutes. Documentary.

Nuremberg: The Nazis Facing their Crimes (*Nuremberg: Les nazis face à leurs crimes*; 2006). Dir. Christian Delage. Prod: La Compagnie des Phares et Balises and ARTE France. 90 minutes. Documentary.

Ordinary Fascism (*Obyknovennyy fashizm*; 1965). Dir: Mikhail Romm. Prod: Mosfilm. 131 minutes. Documentary.

Paper Clips (2003). Dir: Elliot Berlin and Joe Fab. Prod: The Johnson Group/ Ergo Entertainment. 84 minutes. Documentary.

Passenger (*Pasażerka*; 1963). Dir: Andrzej Munk and Witold Lesiewicz. Prod: Zespol Filmowy "Kamera." 58 minutes. Feature film.

Photographer (*Fotoamator*; 1998). Dir: Dariusz Jabłoński. Prod: Apple Film Productions/ Broadcast AV. 52 minutes. Documentary.

The Pianist (2002). Dir: Roman Polanski. Prod: R. P. Productions/Heritage Films/Studio Babelsberg/Runteam/Canal+/StudioCanal/Bac Films/Canal+. 150 minutes. Feature film.

Pourquoi Israël (1973). Dir. Claude Lanzmann. Prod: Stéphan Films. 185 minutes. Documentary.

Respite (*Aufschub*; 2007). Dir: Harun Farocki. Prod: Harun Farocki Filmproduktion. 40 minutes. Documentary.

S21: The Khmer Rouge Killing Machine (2003). Dir: Rithy Panh. Prod: Institut National de l'Audiovisuel (INA)/ arte France Cinéma. 101 minutes. Documentary.

Schindler (1983). Dir: Jon Blair. Prod: Thames Television. 80 minutes. Documentary.

Schindler's List (1993). Dir. Steven Spielberg. Prod: Universal Pictures/ Amblin Entertainment. 195 minutes. Feature film.

Shoah (1985). Dir. Claude Lanzmann. Prod: Les Films Aleph/ Historia/ Ministère de la Culture de la Republique Française. 566 minutes. Documentary.

Shoah by Bullets (*Shoah par balles: l'Histoire oubliée*; 2008). Dir: Romain Icard. Prod: Mano a Mano/ France 3. Documentary.

Sobibor (*Sobibor, 14 octobre 1943, 16 heures*; 2001). Dir: Claude Lanzmann. Prod: Claude Lanzmann/ Les Films Aleph/ Why Not Productions. 95 minutes. Documentary.

The Sorrow and the Pity. Chronicle of a French City Under the Occupation (*Le chagrin et la pitié*; 1969) Dir: Marcel Ophüls. Prod: Télévision Rencontre/ Norddeutscher Rundfunk/ Télévision suisse romande. 251 minutes. Documentary.

The Specialist (*Un spécialiste*; 1999). Dir: Rony Brauman and Eval Sivan. Prod: Momento!/ France 2 Cinéma/ BIFF/ WDR/ Image Création/ RTBF/ Amythos/ Lotus Film. 128 minutes. Documentary.

Spielberg's List (2003). Artist: Omer Fast. gb Agency, Paris. 60 minutes (loop). Video installation/ 2 synchronized channels.

Tango of Slaves (1993). Dir: Ilan Ziv. Prod: Tamouz Media/ IKON Televisie/ Channel Four Productions/ Israel Broadcasting Authority. 107 minutes. Documentary.

Theresienstadt: A Documentary about the Jewish Settlement (*Theresienstadt—Ein Dokumentarfilm aus dem Juedischen Siedlungsgebiet*; 1944). Dir: Kurt Gerron (under duress). Aktualita/ Zentralamt zur Regelung der Judenfrage in Böhmen und Mähren. 23 minutes. Propaganda film (fragment).

The Time of the Ghetto (*Le temps du ghetto*; 1961). Dir: Frédéric Rossif. Prod: les films de la pléiade. 89 minutes. Documentary.

Triumph of the Will (*Triumph des Willens*; 1935). Dir: Leni Riefenstahl. Prod: Leni Riefenstahl-Produktion/ Reichspropagandaleitung der NSDAP. 110 minutes. Propaganda film.

Universal Hotel (1986). Dir: Peter Thompson. Prod: Thompson Films. 20 minutes. Documentary.

Victory of the Faith (*Der Sieg des Glaubens*; 1933). Dir: Leni Riefenstahl. Prod: Reichspropagandaleitung der NSDAP. 61 minutes. Propaganda film.

A Visitor from the Living (*Un vivant qui passe*; 1997). Dir: Claude Lanzmann. Prod: Claude Lanzmann/ Les Films Aleph. 65 minutes. Documentary.

The Wonderful, Horrible Life of Leni Riefenstahl (*Die Macht der Bilder: Leni Riefenstahl*; 1993). Dir: Ray Müller. Prod: Arte/Channel Four Films/Nomad Films/Omega Film GmbH/Without Walls/Zweites Deutsches Fernsehen (ZDF). 180 minutes. Documentary.

The Yellow Star: The Persecution of the Jews in Europe, 1933–1945 (1981). Dir: Dieter Hildebrandt. Prod: Chronos-Film/Michael Arthur Films. 89 minutes. Documentary.

Works Cited

Adorno, Theodor W. "Reply to Peter R. Hofstätter's Critique of *Group Experiment*." In *Guilt and Defense: On the Legacies of National Socialism in Postwar Germany*. Edited and translated by Jeffrey K. Olick and Andrew J. Perrin. Cambridge, MA: Harvard University Press, 2010, 197–209.
—"Education after Auschwitz." In *Can One Live after Auschwitz? A Philosophical Reader*. Edited by Rolf Tiedemann. Stanford, CA: Stanford University Press, 2003a.
—"The Meaning of Working through the Past." Translated by Henry W. Pickford. In *Can One Live after Auschwitz? A Philosophical Reader*. Edited by Rolf Tiedemann. Stanford, CA: Stanford University Press, 2003b, 3–18.
Améry, Jean. *At the Mind's Limits: Contemplations by a Survivor on Auschwitz and Its Realities*. Translated by Sidney Rosenfeld and Stella P. Rosenfeld. Bloomington, IN: Indiana University Press, 1980.
Arendt, Hannah. *Eichmann in Jerusalem: A Report on the Banality of Evil*. New York: Penguin Books, 1994.
—*The Human Condition*. Chicago: University of Chicago Press, 1998.
"At Auschwitz, a Discordant Atmosphere of Tourism." *New York Times*, November 3, 1974, 14.
Atlas. Zusammengestellt von deutschen Autoren. Berlin: Wagenbach, 1965.
Baer, Ulrich. *Spectral Evidence: The Photography of Trauma*. Cambridge, MA: MIT Press, 2002.
Ball, Karyn. "For and Against the *Bilderverbot*: The Rhetoric of 'Unrepresentability' and Remediated 'Authenticity' in the German Reception of Steven Spielberg's *Schindler's List*." In *Visualizing the Holocaust: Documents, Aesthetics, Memory*. Edited by David Bathrick, Brad Prager, and Michael D. Richardson. Rochester, NY: Camden House, 2008, 162–84.
Bangert, Axel, Robert S. C. Gordon and Libby Saxton, "Introduction." In *Holocaust Intersections: Genocide and Visual Culture at the New Millennium*. Edited by Axel Bangert, Robert S. C. Gordon, and Libby Saxton. London: Legenda, 2013.
Baron, Lawrence. *Projecting the Holocaust into the Present: The Changing Focus of Contemporary Holocaust Cinema*. Lanham, MD: Rowman and Littlefield, 2005.
Barthes, Roland. *Camera Lucida: Reflections on Photography*. Translated by Richard Howard. New York: Noonday Press, 1981 (orig. 1980).
Bartov, Omer. "Spielberg's Oskar: Hollywood Tries Evil." In *Spielberg's Holocaust: Critical Perspectives on* Schindler's List. Edited by Yosefa Loshitzky. Bloomington, IN: Indiana University Press, 1997, 41–60.

Bathrick, David. "Billy Wilder's Cold War Berlin." *New German Critique* 37, 2 (2010): 31–47.

Beck, Eldad. "The Nazi's Grandson." May 18, 2011. *ynetnews.com*, http://www.ynetnews.com/articles/0,7340,L-4070115,00.html

Blum, Thomas. "Mauthausen is' no' net untaganga!" *Jungle World* 5, February 1, 2007, http://jungle-world.com/artikel/2007/05/19008.html

Boas, Jacob. "A Nazi Travels to Palestine." *History Today* 30, 1 (1980): 33–8.

Bolter, Jay David and Richard Grusin. *Remediation: Understanding New Media*. Cambridge, MA: MIT Press, 1999.

Böser, Ursula. "*A Film Unfinished*: Yael Hersonski's Re-representation of Archival Footage from the Warsaw Ghetto." *Film Criticism* 37, 2 (2013): 38–56.

Braiterman, Zachary. "Against Holocaust-Sublime: Naïve Reference and the Generation of Memory." *History & Memory* 12, 2 (2000): 7–28.

Brecher, Elinor J. *Schindler's Legacy: True Stories of the List Survivors*. New York: Dutton, 1994.

Brink, Cornelia. "Secular Icons: Looking at Photographs from Nazi Concentration Camps." *History & Memory* 12, 1 (2000): 135–50.

Broder, Henryk M. *Der ewige Antisemit: Über Sinn und Funktion eines beständigen Gefühls*. Frankfurt am Main: Fischer-Taschenbuch-Verlag, 1986.

—*Vergesst Auschwitz! Der deutsche Erinnerungswahn und die Endlösung der Israel-Frage*. Munich: Albrecht Knaus, 2012.

—"Auschwitz ist heute ein Disneyland des Todes." *Die Welt*, January 27, 2014, http://www.welt.de/kultur/article124251623/Auschwitz-ist-heute-ein-Disneyland-des-Todes.html.

Brumlik, Micha and Lena Inowlocki. "Die grundlegende Bedeutung der Vergebung. Antwort auf Harald Welzers Umgang mit der Trauma-Therapie." *Frankfurter Rundschau* 142 (June 23, 2003): 7.

Buerkle, Darcy C. "Affect in the Archive: Arendt, Eichmann and *The Specialist*." In *Visualizing the Holocaust: Documents—Aesthetics—Memory*. Edited by David Bathrick, Brad Prager, and Michael D. Richardson. Rochester, NY: Camden House, 2008, 211–38.

Cesarani, David. *Becoming Eichmann: Rethinking the Life, Crimes, and Trial of a "Desk Murderer."* Cambridge, MA: Da Capo Press, 2004.

Chevrie, Marc and Hervé Le Roux. "Site and Speech: An Interview with Claude Lanzmann about *Shoah*." Translated by Stuart Liebman. *Claude Lanzmann's* Shoah: *Key Essays*. Edited by Stuart Liebman. Oxford: Oxford University Press, 2007, 37–49.

Cole, Tim. *Selling the Holocaust: From Auschwitz to Schindler—How History Is Bought, Packaged, and Sold*. New York: Routledge, 1999.

—"Crematoria, Barracks, Gateway: Survivors' Return Visits to the Memory Landscapes of Auschwitz." *History & Memory* 25, 2 (2013): 102–31.

Corrigan, Timothy. *The Essay Film: From Montaigne, after Marker*. Oxford: Oxford University Press, 2011.

Crowe, David M. *Oskar Schindler: The Untold Account of his Life, Wartime Activities, and the True Story Behind the List*. New York: Basic Books, 2004.

Daniell, Raymond. "War-Crimes Court Sees Horror Films. Motion Pictures of German Concentration Camps are Displayed as Evidence." *The New York Times*, November 30, 1945, 6.

D'Arcy, Michael. "Claude Lanzmann's *Shoah* and the Intentionality of the Image." In *Visualizing the Holocaust: Documents, Aesthetics, Memory*. Edited by David Bathrick, Brad Prager, and Michael D. Richardson. Rochester, NY: Camden House, 2008, 138–61.

"A Daughter's Point of View," *POV*. Interview with Vivian Delman. December 10, 2008. http://www.pbs.org/pov/inheritance/special_survivor.php.

Dawidowicz, Lucy S. *The War against the Jews, 1933–1945*. New York: Holt, Rinehart and Winston, 1975.

—"Visualizing the Warsaw Ghetto: Nazi Images of the Jews Refiltered by the BBC. A Critical Review of the BBC Film, *The Warsaw Ghetto*." *Shoah: A Journal of Resources on the Holocaust* 1, 1 (1978): 5–6, 17.

Derrida, Jacques. *On Cosmopolitanism and Forgiveness*. Translated by Michael Hughes. New York: Routledge, 2001.

Didi-Huberman, Georges. "The Site, Despite Everything." Translated by Stuart Liebman. In *Claude Lanzmann's* Shoah*: Key Essays*. Edited by Stuart Liebman. Oxford: Oxford University Press, 2007, 113–23.

—*Images in Spite of All: Four Photographs from Auschwitz*. Translated by Shane B. Lillis. Chicago: University of Chicago Press, 2008.

Distel, Barbara. "Neue Formen der Erinnerung." In *Realität, Metapher, Symbol. Auseinandersetzung mit dem Konzentrationslager*. Dachauer Hefte, vol. 22. Dachauer Hefte Verlag: Dachau, 2006, 3–10.

Dollinger, Roland. "Anti-Semitism *Because of* Auschwitz: An Introduction to the Works of Henryk M. Broder." In *Rebirth of a Culture: Jewish Identity and Jewish Writing in Germany and Austria Today*. Edited by Hillary Hope Herzog, Todd Herzog, and Benjamin Lapp. New York: Berghahn Books, 2008, 67–82.

Douglas, Lawrence. *The Memory of Judgment: Making Law and History in the Trials of the Holocaust*. New Haven, CT: Yale University Press, 2001.

Ebbrecht, Tobias. *Geschichtsbilder im medialen Gedächtnis. Filmische Narrationen des Holocaust*. Bielefeld: Transcript Verlag, 2011.

Edkins, Jenny. "Authenticity and Memory at Dachau." *Cultural Values* 5, 4 (2001): 405–20.

Engelking, Barbara and Jacek Leociak. *The Warsaw Ghetto: A Guide to the Perished City*. Translated by Emma Harris. New Haven, CT: Yale University Press, 2009.

Evans, Becky. "Amon Goeth: Did 'Executed' Nazi Criminal in *Schindler's List* Escape Justice?" *Mail Online*, March 21, 2013, http://www.dailymail.co.uk/news/article-2296911/Amon-Goeth-Did-executed-Nazi-murderer-Schindlers-List-escape-justice.html

Evans, Richard J. *Lying about Hitler: History, Holocaust, and the David Irving Trial*. New York: Basic Books, 2001.

Frankfurter, Bernhard (ed.), *The Meeting: An Auschwitz Survivor Confronts an SS Physician*. Translated by Susan E. Cernyak-Spatz. Syracuse, NY: Syracuse University Press, 2000.

Friedländer, Saul. *The Years of Extermination: Nazi Germany and the Jews, 1939–1945*. New York: Harper Perennial, 2008.

Friedman, Norman. "Point of View in Fiction: The Development of a Critical Concept." *PMLA* 70, 5 (1955): 1160–84.

Giesen, Bernhard and Christoph Schneider (eds), *Tätertrauma: Nationale Erinnerungen im öffentlichen Diskurs*. Konstanz: UVK-Verlagsgesellschaft, 2004.

Godfrey, Mark. *Abstraction and the Holocaust*. New Haven, CT: Yale University Press, 2007.

Goldberg, Vicki. *The Power of Photography: How Photographs Changed our Lives*. New York: Abbeville Press, 1991.

Göth, Monika. (As Knauss geb. Göth, Monika). "Rettung durch Schweigen." *Der Spiegel* 11 (March 14, 1983): 12.

Gladstone, Kay. "Separate Intentions: The Allied Screening of Concentration Camp Documentaries in Defeated Germany in 1945–46: *Death Mills* and *Memory of the Camps*." In *Holocaust and the Moving Image: Representations in Film and Television Since 1933*. Edited by Toby Haggith and Joanna Newman. London: Wallflower Press, 2005, 50–64.

—"Memory of the Camps: The Rescue of an Abandoned Film." In *Concentrationary Cinema: Aesthetics as Political Resistance in Alain Resnais's* Night and Fog *(1955)*. Edited by Griselda Pollock and Max Silverman. New York: Berghahn Books, 2011, 71–83.

Gouri, Haim. *Facing the Glass Booth: The Jerusalem Trial of Adolf Eichmann*. Translated by Michael Swirsky. Detroit, MI: Wayne State University Press, 2004.

Grodin, Michael A., Eva M. Kor, and Susan Benedict. *The Trial That Never Happened: Josef Mengele and the Twins of Auschwitz*. Berkeley, CA: Berkeley Electronic Press, 2011, http://works.bepress.com/michael_grodin/1

Gross, Jan Tomasz with Irena Grudzińska-Gross. *Golden Harvest: Events at the Periphery of the Holocaust*. New York: Oxford University Press, 2012.

Hansen, Miriam Bratu. "*Schindler's List* Is Not *Shoah*: Second Commandment, Popular Modernism, and Public Memory." In *Visual Culture and the Holocaust*. Edited by Barbie Zelizer. New Brunswick, NJ: Rutgers University Press, 2001, 127–51.

Heckner, Elke, "Whose Trauma Is It? Identification and Secondary Witnessing in the Age of Postmemory." In *Visualizing the Holocaust: Documents, Aesthetics, Memory*. Edited by David Bathrick, Brad Prager, and Michael D. Richardson. Rochester, NY: Camden House, 2008.

Herzinger, Richard. "Ernst von Salomon: Konservativ-revolutionäre Literatur zwischen Tatrhetorik und Resignation." *Zeitschrift für Germanistik*, n.s. 8, 1 (1998): 83–96.

Hicks, Jeremy. *First Films of the Holocaust: Soviet Cinema and the Genocide of the Jews, 1938-1946*. Pittsburgh, PA: University of Pittsburgh Press, 2012.

Hilberg, Raul. *Perpetrators, Victims, Bystanders: The Jewish Catastrophe, 1933–1945*. New York: Harper-Collins, 1992.

—*The Destruction of the European Jews*, 3rd edn, vol. II. New Haven, CT: Yale University Press, 2003.

Hilberg, Raul, Stanislaw Staron, and Josef Kermisz (ed.), *The Warsaw Diary of Adam Czerniakow: Prelude to Doom*. Translated by Stanislaw Staron and the staff of Yad Vashem. New York: Stein and Day, 1979.

Hippler, Fritz. *Die Verstrickung: Einstellungen und Rückblenden*. Düsseldorf: Verlag Mehr Wissen, 1981.

Hirsch, Joshua. *Afterimage: Film, Trauma, and the Holocaust*. Philadelphia: Temple University Press, 2004.

Hirsch, Marianne. *Family Frames: Photography, Narrative, and Postmemory*. Cambridge, MA: Harvard University Press, 1997.

—"Nazi Photographs in Post-Holocaust Art: Gender as an Idiom of Memorialization." In *Phototextualities: Intersections of Photography and Narrative*. Edited by Alex Hughes and Andrea Noble. Albuquerque: University of New Mexico Press, 2003, 19–40.

—*The Generation of Postmemory: Writing and Visual Culture after the Holocaust*. New York: Columbia University Press, 2012.

Höhne, Heinz. "Der Orden unter dem Totenkopf: Die Geschichte der SS." *Der Spiegel* 42, October 10 (1966a): 94–109.

—"Der Orden unter dem Totenkopf. Die Geschichte der SS—10. Fortsetzung: Die antijüdische Politik der SS." *Der Spiegel* 52 (December 19, 1966b): 66–84.

Horowitz, Sara R. "But Is It Good for the Jews? Spielberg's Schindler and the Aesthetics of Atrocity." In *Spielberg's Holocaust: Critical Perspectives on* Schindler's List. Edited by Yosefa Loshitzky. Bloomington, IN: Indiana University Press, 1997, 119–39.

Horstmann, Anja. "'Judenaufnahmen fürs Archiv'—Das dokumentarische Filmmaterial *Asien in Mitteleuropa*, 1942." *Medaon: Magazin für Jüdisches Leben in Forschung und Bildung* 4 (2009): 1–11.

Huyssen, Andreas. *Twilight Memories: Marking Time in a Culture of Amnesia*. New York: Routledge, 1995.

—"Of Mice and Mimesis: Reading Spiegelman with Adorno." *New German Critique* 81 (2000): 65–82.

Insdorf, Annette. *Indelible Shadows: Film and the Holocaust*, 2nd edn. Cambridge: Cambridge University Press, 1989.

Jacobs, Leonard. "How Yael Hersonski Finished *A Film Unfinished*." In *The Clyde Fitch Report*. September 6, 2010, http://www.clydefitchreport.com/2010/09/how-yael-hersonski-finished-a-film-unfinished/.

Jacobs, Steven. "Hitchcock, the Holocaust, and the Long Take: *Memory of the Camps*," *arcadia* 45, 2 (2011): 265–76.

Jansen, Ludiger. "Alles Schlußstrich – oder was? Eine philosophische Auseinandersetzung mit Martin Walsers Friedenspreisrede." *Theologie und Philosophie* 80 (2005): 412–22.

Jaubert, Alain. "Filmer la photographie et son hors-champ." In *Clio de 5 à 7. Les actualités filmées de la Libération: archives du future*. Edited by Sylvie Lindeperg. Paris: CNRS éditions, 2000.

Jenny, Urs. "Holocaust mit Happy-End?" *Der Spiegel* 21 (May 24, 1993): 208–13.

Jockusch, Laura. *Collect and Record! Jewish Holocaust Documentation in early Postwar Europe*. Oxford: Oxford University Press, 2012.

Kacandes, Irene. "'When facts are scarce': Authenticating Strategies in Writing by Children of Survivors." In *After Testimony: The Ethics and Aesthetics of Holocaust Narrative for the Future*. Edited by Jakob Lothe, Susan Rubin Suleiman, and James Phelan. Columbus, OH: Ohio State University Press, 2012, 179–97.

Kaes, Anton. *From 'Hitler' to 'Heimat': The Return of History as Film*. Cambridge, MA: Harvard University Press, 1989.

Kapczynski, Jennifer M. *The German Patient: Crisis and Recovery in Postwar Culture*. Ann Arbor, MI: University of Michigan Press, 2008.

Kaplan, Chaim A. *The Warsaw Diary of Chaim A. Kaplan*. Translated by Abraham I. Katsh. New York: Collier Books, 1973.

Keller, Werner. *Diaspora: The Post-Biblical History of the Jews*. Translated by Richard and Clara Winston. New York: Harcourt, Brace & World, 1969.

Keneally, Thomas. *Schindler's List*. 1982. New York: Scribner, 2000.

Kerner, Aaron. *Film and the Holocaust: New Perspectives on Dramas, Documentaries, and Experimental Films*. New York: Continuum, 2011.

Kessler, Matthias with Monika Göth. *"Ich muß doch meinen Vater lieben, oder?": Die Lebensgeschichte der Monika Göth, der Tochter des KZ-Kommandanten aus Schindlers Liste*. Frankfurt am Main: Eichborn, 2002.

Kite, Buddy. "The Man Turning the History of Our Time into Art." *Esquire.com*, December 15, 2008, http://www.esquire.com/features/best-and-brightest-2008/video-artist-omer-fast-1208

Kligerman, Eric. "Celan's Cinematic: Anxiety of the Gaze in *Night and Fog* and 'Engführung.'" In *Visualizing the Holocaust: Documents—Aesthetics—Memory*. Edited by David Bathrick, Brad Prager, and Michael D. Richardson. Rochester, NY: Camden House, 2008, 185–210.

Klüger, Ruth. "Dichten über die Shoah. Zum Problem des literarischen Umgangs mit dem Massenmord." In *Spuren der Verfolgung: Seelische Auswirkungen des Holocaust auf die Opfer und ihre Kinder*. Edited by Gertrud Hardtmann. Gerlingen: Bleicher, 1992, 203–21.
—*Katastrophen: Über deutsche Literatur*. Göttingen: Wallstein, 1994, 39–58.
—*Still Alive: A Holocaust Girlhood Remembered*. New York: Feminist Press at CUNY, 2001a.
—"Wiener Neurosen. Eine Rede." *Hören: Zeitschrift für Literatur, Kunst und Kritik* 46 (2001b): 21–29.
—"Forgiving and Remembering." *PMLA* 117, 2 (March 2002): 311–13.
—"The Future of Holocaust Literature: German Studies Association 2013 Banquet Speech." *German Studies Review* 37, 2 (2014): 391–403.
—*Gelesene Wirklichkeit. Fakten und Fiktionen in der Literatur*. Göttingen: Wallstein, 2006.
—(As Ruth K. Angress). "Lanzmann's *Shoah* and Its Audience." Museum of Tolerance Online Learning Center, http://motlc.wiesenthal.com/site/pp.asp?c=gvKVLcMVIuG&b=395045
—*unterwegs verloren. Erinnerungen*. Wien: dtv, 2010 (orig. 2008).
Knigge, Volkhard. "Gedenkstätten und Museen." In *Verbrechen erinnern. Die Auseinandersetzung mit Holocaust und Völkermord*. Edited by Volkhard Knigge and Norbert Frei. Munich: Beck, 2002, 378–89.
Koch, Gertrud. "The Angel of Forgetfulness and the Black Box of Facticity: Trauma and Memory in Claude Lanzmann's *Shoah*." *History and Memory* 3, 1 (1991): 119–34.
—"Schindler's List: Myth, Movie, and Memory." *Village Voice* (March 29, 1994): 24–31.
Kohen-Raz, Odeya. "Arnon Goldfinger's *The Flat* (2011): Ethics and Aesthetics in Third Generation Holocaust Cinema." *Studies in Documentary Film* 6, 3 (2012): 323–38.
Köppen, Manuel. "Erinnerungslandschaften. Claude Lanzmanns *Sobibor* (2001) und Romuald Karmakars *Land der Vernichtung* (2004)." In *NachBilder des Holocaust*. Edited by Inge Stephan and Alexandra Tacke. Cologne: Böhlau Verlag, 2007, 77–90.
Kor, Eva. "Heilung von Auschwitz und Mengeles Experimenten." In *Die Verbindung nach Auschwitz: Biowissenschaften und Menschenversuche an Kaiser-Wilhelm-Instituten—Dokumentation eines Symposiums*. Edited by Carola Sachse. Göttingen: Wallstein Verlag, 2003, 59–70.
Kor, Eva Mozes and Lisa Rojany-Buccieri. *Surviving the Angel of Death: The True Story of a Mengele Twin in Auschwitz*. Terre Haute, IN: Tanglewood Press, 2009.
Kracauer, Siegfried. *Theory of Film: The Redemption of Physical Reality*. Oxford: Oxford University Press, 1960.
—"Photography." Translated by Thomas Y. Levin. *Critical Inquiry* 19, 3 (1993): 421–36.
Krojanker, Gustav. *The Transfer: A Vital Question of the Zionist Movement*, English edn. Tel Aviv: Publications of the Hitachduth Olei Germania, 1936.

Kurlansky, Mark. *A Chosen Few: The Resurrection of European Jewry*. Reading, MA: Addison-Wesley, 1995.

LaCapra, Dominick. *History and Memory after Auschwitz*. Ithaca, NY: Cornell University Press, 1998.

—"Holocaust Testimonies: Attending to the Victim's Voice." In *Catastrophe and Memory: The Holocaust and the Twentieth Century*. Edited by Moishe Postone and Eric Santner. Chicago: University of Chicago Press, 2003, 209–31.

Lang, Berel. *The Future of the Holocaust: Between History and Memory*. Ithaca, NY: Cornell University Press, 1999.

—*Act and Idea in the Nazi Genocide*. Syracuse, NY: Syracuse University Press, 2003.

Langford, Barry. "'You cannot look at this': Thresholds of Unrepresentability in Holocaust Film." *Holocaust Studies: A Journal of Culture and History* 8, 3 (1999): 23–40.

Lanzmann, Claude. "From the Holocaust to the *Holocaust*." *Telos* 42 (1979/80): 137–43.

—*Shoah: An Oral History of the Holocaust: The Complete Text of the Film*. New York: Pantheon, 1985.

—"Le Lieu et la parole." In *Au sujet de Shoah: le film de Claude Lanzmann,* Edited by Bernard Cuau, Michel Deguy and Rachel Ertel. Paris: Belin, 1990, 293–305.

—"Holocauste, la représentation impossible." *Le Monde* (March 3, 1994): AS 1+.

—*The Patagonian Hare: A Memoir*. Translated by Frank Wynne. New York: Farrar, Straus and Giroux, 2012.

Lanzmann, Claude, Ruth Larson, and David Rodowick, "Seminar with Claude Lanzmann, 11 April 1990." *Yale French Studies* 79 (1991): 82–99.

Lax, Martin H. *Caraseu: A Holocaust Remembrance*. With Michael B. Lax. Cleveland, OH: Pilgrim Press, 1996.

Lewis-Kraus, Gideon. "Infinite Jetzt." In *In Memory: Omer Fast*. Edited by Sabine Schaschl and Kunsthaus Baselland. Berlin: Green Box, 2010, 26–81.

Levi, Primo. *The Drowned and the Saved*. Translated by Raymond Rosenthal. New York: Vintage, 1989.

Liebman, Stuart. "Introduction." In *Claude Lanzmann's* Shoah*: Key Essays*. Edited by Stuart Liebman. Oxford: Oxford University Press, 2007, 3–24.

—"Historiography/ Holocaust Cinema: Challenges and Advances." In *Cinema & the Shoah: An Art Confronts the Tragedy of the Twentieth Century*. Edited by Jean-Michel Frodon. Albany, NY: State University of New York Press, 2010, 205–16.

—"The Never-Ending Story: Yael Hersonski's *A Film Unfinished*." *Cineaste* 36, 3 (2011): 15–19.

Lindeperg, Sylvie. *"Night and Fog": A Film in History*. Translated by Tom Mes. Minneapolis, MN: University of Minnesota Press, 2014.

—"*Night and Fog*: Inventing a Perspective." *Cinema & the Shoah: An Art Confronts the Tragedy of the Twentieth Century*. Translated by Tom Mes, edited by Jean-Michel Frodon. Albany, NY: State University of New York Press, 2010, 71–91.

Lipstadt, Deborah E. *The Eichmann Trial*. New York: Nextbook/Schocken, 2011.

Liss, Andrea. *Trespassing through Shadows: Memory, Photography, and the Holocaust*. Minneapolis, MN: University of Minnesota Press, 1998.

Loshitsky, Yosefa. "Holocaust Others: Spielberg's *Schindler's List* versus Lanzmann's *Shoah*." In *Spielberg's Holocaust: Critical Perspectives on* Schindler's List. Edited by Yosefa Loshitzky. Bloomington, IN: Indiana University Press, 1997, 104–18.

Ludin, Malte. "Nazi-Lügen verbreitet: zum Film *Hitler—eine Karriere*." In *Neofaschismus: Die Rechten im Aufwind*. Edited by Jan Peters. Berlin: Sozialpolitischer Verlag, 1979, 45–51.

—*Wolfgang Staudte*. Reinbek bei Hamburg: Rowohlt, 1996.

Luhmann, Niklas. *Art as a Social System*. Translated by Eva M. Knodt. Stanford, CA: Stanford University Press, 2000.

Luhmann, Susanne. "Filming Familial Secrets: Approaching and Avoiding Legacies of Nazi Perpetration." *New German Critique* 112 (2011): 115–34.

Łysak, Tomasz. "On the Impossibility of Believing in the Documentary: Dariusz Jabłoński's *Photographer*." Special issue, *Kwartalnik Filmowy* (2013): 128–39.

MacCabe, Colin. *Godard: A Portrait of the Artist at 70*. London: Bloomsbury, 2004.

Macnab, Geoffrey. "Packaging the Holocaust." *The Independent*, August 5, 1999, http://www.independent.co.uk/arts-entertainment/film-packaging-the-holocaust-1110951.html

Magilow, Daniel H. "The Interpreter's Dilemma: Heinrich Jöst's Warsaw Ghetto Photographs." In *Visualizing the Holocaust: Documents—Aesthetics—Memory*. Edited by David Bathrick, Brad Prager, and Michael D. Richardson. Rochester, NY: Camden House, 2008, 38–61.

Mandelbaum, Jacques. "Recovery." In *Cinema and the Shoah: An Art Confronts the Tragedy of the Twentieth Century*. Edited by Jean-Michel Frodon. Translated by Anna Harrison and Tom Mes. Albany, NY: SUNY Press, 2010, 25–42.

Marcuse, Harold. *Legacies of Dachau: The Uses and Abuses of a Concentration Camp, 1933–2001*. Cambridge: Cambridge University Press, 2001.

Margry, Karel. "The First Theresienstadt Film (1942)." *Historical Journal of Film, Radio and Television* 19 (1999): 309–37.

Maynard, Patrick. "The Secular Icon: Photography and the Functions of Images." *The Journal of Aesthetics and Art Criticism* 42, 2 (1983): 155–69.

McGlothlin, Erin. "Autobiographical Re-vision: Ruth Klüger's *weiter leben* and *Still Alive*." *Gegenwartsliteratur* 3 (2004): 46–70.

—*Second-Generation Holocaust Literature: Legacies of Survival and Perpetration*. Rochester, NY: Camden House, 2006.

—"Listening to the Perpetrators in Claude Lanzmann's *Shoah*." *Colloquia Germanica* 43, 3 (2010): 235–71.

McLuhan, Marshall and Harley Parker. *Counterblast*. Toronto and Montreal: McClelland Stewart, 1969.

Melamed, Laliv. "A Film Unraveled: An Interview with Yael Hersonski." *International Journal of Politics, Culture, and Society* 26, 1 (2013): 9–19.

Mesnard, Philippe. "La mémoire cinématographique de la Shoah." In *Parler des camps, penser les genocides*. Edited by Catherine Coquito. Paris: Éditions Albin Michel, 1999, 473–90.

Morag, Raya. "Perpetrator Trauma and Current Israeli Documentary Cinema." *Camera Obscura* 27, 2 (2012): 93–133.

Morris, Leslie. "Berlin Elegies: Absence, Postmemory, and Art after Auschwitz." In *Image and Remembrance: Representation and the Holocaust*. Edited by Shelley Hornstein and Florence Jacobowitz. Bloomington, IN: Indiana University Press, 2003, 288–304.

Mostowicz, Arnold. *With a Yellow Star and a Red Cross: A Doctor in the Łódź Ghetto*. London and Portland, OR: Vallentine Mitchell, 2005.

"Munich-Allach." In *The United States Holocaust Memorial Museum Encyclopedia of Camps and Ghettos, 1933–1945*. Edited by Geoffrey P. Megargee. Bloomington, IN: Indiana University Press in association with the United States Holocaust Memorial Museum, 2009, 516–18.

Nichols, Bill. *Introduction to Documentary*, 2nd edn. Bloomington: Indiana University Press, 2010.

Niederland, William G. "Psychiatric Disorders Among Persecution Victims: A Contribution to the Understanding of Concentration Camp Pathology and Its After-effects." *Journal of Nervous and Mental Disease* 139, 5 (1964): 458–74.

Niethammer, Lutz. "Widerstand des Gesichts? Beobachtungen an dem Filmfragment 'Der Führer schenkt den Juden eine Stadt.'" *Journal Geschichte* 2 (1989): 34–47.

Neurath, Paul Martin. *The Society of Terror: Inside the Dachau and Buchenwald Concentration Camps*. Edited by Christian Fleck and Nico Stehr. Boulder, CO and London: Paradigm, 2005.

Obenaus, Herbert. "Das Foto vom Baumhängen—ein Bild geht um die Welt." *Gedenkstättenrundbrief* 68 (October 1995): 3–8.

Ophüls, Marcel. "Closely Watched Trains." In *Claude Lanzmann's Shoah: Key Essays*. Edited by Stuart Liebman. Oxford: Oxford University Press, 2007, 77–87.

Pingel, Falk. "Building X at Dachau: A Special Case." In *Nazi Mass Murder: A Documentary History of the Use of Poison Gas*. Edited by Eugen Kogon, Hermann Langbein, and Adalbert Rückerl. New Haven, CT: Yale University Press, 1993, 202–4.

Pickford, Henry W. *The Sense of Semblance: Philosophical Analyses of Holocaust Art*. New York: Fordham University Press, 2013.

Pollock, Griselda. "Death in the Image: The Responsibility of Aesthetics in *Night and Fog* (1955) and *Kapò* (1959)." In *Concentrationary Cinema: Aesthetics as Political Resistance in Alain Resnais's* Night and Fog *(1955)*. Edited by Griselda Pollock and Max Silverman. New York: Berghahn Books, 2011, 258–301.

Pollock, Griselda and Max Silverman, "Introduction: Concentrationary Cinema." In *Concentrationary Cinema: Aesthetics as Political Resistance in Alain Resnais's Night and Fog (1955)*. Edited by Griselda Pollock and Max Silverman. New York: Berghahn Books, 2011, 1–54.

Prager, Brad. "Interpreting the Visible Traces of Theresienstadt." *Journal of Modern Jewish Studies* 7, 2 (2008): 175–94.

—"Leben heißt Posieren: Bilder aus dem Warschauer Ghetto—mit Susan Sontag betrachtet." *Fotogeschichte* 126 (2012): 37–48.

"Ralph Izzard Exposes: The Nazis behind the Egyptian Propaganda War—Goebbels Men Help Nasser." *Daily Mail*, December 10, 1956.

Renov, Michael. "Toward a Poetics of Documentary." In *Theorizing Documentary*. Edited by Michael Renov. New York: Routledge, 1993, 12–36.

—*The Subject of Documentary*. Minneapolis, MN: University of Minnesota Press, 2004.

Rentschler, Eric. *The Ministry of Illusion: Nazi Cinema and its Afterlife*. Cambridge, MA: Harvard University Press, 1996.

Richardson, Michael D. "Reenacting Evil: Giving Voice to the Perpetrator in *Das Himmler-Projekt* and *Das Goebbels-Experiment*." *Colloquia Germanica* 43, 3 (2010): 175–94.

Ringelblum, Emmanuel. "Inside the Ghetto: Emmanuel Ringelblum." In *The Holocaust: A Reader*. Edited by Simone Gigliotti and Berel Lang. Malden, MA: Blackwell, 2005, 313–33.

Rose, Sven-Erik. "Auschwitz as Hermeneutic Rupture, Differend, and Image *malgré tout*: Jameson, Lyotard, Didi-Huberman." In *Visualizing the Holocaust: Documents—Aesthetics—Memory*. Edited by David Bathrick, Brad Prager, and Michael D. Richardson. Rochester, NY: Camden House, 2008, 114–37.

Rothberg, Michael. *Traumatic Realism: The Demands of Holocaust Representation*. Minneapolis, MN: University of Minnesota Press, 2000.

—*Multidirectional Memory: Remembering the Holocaust in the Age of Decolonization*. Stanford, CA: Stanford University Press, 2009.

Rothe, Anne. *Popular Trauma Culture: Selling the Pain of others in the Mass Media*. New Brunswick, NJ: Rutgers University Press, 2011.

Rupnow, Dirk. "Die Spuren nationalsozialistischer Gedächtnispolitik und unser Umgang mit den Bildern der Täter: Ein Beitrag zu Yael Hersonskis *A Film Unfinished/ Geheimsache Ghettofilm*." *Zeitgeschichte online*, October 2010. www.zeitgeschichte-online.de/film/die-spuren-15nationalsozialistischer-gedaechtnispolitik-und-unser-umgang-mit-den-bildern-der.

"Ruth Klüger: 'Wien schreit nach Antisemitismus.'" Interview with Ruth Klüger. *Der Spiegel* online, August 31, 2006, http://www.spiegel.de/panorama/ruth-klueger-wien-schreit-nach-antisemitismus-a-434150.html.

Ryback, Timothy W. *The Last Survivor: Legacies of Dachau*. New York: Vintage, 1999.

Sachslehner, Johannes. *Der Tod ist ein Meister aus Wien. Leben und Taten des Amon Leopold Göth*. Styria: Wien, 2008.

Santner, Eric L. *Stranded Objects, Mourning, Memory and Film in Postwar Germany*. Ithaca, NY: Cornell University Press, 1990.
Sanyal, Debarati. "Auschwitz as Allegory in *Night and Fog*." In *Concentrationary Cinema: Aesthetics as Political Resistance in Alain Resnais's* Night and Fog *(1955)*. Edited by Griselda Pollock and Max Silverman. New York: Berghahn Books, 2011, 152–82.
Sarkar, Bhaskar and Janet Walker. "Introduction: Moving Testimonies." In *Documentary Testimonies: Global Archives of Suffering*. Edited by Bhaskar Sarkar and Janet Walker. New York: Routledge, 2010, 1–34.
Sartre, Jean-Paul. *On Genocide*. Boston: Beacon Press, 1968.
Saxton, Libby. *Haunted Images: Film, Ethics, Testimony and the Holocaust*. London: Wallflower Press, 2008.
—"*Night and Fog* and the Concentrationary Gaze." In *Concentrationary Cinema: Aesthetics as Political Resistance in Alain Resnais's* Night and Fog *(1955)*. Edited by Griselda Pollock and Max Silverman. New York: Berghahn Books, 2011, 140–51.
Schirra, Bruno. "Die Erinnerung der Täter." *Der Spiegel* 40 (1998): 90–100.
Schweinitz, Jörg. *Film and Stereotype: A Challenge for Cinema and Theory*. Translated by Laura Schleussner. New York: Columbia University Press, 2011.
Segev, Tom. *Soldiers of Evil: The Commandants of the Nazi Concentration Camps*. New York: McGraw-Hill, 1987.
Senfft, Alexandra. *Schweigen tut weh—Eine deutsche Familiengeschichte*. Berlin: Claassen, 2007.
Shenker, Noah. "Embodied Memory: The Institutional Mediation of Survivor Testimony in the United States Holocaust Memorial Museum." In *Documentary Testimonies: Global Archives of Suffering*. Edited by Bhaskar Sarkar and Janet Walker. New York: Routledge, 2010, 35–58.
Sierakowiak, Dawid. *Diary of Dawid Sierakowiak: Five Notebooks from the Lodz Ghetto*. Translated by Kamil Turowski. New York: Oxford University Press, 1996.
Smale, Catherine. "'Ungelöste Gespenster?': Ghosts in Ruth Klüger's Autobiographical Project." *Modern Language Review* 104, 3 (2009): 777–89.
Stanzel, F. K. *A Theory of Narrative*. Cambridge: CUP Archive, 1986.
Struk, Janina. *Photographing the Holocaust: Interpretations of the Evidence*. London: I. B. Tauris, 2004.
Stuhlpfarrer, Karl. "Österreich." In *Verbrechen erinnern: Die Auseinandersetzung mit Holocaust und Völkermord*. Edited by Volkhard Knigge and Norbert Frei. Munich: Beck, 2002, 233–52.
Sznaider. Natan. "Grenzen der Vergebung: Vesöhnung ist ein politischer Prozess." *Frankfurter Rundschau*, June 30, 2003.
Tacke, Alexandra. "Zwei oder drei Dinge über Malte Ludins Film *2 oder 3 Dinge, die ich von ihm weiß*." In *Das Böse im Blick: Die Gegenwart des Nazionalsozialismus im Film*. Edited by Margrit Frölich, Christian Schneider, and Karsten Visarius. Munich: Text + kritik, 2007, 191–203.

Teege, Jennifer. *Amon: Mein Grossvater hätte mich erschossen (Amon: My Grandfather Would Have Shot Me)*. With Nikola Sellmair. Reinbek: Rowohlt, 2013.

Thomas, David. *Vertov, Snow, Farocki: Machine Vision and the Posthuman*. New York: Bloomsbury, 2013.

Trezise, Thomas. *Witnessing Witnessing: On the Reception of Holocaust Survivor Testimony*. New York: Fordham University Press, 2013.

Trial of the Major War Criminals Before the International Military Tribunal. Nuremberg 14 November 1945—1 October 1946. Volume 2. Nuremberg: Secretariat of the Tribunal, 1947.

Trunk, Isaiah. *Łodz Ghetto: A History*. Translated and edited by Robert Moses Shapiro. Bloomington, IN: Indiana University Press, 2006.

Tuchler, Kurt. "Erlebnisse und Beobachtungen in den ersten vier Hitlerjahren." Yad Vashem Archives, Ball-Kaduri Collection, Archive Number 01/24 (1945).

van der Knaap, Ewout (ed.), *Uncovering the Holocaust: The International Reception of Night and Fog*. London: Wallflower Press, 2006.

Vice, Sue. *Shoah*. London: Palgrave Macmillan/BFI, 2011.

Vitiello, Guido. "Portrait of the Chimpanzee as a Metaphysician: Parody and Dehumanization in *Echoes from a Somber Empire*." In *A Companion to Werner Herzog*. Edited by Brad Prager. Malden, MA: Blackwell, 2012, 547–65.

von Mildenstein, Leopold. *Rings um das brennende Land am Jordan: Eine Fahrt bis zu den Quellen des flüsigen Goldes*. Berlin: Verlagsanstalt Otto Stollberg, 1938.

—*Naher Osten—vom Straßenrand erlebt. Ein Reisebreicht mit sechzehn Frabblidern*. Stuttgart: Union Deutsche Verlagsgesellschaft, 1941.

von Salomon, Ernst. *Der Fragebogen*. Reinbek bei Hamburg: Rowohlt, 1969.

Walker, Janet. *Trauma Cinema: Documenting Incest and the Holocaust*. Berkeley: University of California Press, 2005.

—"Moving Testimonies: 'Unhomed Geography' and the Holocaust Documentary of Return." In *After Testimony: The Ethics and Aesthetics of Holocaust Narrative for the Future*. Edited by Jakob Lothe, Susan Rubin Suleiman, and James Phelan. Columbus, OH: Ohio State University Press, 2012, 269–88.

Walser, Martin. "Erfahrungen beim Verfassen einer Sonntagsrede." In *Die Walser-Bubis-Debatte. Eine Dokumentation*. Edited by Frank Schirrmacher. Frankfurt: Suhrkamp, 1999, 7–17.

Weckel, Ulrike. *Beschämende Bilder: Deutsche Reaktionen auf alliierte Dokumentarfilme über befreite Konzentrationslager*. Stuttgart: Franz Steiner Verlag, 2012a.

—"The Power of Images. Real and Fictional Roles of Atrocity Film Footage at Nuremberg." In *Reassessing the Nuremberg Military Tribunals: Transitional Justice, Trial Narratives, and Historiography*. Edited by Kim C. Priemel and Alexa Stiller. New York: Berghahn Books, 2012b, 221–48.

Weiss, Peter. "Meine Ortschaft." In *Rapporte*. Suhrkamp: Frankfurt a.M., 1968, 113–24.

— "My Place." Translated by Roger Hillman. *TRANSIT* 4, 1 (2008): 1–14.

Weissman, Gary. *Fantasies of Witnessing: Postwar Efforts to Experience the Holocaust*. Ithaca, NY: Cornell University Press, 2004.

—"A Filmmaker in the Holocaust Archives: Photography and Narrative in Peter Thompson's *Universal Hotel*." *Post Script: Essays in Film and the Humanities* 32, 2 (2013): 34–52.

Welzer, Harald. "Vergeben ist ein Recht aller Opfer. Rückgewinnung der eigenen Autonomie ist das entscheidende Ziel." *Frankfurter Rundschau*, June 30, 2003.

Wenders, Wim. "That's Entertainment: Hitler." In *West German Filmmakers on Film: Visions and Voices*. Edited by Eric Rentschler. New York: Holmes and Meier, 1988, 126–31.

Wheeler, Duncan. "Godard's List: Why Spielberg and Auschwitz Are Number One." *Media History* 15, 2 (2009): 185–203.

Wiener, Reinhard. "Mr Wiener's Interview Re Libau." Transcribed March 1992. Interview originally held on September 27, 1981, http://www.ushmm.org/online/film/display/detail.php?file_num=5507

Wiesenthal, Simon. *The Sunflower: On the Possibilities and Limits of Forgiveness*, 1969. rev. edn. Edited by Harry J. Cargas and Bonny V. Fetterman. New York: Schocken Books, 1997.

"Wir waren zu viert: Leon de Winter im Gespräch mit Roman Polanski über eine Jugend im Krakauer Getto." *Die Welt*, November 30, 2002, http://www.welt.de/print-welt/article278631/Wir-waren-zu-viert.html.

Young, James E. *At Memory's Edge: After-Images of the Holocaust in Contemporary Art and Architecture*. New Haven, CT: Yale University Press, 2000.

Index

Act of Killing, The 18, 188
Adizes, Topaz 89–90
Adler, Michael 172
Adorno, Theodor W. 48–9
   and Auschwitz 29, 48–9
   and the ghost of National Socialism 141
   and *Guilt and Defense* 145–6
   and poetry after Auschwitz 98
   and the *Schlussstrich* 253n. 44
Alexandrowicz, Ra'anan 28, 32, 47, 50–67
Alien 38
Allach concentration camp 64
Améry, Jean
   and resentment 120–1, 123, 127, 129–31, 134, 137, 141, 143
   and torture 22, 62
Anne Frank House 28
Arad, Boaz 92
archival footage 8, 10–11, 14–15, 70–2, 86–8, 190, 203, 206, 229, 233
Arendt, Hannah
   and banality 125
   and Chaim Rumkowski 219
   and forgiveness 120–1, 251n. 15, 251n. 16
Auerbach, Rachel 190
Auschwitz concentration camp
   and Charlotte Delbo 7
   and Eva Kor 114–15, 117–19, 121–2, 127–8
   and Facebook 28
   and Hans Münch 125–7
   and Jean Améry 62, 120
   and medical experiments 117
   and *Night and Fog* 6, 41
   and Peter Weiss 30–1
   and Primo Levi 133, 218
   and Rainer Höss 84, 111–12
   and Ruth Klüger 130, 133, 135
   and *Shoah* 27, 103, 139
   and Steven Spielberg 98–9
   and Theodor Adorno 48–9
   and tourism 28–9

Bachmayer, Georg 40
Baer, Ulrich 211–12
Baron, Lawrence
   and *Schindler's List* 109, 247n. 49
Barthes, Roland 200
Bartov, Omer
   and *Schindler's List* 95, 103, 244n. 11, 247n. 50
Beck, Eldad 111–12
Bełżec 226–9
Bełżec extermination camp 3, 7, 80, 150, 226–9
ben-Menachem, Arie 8
Benstock, Jes 28
Bergen-Belsen 14
   and Ruth Klüger 17, 137–8
Betroffenheit 48
Bieber, Justin 28
Biebow, Hans 213, 219–21
Bilderverbot 8, 103
Blaha, Franz 241n. 50
Blair, Jon 78–80, 245n. 27
Blair Witch Project, The 47
Blind Spot: Hitler's Secretary 85
Bloomstein, Rex 32–46, 50, 52, 53, 226–7, 229
Blum, Thomas 46
Boas, Jacob 174, 176
Bomba, Abraham 149, 198–9, 228
Böser, Ursula 191
Bouquet, Michel 6
Boys from Brazil 118
Brachner, Harald 41–3, 45–7, 227
Braiterman, Zachary 234n. 33
Branko: Return to Auschwitz 89
Brink, Cornelia 8, 93
Broder, Henryk 28–9, 238n. 3

Brumlik, Micha   128
Buchenwald   3, 4
  and tree-hanging photo   60–1
Buerkle, Darcy   188
Bulldozer (at Bełżec)   228–9
Bulldozer (at Bergen-Belsen)   14, 229, 236n. 52, 260n. 2
Burger, Hanuš
  and *Death Mills*   232n. 10

camera-eye narration   30, 31, 238n. 9
  and *KZ*   67
  and *Martin*   67
Cayrol, Jean   5, 6, 13, 19, 196
Cesarani, David   175–6
Chełmno   212–13, 215
Citizen Kane   69, 95
Clauberg, Carl   126
CNN Concatenated   91–2
Cole, Tim   28–9, 236n. 61, 238n. 4
compilation films   3, 232n. 8, 232n. 9
complicit onlooking   6
concentration camp syndrome   130
Congo, Anwar   188
Corrigan, Timothy   160
Czerniakow, Adam   190, 192, 201, 204, 266n. 77

Dachau   50, 52–5, 61–5
  and tourism   29
Dachau 1974   92–3
Dachau concentration camp gas chamber   56
Dachau memorial museum   17, 22, 30, 49–51, 56, 62, 66–7
Davidtz, Embeth   76
Dawidowicz, Lucy   177, 180, 195, 264n. 42
Death Mills   3–5, 14, 63, 232n. 10
Delage, Christian   231n. 5
Delbo, Charlotte   7
Delman, Vivian   80–1, 84, 246n. 35
Demjanjuk, John   121
Derrida, Jacques   113
Desbois, Patrick   15
Desplechin, Arnaud   226
Diary of Anne Frank, The   80
Didi-Huberman, Georges   8, 10, 15, 20
disjunctive layering   205, 264n. 43

Dodd, Thomas J.   1
domestic ethnography   151–2, 170
Donovan, James Britt   231n. 3
Dössekker, Bruno   51–2, 63
Douglas, Lawrence   1

Ebbrecht, Tobias   25, 102, 263n. 29
Edkins, Jenny   64
Eichmann, Adolf   187–8, 213
  and banality   121
  and Leopold von Mildenstein   174–6, 180, 182
Eichmann Trial
  and *The Eighty-First Blow*   11
  and *The Flat*   180
  and *Night and Fog*   187, 260n. 2
  and *Schindler's List*   71, 101, 243n. 8
Eighty-First Blow, The   11
empathic unsettlement   51, 193, 201, 206, 241n. 38
Eternal Jew, The   154, 193, 207–8
Execution of Jews in Liepaja   13–14
Exit/Dachau   49
expository mode   18–19, 34, 62, 74, 91, 135

Farocki, Harun   14, 38
Fassbinder, Rainer Werner   165–6
Fast, Omer   20, 23, 90–110
Fiennes, Ralph   74–6, 87
Film Unfinished   11, 24, 189–208, 209, 217
Firestone, Renée   124–5
Fischer, Ludwig   87, 247n. 43
Flat, The   20, 23, 149, 170–85
forgiveness   78, 81, 111–14, 116–17, 119–23, 125, 127–8, 131–3, 147–8, 251n. 15, 251n. 16
Forgiving Dr. Mengele   23, 81, 114–29, 131, 135, 140, 147
Fortunoff Video Archive   16
Frank, Anne   137, 246n. 32
Freud, Sigmund   140–1
Friedländer, Saul   220

Gable, Clark   80
Geissler, Christian   164
Genewein, Walter   208–23
Gerron, Kurt   9, 210
Gerz, Jochen   49–50

Geyrhalter, Nikolaus 38
Gladstone, Kay 5, 232n. 11, 232n. 12
Godard, Jean-Luc
   and the essay film 160
   and Holocaust images 98–9, 248n. 58
   and Spielberg's *Schindler's List* 90, 97–9
Godfrey, Mark 93
Goebbels, Joseph
   and *A Film Unfinished* 207–8, 261n. 10
   and Hitler images 153, 155
   and Leopold von Mildenstein 175
   and propaganda 195, 202
Goering, Hermann 79
Goethe, Johann Wolfgang von 172–3
   and *Faust* 161
Goldfinger, Arnon 20, 24, 170–85
Goldfinger, Hannah 181, 183, 185
Gone with the Wind 80, 90
Göth, Amon 17, 23, 69, 73–81, 84–8, 94, 104, 105, 157, 245n. 28
   and execution 87–8
Gouri, Haim 187
Gross, Jan 228
Grossman, Mordechaj Mendel 8
Guerin, Frances 214

Haavara Agreement 174, 259n. 53
Haider, Jörg 33
Hämmerle, Josef 221
Hansen, Miriam
   and *Schindler's List* 69–70, 103
Hareven, Alouph 10
Hart, Kitty 89, 117, 135, 137, 140
Hebrew Lesson 92
Heine, Heinrich 172
Hersonski, Yael 11, 14, 189–208, 210
Hertwig, Monika 17, 74–87, 90
Herzinger, Richard 156
Heydrich, Reinhard 175–6, 252n. 26
Hilberg, Raul 149, 155, 192
Himmler, Heinrich 13, 79, 173, 221
Himmler Project, The 167
Hippler, Fritz 193, 204, 207, 264n. 46, 265n. 47
Hirsch, Joshua 13, 71, 232n. 8
Hirsch, Marianne
   and perpetrator images 105, 193, 215–16, 261n. 6
   and postmemory 21

Hitchcock, Alfred 4, 232n. 12
Hitler, A Career 153–5
Hitler's Children 17, 79, 84, 111
Höhne, Heinz 174–5
Holocaust (NBC miniseries) 76, 97
Holocaust sublimity 103
Holocaust tourism 22–3, 28–31, 35–6, 41, 53, 138
Holocaust Tourist, The 90
Holy Mountain, The 163
Horowitz, Helen Hirsch 77, 245n. 26
Horowitz, Sara 70
Horstmann, Anja 191
Höss, Rainer
   and *Hitler's Children* 79, 84, 111–12
Höss, Rudolf
   and *Hitler's Children* 84
Howard, Trevor 4
Hurwitz, Leo 187–8
Huyssen, Andreas
   and Anselm Kiefer 146
   and *Maus* 249n. 69

Icard, Romain 15
Inheritance 16, 17, 23, 73–90, 110
Inowlockia, Lena 128
International Tracing Service (ITS) 64
Izkor: Slaves of Memory 241n. 37

Jablonski, Dariusz 11, 189, 208–24
Jacobowitz, Florence 150
Jenny, Urs 76
Joel, Billy 77
Joel Files, The 77, 84
Jonas, Joseph 83
Jonas-Rosenzweig, Helen 74, 76–8, 80–6, 88, 244n. 15, 245n. 26
Jöst, Heinrich 214
Junge, Traudl 85

Kacandes, Irene 256n. 9
Kaes, Anton 153
Kafka, Franz 139, 142
Kalder, Agnes 79
Kalder, Ruth Irene 76–80, 83–6, 88, 90, 245n. 28
   and *Gone with the Wind* 80, 90
Kaplan, Chaim 190, 204

Karmakar, Romuald   28, 167
Karski, Jan   206
Karski Report, The   8
Keller, Werner   172–3
Kellogg, Edgar Ray   1
Kenan, Rona   196
Ken Burns effect   211
Keneally, Thomas   75–7, 245n. 24
Kerner, Aaron   16, 236n. 58, 237n. 69
Kessler, Matthias   79
Kiefer, Anselm   146
Kitty: Return to Auschwitz   16, 31, 117, 135, 137
Klüger, Ruth   17, 113, 125, 129–48, 217, 234n. 34
Knigge, Volkhard   47–8
Koch, Gertrud   103, 248n. 52
Koelle, Fritz
    and *Concentration Camp Inmate*   54
Kohen-Raz, Odeya   184
Kola, Andrzej   227
Kołodziejczyk, Wacław   228
Kor, Eva   81, 113–29, 131, 140, 147, 250n. 5
Kor, Michael   118
Korot, Beryl   92, 96
Koyaanisqatsi   18
Kracauer, Siegfried   17–18
Kriegel, Vera   126
KZ   22, 32–47, 50, 52, 53, 55, 67, 90, 226–8

LaCapra, Dominick   51, 193, 206
Landscapes of Memory: The Life of Ruth Klüger   17, 23, 113, 129–48, 253n. 43
Lang, Berel   20, 123, 239n. 18
Lanzmann, Claude   3, 25
    and aniconism   7–10
    and archival images   8, 11, 24, 194, 199, 212–14, 216, 228–9
    and interviews   34, 43, 126, 136–7, 139, 149–51, 166, 228
    and Jan Karski   206
    and landscapes   27
    and *The Last of the Unjust*   9
    and mise-en-scène   103, 108, 198
    and reenactment   108
    and *Sobibor*   225–6
    and sound editing   225–7
    and Spielberg's *Schindler's List*   23, 69–70, 72, 90, 97–8, 106–7
    see also Shoah
Last Days, The   124
Last of the Unjust, The   8, 9, 210, 262n. 21
Lehmann, Heinrich   184–5
Lehmann, Susanne   183–4
Lehnert, Herbert   142–4
Leiser, Erwin   10
Lerner, Yehuda   225–6
Lesiewicz, Witold   58
Levi, Primo
    and Chaim Rumkowski   219
    and forgiveness   114
    and the gray zone   218–22
    and shame   222
    and survival   138
    and witnessing   133
Lewin, Abraham   190
Lewis-Kraus, Gideon   105
Libau (Latvia)   12
Liebman, Stuart   192, 233n. 24, 236n. 61
Lindeperg, Sylvie   14, 236n. 53, 260n. 4
Lipstadt, Deborah   122
Liss, Andrea
    and postmemories   21
Loshitzky, Yosefa   95
Ludin, Barbara   159, 161–3, 166–8
Ludin, Erla   158, 163–6
Ludin, Hanns   152, 155–8, 160–1, 164–7
Ludin, Malte   25, 152–69, 184
Luhmann, Niklas   235n. 44
Lustig, Branko   89
Łysak, Tomasz   223

MacCabe, Colin   98
McGlothlin, Erin   149–50, 155–6
McLuhan, Marshall   30, 36
Macnab, Geoffrey   125
Madagascar Plan   176–7, 180, 207–8
Mandelbaum, Jacques   226
Mann, Thomas   143
Marathon Man   117
Marcuse, Harold   53–4
Margalit, Ruth   28
Martin   17, 22, 27, 32, 33, 50–67

Mauthausen 54–5
  and Jean Cayrol 13
  and Memorial and Museum 22, 32, 33–47
Mein Kampf 10, 195, 201–2, 208
Memory of the Camps 4, 5, 14
Mengele, Josef 113–17, 119, 121–6, 218, 250n. 4, 250n. 7, 252n. 25
Mesnard, Philippe 24
Michelsohn, Martha 136–7
Miller, J. Hillis 44
Mirroring Evil (exhibition) 92
Mitchell, Margaret 88
Moll, James
  and *Inheritance* 73–90
  and *The Last Days* 124–5
Morley, Peter 16, 89
Morris, Leslie 240n. 25
Moscovitz, Guillaume 226–9
Mostowicz, Arnold 209–10, 213–23
Mozes, Miriam 114, 119
Münch, Hans 119, 121–8, 135
Munk, Andrzej
  and *Passenger* 58
Murderers Are Among Us, The 168–9
Murmelstein, Benjamin 9

Naftali, Timothy 175
Nazi Concentration Camps 1, 2, 14, 63, 70, 229
Neckermann, Josef 77
Neuengamme concentration camp 3
Neurath, Paul Martin 61, 242n. 55
Nichols, Bill
  and modes of documentary 13, 17–19, 37
Nietzsche, Friedrich 130
Night and Fog 3
  and archival materials 14–15, 24, 70, 196
  and Claude Lanzmann 233n. 23
  and documentary modes 19, 51
  and the Eichmann Trial 187–8, 260n. 4
  and *Schindler's List* 100
  and tourism 29, 31
  and witnessing 5–7, 12, 13, 18
No Place on Earth 17, 73, 213

Nuremberg: The Nazis Facing their Crimes 231n. 5
Nuremberg Trials 1, 2, 56
Nyiszli, Miklós 218

Obenaus, Herbert 60–1
Oberhauser, Josef 150–1
observational mode 18, 85, 129, 160, 198, 201
Occupations (Kiefer) 146
Ophüls, Marcel 149, 234n. 42
Oppenheimer, Joshua 18, 188
Ordinary Fascism 11
Ostermann, Dagmar 125

Palestine 171–2, 174, 176–80
Panhölzl, Florian 39–40, 46, 240n. 24
Paper Clips 115
Paranormal Activity 47
participatory mode 18, 23, 47, 151–2
Pemper, Mietek 74–5
performative mode 18, 19, 24, 51, 170
perpetrator photographs 8, 118, 215
Photographer 11, 24, 189, 208–24
Pianist, The 197–8, 208
Pickford, Henry 7
Pingel, Falk 56
Plath, Sylvia 29
poetic mode 18, 37, 47
Polanski, Roman 197–8
Pollock, Griselda 15, 233n. 21
Pourquoi Israël 10
prosthetic memory 22, 237n. 79

Rascher, Sigmund 56, 241n. 48, 241n. 50
Rauffmann, Braha 227
Reichenberg, Ephraim 122
Renov, Michael 14, 151, 170, 235n. 51, 249n. 74, 264n. 43
Resnais, Alain 3, 5–7, 11, 14, 19, 24, 25, 31, 70, 100, 187–8, 196
Respite 14, 192–3, 210
Riefenstahl, Leni 153, 160, 163, 194, 204
Riis, Jacob 214
Ringelblum, Emmanuel 190–2
Rosenberg, Alfred 174
Rothberg, Michael 235n. 45
  and *Schindler's List* 244n. 13

Rouch, Jean 149
Rumkowski, Chaim 212, 218–23, 266n. 77
Rupnow, Dirk 192, 194–6
Ryback, Timothy W.
 and *The Last Survivor: Legacies of Dachau* 51–2, 56, 63–4

Santer, Eric 153, 256n. 10
Sanyal, Debarati 6
Sartre, Jean-Paul 20
Saxton, Libby 6, 10, 98, 198
Schechner, Alan 28, 53
Schindler, Oskar 23, 69, 71, 75, 85, 89, 97, 101
Schindler's List
 and Amon Göth 73, 76, 83, 104, 105
 and Claude Lanzmann 70, 97–9
 and documentary film 71–3
 and Germany 248n. 52
 and the girl in the red coat 71, 101, 103, 203, 243n. 8
 and Hans Münch 126
 and Hollywood 95
 and *Inheritance* 74–6, 78, 80–1, 89
 and Kraków 69
 and *KZ* 39
 and newsreel images 71, 216, 243n. 9
 and opening image 99–100, 116
 and *Spielberg's List* 23, 90–110
 and witnessing 32
 see also Spielberg, Steven
Schirra, Bruno 125–7
Schlussstrich 46, 132, 146, 253n. 44
Schmidtkunz, Renata 134, 137, 139
Scholl, Sophie 85
secondary anti-Semitism 130
Seidl, Karl 113
Seidlin, Oskar 232n. 14
selfies at Auschwitz 28
Senfft, Alexandra 156, 164, 258n. 29
Seuß, Josef 61, 242n. 55
Shoah 3, 10
 and archival images 7, 9
 and documentary 13, 72
 and interviews with perpetrators 136, 149–51, 166
 and landscapes 22, 27

 and mise-en-scène 103, 149, 198, 206, 263n. 30
 and outtakes 8–9
 and performance 15, 198–9
 and *Schindler's List* 69–70, 97, 103
 and witnessing 30, 32
 see also Lanzmann, Claude
Shoah by Bullets 15
Sierakowiak, Dawid 218
Sobibor 8, 225–7
Sontag, Susan
 and Auschwitz tourism 29–30
Sophie's Choice 89
Sorrow and the Pity, The 10
Specialist, The 188, 200
Spiegelman, Art
 and postmemory 21
 and *Schindler's List* 106–7
Spielberg, Steven
 and archival history 71–2
 and Claude Lanzmann 97–8, 106–7
 and fictionalization 77, 90, 91, 94, 105, 109
 and Göth's execution 87–8
 and Jean-Luc Godard 90, 97–9
 and Monika Hertwig 75–6
 and *Night and Fog* 70
 and technique 69
 see also Schindler's List
Spielberg's List 20, 23, 90–110
Stanzel, F. K. 30–1
Staudte, Wolfgang 168–9
Steinmayr, Joachim 53
Stern, Hermann 165
Stevens, George 1, 229
strappado 61
Stroop Report 215
Struk, Janina 214–15
Suchomel, Franz 126, 136, 150, 166
Sunflower, The 113–14
Super Size Me 18
survivor testimony 2, 12, 108
Sztab, Adam 82–3

Tacke, Alexandra 158
Teege, Jennifer 81, 246n. 37, 246n. 38
Theresienstadt 9–10, 133, 172, 184, 191, 217

Theresienstadt: A Documentary Film from the Jewish Settlement Area 9, 191–2, 210
Thompson, Peter 241n. 48
Time of the Ghetto, The 10, 195, 201–2
Treblinka extermination camp 7, 56, 126, 136, 149, 150, 166, 198, 207, 219
tree-hanging photo 60–2
Trezise, Thomas 15–16
Triumph of the Will 154, 159
Tuchler, Gerda and Kurt 170–80, 182, 184
Turkow, Jonas 190
2 or 3 Things I Know about Him 23, 152–69, 184–5, 209
2001 100

United States Holocaust Memorial Museum (USHMM)
 and photo archive 15, 59–60
 and tourism 28
USC Shoah Foundation 16, 69

Vice, Sue 206
Visitor from the Living 8, 9
Vitiello, Guido 196
Vogler, Rüdiger 203–7, 264n. 39
von Mildenstein, Edda Milz 173, 181–3
von Mildenstein, Leopold 172–83, 258n. 44
von Salomon, Ernst
 and *The Questionnaire* 156–8, 160, 164, 169, 257n. 20

Waldheim, Kurt 33
Walker, Janet 16, 69
Walser, Martin 46, 132, 144, 146
Weckel, Ulrike 5, 231n. 2, 232n. 15, 242n. 57
Weiss, Peter 30–1
Weissman, Gary 22, 32, 237n. 75, 237n. 79
Welzer, Harald 127–8
Wenders, Wim 153–4, 203
Westerbork concentration camp 14, 192–3, 210
Wiener, Reinhard 12–14
Wiener Neurose (poem) 145
Wiesenthal, Simon 113–14, 119–20
Wilder, Billy 232n. 10
Wirth, Christian 150
Wiseman, Frederick 18, 160
Wist, Willy 203–7, 264n. 38
Wonderful, Horrible Life of Leni Riefenstahl, The 163, 204

Yad Vashem
 and archives 59, 112, 174
 and Ruth Klüger 147
 and tourism 28, 44
Yellow Star: The Persecution of the Jews in Europe, 1933–1945 195, 201–2, 208
Young, James 49–50, 146

Zaidenstadt, Martin 17, 22, 50–67, 240n. 35
Zaillian, Steven 77, 88
ZDF 119
Ze'evi, Chanoch 79, 111
Ziereis, Franz 41

www.ingramcontent.com/pod-product-compliance
Lightning Source LLC
Chambersburg PA
CBHW070751020526
44115CB00032B/1676